Teaching Music Through Performance in Band

Teaching Music Through Performance in Band

Larry Blocher
Ray Cramer
Eugene Corporon
Tim Lautzenheiser
Edward S. Lisk
Richard Miles

Compiled and Edited by Richard Miles

78376   GIA Publications, Inc.
Chicago

Library of Congress Cataloging-in-Publication Data
Teaching music through performance in band / compiled and edited by
    Richard Miles; [contributions by] Larry Blocher . . . [et al.].
        p. cm.
    Includes bibliographical references and index.
    ISBN 0-941050-93-9
    1. Band music—Analysis, appreciation. 2. Bands (Music)-
-Instruction and study. 3. School music—Instruction and study.
I. Miles, Richard B., 1951- . II. Blocher, Larry.
MT125.T43   1996   96-38981
784. 4'4' 07—dc20   CIP
                                                             MN

G-4484

Copyright © 1997 GIA Publications, Inc.
7404 S. Mason Ave.
Chicago, IL 60638
Printed in the United States of America

Table of Contents

ACKNOWLEDGEMENTS

The following RESEARCH ASSOCIATES are
gratefully acknowledged for outstanding scholarly contributions of the
TEACHER RESOURCE GUIDES

Jeff Emge
Assistant Director of Bands
East Texas State University • Commerce, Texas

Kenneth Kohlenberg
Director of Bands
Sinclair Community College • Dayton, Ohio

Matthew Mailman
Director of Bands
Oklahoma City University • Oklahoma City, Oklahoma

Matthew McInturf
Director of Bands
Florida International University • Miami, Florida

Craig Paré
Director of University Bands
DePauw University • Greencastle, Indiana

Edwin Powell
Doctoral Conducting Associate
University of North Texas • Denton, Texas

Robert Spittal
Director of Bands
Gonzaga University • Spokane, Washington

Thomas Stone
Director of Bands and Orchestra
Centenary College • Shreveport, Louisiana

Introduction

Larry Blocher

A word of explanation to anyone who is about to read or use this book: this is a book about **teaching music**, using band and student performance in band as a means to that end. While we do have a passion for bands and our own collective "understanding" of the many roles band directors are expected to play in today's schools, we believe that band directors and/or conductors in schools at all levels should be first and foremost **music teachers**.

Music teachers and band directors, like all teachers, are decision makers. Band directors, as music teachers, must decide what and when to teach. Band directors must decide what techniques they will use to teach whatever they decide to teach. Band directors must decide what procedures they will use to determine whether or not they were successful in teaching whatever they decided to teach. And perhaps before they begin the decision-making processes about the "what" or "when", "how", and "if" in teaching music, band directors should carefully consider why anyone would need to know or be able to do whatever they have decided to teach. All of these decisions are important, personal, and sometimes "sobering".

For band directors in schools, one opportunity to teach music to students commonly occurs in a band performance setting: a band rehearsal. What the band director does to, for, and with students during this music rehearsal has the potential to directly affect student learning.

The focus of this text is on teaching music through performance in band. It is written for teachers, prospective teachers, and other professionals who interact with students in band rehearsal and performance settings. This volume is presented in three parts. Part I provides an overview of ideas basic to teaching music through performance in band. Part II provides a guide for the practical application of teaching music through performance in band. Part III is a resource guide containing teaching "outlines" for one hundred graded band works (II-VI) designed for individual band director selection and adaptation to fit specific rehearsal situations.

This resource represents a team effort. We are deeply indebted to the many outstanding teachers who have led and continue to lead by example. We are hopeful that this introductory volume will be an impetus for band directors to make a personal transfer in teaching music through performance in band.

PART I

THE BAND CONDUCTOR
AS A MUSIC TEACHER
(IN THEORY)

CHAPTER 1

Why We Wrote This Book

Larry Blocher

*"If you get a big enough why,
you can always figure out the how."*
··· Anthony Robbins ···

Music in the School Curriculum

"What shall we teach and to what end?"[1] Recent attempts to provide answers to this ongoing question have generated educational reform initiatives designed to transform, realign, restructure, and generally "overhaul" many aspects of public school education. The role of the arts has been addressed in many of these national reform efforts.[2]

With the passage of *Goals 2000: Educate America Act*, the arts were recognized as a core subject in the school curriculum. In anticipation of the need for national arts standards, the Consortium of Arts Education Associations developed the *National Standards for Arts Education*. These voluntary guidelines outline knowledge and performance standards for all students in the arts, including students in general music and performance groups, as follows:

Content Standards what students should know and be able to do in
music:
1. Singing alone, and with others, a varied repertoire of music.
2. Performing on instruments, alone and with others, a varied
repertoire of music.
3. Improvising melodies, variations, and accompaniments.
4. Composing and arranging music within specific guidelines.

5. Reading and notating music.
6. Listening to, analyzing, and describing music.
7. Evaluating music and music performances.
8. Understanding relationships between music, the other arts, and disciplines outside the arts.
9. Understanding music in relation to history and culture.

National Standards for Arts Education (1994). *Dance, Music, Theatre, Visual Arts: What Every Young American Should Know and Be Able to Do in the Arts.* Reston, VA: Music Educators National Conference.

While band, as a part of a school music program, may be included as part of the core curriculum in the schools, the actual "role" of band in the school curriculum as an academic subject has remained unclear.

Band in the School Curriculum

In the fall of 1991, the College Band Director's National Association (CBDNA) appointed a national task force to study current academic problems facing public school bands. The National Task Force, supported by funds from CBDNA, the National Band Association (NBA), the American Bandmasters Association (ABA), the Texas Music Educator's Association (TMEA), and the American School Band Director's Association (ASBDA), solicited information from more than 2,000 high school band directors, 700 high school principals, and more than 500 college/university band directors from across the country over a two-year period. Major findings contained in the Task Force Final Report related to the academic role of high school band in the public school curriculum included:

1. A majority of public high schools awarded a full academic credit for high school band.
2. The average high school band was performance-oriented, presenting more than forty-two public performances each year.
3. Academic values associated with high school bands included teaching performance skills and concepts, providing students opportunities to perform quality music at a quality level, and promoting lifelong student involvement with music.[3]

The Band Director as Music Teacher

High school bands, then, spend a great deal of time performing. Consequently, high school band directors must spend a great deal of time preparing bands for performances. It is during this music rehearsal time that band directors have the opportunity to address the academic role of school bands—by teaching not only the performance skills and knowledge that band students need to perform specific music, but also by teaching for understanding "about the music" and music in general. Formal observation of band directors in rehearsal, however, indicates that band directors spend a majority of rehearsal time teaching "the music," with little attention to conceptual teaching—teaching for musical awareness, understanding, and application possibilities to transfer to other musical situations.[4]

Teaching either the knowledge and performance skills necessary to perform the music or teaching for musical understanding need not be an "either/or" proposition for band directors in rehearsal. Teaching music through performance in band does require a band director's desire, planning, and resources, as well as a personal teaching approach. The primary purpose of the material that follows is to provide a basis for beginning the process of *Teaching Music Through Performance in Band*.

Notes

1   J. Bruner, *The Process of Education* (Cambridge: Harvard University Press, 1977), 1.
2   R. Miles, "Current Academic Problems Facing Public High School Bands in the United States: Survey, Analysis, and Comparisons" (Ph.D. diss., The Florida State University, 1993).
3   R. Miles, R. Greenwood, P. Dunnigan, and L. Blocher, "Current Academic Problems Facing Public School Bands" (Columbus, OH: Twenty-Seventh National College Band Directors National Association Conference, 1993).
4   L. Blocher, R. Greenwood, and B. Shellahamer, "Teaching Behaviors Exhibited by Middle School and High School Band Directors in the Rehearsal Setting" (Valencia, Spain: Sixth World Association for Symphonic Bands and Ensembles International Conference, 1993).

CHAPTER 2

What Materials Are You Going To Teach "About Music" "Through Music" While "Performing Music?"

Ray Cramer

*"Music making begins in the mind,
not in the stick."*

··· L. Bernstein ···

As I recall my early years of teaching, perhaps the most difficult decisions I faced were those requiring my choice of literature for rehearsals and performances by my bands at the junior and senior high school level. Mostly, I relied on experienced directors or my college band director for suggestions. At the time, it seemed to me the most important questions about making those choices involved the following:

1. Will the students "like" the music?
2. Are my players "competent enough" to perform the music?
3. Do we have enough "rehearsal time" to learn the music?
4. Will the parents and school personnel "enjoy" the music?

While these questions were, and continue to be, important in our decision process, I know they only cover a small part of this complex problem of choosing fine literature. Selecting quality music must be our top priority in our responsibility as teachers and conductors. A main focus of this publication is to provide a list of quality band music to assist in establishing a *plan* and *procedure* for you and your students to achieve musical satisfaction and excitement. When realized, this goal will have a positive impact on your students, parents, and school colleagues. After all, our basic aim is to make the preparation and performance of music as exciting for *everyone* as possible. To accomplish this task, we need to enliven our work so that our students may see in us knowledge, creativity, positive communication, and above all, enthusiasm.

Before we look at our list of selected works, it might serve us well to examine criteria that one usually uses in making decisions regarding music of artistic merit. Please understand, this is a representative list and certainly does not reflect the only choices that could have been made in each grade level. It is a starting point and a place to embark on our goal of *teaching music through performance in band*.

Without question, there are many philosophical viewpoints regarding the selection of quality music. Some are rather direct and simplistic while others require careful examination based on a set of guidelines. Kurt Weill (1900-1950), a contemporary German composer, once made the statement, "I have never acknowledged the difference between 'serious' music and 'light' music, there is only good music and bad music." A highly respected band director of our time makes the simple statement regarding choosing literature, "Play only music you can respect." A distinguished composer of band music during the past twenty-five years simply asks the question, "Does the music *say* anything or *go* anywhere?" While each of these statements has its own merits, let's concentrate on a few basics for clarification in covering the wide range of material on our list.

Just for a moment we should consider the age-old question, "What comprises music of artistic merit?" One must conclude the music must characterize itself by having special effectiveness or is set apart by qualitative depth and must stand on its own. Criteria used in this study by which we may evaluate literature can be broken down into seven simple steps.

DOES THE MUSIC HAVE ....
1. a well-conceived formal structure?
2. creative melodies and counterlines?
3. harmonic imagination?
4. rhythmic vitality?
5. contrast in all musical elements?
6. scoring which best represents the full potential for beautiful tone and timbre?
7. an emotional impact?

If we are going to teach *about music, through music while performing music*, then all of these elements need to be incorporated into our rehearsal planning as we prepare our students for performance.

Let's look at a few selections from each level on our list and highlight just why they were included.

SNAKES! by Thomas Duffy (grade II) is a wonderful example of how exciting and accessible a contemporary work can be without great range and technical demands. This piece shows great creativity and explores a whole new gamut of different sounds, textures, and colors. Young players can have a wonderful learning experience and become totally involved in the music making process.

AIR FOR BAND by Frank Erickson (grade III) has been performed by the youngest of bands and by fine university bands around the world. *Air for Band* is beautifully scored, exhibiting the richness of tone we have all come to appreciate in a fine band. The melody is constructed in such a manner to draw your attention to its outstanding contour and expressive quality. It is a musical gem.

THE SUITES IN E-FLAT AND F by Gustav Holst (grade IV) have been hailed by many as the "cornerstones" of contemporary band literature in this century. Examine them carefully by the seven simple steps and you will quickly discover the genius and creative talent of this great composer. These magnificent works have withstood the "test of time" and will continue to do so based on the strength of their musical sensitivity.

DIVERTIMENTO FOR BAND by Vincent Persichetti (grade V) represents a whole new genre of literature for band. Composed in 1950, *Divertimento* was his first composition for band and brought forth several new concepts in writing for winds. First, there was a greater emphasis on individual tonal colors represented by each section of the ensemble. Second, the scoring was much more transparent. Third, the percussion section took on a more important function, particularly in regard to melodic representation. This work set the pace for a whole new era of compositional style and tonal color for bands. Other major composers took note of this potential and began contributing major works of their own to our medium during the decade of the '50s.

VARIANTS ON A MEDIEVAL TUNE by Norman Dello Joio (grade V) is a masterful setting of a famous Renaissance melody "In dulci jubilo." The variations are magnificently conceived and demonstrate sensitive writing for solo and full-ensemble scoring. The contrast in style, dynamics, and tempi contribute to the musical energy as the piece moves toward a dramatic finale. *Variants on a Medieval Tune* provides an ideal vehicle of how music from the Renaissance period can be utilized in a most effective contemporary setting.

LINCOLNSHIRE POSY by Percy Grainger (grade VI), as examined in two different doctoral studies during the past twenty years, was determined to be one of the most respected and well-known works for band composed in this century. Little explanation as to why it is included on this list seems necessary. However, the skill and creative talent of Mr. Grainger are certainly best portrayed in this fabulous score. The careful representation of the original folk songs and how they were sung, the rhythmic vitality and challenges, the colorful scoring, and the emotional sensitivity all contribute to the artistic merit of his masterwork. Certainly there is much to be taught about the piece, but also of the life of a great composer.

There is so much *great* music to share with our students. Why should we settle for less? We need to capitalize on every aspect of music to bring the "whole package" into our performance experiences, which will enhance the students involvement and musical fulfillment. Correct notes are obviously important as are attacks, releases, good balance, blend, careful intonation, clarity in texture, and articulation style. But these are all stepping stones to generating musical electricity and excitement. To accomplish this, we must, as teachers and conductors, give our students *more* than the basic musical stepping stones. They need our musical heart and soul, which can only be communicated by sharing everything we have compiled about the period, style, composer, and structure of the composition. In other words, involve the students totally, teach them *about the music, through the music* we choose. Ours is an awesome responsibility, but our energy and enthusiasm for the task must infect those over whom we have been put in charge.

A Tribute to Teachers

In the fall of 1963, Leonard Bernstein, on his first *Young People's Concert* of the season, presented "A Tribute to Teachers." His comments were powerful then and remain just as significant over thirty years later:

> You may think it is strange that I have chosen to open this new season of *Young People's Concerts* with the subject of *teachers*. After all, aren't these programs always about *music*? And what have teachers got to do with music? The answer is: everything! We can all imagine a painter or writer who is self-taught, but it is almost impossible to imagine a professional musician who doesn't owe *something* to one teacher or another. The trouble is that we don't always realize how important teachers are, in music or in anything else. Teaching is probably the noblest profession in the world—the most unselfish, difficult, and honorable profession. But it is also the most unappreciated, underrated, underpaid, and underpraised profession in the world. And so today we are going to praise teachers. And the best way I can think of for me to do this is by paying tribute to some of my own teachers...and...all the great teachers on earth who work so hard to give young people a world that is better, richer, and more civilized.[5]

None of us knows who among our students will become the next Leonard Bernstein, Percy Grainger, William Revelli, Herbert L. Clarke, or William Bell. However, it is *our* responsibility to be the strongest musical influence in their lives as we possibly can be. Through that effort will come inspiration and joy in making music a vivid and vital part of their life's existence.

Notes

5   Leonard Bernstein, *Findings*, (New York: Simon and Schuster, 1982) 182-183, 205.

CHAPTER 3

The Quantum Conductor

Eugene Corporon

Learning is finding out what you already know.
Doing is demonstrating that you know it.
Teaching is reminding others that they know just as well as you.
You are all Learners, Doers, Teachers.
··· RICHARD BACH ···

Everyone has a purpose in life...a unique gift or special talent to give to others.
And when we blend this unique talent with service to others, we experience the ecstasy and
exaltation of our own spirit which is the ultimate goal of all goals.
··· DEEPAK CHOPRA ···

PART ONE: The Process of Learning

The act of learning a piece of music involves a never-ending process of exploration and discovery that turns ideas into actions. Acquiring knowledge can be described as a constant interplay of energy and information. Energetically collecting information is very much like going on a firefly hunt in the woods on a summer evening at twilight: The lights never come on all at once. More often than not we find ourselves discovering one little firefly at a time and putting it in the jar. With care, patience, and persistence we eventually fill the jar...collecting enough fireflies to create an incredible source of living light. While the product is miraculous, in the end it is the process that we carry in our memory and treasure the most. I am a strong advocate of the importance of approaching learning as a process, not a product. In music especially, the process becomes the product. A process-oriented approach must be thorough, effective, thought-provoking, enlightening, expressive, and above all creative. Music is designed to be innately enjoyable. It is incumbent upon us as teachers of music to amplify that joy! Tim Galway, author of *The Inner Game of Tennis*, has said "...the teaching of music should be more musical..." and I could not agree more. The ultimate goal is to connect with the work of art and with the people who bring it to life.

In most settings the amount of time we have to devote to a project is finite. It seems as though there is never enough time to accomplish all that needs to be done: Invariably, it takes as much time as you have and sometimes even more. I remember saying to a friend once that I wished I had *just one more rehearsal.* His response was filled with wisdom: "You've already had it; you just didn't use the time very well." His point is well taken. Very often the amount of time we waste is equivalent to at least one full rehearsal. We must investigate ways to use our time as efficiently and effectively as possible while producing quality work that is painstakingly thorough! Above all else, it is essential that we teach musicianship.

A balanced learning process should be concerned with the Technical, Intellectual, Musical and Personal growth of the musicians. This can be represented in this way:

Craft *Objective* Development	Technical - Work for the Body Intellectual - Work for the Mind	Teach Skill
Inspiration *Subjective* Growth	Musical - Work for the Soul Personal - Work for the Heart	Teach Musicianship

Our approach must allow all four of these areas to grow evenly. The growth environment must be nurturing and facilitate the goal of teaching musical concepts which create knowledgeable and feelingful performers. The process must encourage creativity and stimulate curiosity. Some bit of knowledge must be transferred every day. The conscientious accumulation of meaningful information can lead us to our expressive selves. There can be no room in the teaching environment for anger or sarcasm because they create fear and self-doubt. We must replace these non-productive, dehumanizing actions with patience and understanding while building confidence and accountability in the players. We have to avoid forced response and move towards natural learning, doing so in an atmosphere which is safe and encouraging.

The teacher should be a person of vision, imagination, persistence, humor and discipline. In addition, self-control and honesty will help to develop the players' commitment to personal responsibility and accountable actions. Of course, the students must also bring something to the party. They must be attentive, involved, interactive, and thoughtful, and understand the importance of contributing. Everyone involved contributes continually to everyone else; that's one of the beautiful things about music: making it establishes a community.

The key to success is understanding the importance of developing individual responsibility. ("No deposit, no return.") If you are not contributing, you are taking away. Deepak Chopra offers this description:

> Every relationship is one of give and take. Giving engenders receiving, and receiving engenders giving. What goes up must come down, what goes out must come back. In reality, receiving is the same thing as giving because giving and receiving are different aspects of the flow of energy in the universe. And if you stop the flow of either, you interfere with nature's intelligence.

There is no neutral position. We must find ways to help the individual musician become a partner in the firm, assume ownership, and make daily contributions for the good of the community or ensemble. Players must turn good intentions into thoughtful actions. There must be a consensus, an understanding, that progress must be made, and that the process must involve moving ahead, no matter how slowly! Imagine that every musician represents one cell in the body that is the ensemble. In that light, Deepak Chopra's analogy of the law of giving is a perfect metaphor for what it means to be a member of an ensemble.

> A cell is alive and healthy when it is in a state of balance and equilibrium. This state of equilibrium is one of fulfillment and harmony, but it is maintained by a constant give and take. Each cell gives to and supports every other cell, and in turn is nourished by every other cell. The cell is always in a state of dynamic flow and the flow is never interrupted. In fact, the flow is the very essence of the life of the cell. And only by maintaining this flow of giving is the cell able to receive and thus continues its vibrant existence.

In addition to generating energy, the conductor often acts like a solar energy collector, drawing energy in and storing it when things are sunny, then dispersing it when things get cloudy. Because the energy of the rehearsal or performance is continually cycling through the conductor, it is important that we learn to control and guide its flow. We empower and excite, we detonate and ignite. We cause things to happen. Above all, we facilitate the learning process by being non-defensive and eliminating interference. The goal is to create a state of relaxed, focused concentration in the musicians so they can succeed and fulfill 100% of their potential. It is the conductor's job to make the players' job easier.

While correctness is one of our goals, we must realize that "making right" is not necessarily "making music." The objective elements in music are much more easily observed and modified than the subjective feelings that music is about. It is important to understand that simply eliminating error is useless unless we find expression in the process. An over-concern for accuracy may drain the spontaneity of a group, and spontaneity is the ally of great music making. At some point we must stop correcting the grammar and start reading the story. The process must be about creation, not mindless repetition. Without discovery and discussion there can be no insight. It is necessary to discover the composer's ideas and patterns of thought, remembering that we are the translators of the symbolic language of the composer called notation. We can bring understanding to the listener only if our work is clearly perceivable. Clarity is a primary factor in transmitting ideas. Being sensitive to the smallest ingredient and perceiving it as a major event will produce clarity of purpose. Subscribing to the following four principles (in order) will help establish ensemble clarity in the music making process.

In Tone - Quality of Sound (air is the ally)

In Time - Internalized Cumulative Pulse (moving together in time)

In Tune - Matching Pitch (an illusion created by stopping the beats)

In Touch - Fluid, Natural, Technique (effortless in the service of music)

The learning process should uncover emotion and meaning. We must show the player what to listen for in the music. We must help the musician hear what we hear in our mind's ear, feel what is in our heart, and discover what is in theirs. Our players perform from a single line of music while the conductor is privileged to work from the full score. We have the advantage of seeing the entire work of art throughout the process; players only see an extracted part. Finding creative ways to help them hear what we see in the score is our challenge. Choral musicians have a distinct advantage in this regard for very often, if not always, they sing from a complete score, allowing them to see the entire work of art everytime they sing. I believe that the great musicality that so many choirs achieve has much to do with this issue.

Another goal of the learning process is to compress the margin of error. We need to develop accuracy and consistency, both within the individual and through-out the ensemble. The difference between a student performer and professional is often a matter of consistency. A professional may have only a 5% margin of error while a student's margin may vary drastically. Defining our goals early in the process is very important. Clarifying the difference between planning, practicing, rehearsing and performing is essential; each serves a very different function in the music making process.

One purpose of the rehearsal is to determine what needs to be practiced. I can not stress enough how crucial it is to the success of an ensemble for its individual members to practice away from the rehearsal. Do not assume that the players know how to practice. We must help them set short- and long-term goals and organize their practice sessions. The amount of practice time invested does not need to be overwhelming, but it does need to be regular and focused. Good performances require developing good planning, practice and rehearsal habits.

The conductor's role in the process has a lot in common with an archaeologist's role on a dig. Sometimes he works with dynamite to clear away large amounts of superfluous material, while at other times a bulldozer is used to move things out of the way. As one gets closer to the discovery, one is more apt to take greater care and use a small shovel to uncover the find. Eventually, time on hands and knees is needed to brush away the dust and expose the minute details of the treasure. The more we uncover and make visible in the work of art, the more reverent and respectful we become of the composer's artistry and achievement.

PART TWO: The Four Stages of Development

The process of learning and then teaching a piece can be diagrammed in a way representing what I call the **Quantum Conductor Sphere**. All stages appear as part of a whole; they are connected to each other and interact with each other simultaneously and continuously. Because each stage is in constant communication, improvement in any single stage benefits all the others. Each stage contributes equally to the growth process, and the process would be incomplete if any stage was missing.

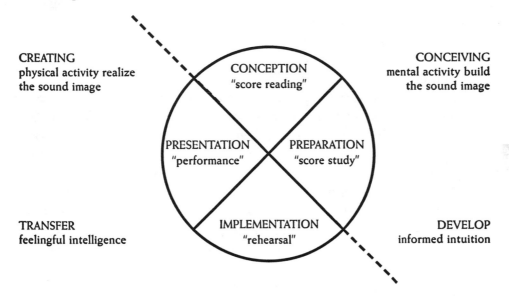

CREATING
physical activity realize
the sound image

CONCEPTION
"score reading"

CONCEIVING
mental activity build
the sound image

PRESENTATION
"performance"

PREPARATION
"score study"

TRANSFER
feelingful intelligence

IMPLEMENTATION
"rehearsal"

DEVELOP
informed intuition

Conception

In the conception stage the imagined ideal of the work is developed. Pierre Boulez has said, "the conductor is looking at the painting and painting it at the same time." Every piece of music begins in the mind and moves through the heart. The composer conceives the sounds and organizes them into ideas which in turn are presented by some system of notation. The teacher's job is to translate and make clear that system of notation. This requires imagination (seeing the music in our mind's "eye") and audiation (hearing the music in our mind's "ear"). We learn to hear in our mind what we see with our eyes. This, in fact, becomes the pressing question when we work. Do we hear what we see on the page? When converting what we hear into a physical presentation or conducting technique, remember that the character of the desired sound determines the quality of the gesture. No gesture can have meaning without conception. You must conceive the sound before you choose a gesture. All gestures begin with a sound image conceived in our mind. Conducting is, after all, showing how sound looks and feels.

Using a recording to facilitate or accelerate the conception development process can be beneficial. However, one must remain aware of the danger of being overwhelmed by a single interpretation. The goal is to develop our own unique expression of the art work that is faithful to the composer's intentions or at the very least, in the range of the composer's intentions. If a recording is going to be used it is better to sample a number of different ones in order to allow for personal musical growth which is free of imitation. The music must come from you, and no one else.

At this stage of the process we are score reading much the way we would read a magazine. We keep our eyes moving and do our best to hear the music in our mind. We need to alternate between audiating and actually listening so that we can develop our ability to hear the piece in our "inner ear." In a sense at this stage, our mind is our instrument.

Preparation

In the preparation stage we take time to study and analyze the score. The goal being to develop a uniform memory of the piece. To quote Walter Piston, "the bringing to light of the inevitable deviations from the commonplace on the part of every composer is perhaps the most interesting and profitable result to be obtained through analysis." We also introduce the ensemble into the equation and begin thinking in terms of devising a rehearsal plan which will facilitate problem solving and musical growth. Unlike the conception stage we stop often while going through the score, zooming in on the details of the music, noting the compositional, structural, formal, and interpretative elements which create an understanding of the relationships that exist in the music.

Developing a concept of the skeletal phrasal shape helps us to make observations about the composer's plan of presentation. We begin to determine what choices the composer has made and to think about why they may have made them. Since every composition represents a series of choices, there is much to be gleaned from observing and acknowledging those choices. Pondering the potential choices that went unused can also be enlightening. Thinking about why the composer made a specific choice over the others often yields great insight. David Elliot, author of *Music Matters* suggests that a composition is "a thought generator." I believe that it is also "a feeling instigator." Learning how a piece is put together enables us to take it apart, and we must be able to disassemble the music in order to rehearse. Understanding and being able to explain how it goes back together is paramount, otherwise we will be left with lots of cleaned parts laying on the podium with no hope of reconstructing the work of art.

Great preparation will yield a great rehearsal plan. Our level of achievement is directly related to our mastery of the score, the flexibility and effectiveness of our rehearsal plan, and our ability to communicate. Knowing and being able to show what comes next in the music is essential. We must be aware of where we have been, where we are, and where we want to go. In this regard we are a sort of time traveler moving freely at will through the past, present, and future of the work. Preparation allows us to develop this ability. Score study is an ongoing process of filling out the substance of the work, much like packing clay on a skeleton to create the shape of a body. Study is to conducting what practice is to playing. We must do our work in order to succeed!

Implementation

In the implementation stage the imagined ideal of the piece meets up with the reality of our ensemble. As Richard Bach says, "You are never given a wish without also being given the power to make it true... you have to work for it however." While the first two stages involve mental activity, the next two require physical action. The time has come to turn ideas into sound. We have moved from conceiving the work of art to creating the work of art. The goal of the first two stages was to develop our informed intuition. Now we must transfer it to the players as feelingful intelligence. In other words, we can now realize our intentions. The stuff that makes conductors and performers different from theorists and historians can be found in the implementation and presentation stages. Studying and audiating the piece is not enough, performing artists must make the music in order to feel complete. The rehearsal and performance are truly their "reason for being." They are the reward for doing all that detailed solitary work. Conception and Preparation have been done in the quiet solitude of our "study place." Now, we finally get to enthusiastically share our vision with living, breathing musicians. Through diligent study we have earned the right to act as the composer's representative.

The rehearsal goals are clear: make it better every time you work on it, recreate the composer's intentions to the best of our ability and be uniquely and creatively expressive in the process. Transcending technique is key to connecting with the composer's inspiration. We have to get past the problems of the individual parts in order to discover the significance of the entire piece. Our goal is to give the gift that every composer dreams of... a performance that goes beyond his or her own conception of the work. We must illuminate concepts not just fix problems. The rehearsal provides the perfect opportunity to help musicians learn to target their powers of attention, creating an awareness which allows them to focus more and more on the subtle details of the music. This laser-like "relaxed focused concentration" helps us to listen and perform with depth, and intelligence. We cannot perform without knowing how to listen, or what to listen for. Good listening skills are a prerequisite to successful performance! Our challenge is to create a collective uniform memory of the work in the minds of our players while teaching them to listen. A process which is natural, effortless, focused and relaxed will produce music that is the same. We can only make it work if we understand the score and communicate what we know and feel in a positive and caring way.

Presentation

In the presentation stage we culminate our work on a given piece of music. To quote Edward T. Cone, "The convincing performance is one that absorbs the listener so deeply into the flow of the music that even though he may know perfectly everything that lies ahead, he can still savor each moment as if for the first time." If the composition is of serious artistic merit, and we perceive it as being so, we will probably plan to repeat it at some point in our future. At this moment we realize we are going to be in a relationship with this particular work of art for the rest of our creative life. Our study of the piece becomes a work in progress. If our approach in each of the previous stages has been thoughtful, thorough and heartfelt, the presentation can not help but be successful. Throughout all of the stages our goal has been to teach the whole piece to everyone and to share our feelings about the work with anyone who hears it. We want to experience the music not just perform it. We want to be connected to one another as the music unfolds, making the vision and intent of the composer clear. It is important that self-expression not be distorted and turned into self-exposure. The music must come before the ego of the conductor. Music must be viewed as an end in itself not a means to an end. The hope is that mind and body will work together, and that feeling and knowing will combine to express and communicate ideas and emotions. Even though we know that perfection is an unattainable idealized goal, we continue to pursue it with a passion. Can a work be performed musically and not be 100% correct? Can a performance be absolutely correct and have nothing musical to say? These questions help us to remember the importance of balancing craft and inspiration in our performances. We must do more than teach band. We must teach musicianship. Our purpose should be to take what we have made right and turn it into something significant and feelingful. A great performance is one that uses uncompromising craft to create inspirational soul-to-soul music making.

PART THREE: Planning/Pacing/Evaluating

Planning

The conductor needs to provide a firm but flexible rehearsal plan that captivates the players. It is always better to have a plan and not need it than to need a plan and not have it. Beginning work on a composition is very much like turning over an hour glass. Consider that the process is represented by the sand in the container. When we flip it the sand begins to flow, giving us a limited amount of time to complete our work. The rehearsal provides an opportunity to bring our imagined ideal of the sound image to life. An overall plan with a sample timing can be diagramed as follows:

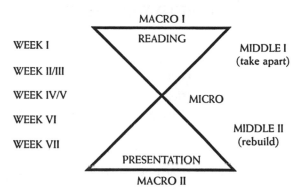

You will notice that the process begins with allowing the group to not only experience, but become familiar with the whole piece before starting to deal with the more specific Middle and Micro level issues. You can lose a great deal of the energy and excitement that surrounds a first encounter by beginning detailed work too soon. The players must be given time to buy into the project and experience the sounds. It is during the Middle I and Micro stages that we do the majority of our intricate work. Sometimes we zoom in on a Middle or Micro level issue not because it needs to be fixed but because we simply want the players to notice the musical significance of the fragment being investigated. The sand in the container can also represent the fluidity of the composition itself. As the piece works its way from the top to the bottom of the hour glass, the musicians develop skill while learning more and more about the music. This provides insight into the workings of the composer's mind and connects us to his feelings. The players learn about the composer (who), the historical circumstances (when) surrounding the creation of the composition, as well as the cultural environment (where) influencing its conception. They grasp the theoretical aspects (how), and become aware of the interaction of the compositional, structural, and formal elements (what) listed below.

COMPOSITIONAL ELEMENTS	STRUCTURAL ELEMENTS	FORMAL ELEMENTS
Sound	New	Statement
Melody	Repeated	Digression
Harmony	Varied	Return
Rhythm	Developed	
Scoring		

Monitoring, controlling and adjusting the following interpretive elements allows us to become the composer's advocate and ally.

INTERPRETIVE ELEMENTS

SOUND		SILENCE
ENERGY	*(low to high)*	
VOLUME	*(soft to loud)*	QUALITY
SPEED	*(slow to fast)*	LENGTH
LENGTH	*(long to short)*	PURPOSE
TIMBER	*(dark to bright)*	CLARITY
TEXTURE	*(thick to thin)*	
NOTE MORPHOLOGY	*(how a sound begins/sustains/ends)*	
GROWTH	*(vertical shape/horizontal movement)*	
RT FACTOR	*(degree of repose or tension)*	
PHRASE	*(organization of musical thought)*	
NOTE GROUPING	*(inflection within the phrase)*	

As we work to realize the ideal sound image, a great deal of time and energy is spent revealing the implied meaning which is hidden in the written symbol. We rely on memory, expectation, illusion, suspense and surprise to create a musical experience. Discovering what is in the music, developing a genuine feeling for it, and communicating it's meaning is crucial. Rather than just isolating and fixing tones, the conductor must highlight the relationships between the tones.

Asking questions is a great method to promote student involvement in developing a rehearsal plan. This can be done informally on a regular basis throughout rehearsals or formally with a questionnaire. A "learning goal survey" can be distributed to involve the players in the process of planning. The questions help the students to develop short term goals, which lead to long term solutions. Hand the questionnaire out at the first rehearsal. Let everyone know they will be filling out the questionnaire at the completion of the first reading. Once filled out, have the players sign and date them, then collect them. A few weeks later hand them out again. Allow the students to evaluate their progress and review their initial reactions and evaluations, amending as needed. Repeat the exercise and compare the answers. A sample questionnaire follows:

1. Is this the best that you can play this piece?
2. What passages went well?
3. What passages will need the most work?
4. How will you practice the difficult passages?
5. What makes the passage difficult?
6. What is the general style of this piece?
7. What is the form of this piece?
8. Describe this piece in one or two word phrases.
9. Will this piece be difficult to learn?
10. How long will it take to learn this piece?
11. Is this a good piece? Why?

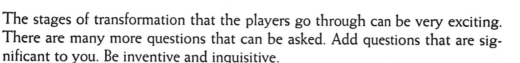

The stages of transformation that the players go through can be very exciting. There are many more questions that can be asked. Add questions that are significant to you. Be inventive and inquisitive.

The simplified goal of the rehearsal is to "transfer ownership" from you to them. The idealized goal of the rehearsal is to discover how a piece works, not to fix problems. The discovery process will expose problems, which in truth, can only be solved by the players. The conductor facilitates that process by offering solutions. The players are the only ones who can take action to implement the change. Taking action is the only way to improve. It is important to understand that the rehearsal is the place to do the work together that can't be done alone.

Our goals can be achieved through engaging the players in the project. Capturing their attention is paramount. Activity and responsibility are the two things that keep them connected. They need to feel they are getting an aesthetic return on their investment of time and energy. Sharing the insights and information we have gleaned through our preparation and study is most important. The goals are many, but primarily we hope to establish an emotive link with others through our performance. The process is not about being the best it is about doing our best. Rather than impressing the listener, our performance goals should include the following.

Engage and **Impact** the listener/player
Affect and **Reach** the listener/player
Move and **Enrich** the listener/player
Elevate and **Captivate** the listener/player

With a comprehensive approach, it becomes apparent that we have the ability to make a wonderful contribution. In a world that has become so quantity oriented, our art is uniquely suited to improve the quality of the lives of those who are touched by what we do.

Pacing

We can use the same diagram of the hour glass shown earlier to illustrate rehearsal pacing. When laid it on its side, it becomes a useful visual for describing the flow of the rehearsal. Great rehearsals should include a series of multiple zooms (in and out). They can also begin with very detailed work and progress to the whole. Avoid getting caught doing detailed work with a select few as the rehearsal time runs out.

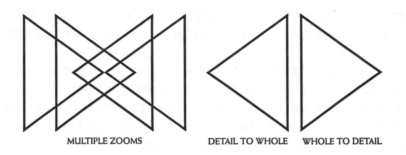

MULTIPLE ZOOMS   DETAIL TO WHOLE   WHOLE TO DETAIL

Keep the tempo of the rehearsal moving. Use instructions that are simple and doubt free. Avoid confusion by giving instructions which focus on one primary issue at a time. Let them know why you stopped and what to do to make it better. Avoid letting the rehearsal lapse into a practice session. Be sure you are clear about whether you are dealing with an error of preparation or an error of concentration before you begin to fix a problem. After all, it may not be broken, only out of focus. Thought must be present in order for change to occur. Time spent acknowledging accomplishment should, at the very least, be equal to the time spent calling attention to the problem. Let the players know you appreciate their good work. As the leader of the process, showing appreciation is one of our primary responsibilities.

The most successful rehearsals usually involve a series of quick raids on problems, separating out an issue, and working on it in a way that involves those who are *not* playing as well as those who are. Getting stuck in one place can quickly bring a rehearsal to a grinding halt. We must continue to monitor the atmosphere and attitudes in the room. If you think you are beginning to lose them you probably already have. To accomplish a change you must do the following:

1. Identify the problem.
2. Recommend a solution.
3. Experience the solution.
4. Catalog the feeling that caused the change so that muscle memory can help you duplicate the solution.
5. Acknowledge the accomplishment or change.

Be persistent with the understanding that not all problems can be solved in one rehearsal. Before you go on, be sure the players know what to do and how to practice to make it better. There is no short cut to improvement. We come together as individuals to form an ensemble which has as its purpose the recreation of a work of art. Players will have to practice away from the rehearsal. Everyone should think of the rehearsal as an artistic assembly plant. The music gets put together at the plant. It is assembled each day and we listen to it work, all the while noticing what still needs to be improved. At the end of the rehearsal we disassemble the art work and send a part of it home with every musician. Each agrees to work on their part so that it will fit better the next time the piece is reassembled. Obviously, when a part is missing or not being played well, the composition is less than whole and progress is impeded. In a very real sense, all musicians have the opportunity to bring a gift to rehearsal, something they make themselves at home... a beautiful part.

We are responsible for using the time we have wisely. Some of the most effective rehearsal approaches are those offered by Barry Green in the *Inner Game of Music*. With this concept we use our Will to create Trust and Respect and increase Awareness. Things cannot get better without first increasing awareness. Trying often fails. Avoid using the word try in rehearsals. Instead, ask the players to think about, look for, focus on, listen to, make clear, and bring out. This type of request creates failure proof instruction. Good rehearsals develop feeling as well as skill. Most rehearsal instructions are based on one of the six skills of awareness listed below. In order to have a well balanced rehearsal it is important to give as many subjective instructions as objective ones. David Perkins suggests that the ensemble will become more and more musical as they learn to identify and understand the relationships of the different aspects of playing also listed below. Both objective and subjective directions can lead us to improving their ability to identify and understand musical relationships.

INSTRUCTIONS		UNDERSTANDING
OBJECTIVE +	SUBJECTIVE =	RELATIONSHIPS
SEE	FEEL	CAUSE - EFFECT
REMEMBER	HEAR	WHOLE - PART
UNDERSTAND	IMAGINE	FOREGROUND-BACKGROUND
		FORM - FUNCTION
		UNITY - VARIETY
		LINES - LAYERS
		HORIZONTAL - VERTICAL - DIAGONAL
		COMPARISON - CONTRAST
		SUCCESSIVE - SIMULTANEOUS
		REPLICATE PRODUCT -
		CREATE INTERPRETATION

A primary goal is to assist the players in fulfilling their potential by eliminating anything that interferes with the process. We accomplish this by giving simple instructions which elicit an immediate response and create change. Remember to work on one issue at a time, simplify the instructions, avoid fear and confusion, and have them participate in the solution.

Evaluating

While it is necessary and productive to critique and review our work, we must avoid becoming overly critical of our students as well as ourselves. Acknowledging accomplishment is equal in importance to suggesting improvement. We need to develop ways to monitor the students progress during the process rather than focusing on an evaluation of the product at the end. David Elliot, in his book *Music Matters*, reminds us "it is imperative that we help our students to assess and evaluate their own developing musicianship." His options which can help them map their progress include:

COMPILING A "MUSICAL - PROCESS FOLIO"
which can include audio and video tapes of students efforts in group rehearsals and individual practice sessions; tapes of solo and small group performances during class and outside of class; students self evaluation of their progress; lists of future rehearsal goals; written or recorded feedback from peers, teachers, or outside guests.

WRITING AN "ENSEMBLE REHEARSAL CRITIQUE"
similar to the many standardized evaluation forms used at festivals throughout the country. Additionally, students could write comments as they listen to or observe a recording of a rehearsal or performance.

KEEPING A "PRACTICE JOURNAL OR DIARY"
which is the students personal record of plans, achievements and self-reflection that can be shared with peers and teachers for feedback and coaching. This is a terrific means of setting short-term and long-term goals as well as organizing their practice time.

NOTATING A "LISTENING LOG"
encourages students to listen to recordings of works they are learning to interpret and perform. Listening more widely to other works by the same composer or from the same style period can also be helpful. This process might also involve making interpretive comparisons of the same piece performed by different conductors or performers. Reading reviews can also be interesting and thought provoking.

In addition, structured debriefing sessions following rehearsals or performances can be beneficial. Here are some sample questions which can be used to help the musicians focus on their achievement and set new goals.
1. What did you like about your performance?
2. Is there still room for improvement?
3. Do you think any performance can be absolutely perfect?
4. If perfection is an impossible goal, what is the goal?
5. Did you experience something in this performance that was new?
6. Did you hear something in the music that was new?
7. Did you see anything that you hadn't noticed before?
8. Did you remember things that you forgot you knew?

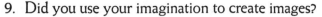

9. Did you use your imagination to create images?
10. Were you moved by this experience?
11. Do you think you moved the audience?
12. Did you feel connected to the music?
13. Did you feel connected to your fellow musicians?
14. Do you have any other comments or thoughts about this experience?
15. What do you think you will remember most about this experience ten years from now?

Often in this setting the responses can be sensitive, perceptive, expressive and quite simply, overwhelming. Providing a forum in which the players can articulate their ideas, acknowledge their feelings, and share pride in their accomplishments will lead to many new discoveries!

In leading a closure session of this sort one becomes immediately aware of David Elliot's premise that "music education is a unique and major source of several fundamental life values which include self-growth, self-knowledge, self-esteem, and musical enjoyment." Additionally, we recognize the value in his belief that "understanding and feeling music is achievable, accessible, and applicable to all students, not just the talented few."

SUMMARY

An educational approach which emphasizes the development of comprehensive musical knowledge and teaches musicianship will lead to broader and more meaningful experiences for everyone involved. At the very least, participation in a music program should create feelingful people who understand and enjoy music. Music creates a pathway to the center of our soul and provides a renewable resource for exploring and expressing our emotions. There is no doubt that music has the power to enhance and enrich human beings and helps to define what being human means.

Music captures moments and preserves the essence of the various paradigms in the world that we call culture. As teachers and professionals we must be careful not to limit ourselves to the most familiar or comfortable paradigms. The truth of the matter is that our limitations are too soon passed on to our students. If we make an eternal commitment to growth and remain open and curious, music can provide a unique way of knowing and experiencing each other. While music is not a language it can express the thoughts and emotions of a culture or individual in a way that nothing else can. Music is and has always been multicultural because it exists within a context of people and places. It is wonderfully diverse and if we are to continue to learn and grow we must embrace that diversity.

Music is a primary condition of the human experience. In the history of man on earth many civilizations have been identified that could not read, write or calculate. None have been discovered that did not make music. It is also interesting to note, that of all the species on earth only humans purposefully engage in making music. There are so many feelings in our heart and images in our mind that can only be accessed through creating, performing, and audiating great music. When those thoughts and feelings are activated and engaged we can experience the profound impact of music making as an endless source of inspirational energy that flows continually through our lives; elevating, expanding, and deepening our spirits.

Our interaction with music as performers and teachers is both cognitive and intuitive. The profession has coined phrases like; *informed intuition* and *feelingful intelligence* in an attempt to explain this phenomenon. Increasing the depth of our musicianship gives us the ability to express our feelings while leading others to discover theirs.

As conductors and teachers we have found that teaching and performing music is not something we do to make a living, it is something we do to make a life. I have heard it said that if you want to be a good conductor you should only conduct good players. However, in our profession if we want to conduct good players we must become good teachers.

CHAPTER 4

The Assessment
of Student Learning
In Band

Larry Blocher

The term *music education* implies musical learning.[6] At frequent points in the teaching and learning process, it is important for teachers to assess the affect of music teaching on student learning. "What did the students learn" is still an important question. In order for learning to take place, teachers must recognize exactly what students must know, how to teach it to them, and how to determine if they have learned it.[7] While there is a wealth of valuable information available on the topic of assessment in education and music education, the focus of this chapter is on the *assessment* of *student learning in band* as a basis for student evaluation.

Assessment: A Starting Point

Assessment involves gathering information about the learning process. Student assessment refers to some form of direct examination of student performance in tasks that are considered significant.[8] An important relationship exists between teacher rehearsal and performance objectives and assessment "procedures" selected to measure student learning in rehearsal and performance settings. While objectives identify important musical behaviors for students to acquire, assessment determines if the designated behaviors have, in fact, been met.[9]

Achieving the aims of education depends on assessment that provides "accurate and constructive feedback to students about the quality of their growing musicianship."[10] Assessment as an active part of music instruction provides opportunities for students not only to receive feedback, but also to participate in ongoing feedback on both music process and product. Assessment—an essential part of the teaching/learning process—is a joint responsibility of teachers and students in a performance setting.

Assessment Versus Evaluation

A number of authors have reported general public, administrator, and teacher confusion about the terms *assessment* and *evaluation*. While a detailed discussion of these terms is beyond the scope of this chapter, *assessment*, for the purposes of this discussion, refers to the means and tools used to gather information about students and their achievement. *Evaluation* refers to judgments and decisions made about students and their work as a result of assessment.[11]

Assessment, Evaluation, and Band Directors

Band directors, as music teachers, must, and do, make decisions regarding the various ways of gathering information about individual and group learning in music performance settings. The value of any assessment technique as a basis for student evaluation is determined by how well it serves the purposes for which it was administered. For example, each time a band director rehearses, he or she is involved in assessing a number of performance elements using performance-based assessment as a basis for diagnostic evaluation, "determining whether there are problems and how to address them."[12] The performance-based assessment techniques used in this case become the tools for diagnostic evaluation. The exact performance-based assessment techniques used, determined by the individual band director, are selected based on the band director's need to determine where the problems are and how to fix them.

Band directors have been described as masters of diagnostic evaluation and proficient with placement evaluation, based on student background and initial performance level and summative evaluation based on student final achievement or product. However, band directors often neglect formative evaluation that involves assessment techniques designed to monitor the ongoing learning of individuals in rehearsal.[13]

Alternative Assessment in Band

Alternative assessment, sometimes referred to as "authentic assessment," "direct assessment," or "performance assessment," is a generic term that reflects, as of this writing, a growing support for alternative methods to assess public school students' achievements. Portfolio Assessment, a common form of alternative assessment, involves sampling and compiling individual students' work over time. It seems unclear, at this time, exactly what Portfolios can measure in a music performance setting. However, Portfolio Assessment may have direct application in *formative evaluation*—ongoing individual evaluation—of students involved in performance preparation in band. While there is little agreement on what should be included in a band student's Portfolio, clearly the Portfolio should include some type of statement of purpose written by the student and the teacher (band director) that clearly establishes goals and objectives. The purpose statement would form the basis for determining what should be included in the Portfolio.

The Assessment of Student Learning in Band

The *National Standards for Arts Education*, as previously discussed, provide all students, including students in general music and students in performing groups, with suggested knowledge and performance standards in the arts. Overall, these standards involve performing, creating, and responding to music. In a broad sense, these standards may provide a foundation for student assessment in performing groups by affirming that knowledge and skills matter, and that aspects of musical learning in performing groups can be measured in a variety of ways.

What follows is a general listing of sample assessment possibilities for use in band. Each assessment technique offers a way to gather a variety of information about student learning in music. The intended *purpose* of any assessment procedure should be carefully considered before implementation. The band director is challenged to use this list as a basis for continuation of his or her own decision-making concerning student assessment and evaluation in band, and to interpret and make the selected ideas fit individual situations.

Assessment Possibilities in Band

Standardized Tests (performance skills, factual knowledge)
Band Director-Constructed Tests (skills, knowledge)
Band Director Critiques (student skills, knowledge)
Band Director/Student Interviews
Band Director/Student Anecdotal Records
Band Director/Student Contracts
Student Audio/Video Recordings (individual/ensemble)
Student Self-Critiques (process, product)
Student Peer Critiques (process, product)
Student Rehearsal Critiques (individual/ensemble)
Music Festival Participation (individual/ensemble)
Private Lessons (individual/group)
Student Rehearsal/Performance Logs/Journals
Student Attitude Surveys
Student Performance Surveys
Student Demonstration (skills, knowledge)
Student Checklists (skills, knowledge)
Portfolios
Student Conferences/Group Discussions
Individual/Section Progress Charts (skills, knowledge)
Student Listening Activities (individual/group)
Consultant Critiques of Student Performances (individual/ensemble)
Student Creative Projects (individual/group)
Written Essays by Students
Student Performance Skill Inventories

Assessment: Initial Closure

Selecting an appropriate assessment procedure to determine the musical "it" that band students learned during the rehearsal and performance process, and deciding how to use this information, involve informed decision-making by band directors. Informed decision-making about assessment in a performance setting forces band directors to ask "what is it that I want my students to learn and remember from the rehearsal and performance experience in band?" When the band rehearsal and performance are viewed as an opportunity for teaching the skills and knowledge required for musical performance and musical understanding, any number of assessment strategies may be appropriate.

Notes

6   C. Leonard, "Evaluation in Music Education," in *Basic Concepts in Music Education*, ed. N. Henry (Chicago: The University of Chicago Press, 1958), 312.

7   C. Madsen, & C. Madsen, *Teaching Discipline* (Raleigh: Contemporary Music Publishing, 1983), 39.

8   T. Goolsby, "Music Portfolios in Secondary Music Classes: What Do They Measure?," in *SRIG Measurement and Evaluation* eds. R. Colwell and J. Holly, (Reston, VA: Music Educators National Conference, 1994) 17.

9   J. Labuta, *Guide to Accountability in Music Instruction* (West Nyack, NY: Parker Publishing Company, 1974), 117.

10   D. Elliott, *Music Matters* (New York: Oxford University Press, 1995), 264.

11   T. Goolsby, "Portfolio Assessment in Secondary Music Classes," University of Washington, 1995.

12   T. Goolsby.

13   Ibid., p.4.

PART II

THE BAND CONDUCTOR AS A MUSIC TEACHER (IN PRACTICE)

Chapter 5

Units of the Teacher Resource Guide

Richard Miles

A Teacher Resource Guide is provided for each of the one hundred select works for band. These guides are designed to assist the director in providing a balanced, comprehensive, and sequential program of instruction while preparing for performance. Many important aspects are addressed concerning musical elements, structure, and style in order to develop musicianship.

Each guide is divided into nine units, seven for instruction and two for reference. The information in the seven instructional units can be presented in a variety of formats. The units may be presented entirely at one time, integrated with other information, presented as an individual concept or skill, or (preferably) presented in one- to two-minute segments of information over an extended period while preparing the work for performance.

Chapter five describes the function and the type of information included in each unit of the Teacher Resource Guides. The most important and relevant aspects are addressed in a brief and concise manner. The unit examples that follow are based on Gordon Jacob's *An Original Suite*.

Unit 1: Composer

Background information about the composer allows the teacher and student to have a better understanding and appreciation of both music and composer. Unit one presents information such as the composers' birth and death dates, national origin, and where the composer lived when writing the selected work. Other aspects are sometimes presented, such as education of the composer, famous teachers or students of the composer, characteristics of his compositional style, major composition awards, and other works composed for the wind band. Example:

Gordon Percival Septimus Jacob was born in London in 1895.

Jacob studied music at the Royal College of Music, and in 1926, became a member of the music faculty, a position which he held for forty years. A teacher, conductor, orchestrater, composer, and author, Jacob contributed several important compositions to the wind band repertoire at a time when bands had limited original literature. Notable works by Jacob include: *An Original Suite, William Byrd Suite, The Battell, Fantasia on an English Folk Song, Tribute to Canterbury,* and *Music for a Festival.*

Unit 2: Composition

Unit 2 information focuses on the origin of the work, the possible meaning or importance of the title, and when it was composed. General characteristics (Romantic, Classical, etc.), along with compositional techniques utilized, are described to give additional insight into the style of the composition. In some instances, the work is related to other compositions by the same composer; those other works are referenced. An overview of the work, the number of movements, form, length and difficulty of the work are also provided to assist the director in the selection of this work for teaching.

Example:

An *Original Suite* was Jacob's first original work for band. There is speculation that the word "original" in the title may refer to the original folk song melodies used by Jacob in the suite. These original melodies helped to distinguish Jacob's composition from the transcriptions which made up the "core" of the bands repertoire at the time. Jacob's folk-song-like melodies were similar in style to his British counterparts Holst and Vaughan Williams. The suite, approximately nine and a half minutes in length, has three contrasting movements, *March* (Allegro di Marcia), *Intermezzo* (Andante ma non troppo), and *Finale* (Allegro Con Brio).

Unit 3: Historical Perspective

The relation to history and culture is the central focus of the information provided in Unit 3. The unit indicates when the selected work was composed, transcribed, and arranged, and presents the historical period and the relation to style and interpretation (e.g., Baroque, Classical, Romantic, Contemporary). The expression, dynamics, and articulation typical of the period or style are often addressed. Other important parallel composers and works for wind band are presented.

Example:

An *Original Suite* was composed during the early years of the development of the repertoire composed specifically for the wind band, often referred to as the "Military Band." The majority of works being performed were transcriptions or arrangements of piano, vocal, or orchestral compositions. *An Original Suite*, composed in 1928, follows other similar British Military Band compositions, including Gustav Holst's *First Suite in Eb* (composed in 1909), the *Second Suite in F* (composed in 1911) and Ralph Vaughan Williams' *English Folk Song Suite* (composed in 1924). Nationalism in music continued to flourish in the years between the World Wars. Folk music was used as a major expression of this stylistic period. Jacob's *An Original Suite* was nationalistic in character although not connected to traditional folk songs.

Unit 4: Technical Considerations

Unit 4 presents the technical skills needed by the student to perform the selected work adequately. Each teacher may need to establish long range technical development exercises in order to achieve the skill level needed for performance. Although some students may not currently possess the technical skills required to perform the work, the teacher may still use the piece by utilizing selected excerpts to assist in the technical development of the needed skills. As technical skills are being developed, the teacher can present and apply other specific concepts.

The major keys, or tonal centers, are outlined with the needed mastery of specific scales to perform the work. Rhythmic considerations are presented, such as the use of syncopation, dotted-eighth-note patterns, 6/8 time, polyrhythms, ostinato, hemiola, and asymmetrical patterns. Performance demands vary with each selected work. Specific demands presented include range, rapid articulation, extended and sustained lines, chromaticism, non-idiomatic treatment of parts, and unusual instrumentation or voicing.

Each of the identified technical considerations can become an additional concept or a "one-to-two minute unit" of instruction.
Example:

The scales of Bb Major, G minor, and F Major are required for the full ensemble. Flutes, Eb Clarinet, Solo and first Clarinets must play ascending and descending arpeggios (two octaves) in Bb Major in sixteenth notes at approximately 120 beats per minute. Flutes, Piccolo, Eb Clarinet, Solo and first Clarinets, and Solo Cornet must play the F Major scale in sixteenth notes at approximately 120 beats per minute. The rhythmic demands are very basic, with the use of eighth- and sixteenth-note combinations. Jacob occasionally utilizes runs which incorporate quintuplets and sextuplets, but these are found only in the woodwinds and baritones.

Unit 5: Stylistic Considerations

Addressed are the primary stylistic considerations of articulation, bowing relationship to articulation (when applicable), stylistic period and interpretation, expression, and phrasing. Performance requirements include the presentation and understanding of specific interpretation parameters. For example, in order to perform a work from the Classical period, students need to know that Classical style requires the use of precise, carefully controlled and restrained articulation. Staccato notes are performed with light separation. Dynamics of this era are more refined and restrained than dynamics used in the Romantic and Contemporary periods. Brass instruments are less dominant and the melodic line needs to project—with clarity—in a tuneful and folk-like manner.

Specific indicators of the interpretation are presented. The expression marks, dynamics, tempo, and style or mood of the work are presented, along with the relation of expression to the musical structure.
Example:

> The contrasting styles of legato, staccato, and marcato are utilized throughout the first movement in the traditional style of earlier British wind band compositions. Dynamics encompass a wide range of intensity, with numerous, sudden contrasts, crescendos, and diminuendos. Rich, full and sonorous tone quality is required for the themes, especially the trio. All melodies should be played in a singing style. The rhythmic accompaniment needs to be metronomically precise with varied (heavy and intense to light) and separated articulation. The tempo should remain constant throughout, with a feeling of "bounce" to the pulse.

Unit 6: Musical Elements

Harmony, melody, rhythm, and timbre are the focus of Unit 6. The harmony area may include information concerning the tonality and chord construction, cadences, dissonance and consonance, and harmonic progression. Other relevant harmonic techniques are addressed as necessary, such as the use of polytonality and serial harmony. The treatment of the voice movement or texture is addressed and identified as being either monophonic, homophonic, or polyphonic.

The melody (or theme) area includes information concerning the use of tonality, scales, motives, sequence, phrases, diatonic structure and melodic design, chromatic melody, serial melody, or themes.

The rhythm area addresses beat and meter, as well as the possible use of polymeter, uneven meter, changing meters, and nonmeters.
Example:

> The main theme in the first movement is stated in G minor with tonal centers of Bb Major and F Major being dominant throughout. The harmony parallels the clarity and pureness of Purcell's 17th Century style while adding contemporary melodic complexity and rhythmic development. Three contrasting themes are used (as outlined in Unit 7). Compositional devices include the use of counter-melodic material (6 before D - E), chromatic harmonic accompani-

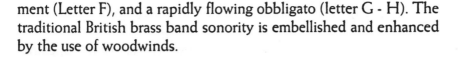

ment (Letter F), and a rapidly flowing obbligato (letter G - H). The traditional British brass band sonority is embellished and enhanced by the use of woodwinds.

Unit 7: Form and Structure

The study of the form and structure of a composition can help the teacher and student better understand the construction outline. Composers use these organizational or design tools to create expression in their music. Unit 7 provides information concerning these organizing forces by outlining the melodic and harmonic functions.

The design of the music is identified through the varied use of phrases, themes, or sections. Tonal structure (or movement) is identified through the organization of key or tonal centers, often influenced by the organization and intent of the cadences. Many formal types of composition construction are presented in the one-hundred select works. These formal types may include binary or two-part, ternary, rondo, arch, theme & variation, sonata, ostinato (forms such as the passacaglia and chaconne), free (forms such as the symphonic poem, toccata, and prelude), and multiple (forms such as the suite and symphony). Example:

OPENING		Introduction (2 measures, stated in the snare drum)
THEME 1		3rd measure, Letter A (Flowing melody in G minor) stated in the upper woodwinds and Solo and first Cornets Repeated at Letter A, instrumentation for the theme is enlarged to include baritones, saxophones, trumpets, and piccolo with flutes an octave higher.
THEME 2		Letter B (contrasting detached melody) stated in the woodwinds and brass
THEME 3		Trio (lyrical melody in Bb Major stated in the lower range)
THEME 1	REPEATED	Letter F (return to melody in G minor, use of countermelody in the cornets, trumpets, and trombones)
THEME 2	REPEATED	Letter G (obbligato embellishment in the flutes, piccolo, upper clarinets, and solo cornet)
THEME 1	REPEATED	Letter H (chromatic harmony accompaniment

to the melody)

CODA   Last three measures (repeat of the opening
                                    snare drum rhythmic figure followed by
                                    closure with a G Major chord)

Unit 8: Suggested Listening

Developing appreciative and discriminating listening skills are important
and are part of the *National Standards for Arts Education* Music Content Standard 6:
Listening to, Analyzing, and Describing Music. Unit 8 provides a suggested listening list
of works which parallel historical period, style, form, tonality, or other relevant
musical aspects.
Example:

> *First Suite in Eb*, Gustav Holst
> *Second Suite in F,* Gustav Holst
> *English Folk Song Suite*, Ralph Vaughan Williams
> *The Battell*, Gordon Jacob
> *Fantasia on an English Folk Song*, Gordon Jacob
> *Music for a Festival*, Gordon Jacob
> *Tribute to Canterbury*, Gordon Jacob
> *William Byrd Suite*, Gordon Jacob
> *Air and March*, Henry Purcell
> *Dido and Aeneas*, Henry Purcell

Unit 9: Additional References and Resources

Sources used for reference in the units are listed for each selected work.
Additional sources (dissertations, books, journals, or articles) are listed that may
address a specific work or composer.
Examples:

Dvorak, Thomas L., Robert Grechesky, and Gary M. Ciepluch. *Best Music for
     High School Band*, edited by Bob Margolis. Brooklyn: Manhattan Beach
     Music, 1993.

Kopetz, Barry, "Gordon Jacob's An Original Suite," *The Instrumentalist*, XLIV June
     1990, 22-30, 53-56.

Kreines, Joseph. *Music for Concert Band*. Tampa: Florida Music Service, 1989.

Rehrig, William H. *The Heritage Encyclopedia of Band Music*. Edited by Paul E.
     Bierley. Westerfield, OH: Integrity Press, 1991.

Smith, Norman, and Albert Stoutamire. *Band Music Notes*. Third

ed. San Diego: Kjos West, 1982.

Stycos, Roland. *Listening Guides for Band Musicians*. Portland, ME: J. Weston Walch, 1991.

Thompson, Kevin. "Gordon Jacob - I Aim at Greater Simplicity Nowadays," *The Instrumentalist*, XXXVIII September 1983, 38-39.

Whiston, J. Alan. "Gordon Jacob. A Biographical Sketch and Analysis of Four Selected Works for Band" (Ph.D. diss., The University of Oklahoma, 1987).

CHAPTER 6

Making the Connection: Academic, Rehearsal, Curriculum

Edward S. Lisk

The major current emphasis in education is the development of new curriculum design, standards, and assessment for all disciplines. The new paradigm for education provides directors opportunities to establish academic importance for their band programs and remove the long-held perception that band is an extra-curricular activity. The expansive amount of information found in this text provides the necessary curriculum materials to establish academic recognition for a wide range of band programs.

An instrumental music program serves as an important component to education. Research and statistical evidence support the significance of playing an instrument. Researchers such as Howard Gardner, David Perkins, Frank Wilson, David Elliott, and Frances Rauscher provide our profession with sufficient reason for inclusion as part of an academic process. The complexities of performing in an instrumental ensemble are massive, and considering current research and information about cognition, extend far beyond the normal school learning experience.

The basic principle *"all children can learn"* is propelling change, as well as new considerations, in teaching techniques. In the past, people often viewed band participation as something for those with a special talent or gift. Not everyone was viewed as capable of playing an instrument. With this basic principle still in place, the removal of the old paradigm of *'selected students'* provides an entire student population of a school district with the opportunity to study instrumental music. This may become a significant factor in the hiring of additional band directors to accommodate increased participation and enrollment. This assumption would require training band directors to design band programs within the new educational framework of academic accountability.

The rehearsal period and instruction must address key issues: *What is expected of students and from the band program? What are students expected to know and be able to do through the study of instrumental music?* The statement is critical and has far-reaching implications when designing a band program of excellence and academic accountability. All students participating in an instrumental program will ideally demonstrate the highest levels of musical literacy and be able to function through the life-long learning experience of instrumental music as participants, consumers, or advocates.

The new paradigm for education, and its implications on our conventional rehearsal structure (warm-up, literature preparation, and evaluation and assessment), require change to accommodate new curriculum demands and student learning expectations. Rehearsal planning should consider how students learn and how *specialized* skill development expands an individual's knowledge base and contributes to the whole of academic achievement. An effective and well-designed rehearsal will provide ongoing, spontaneous opportunities for students to exercise and develop their critical listening and thinking skills supported by musical decision-making opportunities.

The ensemble experience allows the band student to become *actively involved in a decision making process* that ultimately determines the band's quality and excellence. Each participant must be responsible for tuning, balance, blend, rhythm, dynamics, and phrasing. If the director assumes the responsibility in making all musical decisions and denies students the opportunity to develop *their* critical listening and thinking skills, the student becomes a *passive participant waiting to be told what to do.* The director must instruct and guide the student through the process of musical decisions relative to performance demands. Each participant challenged to the highest degree. The challenge can be expanded considerably when the individual is placed in a section setting and experiences how his or her decisions impact the final performance.

The instrumental ensemble addresses the importance of inter and intrapersonal skill (intelligence) development. It is perhaps the only learning situation found in a school setting that allows a student to be autonomous while, at the same time, make musical decisions that affect the full ensemble (synergy). A superior band program results from student musicians who understand, appreciate, and are sensitive to each other in this musical world of communication and expression. All areas are critical in the development of musicianship and significantly contribute to the students' total educational process. There is no other subject or discipline like instrumental music that so effectively spans the entire universe of learning.

The Rehearsal Period

The changing time configuration from a traditional six to eight-period school day to an extended 90 to 120-minute period (the "block schedule") creates new advantages and opportunities for directors. Increased rehearsal time allows the director to focus greater attention toward performance fundamentals, curriculum design, literature selection, and performance concepts. The biggest change will be for the director to expand and upgrade rehearsal techniques from the established and comfortable pattern of a 45-50 minute period.

The rehearsal warm-up should provide students sufficient time to prepare both physically and mentally for the pace and intensity of an extended instructional period (60-120 minutes). This segment usually contains some form of tuning process as well as rhythm studies, chorales or technical exercises. Repetition is a high priority when establishing consistent performance standards, but can be detrimental to a rehearsal if students become passive due to monotonous, repetitious exercises that contribute little to any type of musical or mental readiness for the rehearsal.

To remove any type of passive involvement or response from students, the warm-up exercises must be connected or linked to the performance demands of the literature under preparation. This establishes a mindset for the particular musical task to come. Performance demands include balance, blend, intonation, tone quality, rhythmic accuracy, entrance, release, dynamics, style, technic, articulation, phrasing and expressive qualities. All the performance elements and demands of a particular composition cannot be contained in any one specific warm-up exercise. When planning the rehearsal period, the director decides *what* and *where* the band's weaknesses are in regard to the specific literature under preparation. These musical demands become a part of the rehearsal warm-up process. Thus, the warm-up exercises change for each rehearsal to accommodate the musical growth and development of students and the relevant literature. Furthermore, connecting or linking a warm-up process to the literature under preparation elevates it to a more prominent status within the structure of a rehearsal. For the director, this requires literature analysis (found in this text), imagination, and creativity.

The planning or design of a linked warm-up process is quite simple. If, for example, the literature to be rehearsed is in a march style, apply the following options to the warm-up exercises:

1. Play a warm-up exercise in the style and tempo of the selected march.
2. Apply articulation style and patterns with any type of scale exercise or other technical étude.
3. Select any complex rhythmic pattern that may be a problem and apply it to scale exercises.
4. Combine rhythmic accompaniment patterns with scale exercises or other technical study or étude.
5. For intonation or balance problems, take any tutti chord and play slowly through a chromatic scale passage. The chromatic approach to tutti voicing should also be applied to rhythm patterns.

The process is not that difficult. Once applied, imagination and creativity provide unlimited musical possibilities connected to the literature. The goal is to recognize the weaknesses and strengths of a band program and not have to re-teach basic performance skills with every composition.

The question of how much rehearsal time a warm-up consumes has been a longtime concern for band directors. Approximately 20% of the rehearsal period should be devoted to warm-up exercises based upon the musical complexities of the literature being prepared. A 60-minute rehearsal would require 12-15 minutes of rehearsal time, while 15-20 minutes could be used in a 120-minute period. The 120-minute block allows additional opportunities for extended tuning, balance, and blend exercises to be interspersed throughout the rehearsal. The remainder of rehearsal time can be devoted to literature preparation, study, and analysis as outlined in the model Units found in this text.

Students' knowledge and skill of basic performance fundamentals determine the amount of rehearsal time a particular selection will require (one hour, one week, one month, two months, etc.). Tone quality, rhythmic understanding, and technical skills (e.g. scale mastery) are part of all successful performances. Technical demands must not exceed the students' skill level, but should offer a realistic challenge. Too often, when literature surpasses the students technical skills, a tedious and repetitious process produces a mechanical performance with little expressive nuance or understanding. A careful balance must be in place when selecting literature that will effectively motivate, challenge, and inspire student musicians.

The established curriculum serves as the driving force and guidance system for this newly organized band program. The concert performance is the result of a curriculum based upon band 'masterworks,' rather than superfluous literature that adapts to the whims of the time. Thus, instrumental education will receive equal recognition as do all other disciplines of academic worth. This text provides directors with sufficient material to establish a model curriculum to support a superior band program within the new educational framework of academic accountability.

Curricular Models Based on Literature Selection

Richard Miles

There are an infinite number of ways one can select music literature for curricular study. The following models serve as reference for consideration in adapting to a state-wide, regional, district, or individual curriculum. These models provide examples of literature selected to be taught in either a sequential manner, a cyclic approach, an emphasis on the historical perspective, or as a combination of the above.

The Basic Band Curriculum

The following list of 48 compositions is meant as a reference for teaching quality music in a four-year cycle. This "Basic Band Curriculum" appears in the *BD Guide's* September/October 1987 issue. Three levels of difficulty are presented: Grades IV, V, and VI. Each band would study, rehearse, and perform yearly each of the four compositions listed by difficulty level. Two of the works would be performed for festival or concert contest and two in a regularly scheduled concert during the year.

GRADE IV

YEAR 1	Suite No. 1 in Eb	Gustav Holst
	Variations on a Korean Folk Song	John Barnes Chance
	Trauersinfonie	Richard Wagner
	Scenes from the Louvre	Norman Dello Joio
YEAR 2	Suite No. 2 in F	Gustav Holst
	Elsa's Procession ("Lohengrin")	Richard Wagner
	Toccata Marziale	Ralph Vaughan Williams
	Canzona	Peter Mennin

YEAR 3	William Byrd Suite	Gordon Jacob
	Irish Tune/Shepherd's Hey	Percy Grainger
	Chorale and Alleluia	Howard Hanson
	Chorale and Shaker Dance	John Zdechlik
YEAR 4	Folk Song Suite	Ralph Vaughan Williams
	Colonial Song	Percy Grainger
	When Jesus Wept	William Schuman
	Incantation and Dance	John Barnes Chance

GRADE V

YEAR 1	Overture for Band	Felix Mendelssohn
	Symphony VI	Vincent Persichetti
	Suite Francaise	Darius Milhaud
	Chester Overture for Band	William Schuman
YEAR 2	Divertimento	Vincent Persichetti
	Festive Overture	Dmitri Shostakovitch/ Hunsberger
	Fanfare and Allegro	Clifton Williams
	George Washington Bridge	William Schuman
YEAR 3	Celebration Overture	Paul Creston
	Suite of Old American Dances	Robert Russell Bennett
	Outdoor Overture	Aaron Copland
	Variants on a Medieval Tune	Norman Dello Joio
YEAR 4	Variations on America	Charles Ives/ Schuman-Rhoads
	Fantasies on a Theme by Haydn	Norman Dello Joio
	Overture to Candide	Leonard Bernstein/Beeler
	Armenian Dances	Alfred Reed

GRADE VI

YEAR 1	Lincolnshire Posy	Percy Grainger
	Symphony in Bb	Paul Hindemith
	Sinfonietta	Ingolf Dahl
	La Fiesta Mexicana	H. Owen Reed
YEAR 2	Prelude and Scherzo: Hammersmith	Gustav Holst
	Emblems	Aaron Copland
	The Leaves Are Falling	Warren Benson
	Music for Prague 1968	Karel Husa
YEAR 3	Theme and Variations, op 43a	Arnold Schoenberg
	Designs, Images and Textures	Leslie Bassett
	Symphony No. 3	Vittorio Giannini

	Symphony for Band "West Point"	Morton Gould
YEAR 4	Dionysiaques	Florent Schmitt
	Apotheosis of This Earth	Karel Husa
	Concerto for Percussion & Winds	Karel Husa
	Symphony for Drums & Wind Orchestra	Warren Benson

Comprehensive Music Curriculum

Robert Garofalo, in his 1976 book *Blueprint for Band* (published by Meredith Publications), proposes a curriculum based on a multi-faceted approach of comprehensive music instruction containing three principal components: 1) the instructional units, the unit study composition and special study unit, 2) band projects, and 3) the source/reference notebook. Each director utilizes yearly cycles of instruction which focus on instructional units, projects, and activities. Specially selected compositions serve as the core of this proposed curriculum. Teachers create their own curriculum for each composition and the procedure for information sharing. Instruction, or "unit study lesson plans," may take from a few days to weeks to complete. The comprehensive study of each selected composition is to be presented over an extended period.

The following is a representation of the selected repertoire listed in Appendix C of *Blueprint for Band* (pp. 110-114). The repertoire is listed according to historical period and three levels of difficulty: medium (M), moderately difficult (MD), and difficult (D).

Concert Band Literature

TWENTIETH CENTURY

COMPOSER-ARRANGER	TITLE	GRADE
Badings, Henk	Concerto for Flute and Wind Orchestra	D
Barber, Samuel	Commando March	MD
Bassett, Leslie	Designs, Images and Textures	D
Bennett, Robert Russell	Suite of Old American Dances	MD
Benson, Warren	The Leaves are Falling	D
	The Solitary Dancer	M
Copland, Aaron	An Outdoor Overture	MD
	Emblems	D
	Lincoln Portrait (with narrator)	MD
Cowell, Henry	Celtic Set	M
	Hymn and Fuguing Tune No. 1	M
Creston, Paul	Celebration Overture, op. 61	D
	Concerto for Alto Saxophone and Band	D
	Concerto for Marimba and Band	MD
Dahl, Ingolf	Sinfonietta for Band	MD

Dello Joio, Norman	Fantasies on a Theme by Haydn	M
	Songs of Abelard (optional solo voice)	MD
	Variants on a Medieval Tune	MD
Elgar, Edward	The Severn Suite	MD
	(originally for brass band)	
Giannini, Vittorio	Praeludium and Allegro	D
	Variations and Fugue	D
Grainger, Percy	Colonial Song	M
	Children's March	
	(Over the Hills and Far Away)	M
	Irish Tune from Country Derry	M
	Lincolnshire Posy	D
	Shepherd's Hey	MD
Hanson, Howard	Chorale and Alleluia	MD
Hindemith, Paul	Konzertmusik für Blasorchester, op. 41	D
	Symphony in Bb	D
Holst, Gustav	First Suite in Eb	M
	Hammersmith: Prelude and Scherzo	D
	Second Suite in F	MD
Hovhaness, Alan	Symphony No. 4, op. 165	MD
Husa, Karel	Music for Prague	D
Ives, Charles	Country Band March	MD
Mennin, Peter	Canzona	MD
Milhaud, Darius	Suite Francaise	MD
Nelhybel, Vaclav	Two Symphonic Movements	M
Persichetti, Vincent	Chorale Prelude: Turn Not Thy Face	M
	Divertimento	MD
	Masquerade for Band, op. 102	MD
	Psalm	MD
	Symphony No. 6, op. 69	D
Piston, Walter	Tunbridge Fair	MD
Rogers, Bernard	Three Japanese Dances	D
Schoenberg, Arnold	Theme and Variations, op. 43a	D
Schuller, Gunther	Meditations	MD
Schuman, William	Chester Overture	MD
	George Washington Bridge	MD
	When Jesus Wept	MD
Shostakovich, Dimitri	Festive Overture, op. 96	D
Stravinsky, Igor	Circus Polka	D
Vaughan Williams, Ralph	English Folk Song Suite	M
	Flourish for Wind Band	M
	Toccata Marziale	MD
	Sea Songs	M

| Walton, William | Crown Imperial: A Coronation March | D |

ROMANTIC

"Ninetenth-century original band music edited
for modern instrumentation"

Berlioz, Hector	Symphonie Funèbre et Triomphale (Symphony for Band), op. 15	MD
Donizetti, Gaetano	March for the Sultan Abdul Medjid	MD
Mendelssohn-Bartholdy, Felix	Overture for Winds, Op. 24 (based on 1826 autograph score)	MD
Rossini, Gioacchino	Three Marches for the Marriage of the Duke of Orleans	MD
	Scherzo for Band	MD
Wagner, Richard	Huldigungsmarsch (Homage March)	MD
	Trauersinfonie (Funeral Symphony)	M

CLASSICAL

"Late eighteenth-century original band music edited
for modern instrumentation"

Catel, Simone	Overture in C	MD
	Symphonie Militaire	M
Gossec, Francois Joseph	Classic Overture in C	MD
	Military Symphony in F	M
	Suite for Band	M
Hummel, Joseph	Three Marches for Band	M
Jadin, Hyacinthe	Overture in F (1795)	M
Jadin, Louis	Symphonie for Band	M
Mehúl, Éthenne-Henri	Overture in F	M
Paer, Ferdinando	Two Napoleonic Marches	M

BAROQUE - RENAISSANCE

"Illustrative of the many excellent band transcriptions
and arrangements of music from early historical periods"

Bach-Chidester	Passacaglia in C Minor	MD
Bach-Goldman & Leist	Fantasia in G Major	MD
Bach-Holst	Fugue à la Gigue	MD
Bach-Hunsberger	Passacaglia and Fugue in C Minor	MD
Bach-Moehlmann	Preludes and Fugue (in Bb, F, G, and D Minor)	M

Byrd-Jacob	William Byrd Suite	MD
Frescobaldi-Slocum	Toccata	M
Frescobaldi-Brunelli	Preludium and Fugue	M
Gabrieli, A.-Gardner	Chorale St. Marks	M
Gabrieli, G.-Schaefer	Sonata Pian e Forte	M
Handel-Kay	Water Music	M
Handel-Schaefer	Royal Fireworks Music	MD
Purcell-Gardner	Fanfare and Rondo	M
Vivaldi-Cacavas	Concerto Grosso in D Minor	M

The Three Or Four Year Cyclic Curriculum Based On The "Menu Principle"

Joseph A. Labuta, in his book *Teaching Musicianship in the High School Band* (originally published by Parker Publishing Company and revised and republished in 1996 by Merideth Music Publications), presents a curriculum based on instructional content in which students learn more than performance skills. Labuta proposes a cyclic approach to learning "about music" while studying "theory, styles, and values." The following three- to four-year curriculum is based on a sequence of teaching and emphasizing one content area per year, although all content areas would be reviewed to assure continuity and reinforcement.

During the first year, students study the primary topics of "Timbre and materials of music." Tone development, overall band sonority, and timbre and tone color are stressed in both large and small ensemble participation. Individual and group development are emphasized. All of these concepts are taught while rehearsing daily instructional band literature. Also presented are the following musical elements: rhythm, melody and theme, harmony and texture.

The second year focuses on the study of "Forms and styles of music." Music structure and formal types of music are presented through literature for study, rehearsal, and performance. Students learn the components and principles of form and tonal structure. Formal types, such as binary, ternary, rondo, arch, theme and variation, sonata, ostinato, fugue, Concerto grosso, and others, are presented.

The third-year curriculum presents "Interpretation and discrimination of music." The interpretation area focuses on two categories: 1) the use of expression marks, including dynamics, tempo, and style or mood, and 2) the musical structure of the phrasing or musical line. The second area focuses on the development of musical discrimination, as students are presented concepts for evaluating what is good music, performance, and style. The objective of this is to develop the ability to make positive value judgments about music.

A four-year curriculum divides the second year of study into two independent areas. The second year presents only the "forms of music" and the fourth year presents the "styles of music." The study of styles involves two areas: 1) the teaching of general styles of articulation, march and rubato style, and 2) the teaching of historical styles and performance practices of the Baroque, Classical, Romantic, and Contemporary periods. Also presented each year would be general information about timbre, musical elements, and form construction.

Labuta provides a listing of numerous band works to be used for teaching formal structure types and general styles of music. The following compositions are listed as representative works from the different historical periods. Many of these works are out of print. *The following is used with permission, Merideth Music Publications, 170 N.E. 33rd St., Ft. Lauderdale, FL 33334.*

THE BAROQUE ERA (c. 1600-1750)

Bach-Moelhmann, FitzSimmons	Preludes and Fugues (Bb, F, G and D minor)	M
Bach-Falcone	Passacaglia and Fugue in C minor	MD
Bach-Boyd	Little Fugue in G minor	MD
Bach-Leidzen	Toccata and Fugue in D minor	D
Bach-Peterson	Crucifixus	M
Couperin-Scott	Cantus Firmus and Fugue	E
Frescobaldi-Slocum	Toccata	M
Handel-Malin	Concerto Grosso	MD
Handel-Johnson	Messiah Overture (French Overture)	M
Handel-Calliet	Messiah Overture (French Overture)	M
Handel-Osterling	Prelude and Fughetta	ME
Handel-Ades	Hallelujah Chorus	M
Handel-Johnson	Hallelujah Chorus	M
Handel-Sartorius	Royal Fireworks Music (Suite)	M
Handel-Harty	The Royal Fireworks	D
Handel-Kay	Water Music	M
Purcell-Gordon	Air and March	E
Vivaldi-Cacavas	Concerto Grosso in D minor	M
Vivaldi-Lang	Concerto for Two Trumpets	MD

THE CLASSICAL ERA (c. 1750-1820)

Catel-Goldman	Overture in C	MD
Gossec-Goldman	Classic Overture in C	MD
Gossec-Goldman	Military Symphony in F	M
Gossec-Townsend	Suite for Band	M
Jadin-Townsend	Overture in F	M
Jadin-Schaefer	Symphonie for Band	M
Haydn-Isaac	London Symphony, First Movement	M
Haydn-Erickson	Finale from Oxford Symphony	M
Haydn-Gordon	Largo and Menuetto	ME
Haydn-Kiser	Second Movement from	

	Surprise Symphony	M
Haydn-DeRubertis	Orlando Palandrino Overture	M
Haydn-Riley	March for the Prince of Wales	M
Haydn-Wilcox	St. Anthony Divertimento	M
Leopold Mozart-Gordon	Toy Symphony	E
Mozart-Baker	Menuet and Trio from Jupiter Symphony	M
Mozart-Beeler	Menuet and Trio from Linz Symphony	ME
Mozart-Gordon	Alleluia (trumpet solo)	M
Mozart-Isaac	Abduction from the Seraglio	ME
Mozart-Moehlmann	Titus Overture	M
Mozart-Slocum	Marriage of Figaro Overture	MD
Mozart-Tolmage	Menuetto from Symphony No. 39	ME

ROMANTIC ERA (c. 1820-1900)

Brahms-Fote	Finale from Symphony No. 4	MD
Franck-Arlen	Symphonic Variations	M
Franck-Harding	Psyché and Éros	M
Liszt-Duthoit	Les Préludes (Tone Poem)	D
Liszt-Norman	Les Préludes (Tone Poem)	M
Rimsky-Korsakov-Duthoit	Polonaise	M
Smetana-Nelhybel	Three Revolutionary Marches	M
Wagner-Buehlman	Traume	E
Wagner-Cailliet	Elsa's Procession	MD
Wagner-Cailliet	Siegfried's Rhine Journey	MD
Wagner-Johnson	Album Leaf	E
Wagner-Osterling	Die Meistersinger Excerpts	M
Wagner-Osterling	Rienzi Excerpts	M
Wagner-Whear	Siegfried's Funeral Music	ME
Wagner-Leidzen	Trauersinfonie	M

THE CONTEMPORARY PERIOD (c. 1900 to the Present)

Neoromanticism

Hanson-Garland	Merry Mount Suite	MD
Hanson-Maddy	Nordic Symphony, Second Movement	MD
Hanson	Chorale and Alleluia	MD
Mahler-Gardner	March from Symphony No. 2	ME
Saint-Saëns-deRubertis	Finale from Symphony No. 1	MD
Strauss-Davis	Allerseelen	M
Strauss-Harding	Finale to Death and Transfiguration	M
Other Composers:	Mahler, Bruckner, Barber, Sibelius	

Nationalism

Bartok-Suchoff	Four Pieces for Band	E
Holst	First Suite in E-Flat	M
Holst	Second Suite in F	MD
Milhaud	Suite Francaise	D
Grainger	Lincolnshire Posy	D
Grainger	Hill Song No. 2	D
Grainger	Ye Banks and Braes O' Bonnie Doon	E
Vaughan Williams	English Folk Song Suite	M
Shostakovich-Righter	Finale, Symphony No. 5	D
Sibelius-Cailliet	Finlandia	MD
Other Composers:	French Six, Russian Five, Kodaly, Dvorák	

Barbarism and Primitivism

Stravinsky-Wilson	Berceuse from Firebird Suite	M
Stravinsky-Gardner	Petrushka Themes	M
Stravinsky-Gardner	Danse Infernal	M

Impressionism

Debussy-Walker	Arabesque	M
Debussy-Beeler	Clair de Lune	M
Debussy-Schaefer	Fêtes from Three Nocturnes	D
Debussy-Johnson	Reverie	M
Debussy-Wilson	In Moonlight	M
Griffes-Erickson	The White Peacock	MD
DeFalla-Morrisey	Ritual Fire Dance	M
Ravel-Johnson	Pavane	ME
Respighi-Duker	The Pines of the Appian Way	MD
Ravel-Erickson	Bolero	M

Expressionism and Serial Music

Schoenberg	Theme and Variations, op. 43a	D
Erickson	Three Miniatures	M
Latham	Dodecaphonic Set	M
Smith	Somersault	M
Starer	Dirge for Band	M
Schuller	Meditation	D
Other Composers:	Berg, Webern, Krenek	

Neoclassicism

Bright	Concerto Grosso (fl., ob., cl.)	MD
Bright	Prelude and Fugue in F Minor	MD
Carter	Overture in Classical Style	E
Giannini	Symphony No. 3	D
Hindemith	Symphony for Band	D
Ives-Schuman	Variations on America	MD

Joseph Wagner	Concerto Grosso (2 fl., cl.,)	MD
Morrissey	Concerto Grosso (2 trpt., trb.)	M
Nelhybel	Prelude and Fugue	M
Perschetti	Symphony for Band	D
Prokofiev-Lang	Gavotte from Classical Symphony	ME
Schuman	Chester Overture	MD
Stravinsky-Erickson	A Stravinsky Suite	ME
Vaughan Williams	Toccata Marziale	D
White	Miniature Set for Band (Polytonal)	MD

Jazz

Berkowitz	Paradigm	MD
Bernstein-Beeler	Overture to Candide	MD
Bernstein-Gilmore	Prologue from West Side Story	MD
Copland-Lang	Celebration Dance from Billy the Kid	MD
Copland-Lang	Waltz from Billy the Kid	M
Gershwin-Krance	An American in Paris	M
Gershwin-Bennett	Porgy and Bess	MD
Gershwin-Grofe	Rhapsody in Blue	M
Gershwin-Krance	Second Prelude	M
Ward-Steinman	Jazz Tangents	D
Other Composers:	Milhaud, Schuler	

Aleatoric

Gillis	Instant Music	M
Smith	Take a Chance	M

Experimentalism

Bielawa	Spectrum (Prepared tape and band)	MD
Erb	Stargazing (Prepared tape and band)	M
Other Composers:	Cage, Cowell, Boulez, Babbitt, Varese, Ussachevsky, Luenning	

Teaching Strategy For Music Education

The curricular approach advocated by Bruce Pearson supports the teaching of comprehensive musicianship while using a modified "Four Year 'Hybrid Cycle' Curriculum For Literature Selection" (similar to the four year "hybrid" curriculum that follows). His curricular plan includes:

the selection of one composition to study in depth, for each concert season. The work selected would then be the source and model for activities that would include studies in tonality, rhythm, melody, music theory, phrasing, terms and symbols, ear training, composition, music history, multi-cultural and inter-disciplinary studies.

Pearson's approach is represented through the Neil A. Kjos Music Company's *Standard of Excellence Concert* series for beginning and intermediate bands. Nine concert and festival pieces are available and reinforce the concepts presented in Pearson's *Standard of Excellence Comprehensive Band Method*. Each concert and festival piece includes a Teacher's Resource Guide with activities designed to "enrich students' musicical understanding." The following selections are available with accompanying guides:

Wyndham March by Bruce Pearson and Chuck Elledge (Grade 1)
Teacher's Resource Guide by Wendy Barden and Bruce Pearson

Matterhorn Overture by Chuck Elledge (Grade 1 1/2)
Teacher's Resource Guide by Wendy Barden and Bruce Pearson

El Marinero arranged by Mike Hannickel (Grade 1 1/2)
Teacher's Resource Guide by Wendy Barden and Bruce Pearson

Barbarossa by William Himes (Grade 2)
Teacher's Resource Guide by Wendy Barden and Bruce Pearson

Downing Street March by Barry Kopetz (Grade 2)
Teacher's Resource Guide by Wendy Barden and Bruce Pearson

Renaissance Festival and Dances arranged by Bruce Pearson (Grade 2 1/2)
Teacher's Resource Guide by Wendy Barden and Bruce Pearson

Spirituals! arranged by Charlie Hill and Chuck Elledge (Grade 3)
Teacher's Resource Guide by Wendy Barden and Bruce Pearson

Three Chinese Miniatures by Robert Jager (Grade 3)
Teacher's Resource Guide by Wendy Barden and Bruce Pearson

Celebration of Life by Ralph Hultgren (Grade 3)
Teacher's Resource Guide by Wendy Barden and Bruce Pearson

Four Year "Hybrid-Cycle"
CURRICULUM FOR LITERATURE SELECTION

The "Hybrid" curriculum compiles parts of each of the above curricular ideas. This curriculum involves teaching a four-year cycle of literature in which aspects of historical period, form and structure, and musical elements are presented in small units of instruction. Four works per year are selected for this instructional focus, one work for each of four concerts. Two works per year represent a specific historical period, and two works per year are from the "Basic Band Curriculum" or the "Recommended Works" for band which are presented in this project. The following outlines the sequence.

FIRST YEAR   The Baroque and Classical Eras are emphasized for the entire year. One concert work is selected from the Baroque era, one from the Classical era, and two from the "recommended works" for band. Four concerts are presented, with the following topics emphasized per concert period:

CONCERT ONE	CONCERT TWO	CONCERT THREE	CONCERT FOUR
Timbre/Tone & Elements of Music: Rhythm, Melody/Theme Harmony Texture	Musical Forms	Interpretation: Expression Phrasing Structure & Discrimination	Musical Styles: Articulation & Historical

SECOND YEAR   The Romantic Era is emphasized for the entire year. Two concert works are selected from the Romantic era and two from the "recommended works" for band. Four concerts are presented, with the following topics emphasized per concert period:

CONCERT ONE	CONCERT TWO	CONCERT THREE	CONCERT FOUR
Timbre/Tone & Elements of Music: Rhythm Melody/Theme Harmony Texture	Musical Forms	Interpretation: Expression Phrasing Structure & Discrimination	Musical Styles: Articulation & Historical

THIRD YEAR   The Contemporary Era (Part 1) is emphasized for the entire year. Two concert works are selected from the Contemporary era and two from the "recommended works" for band. Four concerts are presented, with the following topics emphasized per concert period:

CONCERT ONE	CONCERT TWO	CONCERT THREE	CONCERT FOUR
Timbre/Tone & Elements of Music: Rhythm Melody/Theme Harmony Texture	Musical Forms	Interpretation: Expression Phrasing Structure & Musical Discrimination	Musical Styles: Articulation & Historical

FOURTH YEAR   The *Contemporary Era (Part 2)* is emphasized for the entire year.

Two concert works are selected from the Contemporary era and two from the "recommended works" for band. Four concerts are presented, with the following topics emphasized per concert period:

CONCERT ONE	CONCERT TWO	CONCERT THREE	CONCERT FOUR
Timbre/Tone & Elements of Music: Rhythm Melody/Theme Harmony Texture	Musical Forms	Interpretation: Expression Phrasing Structure & Discrimination	Musical Styles: Articulation & Historical

In addition to the above, a technical skills development sequence could be incorporated with the proposed Garofalo band projects and source/reference notebook. All aspects of the music content standards that are listed in the *National Standards for Arts Education,* developed by the Consortium of National Arts Education Associations, should be included. The one hundred "Recommended Works" are listed in Part III, "The Band Conductor as a Music Teacher (The Materials)."

CHAPTER 8

The Essential Element to a Successful Band:
The Teacher • The Conductor • The Director • The Leader

Tim Lautzenheiser

The Art of Music and The Art of Teaching

The integration of substantive content and sensitive context is the key to success for any exemplary educator. In the field of music it is an absolute necessity. Bringing the data to the students is only one step in the growth process; presenting it in a fashion they understand and appreciate is equally challenging.

The *art of music* combined with the *art of teaching* creates a forum of opportunity for every aspiring musician. It is necessary to bring both of these components to the rehearsal room if we expect to achieve our professional goals of *teaching music through performance in band*. This important chapter is focused on the *contextual* aspect of the rehearsal; the role of the teacher/conductor.

The Band Director as a Leader

In today's educational system the band director is far more than a trained musician capable of conducting an array of beat patterns. Most of his/her school day is dedicated to a host of other responsibilities and the much-cherished podium time is all too brief; therefore, it is crucial to make use of every moment spent *rehearsing the band*. Time lost during rehearsals is lost forever and the negative results of wasted time far exceed what is casually observed. Students often become frustrated and discouraged, and music rehearsals become an unpleasant experience rather than "the best time of the day." The band director is in a position to organize and lead students to new levels of musical understanding and expression. It is clear the band director must be a leader of people as well as a conductor of music. Blending both of these important aspects of teaching into one personality ensures a successful rehearsal for everyone involved. We cannot ignore the leadership attributes of the band director, but rather must emphasize them in ongoing professional development.

Traditionally, our colleges and universities have not required classes in the area of "people skills." It has always been assumed that a solid library of musical knowledge would suffice in the development of a successful teacher. In defense of these institutions of higher learning there is little if any time for elective courses if one is to complete the mandated requirements in a strict degree program. Additional classes outside the discipline of music are next to impossible. With the present requisites many students need five years to complete and receive their undergraduate diploma. In spite of this we must take note of ongoing research that specifically demonstrates the vital importance of various personality traits in determining success in the rehearsal classroom.

Research Emphasizes Personality Traits Needed for Success

In an ERIC document, *Characteristics of Effective Music Teachers*, (University of Houston, No. ED 237 400), Dr. Manny Brand reported:
Although possession of a high degree of musicianship was assumed, there are other essential qualities that a band director must possess:

1. *Enthusiasm.*
2. *Warmth and personal interest.*
3. *A rehearsal technique combining clarity, brevity, fast pace, and variety.*
4. *A balance of praise and meaningful criticism.*
5. *A discipline technique focusing on communication.*
6. *A desire to improve and learn.*

In a sequel to this study, Dr. Brand concluded:

> *The ingredients of a master music teacher are: a sixth sense of understanding his or her students, pride in his or her remarkable competence, a fertile imagination, a theatrical flair, instructional urgency, a drive to accomplish the highest musical goals, the drive to work hard and obtain enormous satisfaction.*

Clearly, this spotlights the band director as a teacher and communicator as well as a musician.

Mike Manthei of Valley City State University, Valley City, North Dakota co-wrote "A Preliminary Investigation into the Qualities of a Successful Band Director" with Ray Roth of Mackinaw City, Michigan as part of the abstract sponsored by *The American School Band Directors Association*. The two men reached a similar conclusion to Brand's. Quoting P.B. Baker's research, "The Development of a Music Teacher Checklist for Use by Administrators, Music Supervisors, and

Teachers Evaluating Music Teaching," the ten most important characteristics of a successful music teacher/band director are:

1. *Enthusiasm for teaching and caring for students.*
2. *Strong, but fair discipline.*
3. *Observable student enjoyment, interest, and participation.*
4. *Communication skills.*
5. *Sense of humor.*
6. *In depth musicianship.*
7. *Knowledge and use of good literature.*
8. *Strong rapport with the students, both individually and as a whole.*
9. *High professional standards.*
10. *The use of positive group management techniques.*

Manthei and Roth also bring the work of T. C. Saunders and J. L. Worthington ("Teacher Effectiveness in the Performance Classroom," *Update*, 8 (2), 26-29.) to their document with these revealing discoveries:
Saunders and Worthington found that aside from the high level of musical competencies, the successful music educator possesses four skills:

1. *The ability to plan, both on paper and interactively, in the classroom setting.*
2. *The ability to format and pace lessons in a way that maximizes learning and minimizes frustration.*
3. *The ability to communicate with students in a variety of ways that enhance learning.*
4. *The ability to maintain a positive classroom atmosphere where expectations are high and students are constantly reinforced in their progress.*

Certain similarities create a common theme in all of these data. Regardless of a researcher's findings, the qualities of enthusiasm, caring, communication, positive reinforcement, fair discipline, musical competency and high professional standards serve as the suggested personality pillars of the successful band director.

From Research to Reality

- How does one develop these various personality traits?
- What techniques can be brought to the classroom setting that will guarantee a higher degree of musical learning?
- Which teaching skills need to be emphasized and which must be avoided?

- What are the responsibilities of the band director during rehearsals?

Personal development is a way of life for students of human potential. Much like practicing an instrument to attain mastery, outstanding educators are always fine-tuning their communication skills and seeking more efficient and effective ways of bringing the art of music to their students. The combining of the contemporary findings of leadership with traditional band directing has offered an exciting new frontier of possibilities. There is an ever-growing amount of data confirming the educator can program his or her personality to ensure a higher degree of success in daily rehearsals as well as performances. Just as a pilot is required to go through a pre-flight checklist prior to flying a plane, the band director should have a pre-rehearsal checklist prior to standing in front of his/her students:

1. Will my present attitude promote a positive learning atmosphere?
2. Are all my thoughts focused on creating a musical experience throughout the rehearsal?
3. Do I exemplify the standards of excellence I expect from my students?
4. Am I properly prepared to make the best use of time by highlighting the musical growth of every student?
5. Have I dismissed my own agenda of personal considerations so that rehearsal will be directed toward serving students in a disciplined format of measured learning?
6. Am I in touch with my philosophical mission of the importance of teaching music?

It is assumed there will be an affirmative answer to these important pre-rehearsal questions, just as the pilot assumes the airplane is mechanically ready to endure the requirements of the flight. However, the mere process of reminding ourselves of the importance of our state of mind and the impact it will have on what can be accomplished during the upcoming rehearsal will afford us the opportunity to avoid any damaging attitude we might inadvertently bring to the rehearsal setting. We demand total concentration from the musicians and must therefore model this vital discipline. Pilots are not allowed to take off without a perfect score on the pre-flight checklist; directors should have a similar mandate before lifting his/her students to new heights.

The Focal Point: Musical Prosperity for the Band

High-level achievement is attained when the synergy of the students and director is centered on a common goal. This can be accomplished through the guidance of the director based on four cornerstones of leadership effectiveness.

1. *Make the students the emphasis of your teaching.*

The more you can avoid relating your suggestions, corrections, thoughts, and comments in *"I/me"* terms, the more the students will assume personal responsibility. Emphasize *"We/Us"* and *"You"* in your verbal exchange. For example, "I think the trumpet phrase needs to have a gradual crescendo to establish more intensity prior to letter A. Do that for me," becomes, "Trumpets, *you* can generate some real excitement for *us* if you crescendo *your* line as you come up to letter A. *We're* counting on *you.*" Notice how the second instruction puts the responsibility on the players and offers them the chance to expressively contribute to the group, rather than simply "to do as they are told" to appease your request. They take ownership of the musical phrase and simultaneously become aware of their importance to their fellow musicians. The students are key in this process, for they bring life to the music. The director merely guides their energies towards achieving this mutually agreed-upon goal.

2. *Explain clearly what you want from the performers.*

Time is the director's most precious commodity and must be used judiciously. Any waste of time is a loss to everyone in the band. Communication skills—knowing what to say and how to say it—serve as the tools of every competent conductor. Avoid general comments that do not carry corrective instructions for improvement, i.e., "There is a balance problem in the brass. That's unacceptable; let's do it again," becomes, "Trombones, enter softly at letter G. You must be able to hear the clarinets." They now know exactly what to do, how to do it, and how to measure their success. (They must hear the clarinets.) All too often students want to fulfill your instructional expectations, but are really not aware of what to do. In place of asking they will simply repeat their efforts until they either stumble accidentally on the right combination or just run out of time. Another cornerstone of leadership requires competent score-preparation, which guarantees a more effective use of time.

3. *Communicate throughout the rehearsal.*

Communication is far more than words exchanged between playing segments. Communication can be verbal, visual, or tactile, and with music, band directors must incorporate intuitive connections with the musicians. Frequent eye contact is imperative, not with just first chair players, but with every section and member of the band. If musicians are expected to "watch the conductor," the conductor should share the responsibility by visually communicating with the musicians. A picture is worth a thousand words, and facial gestures will bring new dynamics to every rehearsal. When the students are aware of this ongoing forum of communication they will begin to communicate actively with the conductor. Only then can we "make music" as opposed to "playing notes." If the director is focused only on the score, the students will, likewise, focus only on their parts. The rehearsal then becomes a mechanical exercise and the human factor – the truly expressive component – disappears. The greater the frequency of genuine director-student communication during the rehearsal, the greater the musical experience.

4. Take responsibility for every condition in the rehearsal.

If there is a breakdown, an interruption, a discipline problem, or any other situation that threatens the rehearsal atmosphere, assume responsibility for it and move ahead. Stopping the band to justify, excuse, blame, or point out where someone's "wrong" preventing the intended rehearsal plan from taking place is almost always an infringement on valuable group time. If an emergency class meeting or an unscheduled athletic event removes students from the rehearsal, embrace the situation and do not amplify the problem by wasting class time with the remaining musicians. Look for the possibilities the unexpected circumstances can provide, i.e., attention to certain sections of the music, listening to recordings, reviewing tapes, working on technique studies – and a myriad of other positive musical prospects. A verbal protest from the podium dwelling on the obvious encroachment on the group's rehearsal time only adds negative fuel to the present situation. Taking responsibility involves creatively using existing conditions to advance the cause of music for those students who are there, instruments in hand and eager to move ahead.

Intrinsic and Extrinsic Rewards

The joy of playing a musical instrument is an intrinsic experience. In every program there are extrinsic rewards, but it is vital these bonuses be secondary in emphasis. If a student puts greater value on awards, chair placement, ratings, rankings, trips, or trophies, than on the musical experience, the *product* takes precedence over the *process*. However, if the pleasure of playing the instrument is the priority, extrinsic prizes are merely personal premiums along the pathway of artistic expression. Because of our often over-materialistic contemporary values, it is vitally important that the band director repeatedly explain why music is an integral part of our lives and stress the importance of the *language of music*. The director must constantly point out the benefits of mastering technical skills in order to provide an extended musical vocabulary of self-expression. Music accesses a part of the mind unique to every individual. It is a language unto itself; music can only be explained by music. It is, quite literally, feeling described in sound. The more technique available to the musician – i.e., the higher the musical vocabulary – the more successful he or she will be in communicating his or her innermost feelings. Therein lies the benefit of dedicated practice.

Do not assume students will discover the *intrinsic dividends* on their own. Many promising young musicians give up studying music because they feel improperly compensated (with extrinsic payoffs) for their efforts and energies. For them the success of their band experience is based solely on winning the contest, being selected as the soloist, appointed section leader, etc. They may be outstanding students committed to the band's success, but they consider playing their instrument as a means to the end, and when the end does not provide a satisfying extrinsic reward they choose not to continue their study. In this case everyone loses, particularly the students that quit. In contrast if intrinsic value is the mainstay of the band experience, the extrinsic disappointments are far less damaging. Of course there will be setbacks, but they should not be devastating to the individual's relationship with band or music. In this case everyone wins, particularly the student who is ready to move on to the next level of band.

Motivation by Fear or Desire

What is motivation? The word is a derivative of the Latin, *motere*, which means "to motor" or "to move." We envision the motivated student as the one who is moving forward in a positive direction. A motivated band is a group of young musicians moving towards a common goal of excellence.

How do we motivate students? Psychology tells us the only true motivation is *self*-motivation. Therefore, it is important to provide an environment where students will choose to move forward of their own volition rather than await some outside force to manipulate their behavior to accommodate the desired results. How can a director *light the fire* in young musicians?

Fear has long been an effective stimulant to alter behavior. There is no question it plays on the basic human survival mechanism. Pain, blame, guilt, and shame are certain to bring about predictable reactions; however, there are negative residual consequences to be dealt with following these actions. To remove fear as a form of behavior modification is unrealistic–however, a judicious use of this powerful tool is advised. It should be used sparingly and only in extreme circumstances. Rest assured, there will be a needed time of healing for both director and students once fear is purposely injected into the environment. When a person is threatened the natural reaction is to seek safety and choose the path of least resistance to avoid pain or embarrassment. In our case an *extreme* option would be to simply quit the band.

Desire does not carry with it the reaction-urgency of *fear*, however the long-term pro-action effects are certainly more conducive to harmony, balance, blend, and mutual trust. These conditions serve as a better foundation for musical growth and development and support the ideals of a positive band experience for the students. When students are *motivated* by an inner drive to reach the level of *desired* performance the rehearsal atmosphere is dramatically shifted. Each student becomes his or her own source of power. The director can now focus that synergy – the combined energies of the students – to increase the pace of the learning process. Time is not lost in disciplinary measures, but instead devoted to facilitating the path to musical prosperity. Students leave rehearsals enthused about their band class and are eager to recreate a similar set of standards in other facets of their lives as well as continue their musical journey whether at home working on their individual parts or in the next scheduled rehearsal.

Creating a Positive Climate for Learning

Being in the band means devoting time to a common goal. It requires the participants to relinquish much of their "free time" and/or "fun time" and reassign it to rehearsals. While many of their friends may enjoy the social benefits of adolescence, band students are fulfilling the requests of the band director. For a chosen few the intrinsic payoff will warrant the dedication of their efforts and energies. Others, however, will seek additional dividends. All students are not *intrinsically motivated*. If they are properly trained, though, they will begin to comprehend a higher level of understanding, begin to wean themselves from extrinsic payoffs and enjoy music for the sake of music. Herein lies one of the most significant contributions a director can bring to any student: leading a child step-by-step to the joy of music. This metamorphosis will be almost immediate for some, but will require extended patience with others. Persistence alone is omnipotent in this charge. What classroom conditions best serve this goal?

CONDITION #1: SAFETY
Is the rehearsal a *safe* place to reside? Abraham Maslow's *Scale of Hierarchy* is very clear concerning the importance of *survival;* he states that survival is the basic human need, quickly followed by the need for *safety*. If the atmosphere of the rehearsal is threatening, students will put a higher priority on survival (avoidance of pain) and safety (maintaining their dignity) than on extending their talents and skills for the common goal of the ensemble. If the students and/or director assume a defensive posture, it is certain to hinder the group's musical objectives.

CONDITION #2: CHALLENGE
Learning is exciting. Master teachers are well aware of the enthusiasm generated in an exchange of knowledge where student and teacher are both challenged. There is a fine art to establishing challenging attainable goals without overwhelming the students with a barrage of information. Knowing each student learns at his or her own pace, the astute music teacher constantly regulates expectations to establish a challenge for gifted students while supporting the

growth of those who might learn at a slower pace. Although it is difficult to explain how to establish this important teacher-student communication, it appears to fall in the realm of *intuitive sensitivity*. Experience itself could well be the key to mastering this skill. Beware the temptation to focus only on "fun and easy" material; it is deceptive both to the director and to the students. Quality begets quality. The mind left unchallenged will search for another source of inspiration.

CONDITION #3: ENCOURAGMENT

To encourage means; to bring into the presence of *courage*. Although there are times when every band director must confront an uncomfortable situation, admonishment or discouragement should not be the theme of the rehearsal. In most cases students have chosen to participate in band above and beyond other academic requirements. Band often demands more of their time than other classes; therefore, it is important the band director becomes a source of honest encouragement. Highlighting positive behavior is certain to develop a genuine sense of caring and sharing, an atmosphere conducive to musical expression. Encouragement is a necessity. It is the fuel students seek in their journey through life and can often be the deciding factor in lifting the student from the depths of rejection to the infinite possibilities of musical mastery. Do not underestimate the importance of encouragement; use it often to unleash the power to move the group forward.

Effective Communication Translates to Effective Teaching

The world of high technology has dramatically shifted the world of communication for the upcoming generation. Educators must eagerly embrace this reality and adapt their communication skills to the modern-day language of computers, modems, faxes, electronic mail, etc. The underlying theme of contemporary education is: *state the message in brief, understandable terms, avoiding extra verbiage.* Students enter the class with this fast pace in mind and are mentally geared to move quickly in accomplishing the assigned tasks. The perceptive teacher will adjust his or her communication style to the students' gait and take advantage of their ability to consume information at a high rate of exchange. This requires energized communication—the capability to engage the students in the communication process to foster learning at the highest level. Unlike in a traditional lecture procedure, the teacher instead opens the forum of idea-exchange and encourages the students to offer *their* thoughts and opinions. Proper teacher guidance and a prudent use of time are key elements in allowing the students to "own the band" and feel a sense of personal contribution to the organization's success.

Inspired communication involves the love of students. If the students are to be inspired, the teacher must be inspired. The influential conductor demonstrates love for teaching by becoming immersed in the daily agenda. Teaching is not an act, but rather an interact—an ongoing relationship with the students.

A Podium For Educational Success

Components for teacher success can be measured, taught, learned, and, generally, blended into every rehearsal. There is no mystery. What has been labeled as "charisma" is merely an execution of various behavior patterns carefully timed to focus young performers in a purposeful direction. The art of teaching, much like the art of music, is based on the strategic use of personality characteristics every educator can master.

This chapter would be incomplete without mentioning the elusive quality of *passion*. The great conductors are passionately devoted to their art form. They love the music, they love their students, and they are driven to share this passion with everyone. We authors tip our hats in thankful admiration and appreciation to exemplary models of teaching expertise. Outstanding mentors continue to set the standards for the profession as they passionately develop the leaders of tomorrow by *TEACHING MUSIC THROUGH PERFORMANCE IN BAND* today.

PART III

THE BAND CONDUCTOR AS A MUSIC TEACHER (THE MATERIALS)

THE TEACHER RESOURCE GUIDES

*The following RESEARCH ASSOCIATES are
gratefully acknowledged for outstanding
scholarly contributions of the*
TEACHER RESOURCE GUIDES

Jeff Emge
Assistant Director of Bands
East Texas State University • Commerce, Texas

Kenneth Kohlenberg
Director of Bands
Sinclair Community College • Dayton, Ohio

Matthew Mailman
Director of Bands
Oklahoma City University • Oklahoma City, Oklahoma

Matthew McInturf
Director of Bands
Florida International University • Miami, Florida

Craig Paré
Director of University Bands
DePauw University • Greencastle, Indiana

Edwin Powell
Doctoral Conducting Associate
University of North Texas • Denton, Texas

Robert Spittal
Director of Bands
Gonzaga University • Spokane, Washington

Thomas Stone
Director of Bands and Orchestra
Centenary College • Shreveport, Louisiana

Grade 2

Teacher Resource Guide

"Ancient Voices"
Michael Sweeney

(b. 1952)

Unit 1: Composer

Michael Sweeney is a graduate of Indiana University, where he earned a degree in music education. While at Indiana, he composed and arranged for the jazz ensembles and marching band. Sweeney's teaching experience includes five years in the public schools of Ohio and Indiana, where he produced successful concert, jazz, and marching programs from elementary through high school. Since 1982, Sweeney has been a composer and arranger for the Hal Leonard Publishing Corporation. He is currently Instrumental Publications Editor, responsible for the development, production, and marketing of new publications for jazz ensemble and marching band. Known particularly for his writing at the younger levels for concert band and jazz, over 400 of his compositions and arrangements have been published by Hal Leonard.

Unit 2: Composition

Ancient Voices was composed to suggest moods and sounds of early civilizations to young musicians. Published in 1994, the work utilizes a number of contemporary compositional techniques, such as tone clusters, blowing air through an instrument, singing, and pencils tapping on music stands. Players are encouraged to use their imaginations to visualize various scenes from distant eras on Earth, ranging back to prehistoric times.

Unit 3: Historical Perspective

The music of the 20th century is made up of a world of new and interesting compositional techniques through the use of melody and harmony, instrumental textures, and colors. Singing and playing traditional instruments in non-traditional ways are just a few of the numerous new experimental techniques that composers integrate into their works. In addition, the use of different modes, in lieu of major/minor sonorities, also recalls music of a different time in history. Indeed, composers wishing to create new sounds and stretch the boundaries of traditional music have often looked both to the future and the past for musical inspiration.

Unit 4: Technical Considerations

While centered around the concert key of G minor, the work's harmonic movement is not strictly functional in the traditional sense. Modal root and melodic movement both add to the "ancient" sound of the music, and provides a challenge for young ears. Rhythmic notation is based on simple combinations of whole, dotted-half, half, quarter, and eighth notes. The percussion part also includes the motive of eighth/two sixteenths. The work is primarily in 4/4, with a single measure in 2/4. Repeated sections, with first/second endings, are used. The instrumentation is suited for a young band: flutes/oboes (opt.)/bells (opt.)/recorders(opt.), Bb clarinet 1 & 2, alto saxophone, trumpet 1 & 2, F horn(opt.), low brass & woodwinds, and percussion 1 (snare drum, bass drum castanets) & 2 (wind chimes, suspended cymbal, medium tom tom, shaker, triangle, gong, crash cymbals). The composer notes that, if necessary, as few as four percussionists could cover the parts (not including the optional bell part).

Unit 5: Stylistic Considerations

Textures of tone clusters with major/minor seconds are used frequently, requiring attention to balance and tone color, and solid breath control as these clusters are often sustained for long values. In addition, wind and brass instruments need to be able to blend into the "sound masses", with uniform articulation and dynamic contrasts. According to the composer, the pencil tapping (along with other percussive techniques) was inspired by the idea that prehistoric man possibly used animal bones and skins as musical instruments. Percussion sounds, when used for color alone, need to be clear and distinct. Indeed, the variety of instruments called for in percussion section create their own balance and articulation challenges.

Unit 6: Musical Elements

Ancient Voices is made up of a combination of textural elements: "sound masses" using instruments, instrumental sound effects, and voices, homophonic accompaniment of the reiteration of a distinct motive, and unison rhythmic tapping on music stands, all with energetic percussion writing. An eighth-note modal figure, which is present throughout the work, acts as a unifying motive; it is suggested that recorders be used for this part. It is the source of some development, through elongation (mm. 9-18), transposition (m. 30), and, finally, transformation into a "theme" (m. 59).

Unit 7: Form and Structure

A   Introduction: percussion sounds combined with air effects from woodwind and brass instruments; membrane percussion instruments hint at motive by playing its rhythmic outline; tone clusters in woodwinds clash with thirds in trumpets; initial presentation of motive in recorders/flutes; singing introduced, G-D interval; tone clusters and percussion colors continue texture changes of motive, with added chordal accompaniment (m. 18); continued interplay of motive   mm. 1-58

B   Pencil tapping on stand, combined with similar sounds on percussion instruments; unison rhythms in measure phrases; motive introduced in low brass woodwinds, developed from initial motive in m. 9; continued development leading to thematic material in measure 59   mm. 59-68

A   Brief return of A texture, with motive presentations and identical harmonic accompaniment   mm. 69-78

Coda   Parallel fifths in stepwise motion; final presentations of initial motive; modal progression leads to final chord of G minor   mm. 79-89

Unit 8: Suggested Listening

Daniel Bukvich, *Symphony No. 1*
George Crumb, *Ancient Voices of Children*
John Paulson, *Epinicion*
Joseph Schwantner, *and the mountains rising nowhere, From a Dark Millienium*

Unit 9: Additional References and Resources

"The Basic Band Curriculum: Grades I, II, III." *BD Guide,* September/October 1989, 2-6.

Duarte, Leonard P., Daniel S. Hiestand, Carol Ann Prater, Doy E. Prater. *Band Music That Works.* Volume 1. Burlingame, California: Contrapuntal Publications, 1987.

Duarte, Leonard P., Daniel S. Hiestand, Carol Ann Prater, Doy E. Prater. *Band Music That Works.* Volume 2. Burlingame, California: Contrapuntal Publications, 1988.

Dvorak, Thomas L., Cynthia Crump Taggart, and Peter Schmaltz. *Best Music for Young Band.* Edited by Bob Margolis. Brooklyn, New York: Manhattan Beach Music, 1986.

Garofalo, Robert J. *Instructional Designs for Middle/Junior High School Band.* Fort Lauderdale, Florida: Meredith Music Publications, 1995.

Kreines, Joseph. *Music for Concert Band.* Tampa, Florida: Florida Music Service, 1989.

Hal Leonard Corporation, Milwaukee, Wisconsin (publisher of *Ancient Voices*)

Read, Gardiner. *Contemporary Instrumental Techniques.* New York: Schirmer Books, 1976.

Rehrig, William H. *The Heritage Encyclopedia of Band Music.* Edited by Paul E. Bierley. Westerville, Ohio: Integrity Press, 1991.

Teacher Resource Guide

"As Summer Was Just Beginning"
Larry D. Daehn
(b. 1939)

Unit 1: Composer
Larry D. Daehn has been teaching music at the junior and senior high school levels for thirty two years, with the last twenty five at New Glarus, Wisconsin Junior/Senior High School. He started Daehn Publications in 1987, and has arranged works for concert band by Bach, Grainger, Shostakovich and Vecchi. *Renaissance Trilogy* is Daehn's other original published work for band.

Unit 2: Composition
As Summer Was Just Beginning, subtitled *Song for James Dean*, was written in memory of the actor who died in a car crash in 1955. Composed in the summer of 1994, the title is a translation of a Greek inscription that appears on a bronze bust of Dean by the artist Kenneth Kendall, and refers to the tragedy of the actor's death at such an early age. According to the composer, a James Dean enthusiast, the main melody is loosely based on an old British Isles folksong, "The Winter it is past, and the Summer's here at last," recalling Dean's Irish, English, and Scottish heritage.

Unit 3: Historical Perspective
The folksong styles and traditions of the British Isles have inspired many composers to set those tunes for wind bands. Native composers such as Gordon Jacob (*Old Wine in New Bottles*), Gustav Holst (*Suites in Eb and F*), Ralph Vaughan Williams (*Sea Songs, Folk Song Suite*), and Haydn Wood (*Mannin Veen*) provided important settings of these songs for bands. In addition, non-British composers have also found this body of folksongs an inspirational source of ideas for some of their band works. Some of these include Percy Grainger (*Lincolnshire Posy*,

74

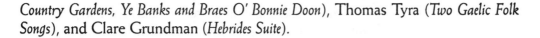

Country Gardens, Ye Banks and Braes O' Bonnie Doon), Thomas Tyra (*Two Gaelic Folk Songs*), and Clare Grundman (*Hebrides Suite*).

Unit 4: Technical Considerations

The scales of Bb Major, Eb Major, and C Major are required from all ensemble members. *As Summer Was Just Beginning* is scored for a standard band instrumentation: piccolo/flute; oboe 1 & 2; Eb clarinet, Bb clarinet I-II-III, alto and bass clarinets; bassoon 1 & 2; alto saxophone I-II-III, tenor and baritone saxophones; cornet I-II-III; horn I-II-III-IV; trombone 1-2-3; baritone; tuba; timpani, suspended cymbal, bells and vibraphone (ad lib.). The written ranges for several brass instruments are extended: cornet I - G5; horns - F5; trombone I - Eb4. Dotted quarter notes and dotted eighth-sixteenth rhythmic cells are prominent in the primary melodic lines.

Unit 5: Stylistic Considerations

Sostenuto and *cantabile* aptly describe the qualities of the melody and harmonic accompaniment. Melodic lines are simply presented in various instruments and registers, with sonorous chordal accompaniment underneath. Expressive characteristics dominate the work, with long crescendos and diminuendos, and delicate writing in the upper woodwind registers. Often three elements exist simultaneouly: primary theme, countermelody, and harmonic accompaniment. Important balance decisions need to be considered as the primary tune must be heard consistently.

Unit 6: Musical Elements

The harmonic foundation of the piece is based on traditional progressions (as a folksong would presumably be), with tonal centers in concert Bb Major, Eb Major, and C Major. The melody is also in a folksong style, with a verse and refrain used identically in both sections of the piece. Development or variation of the melodic line is evident through modulation and changes in instrumentation. The texture, from section to section, remains active through the employment of countermelodies (entire melodies or motives) and rhythmically-active accompaniment figures.

Unit 7: Form and Structure

Section 1	A	Bb Major; initial verse of folksong, composed of two similar phrases	mm. 1-16
	b	Refrain of folksong; contrast in scoring	mm. 17-24
	a	Abbreviated version of initial verse	mm. 25-32
Section 2	A'	Eb Major; verse of folksong, similar melodically to first sixteen measures, varied scoring and texture in accompaniment	mm. 33-48

| b' | Refrain of folksong; similar melodic treatment, embellished with prominent motive from melodic line | mm. 49-56 |

A'   C Major; full version of initial verse, with identical harmonic growth; slowing down, very expressive
mm. 57-72

Unit 8: Suggested Listening
James Barnes, *Yorkshire Ballad*
John Barnes Chance, *Elegy*
Percy Grainger, *Irish Tune from County Derry*
Gordon Jacob, *Old Wine in New Bottles*
Ronald Lo Presti, *Elegy for a Young American*
Vincent Persichetti, *Chorale Prelude: Turn Not Thy Face, Op. 105*
Frank Ticheli, *Amazing Grace*
Ralph Vaughan Williams, *Folk Song Suite, Linden Lea*

Unit 9: Additional References and Resources

"Basic Band Curriculum: Grades I, II, III." *BD Guide*, September/October 1989, 2-6.

Daehn Publications, New Glarus, Wisconsin (publisher of *As Summer Was Just Beginning*).

Duarte, Leonard P., Daniel S. Hiestand, Carol Ann Prater, Doy E. Prater. *Band Music That Works*. Volume 1. Burlingame, California: Contrapuntal Publications, 1987.

Duarte, Leonard P., Daniel S. Hiestand, Carol Ann Prater, Doy E. Prater. *Band Music That Works*. Volume 2. Burlingame, California: Contrapuntal Publications, 1988.

Dvorak, Thomas L., Cynthia Crump Taggart, and Peter Schmaltz. *Best Music for Young Band*. Edited by Bob Margolis. Brooklyn, New York: Manhattan Beach Music, 1986.

Garofalo, Robert J. *Instructional Designs for Middle/Junior High School Band*. Fort Lauderdale, Florida: Meredith Music Publications, 1995.

Kreines, Joseph. *Music for Concert Band*. Tampa, Florida: Florida Music Service, 1989.

Rehrig, William H. *The Heritage Encyclopedia of Band Music*. Edited by Paul E. Bierley. Westerville, Ohio: Integrity Press, 1991.

Teacher Resource Guide

"The Battle Pavane"
Tielman Susato (ca. 1500–ca. 1561-4)
arranged Bob Margolis (b. 1949)

Unit 1: Composer
Though not a very familiar figure today, Tielman Susato (ca. 1500-ca. 1561-4) was a prominent Renaissance musician, composer, and calligrapher. Living primarily in Antwerp, Susato performed as a trumpeter, composed music for a variety of instruments and voices, and is best known today by scholars for establishing a successful music printing shop in 1543. His printing business produced music by many composers of the period (Josquin Dez Prez, Orlando di Lassus, Clement Jannequin, Nicholas Gombert), as well as collections of his own.

Unit 2: Composition
The Battle Pavane is arranged from a collection of popular dance tunes (*Het derde musyck boexken . . . alderhande Danserye*) published by the composer in 1551. Set for band in 1981, this piece is one of a vast array of Renaissance works that have been arranged and adapted for modern concert band instrumentation by Bob Margolis and published by Manhattan Beach Music. *The Battle Pavane* is approximately three minutes in length, and features generous cuing and cross-cuing, enabling young or incomplete bands to perform it.

Unit 3: Historical Perspective
The pavane (which is translated "in Padua") was a sixteenth-century court dance that was Italian in derivation. Initially seen as early as 1508 in Dalza's *Intabolatura di lauto*, this popular dance quickly spread throughout Europe. Specifically, the pavane was a slow, processional type of stately dance which utilized a continuous repetition of basic step/rhythmic patterns, and was usually in duple meter. It was normally paired with a contrasting, faster dance of the period, such as the

galliard, padovana, or saltarello. With the popularity of dancing (from both social and theatrical perpectives) came the demand for an enormous amount of printed music. However, much of the music printed was for keyboard, voice, or instruments that were used during the Renaissance period (i.e., shawms, sackbuts, and crumhorns). Modern bands can now perform music of this period thanks to the publishers and arrangers that provide settings of this literature for 20th-century instrumentation.

Unit 4: Technical Considerations

The work is tonally centered in Bb Major, and its dominant key, F Major. Scales of these keys should be familiar to all players. Rhythmic considerations include the use of dotted-quarters, tied notes (mainly used in suspensions), the rhythmic cell of four sixteenth notes. Percussionists also must be familiar with dotted-eighth/sixteenth combinations. Certain brass instruments have extended written ranges: trumpet I (G5); horn I (F5); trombone I (F4). Several unusual instruments for the young band (piccolo, Eb clarinet, and string bass) are included but are optional. The percussion parts require eight players, but options are made available for four (minimum), five, six, or seven percussionists.

Unit 5: Stylistic Considerations

Transcribed from an original polyphonic four-part setting, doubled instrumental lines predominate the work, requiring careful decisions on balance and color. Sustained, full tones are necessary for proper ensemble sound. Uniform articulation, tonguing, and note lengths from all instruments are important for clarity within this style, especially in order to distinguish individual lines in the texture. Percussion instruments are used in the Renaissance tradition of accompanying with timekeeping, but care should be taken to obtain sounds that are characterisitic of the period, and not the contemporary percussion section (i.e., too "sophisticated" in sound). Remember that the ideal drum sound would come from a deep-shelled wood instrument, with rope tension and calfskin heads, with gut snares.

Unit 6: Musical Elements

Polyphonic, independent lines dominate this period's style, along with homorhythmic vertical textures. Within larger sections of the piece, strains are repeated with identical melodic and harmonic content. Variation is obtained through striking changes in dynamics and instrumentation. Percussion instruments provide both a steady beat and a kaleidoscope of changing colors throughout.

Unit 7: Form and Structure

A   First strain—polyphonic linear texture, homorhythmic texture;
cadence on dominant V chord   mm. 1-9

      First strain repeated, with changes in dynamics, instrumentation,
and register   mm. 9-16

B   Second strain—continued independence of individual
lines; full cadence on tonic I chord   mm. 17-24

      Second strain repeated, with changes in dynamics,
instrumentation, and register   mm. 25-33

C   Third strain—initial motive derived from Second strain;
tonally centered on tonic   mm. 33-40

      Third strain repeated, with changes in dynamics,
instrumentation, and register   mm. 41-48

D   Fourth strain—most rhythmically energetic, and fullest
in instrumentation; tonally centered on tonic   mm. 49-56

      Fourth strain repeated, with changes in dynamics,
instrumentation, and register   mm. 57-64

Unit 8: Suggested Listening

Thoinot Arbeau/arr. Margolis, *Belle Qui Tiens Ma Vie*
Pierre Attaignant/arr. Margolis, *Fanfare, Ode, and Festival*
Jan Bach, *Praetorius Suite*
Giovanni Gabrieli, any brass ensemble music: *Canzon, Sacrae Symphoniae*
Michael Praetorius/arr. Margolis, *Terpsichore*
Tielman Susato/arr. Michael Walters, *Twelve Dances from the "Danserye"*
Guy Woolfenden, *Illyrian Dances*

Unit 9: Additional References and Resources

Apel, Willi, ed. *Harvard Dictionary of Music.* Second Edition. Cambridge,
    Massachusetts: Belknap Press, 1970.

"The Basic Band Curriculum: Grades I, II, III." *BD Guide,* September/October
    1989, 2-6.

Duarte, Leonard P., Daniel S. Hiestand, Carol Ann Prater, Doy E. Prater.
    Band Music That Works. Volume 1. Burlingame, California: Contrapuntal
    Publications, 1987.

Duarte, Leonard P., Daniel S. Hiestand, Carol Ann Prater, Doy E. Prater.
    Band Music That Works. Volume 2. Burlingame, California: Contrapuntal
    Publications, 1988.

Dvorak, Thomas L., Cynthia Crump Taggart, and Peter Schmaltz. *Best Music for Young Band*. Edited by Bob Margolis. Brooklyn, New York: Manhattan Beach Music, 1986.

Farkas, Philip. *The Art of Musicianship*. Bloomington, Indiana: Musical Publications, 1976.

Garofalo, Robert J. *Instructional Designs for Middle/Junior High School Band*. Fort Lauderdale, Florida: Meredith Music Publications, 1995.

Kreines, Joseph. *Music for Concert Band*. Tampa, Florida: Florida Music Service, 1989.

Manhattan Beach Music, Brooklyn, New York

Munrow, David. *Instruments of the Middle Ages and Renaissance*. London: Oxford University Press, 1976.

Rehrig, William H. *The Heritage Encyclopedia of Band Music*. Edited by Paul E. Bierley. Westerville, Ohio: Integrity Press, 1991.

Sadie, Stanley, ed. *New Grove Dictionary of Music and Musicians*. London: Macmillan Publishers Limited, 1980. S.v. "Tielman Susato," by Susan Bain.

Slonimsky, Nicholas, ed. *Baker's Biographical Dictionary of Musicians*. Fifh Edition. New York: G. Schirmer, 1958.

Stolba, K Marie. *The Development of Western Music*. Dubuque, Iowa: William C. Brown Publishers, 1990.

Whitwell, David. *A Concise History of the Wind Band*. Northridge, California: WINDS, 1985.

Teacher Resource Guide

"Carpathian Sketches"
Robert Jager

(b. 1939)

Unit 1: Composer

Robert Jager (b. 1939) was born in Binghamton, New York, and attended Wheaton College and the University of Michigan. He served four years in the United States Navy as a staff arranger at the Armed Forces School of Music. He currently teaches theory, analysis, and composition at Tennessee Tech University. Jager has received a number of awards for his music, including the ABA-Ostwald Award in 1964, 1968, and 1972 (for *Symphony for Band*, *Diamond Variations*, and *Sinfonietta* respectively), and the National School Orchestra Association Roth Award in 1964 and 1966. He has also been awarded Kappa Kappa Psi's Distinguished Service to Music medal. Jager's works, which range from chamber music to orchestra and concert band music, include *Second Suite for Band*, *Third Suite for Band*, *Sinfonia Nobilissima*, and *Colonial Airs and Dances*. His more recent band works include *The Wall* and *Meditation on an Old Scottish Hymn Tune*.

Unit 2: Composition

Carpathian Sketches is a musical impression, using original melodies by the composer, of the strength and beauty of the Czechoslovakian people. The title is taken from the Carpathian mountain range that is an expansion of the Alps, running through eastern Europe. The music captures the flavor and spirit of the Slavic people through its unusual harmonic progressions and dance-like qualities. Composed in 1977, the work is approximately three minutes and forty-five seconds in length.

Unit 3: Historical Perspective

The Carpathian mountain range is a crescent-shaped range in east central Europe that extends for approximately 900 miles from the Danube Gap near Bratislava, the former Czechoslovakia southward to Brasov, Romania, and southeast to the Danube Valley near Orsova, Romania. The folk music of this region has always fascinated composers and listeners, with its unusual characteristics of rhythm, harmony, and melodic line. Béla Bartók (1882-1945), from 1905-1917, collected and studied the folk music of eastern Europe, publishing collections of folk songs he had personally gathered and recorded. This eastern European sound, with its wide variety of styles, is personified in a number of well-known composers: Bartók, Leos Janacek, Zoltan Kodaly, Bedrich Smetana, and Antonin Dvorak.

Unit 4: Technical Considerations

The scales of D minor and G minor are required for all ensemble members. In addition, the phrygian scale beginning on D should also be familiar, both technically and aurally. Accidentals are used frequently in all parts. A 4/4 time signature is used throughout the work. Rhythms are basic, utilizing combinations of whole, dotted half, half, dotted quarter, quarter, and eighth notes. Syncopated rhythms occur in the low brass. Playing ranges are extended for trumpet I (F#5), trombone I (E4), and baritone (Eb4). Percussion requirements include timpani, bells, snare drum, bass drum, and crash cymbals.

Unit 5: Stylistic Considerations

A weighted tone with great depth and sustained length is needed for the many homorhythmic passages. Dark tone colors, with the absence of brilliant highs, are required. Firm attacks and articulations are necessary to add clarity to this style. Additionally, uniform note lengths and attacks are important in this style that prominently features longer note lengths. Tone colors and dynamics shift quickly and regularly, requiring close attention to balance and clear dynamic contrast. Percussion colors, primarily used to complement a melodic line or reinforce a cadence, must blend with the ensemble and not dominate it.

Unit 6: Musical Elements

Using original motives and melodies, *Carpathian Sketches* is dominated by distinct, individual musical ideas that are briefly presented, then left for a new or related idea. Minor tonalites dominate the harmonic foundation (D minor, G minor), with phrygian influences intermingled (i.e., mm. 2-3, letter E, Coda). A pivotal cadence (two measures before letter C) utilizes an *alternate dominant* progression in which the tonic D minor chord is approached by half step from two directions as the "dominant" chords expand up and down. The low brass, at times, function as a rhythmic foundation for melodic or motivic presentations in the remainder of the ensemble (i.e., mm. letters C & E). Unison presentations of motives are a distinguishing characteristic of the work (measure 1, letter C, two measures before F, Coda).

Unit 7: Form and Structure

Introduction   D minor; unison presentation of the A theme (mm. 1-3); tonality shifts to phrygian mode with two-voice cadential figure (mm. 2-3), followed by primary motive; cadence to letter A in phrygian mode; primary motive, and related motive centered on dominant (low brass— three measures after letter A), are briefly presented and developed; trumpet section—alternate dominant, leading to D tonic   mm. 1-letter C

A   D minor; primary motive stated definitively in woodwinds, followed by B theme in flute/clarinet I; shift to G minor; new motive in trumpet—perfect fifth, which develops into third thematic area at letter D; seven-measure phrase begins on dominant of D minor and arrives at tonic at letter E   letter C-E

B   D phrygian tonal center; C theme in flute/clarinet I; change in character and texture; half cadence on A, followed by alternate dominant leading to return to A section   letter E-F+12

A   D minor; primary motive stated definitively in woodwinds, followed by B theme in flute/clarinet I; shift to G minor; new motive in trumpet—perfect fifth, which develops into third thematic area at letter D; seven-mea sure phrase begins on dominant of D minor and arrives at tonic at Dal segno sign   letter C-E

Coda   D phrygian tonality, featuring final appearance of A motive,followed by D minor unison statement of A motive in augmentation; final D minor triad   last seven measures

Unit 8: Suggested Listening

Béla Bartók, *Dance Suite, Mikrokosmos*
Antonin Dvorák, *Slavonic Dances*
Robert Jager, *Second Suite, Third Suite, Diamond Variations, The Wall*
Leos Janácek, *Sinfonietta, Jenufa*
Zoltan Kodály, *Hary Janos Suite, Marosszéki táncok, Galánti táncok*
Bedrich Smetana, *The Bartered Bride, The Moldau*

Unit 9: Additional References and Resources

Apel, Willi, ed. *Harvard Dictionary of Music.* Second edition. Cambridge, Massachusetts: Belknap Press, 1970.

"The Basic Band Curriculum: Grades I, II, III." *BD Guide,* September/October 1989, 2-6.

Duarte, Leonard P., Daniel S. Hiestand, Carol Ann Prater, Doy E. Prater. *Band Music That Works.* Volume 1. Burlingame, California: Contrapuntal Publications, 1987.

Duarte, Leonard P., Daniel S. Hiestand, Carol Ann Prater, Doy E. Prater. *Band Music That Works.* Volume 2. Burlingame, California: Contrapuntal Publications, 1988.

Dvorak, Thomas L., Cynthia Crump Taggart, and Peter Schmaltz. *Best Music for Young Band.* Edited by Bob Margolis. Brooklyn, New York: Manhattan Beach Music, 1986.

Farkas, Philip. *The Art of Musicianship.* Bloomington, Indiana: Musical Publications, 1976.

Garofalo, Robert J. *Instructional Designs for Middle/Junior High School Band.* Fort Lauderdale, Florida: Meredith Music Publications, 1995.

Kreines, Joseph. *Music for Concert Band.* Tampa, Florida: Florida Music Service, 1989.

Edward B. Marks Music c/o Hal Leonard Publishing, Milwaukee, Wisconsin

Rehrig, William H. *The Heritage Encyclopedia of Band Music.* Edited by Paul E. Bierley. Westerville, Ohio: Integrity Press, 1991.

Sadie, Stanley, ed. *New Grove Dictionary of Music and Musicians.* London: Macmillan Publishers Limited, 1980. S.v. "Czechoslovakia," by Karel Vetterl and Oskár Elschek.

Sadie, Stanley, ed. *New Grove Dictionary of Music and Musicians.* London: Macmillan Publishers Limited, 1980. S.v. "Europe § Eastern," by A. L. Lloyd.

Serly, Tibor. *Modus Lascivus.* Ann Arbor: Modus Associates, 1975.

Slonimsky, Nicholas, ed. *Baker's Biographical Dictionary of Musicians.* Fifh Edition. New York: G. Schirmer, 1958.

Stolba, K Marie. *The Development of Western Music.* Dubuque, Iowa: William C. Brown Publishers, 1990.

World Book Encyclopedia, 1993 ed. S.v. "Czechoslovakia," by Vojtech Mastny.

Teacher Resource Guide

"A Childhood Hymn"
David Holsinger

(b. 1945)

Unit 1: Composer

David Holsinger was born in Hardin, Missouri in 1945. He earned a Bachelor of Music degree from Central Methodist College and a Master of Music Degree from Central Missouri State University, with post-graduate work at the University of Kansas, where he was an arranger for university bands and the swing choir. Holsinger currently serves as Composer-in-Residence to Shady Grove Church, Grand Prairie, Texas. A prolific composer for the band medium, his works include *To Tame the Perilous Skies*, *Liturgical Dances*, *Havendance*, *Helm Toccata*, *On a Hymnsong of Philip Bliss*, *Consider the Uncommon Man*, *American Faces* and two ABA-Ostwald award-winning compositions: *The Armies of the Omnipresent Otserf* and *In the Spring at the Time When Kings Go Off to War*.

Unit 2: Composition

A Childhood Hymn was published in 1991 and is based on the children's hymntune, "Jesus Loves Me" (music by William Bradbury). The tune is used, through a variety of interesting harmonic and melodic treatments (i.e., non-traditional harmonic accompaniment and melodic transformation), to introduce a young band to the musical skills necessary for expressive playing, such as pitch and dynamic control, balance, legato tonguing, and rubato. The work is approximately three minutes long.

Unit 3: Historical Perspective

A general trend in band literature for young musicians is to concentrate on "block scoring" where instrumental parts are consistently doubled throughout a work, or on musical elements that make popular music so well-known (bland syncopated melodies with predictable harmonic and rhythmic accompaniment). As a result, less attention has been placed on the elements that young students (through lack of playing technique and experience) rarely encounter: motivic development and transformation, unique and advanced harmonic progressions, lighter scoring with attention to unique instrumental combinations, and a role for the percussion section other than timekeeping. Holsinger, along with a number of other composers, is helping young band musicians experience a variety of interesting compositional techniques at an easier level. In turn, the students' experience in making music can ultimately be more rewarding.

Unit 4: Technical Considerations

The work is based on the concert scales of Bb Major and Eb Major, with the use of the full scale and tonic arppegios in each key. The instrumentation is suited for a young band: flutes/oboes/bells, Bb clarinet 1 & 2, alto saxophone 1 & 2, tenor saxophone, trumpet/cornet 1 & 2, F horn, trombone 1 & 2/baritone/low reeds, tuba, and percussion (small triangle, suspended cymbal, bass drum, and timpani). The work is primarily in 4/4, with a single measure in 2/4. The rhythmic structure is composed of whole, half, quarter, and eighth note combinations.

Unit 5: Stylistic Considerations

A sustained, legato style is required from the entire ensemble (*Slow and expressive, legato in style*), with solid breath control. The dynamic contrast ranges from *piano* to *forte*, with sudden changes, crescendos, and diminuendos. The hymntune is presented in a variety of instruments and registers, indicating important balance and listening considerations. The percussion instruments are used sparingly, but effectively, for color.

Unit 6: Musical Elements

The hymntune is presented both as a complete (though not literal) melody and in motivic fragments. Harmonically, the music is divided into sections that are primarily in Bb Major and Eb Major, with interesting harmonic accompaniments intertwined, such as seventh chords, parallel diatonic harmonies, and modal progressions. The rhythmic texture consists of combinations of homophonic and independent lines.

Unit 7: Form and Structure

Introduction	Varied form of hymntune verse; Bb Major mm. 1-8
Section A	Tonality established, as is accompaniment mm. 9-12 texture; entire verse of hymntune (varied from original tune); interesting harmonic setting mm. 13-21
Section B	Modulation to Eb Major; refrain of hymntune; modal treatment of melody and harmony mm. 22-30

| Section A' | Harmonically and melodically reminicent of Introduction; return to Bb Major; strong half-cadence on bVI chord; closing section mm. 31-36 features arpeggiated motive |
| Coda | Harmony dominated by tonic six-four chord mm. 37-43 |

Unit 8: Suggested Listening

James Barnes, *Yorkshire Ballad*

Percy Grainger, *Irish Tune from County Derry, Ye Banks and Braes O' Bonnie Doon*

Frank Ticheli, *Amazing Grace*

Unit 9: Additional References and Resources

"The Basic Band Curriculum: Grades I, II, III." *BD Guide,* September/October 1989, 2-6.

Duarte, Leonard P., Daniel S. Hiestand, Carol Ann Prater, Doy E. Prater. *Band Music That Works.* Volume 1. Burlingame, California: Contrapuntal Publications, 1987.

Duarte, Leonard P., Daniel S. Hiestand, Carol Ann Prater, Doy E. Prater. *Band Music That Works.* Volume 2. Burlingame, California: Contrapuntal Publications, 1988.

Dvorak, Thomas L., Cynthia Crump Taggart, and Peter Schmaltz. *Best Music for Young Band.* Edited by Bob Margolis. Brooklyn, New York: Manhattan Beach Music, 1986.

Garofalo, Robert J. *Instructional Designs for Middle/Junior High School Band.* Fort Lauderdale, Florida: Meredith Music Publications, 1995.

Kreines, Joseph. *Music for Concert Band.* Tampa, Florida: Florida Music Service, 1989.

Rehrig, William H. *The Heritage Encyclopedia of Band Music.* Edited by Paul E. Bierley. Westerville, Ohio: Integrity Press, 1991.

TRN Music Publishers, Ruidoso, New Mexico

Wingert-Jones Music, Inc., Kansas City, Missouri

Teacher Resource Guide

"Down a Country Lane"
Aaron Copland (b. 1900–d. 1990)

transcribed by
Merlin Patterson (b. 1929)

Unit 1: Composer

Aaron Copland (1900-1990) is unequalled in stature among American composers. Aside from his prodigious output, Copland's role as pioneer and mentor to succeeding generations of American composers was indispensible to the development of a distinctly American style. His early works established him as paradigm in American music. His use of advanced harmonic and rhythmic practices, as well as his incorporation of jazz elements in "serious" concert music, caused him to be viewed in conservative circles as a wild modernist. During the mid-1930's, Copland turned to writing in a more accessible style. His use of American folk tunes and cowboy songs, along with his development of a less complicated harmonic vocabulary (characterized by open intervals), created a prototypical American sound. As a composer and writer, Copland was acclaimed throughout his career: he won the Pulitzer Prize and the New York Critics Circle Award and was Charles Eliot Norton Professor of Poetics at Harvard University, 1951-52. He also published three works on music—*What to Listen for in Music, Our New Music,* and *Music and Imagination.* His works for band include *Emblems* (1964; commissioned by the College Band Directors National Association), and *An Outdoor Overture* (1938/1941; originally for orchestra, arranged for band by the composer).

Unit 2: Composition

Down a Country Lane, commissioned by *Life* Magazine, was first composed as a solo piano work, which appeared in the June 29, 1962 issue. Copland wrote the work specifically with young musicians in mind, stating that "the music is descriptive only in an imaginative, not a literal sense. I didn't think up the title until the piece was finished—*Down a Country Lane* just happened to fit its flowing quality." The work was transcribed for school orchestra by the composer in 1965 and transcribed for band by Merlin Patterson in 1988. It is approximately three and one-half minutes in length.

Unit 3: Historical Perspective

In music history, it is rare to find instances where important composers have created works with the technical and musical limitations of young musicians in mind (Bartok, *Mikrokosmos*; Gustav Holst, *St. Paul's Suite*, *Brook Green Suite*; Schumman, *Album for the Young, Op. 68*, Persichetti, *Little Piano Book*; Hindemith, *Let's build a town*). For years, musicians have sought out major composers to contribute their ingenuity and unique compositional style to writing music for young students. In an effort to do this, *Life* Magazine commissioned Aaron Copland to write a work with young pianists in mind, while giving those young students a taste of Copland's style of composition. The result was a success. *Life* stated that "*Down a Country Lane* helps fill a musical gap: it is among the few modern pieces specially written for young piano students by a major composer."

Unit 4: Technical Considerations

Concert keys of F Major and Db Major should be familiar to all players. Rhythms are basic, consisting of combinations of whole, half, quarter, and eighth notes, as well as dotted values. The meter is 4/4 throughout. The range for trumpet I is extended to G5. Vibraphone is the only percussion instrument needed, and is an optional addition to the scoring.

Unit 5: Stylistic Considerations

Legato, expressive playing is appropriate throughout the work. In accord with the pastoral mood of the piece, dynamic shading within phrases is subtle, with a round, full tone quality required from the ensemble (even in the *fortissimo* dynamic of the final A section).

Unit 6: Musical Elements

The music is tonally based in F Major and Db Major, with an emphasis in the F Major sections on the progression IV-I. In addition, diatonic chords often used either in a non-functional manner (V-IV), and dissonant tones are added to functional chords. The material for both A sections is presented in the first ten measures, forming the harmonic and melodic structure of the remainder of the section; the B section differs in the shape of melodic ideas and in its tonal center. Skips, more often than stepwise motion, dominate the melodic contour of the piece, with two-voice textures prominent in several sections.

Unit 7: Form and Structure

A   Beginning-letter C

F Major; main melodic material presented—descending figures in half and quarter notes; ten measures divided into groups of two-measure phrases; primarily a two-voice texture; light harmonization
beg.-letter A

Opening material presented again, with fuller harmonic accompaniment; IV-I is a dominant chord progression
letter A-B

Transition; tonal shift away from F Major; new melodic material, opening figure distinguished by octave leap and tempo change
letter B-C

B   Letter C-D

New tonal center of Db Major (even though only four flats are in the key signature); final two measures (2 before D) feature tonic/dominant root movement with added major second (Db/Eb, Ab/Bb)
letter C-D

A   Letter D-end

Return of F Major tonality (with IV-I harmonic progression); identical harmonic and melodic structure, with fuller orchestration; final measures reiteration of IV-I movement
letter D-end

Unit 8: Suggested Listening
Works by Aaron Copland:
Aaron Copland, *Emblems*
Aaron Copland, *An Outdoor Overture*
Aaron Copland, *Symphony No. 3*
Aaron Copland, *Appalachian Spring*

Unit 9: Additional References and Resources

Apel, Willi, ed. *Harvard Dictionary of Music.* Second edition. Cambridge, Massachusetts: Belknap Press, 1970.

"The Basic Band Curriculum: Grades I, II, III." *BD Guide,* September/October 1989, 2-6.

Boosey & Hawkes Music Publishers, New York

Duarte, Leonard P., Daniel S. Hiestand, Carol Ann Prater, Doy E. Prater. *Band Music That Works*. Volume 1. Burlingame, California: Contrapuntal Publications, 1987.

Duarte, Leonard P., Daniel S. Hiestand, Carol Ann Prater, Doy E. Prater. *Band Music That Works*. Volume 2. Burlingame, California: Contrapuntal Publications, 1988.

Dvorak, Thomas L., Cynthia Crump Taggart, and Peter Schmaltz. *Best Music for Young Band*. Edited by Bob Margolis. Brooklyn, New York: Manhattan Beach Music, 1986.

Farkas, Philip. *The Art of Musicianship*. Bloomington, Indiana: Musical Publications, 1976.

Garofalo, Robert J. *Instructional Designs for Middle/Junior High School Band*. Fort Lauderdale, Florida: Meredith Music Publications, 1995.

Grout, Donald J. *A History of Western Music*. Third edition. New York: W. W. Norton, 1980.

Kreines, Joseph. *Music for Concert Band*. Tampa, Florida: Florida Music Service, 1989.

Rehrig, William H. *The Heritage Encyclopedia of Band Music*. Edited by Paul E. Bierley. Westerville, Ohio: Integrity Press, 1991.

Sadie, Stanley, ed. *New Grove Dictionary of Music and Musicians*. London: Macmillan Publishers Limited, 1980. S.v. "Aaron Copland," by William W. Austin.

Slonimsky, Nicholas, ed. *Baker's Biographical Dictionary of Musicians*. Fifth Edition. New York: G. Schirmer, 1958.

Stolba, K Marie. *The Development of Western Music*. Dubuque, Iowa: William C. Brown Publishers, 1990.

Vinton, John, ed. *Dictionary of Contemporary Music*. New York: E.P. Dutton, 1974.

Watkins, Glenn. *Soundings*. New York: Schirmer Books, 1988.

Teacher Resource Guide

"Greenwillow Portrait"
Mark Williams

(b. 1955)

Unit 1: Composer

Mark Williams (b. 1955) earned a Bachelor of Arts and Master of Education degrees from Eastern Washington University. He taught elementary band for eleven years in Washington and served as director of the Spokane All-City Band Program and the Spokane Elementary Honor Band. Williams was chief arranger for the 560th Air Force Band and is well-known in the Spokane area as a woodwind performer. He currently is a composer for the Alfred Publishing Company, where he has had over seventy works for band published. In addition, he is also String Music Editor for Alfred and has nine published works for orchestra and two for choir. Along with *Greenwillow Portrait*, Williams' other original works for band include *The Ash Grove, Echoes of the Civil War, Northland Saga, Fantasy on Yankee Doodle, Kentucky Ballad* and *March to the Big Top*.

Unit 2: Composition

Greenwillow Portrait is Williams' first published work for band. Composed in 1986, the work resembles the folktune "Barbara Allen." According to the composer, the tune originally occurred to him as an unknown, subconscious melody. It was only after having composed the work that he realized the tune resembled "Barbara Allen."

Unit 3: Historical Perspective

Depending on the source, "Barbara Allen" is either English or Scottish in origin. Both claim the original ballad in different versions, and both versions were brought to this country by the earliest settlers. Since then there have been countless variations, many in America coming from Virginia and West Virginia. Drawn from the British folk style, the style and source of *Greenwillow Portrait* is influenced by an important body of compositions that are based on a variety of British Isles folk songs. These include Grainger's *Lincolnshire Posy*, Holst's *Suite in Eb*, and Vaughan Williams' *Sea Songs*.

Unit 4: Technical Considerations

The scales of Eb Major and C natural minor (same key signature, different tonic pitches) are required from all players. Articulations range from slurred, legato phrases, to detached lines that need to be tongued clearly. The meter is 3/4 throughout, with rhythmic notation consisting of dotted half, half, quarter, and eighth notes. Ranges are extended for trumpet I (A5), trombone I (G4), and baritone (F4). Percussion requirements include timpani, bells, crash and suspended cymbals, snare drum, bass drum, and triangle.

Unit 5: Stylistic Considerations

As the work is mainly a folksong setting, the emphasis is on flowing lines, sustained note lengths, and lyrical phrases. Rhythmically, there are two important stylistic considerations in the melodic line: eighth notes must be evenly placed without rushing and the distinctive "Scotch Snap" should be played faster than the sixteenth notation might indicate. Subtleties between melody and accompaniment must be observed throughout the work since the melody often changes voice and register. In addition, the listener's interest is clearly on the flow of the melody from voice to voice, so it should be heard clearly at all times without forcing the tone quality of the instruments playing it. Always balance the accompaniment to the melodic line, regardless of the texture.

Unit 6: Musical Elements

The folktune "Barbara Allen" is presented three times in the piece. It is transformed in three ways: transposed to its relative minor key, repeated with varied harmonic accompaniment, and presented in a variety of instrumental colors. No true development of the tune occurs, but motives are borrowed from the A and B themes at the Coda and in a transitional section (mm. 43-50) leading to the work's climax. Tonally, the work is centered in Eb Major and C Aeolian. The Aeolian scale differs from other forms of the minor key in that the seventh degree of the scale, Bb, is not raised as a leading tone. This creates an unusual major VII chord which, in this work, leads to cadences on the tonic i chord (a characteristic of British folk music).

Unit 7: Form and Structure

A   A theme, Eb Major, parallel period; lyrical phrasing; initially presented in middle range by clarinets, tenor saxophone, and baritone; repeated in m. 9 in cornet I; lighter accompaniment texture, countermelody in alto saxophone   mm.1-18

B   B theme, C Aeolian (no raised leading tone), parallel period; melodic outline similar to A theme; cadence with Picardy third

     mm. 19-26

A'   A theme, C Aeolian; three-part texture—polyphonic in style—two voices doubled in octaves   mm. 27-34

B   B theme; identical theme, varied harmonic accompaniment— begins in the relative major—Eb; presented in oboe and alto saxophone   mm. 35-42

     Extension: reiteration of motive from B theme; climax of piece; diatonic ascending thirds above Bb dominant pedal

     mm. 43-50

A   Return of portion of A theme, Eb Major; fuller orchestration; new rhythmic accompaniment in percussion; second phrase interrupted with Fdom9 chord   mm. 51-56

Coda   second phrase of A theme completed; fragments of A theme

     mm. 57-63

Unit 8: Suggested Listening

Ralph Vaughan Williams, *Folk Song Suite, Linden Lea, Sea Songs*
Percy Grainger, *Lincolnshire Posy, Ye Banks and Braes O' Bonnie Doon*
Gustav Holst, *First Suite in Eb, Second Suite in F*

Unit 9: Additional References and Resources

Alfred Publishing Company, Van Nuys, California

Apel, Willi, ed. *Harvard Dictionary of Music.* Second edition. Cambridge, Massachusetts: Belknap Press, 1970.

"The Basic Band Curriculum: Grades I, II, III." *BD Guide,* September/October 1989, 2-6.

Boni, Margaret Bradford, ed. *Fireside Book of Folk Songs.* New York: Simon & Schuster, 1947.

Duarte, Leonard P., Daniel S. Hiestand, Carol Ann Prater, Doy E. Prater. *Band Music That Works.* Volume 1. Burlingame, California: Contrapuntal Publications, 1987.

Duarte, Leonard P., Daniel S. Hiestand, Carol Ann Prater, Doy E. Prater. *Band Music That Works*. Volume 2. Burlingame, California: Contrapuntal Publications, 1988.

Dvorak, Thomas L., Cynthia Crump Taggart, and Peter Schmaltz. *Best Music for Young Band*. Edited by Bob Margolis. Brooklyn, New York: Manhattan Beach Music, 1986.

Farkas, Philip. The Art of Musicianship. Bloomington, Indiana: Musical Publications, 1976.

Garofalo, Robert J. *Instructional Designs for Middle/Junior High School Band*. Fort Lauderdale, Florida: Meredith Music Publications, 1995.

Kreines, Joseph. *Music for Concert Band*. Tampa, Florida: Florida Music Service, 1989.

Luboff, Norman and Win Strake, arr. Songs of Man: *The International Book of Folk Songs*. Englewood Cliffs, New Jersey: Prentice-Hall, 1969.

Rehrig, William H. *The Heritage Encyclopedia of Band Music*. Edited by Paul E. Bierley. Westerville, Ohio: Integrity Press, 1991.

Stolba, K Marie. *The Development of Western Music*. Dubuque, Iowa: William C. Brown Publishers, 1990.

Teacher Resource Guide

"The Headless Horseman"
Timothy Broege

(b. 1947)

Unit 1: Composer

Timothy Broege was born in Belmar, New Jersey in 1947. He earned a Bachelor of Music degree in 1969 from Northwestern University, and has held a number of teaching positions in the public schools and at the university level. A prolific composer for band, Broege has composed over 30 works for band, along with works for keyboard, guitar, and voice. His other works for band include a series of *Sinfonia*, *Three Pieces for American Band (Set 1 & Set 2)*, *Dreams and Fancies*, and *Serenata for Trumpet and Band*.

Unit 2: Composition

The Headless Horseman was composed in 1973 and first performed by the Manasquan, New Jersey Summer School Concert Band. This programmatic work is based on the well-known character in Washington Irving's short story, *The Legend of Sleepy Hollow*. The music depicts the Horseman, his whinnying stallion, and their frightnening ride through the countryside as they snatch unsuspecting souls. With only forty-five measures, the work lasts approximately one and one-half minutes.

Unit 3: Historical Perspective

Programmatic music has been an important part of music history for many years. Composers as varied as Hector Berlioz (*Symphonie Fantastique*), Modest Mussorgsky (*Pictures at an Exhibition*), Richard Wagner (use of *leitmotifs* throughout his opera cycle *Der Ring des Nibelungen*), Richard Strauss (*Till Eulenspiegel, Don Juan*), Claude Debussy (*Prélude à l'après-midi d'un faune*) sought to portray characters, moods, and events through musical means. Late in the 20th century, composers such as John Adams (*Short Ride in a Fast Machine*) and Gunther Schuller (*Studies on Themes of Paul Klee*) still utilize aspects of programmatic music for their own works. In addition, today's motion pictures often rely on the creative and imaginative ideas of composers (John Williams, for example) to bring a complete and effective presentation to an audience. Some programmatic works that have been composed for band include David Maslanka's *A Child's Garden of Dreams*, Michael Colgrass' *Winds of Nagual*, Cindy McTee's *Circuits*, and William Schuman's *George Washington Bridge*.

Unit 4: Technical Considerations

Although there are a number of sections that feature polytonal or nontonal harmonies, the piece is centered in G minor. Some challenging chromatic writing occurs in the low brass (mm. 14-16) and trumpets and horns (mm. 24-32), with glissandi in the trombones (first-to-seventh position Bb-E). 4/4, 2/4, and 6/4 time signatures occur in the piece. 4/4 is the predominant meter, and the 6/4 is consistently divided into 4 + 2 beats to the measure. Rhythmic challenges are basic, with whole, dotted half, half, quarter, and eighth-note combinations, and quarter-note triplets (trumpet I part only). Snare drum player must be secure in maintaining an eighth/two-sixteenth rhythm with consistency of pulse, and the ability to perform that rhythm at a variety of dynamics.

Unit 5: Stylistic Considerations

The Headless Horseman is a brief but rapidly-changing work, requiring players to effectively shift dynamics, articulations, and tone qualities quickly. Staccato and legato articulations are required, with dynamics ranging from *pp* through *fff*. Relative dynamic levels should be considered in order to produce the widest dynamic range and best tone quality possible. The opening *Adagio misterioso* should be allowed to develop slowly, without rushing the tempo or dynamic intensity (the composer states that, if possible, a tempo slower than the indicated quarter-note=60 should be taken). Instruments that share harmonies, both non-tonal chords (mm. 26-33) and tonal harmonies (mm. 20-23), should blend with no specific color dominating. In addition, the percussion combination of snare drum, bass drum, and cymbals should likewise contribute to the sound without dominating.

Unit 6: Musical Elements

The A melodic idea (first presented in mm. 11-13) outlines the dominant D minor key above an active polytonal accompaniment. The B thematic idea (mm. 20-23), chordal in texture, is based on the tonic G minor tonality. Its harmonic form is modal, in that the dominant D chord has no raised leading tone (F-natural). Above each B theme is a motive from the A theme functioning as a decorative obbligato. Contemporary compositional devices include quartal harmony

(m. 26), dissonant tone clusters (m. 8-9), polytonality (m. 10-13), and non-tonal lines (mm. 14-15).

Unit 7: Form and Structure

| Introduction | *Adagio misterioso;* sound mass texture created by percussion rolls, glissandi in trombones, and tone clusters in wood winds and trumpets | mm. 1-9 |

A   Active bi-tonal harmonic texture (staccato eighth notes); A theme presentation in flutes, oboes, and bells; snare drum "stallion" accompaniment; low brass non-tonal unison interjection; initial thematic ideas resume
mm. 10-19

B   B theme; chordal, homorhythmic, 6/4 meter, G minor tonality; A theme fragment appears as obbligato; two-measure transition, arrival signalled with tone cluster from Introductio (m.8)
mm. 20-25

C   Change in texture; harmonic changes primary interest; quartal/bitonal harmonies change timbres, passed from brass to woodwinds; rhythmic snare drum accompani ment resumes
mm. 26-32

B   return of B theme; literal return minus the first measure; two-measure extension using fragment of obbligato (perfect fifth interval);G.P. in 2/4 part of extension
mm. 33-38

A   Coda-like; return of A theme and texture; baritone solo presents non-tonal material, different from initial presentation—arrives on tonic g; trumpet solo brief transformation of A theme fragment
mm. 39-45

Unit 8: Suggested Listening
Michael Colgrass, *Winds of Nagual*
Paul Dukas, *The Sorcerer's Apprentice*
Morton Gould, *Halloween*
David Maslanka, *A Child's Garden of Dreams*
Modest Mussorgsky, *A Night on Bald Mountain*
Richard Strauss, *Till Eulenspigel*

Unit 9: Additional References and Resources

"The Basic Band Curriculum: Grades I, II, III." *BD Guide*, September/October 1989, 2-6.

Bourne Publication Company, New York

Duarte, Leonard P., Daniel S. Hiestand, Carol Ann Prater, Doy E. Prater. *Band Music That Works*. Volume 1. Burlingame, California: Contrapuntal Publications, 1987.

Duarte, Leonard P., Daniel S. Hiestand, Carol Ann Prater, Doy E. Prater. *Band Music That Works*. Volume 2. Burlingame, California: Contrapuntal Publications, 1988.

Dvorak, Thomas L., Cynthia Crump Taggart, and Peter Schmaltz. *Best Music for Young Band*. Edited by Bob Margolis. Brooklyn, New York: Manhattan Beach Music, 1986.

Garofalo, Robert J. *Instructional Designs for Middle/Junior High School Band*. Fort Lauderdale, Florida: Meredith Music Publications, 1995.

Kreines, Joseph. *Music for Concert Band*. Tampa, Florida: Florida Music Service, 1989.

Manhattan Beach Music, Brooklyn, New York

Rehrig, William H. *The Heritage Encyclopedia of Band Music*. Edited by Paul E. Bierley. Westerville, Ohio: Integrity Press, 1991.

Stolba, K Marie. *The Development of Western Music*. Dubuque, Iowa: William C. Brown Publishers, 1990.

Vinton, John, ed. *Dictionary of Contemporary Music*. New York: E.P. Dutton, 1974.

Watkins, Glenn. *Soundings*. New York: Schirmer Books, 1988.

Teacher Resource Guide

"Kentucky 1800"
Clare Grundman

(b. 1913–d. 1996)

Unit 1: Composer

For almost any musician that has played in a band, Clare Grundman is one of the most recognizable names in composition. Born in 1913 in Cleveland, Ohio, Grundman is unmistakably a leader in the development of American wind literature for the young student. He has composed over sixty works for band, as well as having arranging many orchestral works for band by such composers as Leonard Bernstein, Aaron Copland, Sir Edward Elgar, and Gustav Holst. His original works for band include *The Blue and the Gray*, *A Colonial Legend*, four *American Folk Rhapsodies*, *Fantasy on American Sailing Songs*, *Northwest Saga*, *Burlesque for Band*, and *Tuba Rhapsody*.

Unit 2: Composition

Kentucky 1800, published in 1955, is a setting of three American folk songs: *The Promised Land*, *I'm Sad and I'm Lonely*, and *Cindy*. The melodies recall a time in this country's history when the pioneers struggled to move west, settle, and make a new life for themselves and their families. Grundman uses these folk tunes as thematic material and, through the use of colorful scoring and interesting accompanimental figures, creates a rhapsodic tone poem offering a quality musical experience to young musicians. The work is approximately three and one-half minutes in length.

Unit 3: Historical Perspective

Many of the immigrants who came to the American Colonies in the eighteenth century were English-speaking people from the British Isles. Arriving from England, Ireland, and Scotland, they came as indentured servants, farmers, and

100

laborers, escaping tyranny, poverty, and famine. They brought with them their traditions and melodies of folk songs, which varied in subjects from bemoaning their plight in the world to their hope for deliverance to amorous songs about their loved ones. These and many other folk song traditions spread among the new Americans and, as they migrated to new, unsettled areas, the songs followed to comfort and entertain them. This folk song tradition, as a truly unique American source of music, would prove to be an inspiration to a number of American composers in the 20th century (Aaron Copland, for example) who sought to create a uniquely American style of composition. Clare Grundman is one of the few composers to use this wealth of genuine American folksongs in original settings for the concert band.

Unit 4: Technical Considerations

The concert scales of G minor, G Major, Ab Major, and Eb Major are required for the entire ensemble. Rhythmic considerations include the prominent use of three rhythmic motives in the melodies: eighth/dotted quarter, two sixteenth/eighth, and dotted eighth/sixteenth. Cross-cuing is amply provided throughout the work. Trumpet I (A5) and trombone I (F4) have extended ranges, but only for isolated notes. The percussion scoring calls for timpani, snare drum, bass drum, cymbals, triangle, and bells.

Unit 5: Stylistic Considerations

As the primary material is based on folk songs, a singing, lyrical quality is necessary for the proper execution of the melodic elements of this work. Full breaths, with the control to sustain a tone for long note values, are required. With a dynamic range of *p* to *fff*, good tone quality from all instruments must be maintained, regardless of register or dynamic. The folk song melodies are featured in a variety of instruments throughout the work, necessitating careful attention to the balance of melody and accompaniment.

Unit 6: Musical Elements

The melodies *The Promised Land, I'm Sad and I'm Lonely,* and *Cindy* are presented in their entirety after brief introductions, which sometimes consist of a prominent motive from the tune. Grundman juxtaposes the melodies in a variety of voices, adding interest to their presentations and exploiting the band's instrumental colors. Although no metronome marking is indicated, a number of qualitative musical directions are listed: *with motion, cantabile, marcato,* and *broadly.*

Unit 7: Form and Structure

Introduction   Deceptively beginning on a bVII chord, opening the tonality of G minor is established eight motivic material from *The Promised Land* measures

Section 1   *The Promised Land;* eight-measure verse, followed by two eight-measure presentations of the refrain; refrains varied in articulation, rhythmic texture, and scoring
                                                                letter A-C

transition   change in texture, from rhythmic to smooth, sustained sonorities; stepwise harmonic motion—Eb, Db, C—leading to bVII-I arrival in new key of Ab Major
                                                                letter D

Section 2   *I'm Sad* and *I'm Lonely;* new key of Ab Major; prominent pedal fifths add to the folk-like quality of the music; eight-measure melody presented twice, first time with a one-measure extension   letter E-F

Section 3   *Cindy;* brief introduction, acts as a transition to new key of Eb Major; initially, only first phrase of Cindy presented (four measures); eight-measure refrain (letter I); verse and refrain presented in full   letter G-K

Section 4   return of *The Promised Land* refrain and original key of G minor   letter L

Coda   prominent motivic figure from *The Promised Land;* tonal shift to G Major, with added sonority of tonic/dominant pedal (G-D)   letter L

Unit 8: Suggested Listening

Robert Russell Bennett, *Suite of Old American Dances*
Clare Grundman, *American Folk Rhapsodies 1-4, Fantasy on American Sailing Songs*
Grundman at Eighty: A Retrospective of Clare Grundman's Band Music
Promotional cassette available from Boosey & Hawkes
Long Time Ago: Old American Songs—Dawn Upshaw/Thomas Hampson Teldec 9031-77310-2

Unit 9: Additional References and Resources

"The Basic Band Curriculum: Grades I, II, III." *BD Guide,* September/October 1989, 2-6.

Boosey & Hawkes Music Publishers, New York

Duarte, Leonard P., Daniel S. Hiestand, Carol Ann Prater, Doy E. Prater. *Band Music That Works. Volume 1.* Burlingame, California: Contrapuntal Publications, 1987.

Duarte, Leonard P., Daniel S. Hiestand, Carol Ann Prater, Doy E. Prater. *Band Music That Works. Volume 2.* Burlingame, California: Contrapuntal Publications, 1988.

Dvorak, Thomas L., Cynthia Crump Taggart, and Peter Schmaltz. *Best Music for Young Band.* Edited by Bob Margolis. Brooklyn, New York: Manhattan Beach Music, 1986.

Farkas, Philip. *The Art of Musicianship.* Bloomington, Indiana: Musical Publications, 1976.

Garofalo, Robert J. *Instructional Designs for Middle/Junior High School Band.* Fort Lauderdale, Florida: Meredith Music Publications, 1995.

Hamm, Charles. *Music in the New World.* New York: W. W. Norton, 1983.

Kreines, Joseph. *Music for Concert Band.* Tampa, Florida: Florida Music Service, 1989.

"Meet the Composer: An Interview with Clare Grundman." *Conductor's Anthology, Volume 2.* Northfield, Illinois: Instrumentalist Publishing Company, 1989.

Rehrig, William H. *The Heritage Encyclopedia of Band Music.* Edited by Paul E. Bierley. Westerville, Ohio: Integrity Press, 1991.

Teacher Resource Guide

"Korean Folk Rhapsody"
James Curnow
(b. 1943)

Unit 1: Composer
James Curnow (b. 1943) was born in Port Huron, Michigan, and attended Wayne State University and Michigan State University. He is active as a conductor, composer, and clinician throughout the United States, Canada, Australia, and Europe. Curnow's band compositions have won several awards, including the ASBDA/Volkwein Award in 1977 and 1979 (for *Symphonic Tryptich* and *Collage for Band*, respectively), and ABA/Ostwald Awards in 1980 and 1984 (for *Mutanza* and *Symphonic Variants for Euphonium and Band*). Curnow has been a composer/arranger/educational consultant/editor for Jenson Music Publications. In 1995 he founded Curnow Music Press in Wilmore, Kentucky. Some of Curnow's other original works for band include *Five Concord Diversions* and *Lochinvar*.

Unit 2: Composition
Korean Folk Rhapsody is based on the Korean folk song, *Ahrirang*. Previously used by John Barnes Chance in his well-known *Variations on a Korean Folk Song*, the tune is presented in a variety of styles, with a young ensemble in mind. The work, published in 1988, is approximately two minutes and forty seconds in length.

Unit 3: Historical Perspective
The music of Asia and the far east has traditionally emphasized melody and rhythm rather than polyphony or harmony. The musical elements which make it distinctive include the limited range of melodies, the use of pentatonic (sometimes six- and seven-note) scales, and the characteristic instrumental colors of idiophones, such as bells, xylophone, p'yon-kyong (tuned stones), p'yon-jong

(tuned bronze bells), and gongs. Many composers have been influenced through by the musical materials of Asian music, including Claude Debussy (*Prélude à l'après-midi d'un faune*), Maurice Ravel (*Ma mère l'oye*), and Giacomo Puccini (*Madama Butterfly*), or by specific folk songs, such as John Barnes Chance (*Variations on a Korean Folk Song*) and Ray Cramer (*Fantasy on "Sakura Sakura"*).

Unit 4: Technical Considerations

The scales of F Major, Bb Major, and Eb Major are required for all players. Accidentals are used frequently in many parts. 3/4 is the sole time signature in the piece. Rhythms are basic, utilizing combinations of dotted half, half, dotted-quarter, quarter, and eighth notes. Percussion requirements include timpani, bells, vibraphone (with motor), wind chimes (to be set in motion with an electric fan), large and small suspended cymbals, triangle, tambourine, snare drum, temple blocks, and gong.

Unit 5: Stylistic Considerations

Slurred, legato, and staccato articulations are required in this work. With no slurs indicated, the song is still to be performed in a smooth, legato style, with light tonguing and full note lengths. Staccato accompanimental figures (i.e., mm. 23-33) should be attacked lightly, with a lifted quality at the release of each note. The folk song (in its entirety or in the form of prominent motives) is almost always present, so balance decisions should instinctively allow for this line to dominate. Percussion colors must always fit into the sound of the ensemble. When mallet instruments double the prevailing line(s) (i.e., mm. 1-13, 41-43, 76-78) their color should also compliment the ensemble, not dominate. Glass wind chimes will produce a clearer and more distinctive tone, and are preferable to bamboo or wood materials.

Unit 6: Musical Elements

The folk song *Abrirang* is presented in its entirety, with a variety of harmonic settings supporting it. Two types of variety occur in the tune's presentation: it is passed between several instruments (i.e., mm. 5-22), and is presented in different keys (mm. 5-22 vs. 58-72). Tonally, modes are interchanged as new presentations of the tune occur. For example, in measures 23-33, the tonal center is F mixolydian (added Bb and Eb), while the final tune presentation (mm. 58-65) appears to be harmonized in Eb Major. Percussion sounds provide pitched and non-pitched colors to complement the work's Asian flavor, particularly the constant sound of wind chimes. A small development section (mm. 43-57) alters the tune's harmonization (mm. 43-44) and highlights two motives, taken from the song's first and third phrases. The harmonic movement in the Development, above pedals of F-C, then Eb-Bb, leads to the piece's sole modulation, Eb (mm. 54-57).

Unit 7: Form and Structure

Introduction — used to establish key and texture; F Major; modal chord progression provides harmonic foundation (I-bVII7-I); prominent parallel fifths in scoring; percussion colors create atmosphere · · · · · · · mm. 1-4

A — First and second phrases of folk song presented—horn/ alto,tenor saxophone; pentatonic melody; pentatonic melody; eight-measures with one-measure; underlying scoring texture continues · · · · · · · mm. 5-13

B — Third and fourth phrases of folk song—third in trumpet, fourth (repeat of first and second) in alto saxophone and clarinet; pentatonic melody harmonized in F Major; eight-measures with one-measure extension · · · mm. 14-22

A — First and second phrases repeated, preceded by two-measure introduction to establish new texture; faster harmonic and rhythmic accompaniment; tonic pedal (F-C) present throughout · · · · · · · mm. 23-33

B — Third and fourth phrases repeated; eight-measures with one-measure extension · · · · · · · mm. 34-42

Development

Motives from first and third phrases prominent (m. 43-44); tonic pedal in low woodwinds and brass, with shift to F dorian mode in clarinets, where motive is harmonized; continued development of third phrase (mm. 51-55); preparation for modulation to Eb Major · · · · · · · mm. 43-57

A — First and second phrases in Eb Major, transposed pentatonic melody; false entry of third phrase in flute/oboe/bells (m. 61); harmonic foundation (I-IV7-I) · · · · · · · mm. 58-65

B — Third and fourth phrases; simple texture;phrase ending elides with Coda · · · · · · · mm. 66-72

Coda — Incipit motives from first and third phrases present; bVII7-I final cadence in Eb · · · · · · · mm. 73-79

Unit 8: Suggested Listening

John Barnes Chance, *Variations on a Korean Folk Song*

James Curnow, *Five Concord Diversions for Brass Quintet, Symphonic Winds, and Percussion, Fantasia on a Southern Folk Tune, Variants on an Early American Hymn Tune*

Ray Cramer, *Fantasy on "Sakura Sakura"*

Bernard Rogers, *Three Japanese Dances*

Unit 9: Additional References and Resources

Apel, Willi, ed. *Harvard Dictionary of Music.* Second edition. Cambridge, Massachusetts: Belknap Press, 1970.

"The Basic Band Curriculum: Grades I, II, III." *BD Guide,* September/October 1989, 2-6.

Blades, James. *Percussion Instruments and Their History.* London: Faber and Faber, 1984.

Curnow Music Press, Inc., Wilmore, Kentucky

Duarte, Leonard P., Daniel S. Hiestand, Carol Ann Prater, Doy E. Prater. *Band Music That Works.* Volume 1. Burlingame, California: Contrapuntal Publications, 1987.

Duarte, Leonard P., Daniel S. Hiestand, Carol Ann Prater, Doy E. Prater. *Band Music That Works.* Volume 2. Burlingame, California: Contrapuntal Publications, 1988.

Dvorak, Thomas L., Cynthia Crump Taggart, and Peter Schmaltz. *Best Music for Young Band.* Edited by Bob Margolis. Brooklyn, New York: Manhattan Beach Music, 1986.

Farkas, Philip. *The Art of Musicianship.* Bloomington, Indiana: Musical Publications, 1976.

Garofalo, Robert J. *Instructional Designs for Middle/Junior High School Band.* Fort Lauderdale, Florida: Meredith Music Publications, 1995.

Jenson Publications, New Berlin, Wisconsin

Kreines, Joseph. *Music for Concert Band.* Tampa, Florida: Florida Music Service, 1989.

Rehrig, William H. *The Heritage Encyclopedia of Band Music.* Edited by Paul E. Bierley. Westerville, Ohio: Integrity Press, 1991.

Sadie, Stanley, ed. *New Grove Dictionary of Music and Musicians.* London: Macmillan Publishers Limited, 1980. S.v. "Korea," by Byong Won Lee.

Teacher Resource Guide

"Linden Lea"
Ralph Vaughan Williams
(b. 1872– d. 1958)

arranged by
John W. Stout
(b. 1957)

Unit 1: Composer

Ralph Vaughan Williams (1872-1958) was the most important English composer of his generation. A composer, teacher, writer, and conductor, he was a key
figure in the 20th-century revival of English music, a tradition that had not
produced a major composer for over one hundred years. Vaughan Williams,
along with Gustav Holst, are considered two of the most important and influential composers for band, helping establish the traditions of British band literature,
and producing quality original works for band at a time when few composers
were doing so. *Folk Song Suite*, *Toccata Marziale*, *Sea Songs*, and *Flourish for Wind Band*
are standards in today's band libraries and repertoire lists.

Unit 2: Composition

Linden Lea is a song by Vaughan Williams originally set for voice and piano in
1901 on a text by William Barnes. The current arrangement, set for band by John
Stout, was published in 1984. It is approximately two minutes and forty-five seconds in length.

Unit 3: Historical Perspective

The early 20th century saw the renewed interest of composers in the folk music
of their own countries. Béla Bartók, Zoltan Kodály, and Leos Janácek were some

of the first composers to research and catalog the folk music of their peoples, and apply this source to their own compositions. Ralph Vaughan Williams became a member of the Folk Song Society in 1904, collecting hundreds of English traditional tunes and setting many of them for voice or orchestra. He also served, from 1904-06, as a musical editor for the new English hymnal. The style of the English folk song so pervaded his compositional style that many of his original melodies have been mistaken for authentic folk songs, including *Linden Lea*.

Unit 4: Technical Considerations

The piece is exclusively in F Major. That scale, along with the tonic, subdominant, and dominant arpeggios of that key, should be familiar to all players. The rhythmic challenges of the work are basic, with quarter and eighth notes being the primary note values. Slurring within phrases and smooth legato tonguing, are required articulations. Percussion requirements include timpani, suspended cymbal, bells, and chimes.

Unit 5: Stylistic Considerations

As the work is mainly a folk song setting, the emphasis is on flowing lines, sustained note lengths, and lyrical phrases. Subtleties between melody and accompaniment must be observed throughout the work since the melody often changes voice and register. In addition, since the harmony is not complex, the listener's interest is clearly on the flow of the melody from voice to voice and on the variety of orchestration in the accompaniment.

Unit 6: Musical Elements

The setting of *Linden Lea* is primarily a four-part texture of melody versus accompaniment. There is no development of the melodic line, except for its presentations in various instruments. Hamonically, the accompaniment is diatonic, with occasional dominant major/minor sevenths and secondary dominant chords. F Major is clearly the primary tonal center, established immediately with a tonic pedal at the beginning. Each of the first two phrases, forming parallel periods, cadence on the dominant C Major tonal center before returning to the tonic at the end of the second period and forming a double period.

Unit 7: Form and Structure

Introduction	F Major tonality established over F pedal tone	
		mm. 1-4
Section A	Phrase Ia; cadence on I	mm. 5-8
	Phrase IIa; cadence on V	mm. 9-12
	Phrase IIIa; centered on V	mm. 13-16

Phrase IVa; similar to first phrase in construction, with harmonic variations; return to I; five beat extension to phrase; completes a binary form, as a double period

mm. 17-20

Section B   Phrase Ib; change in orchestration/texture: lighter texture with upper woodwinds, tonic pedal tone in string bass and timpani   mm. 21-25

Phrase IIb; change in orchestration/texture: lighter texture with upper woodwinds, tonic pedal tone in string bass and timpani   mm. 26-29

Phrase IIIb; fuller woodwind orhestration   mm. 30-33

Phrase IVb; return to scoring of phrases Ib and IIb; no extension, as previously heard   mm. 34-37

Section C   Phrase Ic; new deceptive cadence (m. 41); brass section soli   mm. 38-41

Phrase IIc; brass soli continued   mm. 42-45

Phrase IIIc; change in accompanimental texture, risoluto; fuller harmonization   mm. 46-49

Phrase IVc; five measure extension (Coda) above F pedal tone to end   mm. 50-57

Unit 8: Suggested Listening

James Barnes, *Yorkshire Ballad*
Benjamin Britten, *Songs and Folksongs (Etcetera Digital KTC 1046)*
    English Folk Songs arranged by Britten
Frank Erickson, *Air for Band*
Percy Grainger, *Irish Tune from County Derry, Ye Banks and Braes O' Bonnie Doon*
Gordon Jacob, *Old Wine in New Bottles*
Peter Pears/Julian Bream, *Sweet, Stay Awhile (RCA GL 42752)*
Ralph Vaughan Williams, *Folk Song Suite, Rhosymedre*

Unit 9: Additional References and Resources

Apel, Willi, ed. *Harvard Dictionary of Music.* Second edition. Cambridge, Massachusetts: Belknap Press, 1970.

"The Basic Band Curriculum: Grades I, II, III." *BD Guide,* September/October 1989, 2-6.

Duarte, Leonard P., Daniel S. Hiestand, Carol Ann Prater, Doy E. Prater. *Band Music That Works*. Volume 1. Burlingame, California: Contrapuntal Publications, 1987.

Duarte, Leonard P., Daniel S. Hiestand, Carol Ann Prater, Doy E. Prater. *Band Music That Works*. Volume 2. Burlingame, California: Contrapuntal Publications, 1988.

Dvorak, Thomas L., Cynthia Crump Taggart, and Peter Schmaltz. *Best Music for Young Band*. Edited by Bob Margolis. Brooklyn, New York: Manhattan Beach Music, 1986.

Farkas, Philip. *The Art of Musicianship*. Bloomington, Indiana: Musical Publications, 1976.

Garofalo, Robert J. *Instructional Designs for Middle/Junior High School Band*. Fort Lauderdale, Florida: Meredith Music Publications, 1995.

Grout, Donald J. *A History of Western Music*. Third edition. New York: W. W. Norton, 1980.

Kreines, Joseph. *Music for Concert Band*. Tampa, Florida: Florida Music Service, 1989.

Rehrig, William H. *The Heritage Encyclopedia of Band Music*. Edited by Paul E. Bierley. Westerville, Ohio: Integrity Press, 1991.

Sadie, Stanley, ed. *New Grove Dictionary of Music and Musicians*. London: Macmillan Publishers Limited, 1980. S.v. "Ralph Vaughan Williams," by Hugh Ottaway.

Slonimsky, Nicholas, ed. *Baker's Biographical Dictionary of Musicians*. Fifth Edition. New York: G. Schirmer, 1958.

Stolba, K Marie. *The Development of Western Music*. Dubuque, Iowa: William C. Brown Publishers, 1990.

Teacher Resource Guide

Little Suite for Band
Clare Grundman
(b. 1913–d. 1996)

Unit 1: Composer

For almost any musician who has played in a band, Clare Grundman is one of the most recognizable names in composition. Born in 1913 in Cleveland, Ohio, Grundman is unmistakably a leaders in the development of American wind literature for the young student. He has composed over sixty works for band, as well as having arranged many orchestral works for band by such composers as Leonard Bernstein, Aaron Copland, Sir Edward Elgar, and Gustav Holst. His original works for band include *The Blue and the Gray*, *A Colonial Legend*, four *American Folk Rhapsodies*, *Fantasy on American Sailing Songs*, *Northwest Saga*, *Burlesque for Band*, and *Tuba Rhapsody*.

Unit 2: Composition

Little Suite for Band, composed in 1957, is dedicated to Richard Otto and the Lyman Hall High School Band of Wallingford, Connecticut. The work is in three short movements: Prelude, Ballad, and Festival. It is approximately four minutes and thirty seconds in length.

Unit 3: Historical Perspective

The suite is a musical form that originated in the Baroque era. Derived from the term *suytte* (meaning pieces that followed one another), early suites, such as Johann Sebastian Bach's *Italian* and *French Suites* for harpsichord, consisted of groups of dance pieces. Composers have since used the form in variety of personal ways, ranging from a collection of musical excerpts taken from a larger work (i.e., Igor Stravinsky's suites from *The Firebird* and *The Soldier's Tale*, Maurice Ravel's suites from *Daphnis et Chlöe*) to completed works that are a series of contrasting movements (Richard Strauss' *Suite in Bb, Op. 4*, Claude Debussy's *Suite Bergamesque*). In the 20th century, British band composers Gustav Holst (*First Suite in Eb, Second Suite in F*), Ralph Vaughan Williams (*Folk Song Suite*), and Gordon Jacob (*An Original Suite, William Byrd Suite, Suite in Bb*) utilized the form with tremendous success. Other composers of suites for winds include Robert Russell Bennett's *Suite of Old American Dances*, Alan Hovhaness' *Suite for Band*, and Darius Milhaud's *Suite Française*.

Unit 4: Technical Considerations
The scales of Bb Major, F Major, F natural minor, and Eb Major are required for the full ensemble. Accidentals are used regularly in many parts. For most of the ensemble rhythms are basic, using combinations of whole, dotted half, half, dotted quarter, quarter, and eighth notes. In addition, cornet, saxophone, and snare drum parts include eighth/two sixteenth rhythms. Flutes, oboes, Eb and Bb clarinet I-II must play a thirty-second note septuplet scale run in Bb at *Allegro moderato*. Playing ranges are extended for trumpet I (G5), trombone I (F4), and baritone (E4). Mutes are needed by all cornet players. Percussion requirements include timpani, vibraphone, bells, snare drum, bass drum, suspended and crash cymbals, and triangle.

Unit 5: Stylistic Considerations
Each movement requires great contrasts in tone quality and articulation. *Prelude*, a brilliant fanfare, calls for a bright, crisp tone quality combining legato, staccato, and marcato articulations. A full-bodied *ff* sound, without harshness, is appropriate for this style. *Ballad* requires a rich, full tone from all players, and full note values with round attacks and releases. Dynamic levels, ranging from *pp* to *mp* in the accompaniment, should be clearly heard, with proper subtlety, and balanced against the melody. *Festival* requires solid breath support behind clean, crisp staccato playing. The rhythmic accompaniment is often dominant in the upper register, requiring careful attention to melodic balance. Additionally, articulations and note lengths in the accompaniment should be uniform in all instruments.

Unit 6: Musical Elements
Borrowed chords, or *mode mixture*, is apparent throughout much of the piece. This compositional tool involves the use of tones from one mode (i.e., major or minor) in a passage that is predominantly in the other mode. For example, in the second movement, *Ballad*, the key signature initially indicates F Major. However, Eb and Ab are used in the harmony immediately in the first measure. The movement ultimately comes to a complete cadence in F Major, but the harmony often borrows chords from the parallel F natural minor scale. Another device, *planing*—the parallel movement of similar chords—is used in the first movement

113

Prelude (mm. 6-9) as an approach to the dominant chord F in the key of Bb. In his use of melodic and motivic material, Grundman presents motives or themes that recur with some variation or development. In *Ballad*, the main theme, presented twice, is slightly developed the second time (letters G-H and H-I). In *Festival*, the main theme (letter J-L), is later transposed and varied in intervallic content (letters N-P and P-R). An exception to this is evident in *Prelude*, where the two-measure Fanfare Motive is presented in the same form throughout the movement (letters A, B, and F). Typically, Grundman provides variety in ensemble color through dramatic changes in scoring for accompaniment. In *Ballad*, for example, interest is added to the second presentation of the main theme by changing the orchestration of the accompaniment and adding rhythmic activity to the harmonic foundation.

Unit 7: Form and Structure

Prelude   Bb Major; Fanfare motive with eighth note melodic motive in clarinets; short extension of Fanfare motive, with modal harmonic movement (planing) to tonic (Db-Eb-F-Bb); brief return of Fanfare; harmonic transition to B theme   letter A-C

B theme, lyrical, upper woodwinds, alto saxophone I; harmony consists of a chain of dominant sevenths leading to tonic Bb at D   letter C-D

Fanfare motive; extended treatment of clarinet A motive (from m. 5); transitional   letter D-E

Brief return of lyrical B material, minor 3rd higher
                    letter E-F

Return of Fanfare motive; circle of fifths progession using borrrowed chords (Ab-Db-Gb), letter F-leading to final V-I in Bb   end

Ballad   F Major, with frequent borrowed chords from F natural minor; two-measure introduction establishes primary harmonic movement; main theme presented in muted solo cornet; homorhythmic chordal accompaniment; two-measure phrase extension   letter G-H

Second presentation of main theme; first two measures varied in pitch; identical harmonic foundation; phrase conclusion elides with beginning of last portion of Ballad
                    letter H-I

Coda; harmony alone—no melody; extension with inverted pedal point on tonic pitch; cadence in

letter I-end

F Major approached by I-bIII-bII-I-ii-I

Festival   Introduction; Bb Major; long preparation on IV-V-I establishes Bb as tonic; introductory motive in Beginning- upper woodwinds, horns, cornets, and snare drum   letter J

Main theme presented in muted cornets; active rhythmic accompaniment (homorhythmic) in woodwinds and horns, isolated harmonic changes in low brass and woodwinds   letter J-L

Transition; false start of main theme in cornets; dominant preparation/modulation to Eb   letter L-M

Eb Major; varied statement of main theme in trombones and horns; similar harmonic foundation and accompanimental texture   letter N-P

Second varied statement of main theme in upper woodwinds, horns, baritone, and bells   letter P-R

Coda; introductory motive in upper woodwinds, horns, cornets, and snare drum; perfect authentic cadence in Eb

letter R end

Unit 8: Suggested Listening
Robert Russell Bennett, *Suite of Old American Dances*
Clare Grundman, *Hebrides Suite, Little English Suite, American Folk Rhapsody No. 1*
Gordon Jacob, *An Original Suite, William Byrd Suite*
Darius Milhaud, *Suite Française*
Vincent Persichetti, *Divertimento for Band*

Unit 9: Additional References and Resources
"The Basic Band Curriculum: Grades I, II, III." *BD Guide*, September/October
    1989, 2-6.

Boosey & Hawkes Music Publishers, New York

Duarte, Leonard P., Daniel S. Hiestand, Carol Ann Prater, Doy E. Prater.
    Band Music That Works. Volume 1. Burlingame, California: Contrapuntal
    Publications, 1987.

Duarte, Leonard P., Daniel S. Hiestand, Carol Ann Prater, Doy E. Prater. *Band Music That Works*. Volume 2. Burlingame, California: Contrapuntal Publications, 1988.

Dvorak, Thomas L., Cynthia Crump Taggart, and Peter Schmaltz. *Best Music for Young Band*. Edited by Bob Margolis. Brooklyn, New York: Manhattan Beach Music, 1986.

Farkas, Philip. *The Art of Musicianship*. Bloomington, Indiana: Musical Publications, 1976.

Garofalo, Robert J. *Instructional Designs for Middle/Junior High School Band*. Fort Lauderdale, Florida: Meredith Music Publications, 1995.

Grout, Donald J. *A History of Western Music*. Third edition. New York: W. W. Norton, 1980.

Hamm, Charles. *Music in the New World*. New York: W. W. Norton, 1983.

Kostka, Stefan and Dorothy Payne. *Tonal Harmony*. Third edition. New York: McGraw-Hill, 1995.

Kreines, Joseph. *Music for Concert Band*. Tampa, Florida: Florida Music Service, 1989.

"Meet the Composer: An Interview with Clare Grundman." *Conductor's Anthology*, Volume 2. Northfield, Illinois: Instrumentalist Publishing Company, 1989.

Rehrig, William H. *The Heritage Encyclopedia of Band Music*. Edited by Paul E. Bierley. Westerville, Ohio: Integrity Press, 1991.

Stolba, K Marie. *The Development of Western Music*. Dubuque, Iowa: William C. Brown Publishers, 1990.

Teacher Resource Guide

"Llwyn Onn"
Brian Hogg

(b. 1953)

Unit 1: Composer

Brian Hogg, born in England in 1953, emigrated to Australia in 1964. As an active performing musician, composer, and conductor, Hogg has been involved with a number of musical organizations throughout Australia, including the Melbourne Staff Band of the Salvation Army and the Australian Band and Orchestra Directors Association. His works for brass band have been performed and recorded in England, the United States, Canada, New Zealand, Sweden, and Australia. Hogg has also won the ABODA Composer of the Year award twice (in 1986 for *March, Theme, and Scherzo*, and in 1989 for *Kelly*). Currently the head of brass studies at Yarra Valley Anglican School in Ringwood, Victoria, his other works for concert band include *The New Anzacs*, *The Stone Guest*, and *Fanfare and Processional*.

Unit 2: Composition

Llwyn Onn is a free pastorale setting based on the Welsh folk song (translated "The Ash Grove"). The original tune is used as the basis for the work, but is treated freely through a series of compositional devices, including a varied harmonic foundation, development of motives taken from the tune, and elongation through extensions of phrases or augmentation. Published in 1990, the piece is approximately four minutes and five seconds in length.

Unit 3: Historical Perspective

Folk music exists in almost every part of the world. It has traditionally been passed on through aural transmission, usually with changes or modifications as it was passed from person to person. As a result, a particular folk tune can at first appear to have a variety of possible original sources. In the case of *Llwyn Onn*, the tune is very old, and bears resemblance to the Irish air "Kitty of Coleraine." It has been mistaken for the old English air "Cease Your Funning," which has historically given the impression that this Welsh air was borrowed from English sources. The song, typical of many Welsh airs, is set in a simple form (AABA). The first part of the phrase is repeated immediately, followed by a second phrase that differs melodically and harmonically. The melodic line is derived from triadic harmony (often an arpeggiation of existing chords), with simple chromaticism supported by secondary dominants.

Unit 4: Technical Considerations

The scales of F Major and F Lydian are required for the entire ensemble. Arpeggios on the tonic, dominant, and subdominant chords are also used, often as part of the melodic line. Rhythms are basic, with combinations of whole, dotted half, half, dotted quarter, quarter, and eighth notes. A scale passage of ascending sixteenth notes on an F Major scale is required for flutes, oboes, clarinets, and alto saxophones. Playing ranges are extended for several brass instruments: trumpet I (G5), horn (G5, opt.), trombone I (F4), and euphonium (G4). Cupped mutes are needed for all trumpet parts. Percussion requirements include timpani, bells, vibraphone, bell tree, finger cymbals, suspended cymbal, and bass drum.

Unit 5: Stylistic Considerations

In keeping with the expressive qualities of this folk song, a secure, warm tone is required from all ensemble members at all dynamics, which range from *ppp* through *f*. Slurred lines and legato tonguing are the primary articulations in the work. Slurred passages should have a solid tone quality, with careful attention to balance and dynamic intensity when full sections are combined (i.e., brass in mm. 44-52). Legato attacks, and subsequent note lengths, should match in all instruments in similar passages (mm. 12-27, 53-59). Decisions regarding balance must be made in thickly-scored areas where several important lines converge (for example, mm. 49-52 and 61-68). Percussion effects, often used for color in the metallophones, should be clearly heard within the instrumental texture (mm. 44-46).

Unit 6: Musical Elements

The first phrase of the folk tune *Llwyn Onn* is presented in its original form throughout the work (i.e., mm. 13-28), but the second phrase is varied by "implying" its presence through the elongation of repeated notes in the original tune (mm. 29-36) and through the underlying harmonic movement of the phrase, coupled with "hints" of the actual song (mm. 61-68). The incipit motive of the melody—the outline of the tonic triad_is a source of development in several sections of the work (mm. 44-48, 77-84). Modal harmony is exploited by juxtaposing modes with the same tonic pitch (F Major/F Lydian/F Mixolydian).

Unit 7: Form and Structure
Introduction

F Lydian; tonic pedal, perfect fifth (F-C) dominating the harmony; tonic chord to #II chord prominent harmonic movement; perfect fourth interval primary motive in Introduction; false entry of incipit thematic motive (mm.7-8); unusual cadence to A section, #II-VII-I

mm. 1-12

A   F Major; folk tune (A section) presented in clarinets; eight-measure phrase; first measure 4/4, then to tune's true time signature, 3/4; tonic pedal continues

mm.13-20

A section of tune repeated in clarinets, with trombones/euphonium added; tonic pedal continues

mm. 21-28

B   B section of tune presented freely from original (sustained melodic pitches used where active quarters appear in the original melody (i.e., m. 29); harmonically varied from original   mm. 29-36

A   return of tune's A section (clarinets); false entries of theme in flute/oboe/saxophone/trumpet; fuller chordal accompaniment; seven-measure phrase—elision with development section   mm. 37-43

C   incipit motive of theme exploited; I-bVII7 sole harmonic foundation, with tonic pedal in timpani/tuba/baritone saxophone; brief change to 4/4 meter; accompanying eighth-note figure based on bVII7 arpeggiation; return to 3/4 with exploitation of eighth-note figure; dominant half-cadence arrival   mm. 44-52

A   return of folktune in trombones; imitation of B section incipit in trumpet; false entry of theme in horn (m. 59);
mm. 53-60

B   B section of tune varied, folktune melody disguised; prominent scalar eighth-note passages and syncopated motor rhythm in saxophones; eight-measure phrase; tonic cadence   mm. 61-68

	B section variation, similar in texture to initial presentation (mm. 29-36); dominant V cadence	mm. 69-76
A	A section of folktune returns, harmonized in thirds; imitative motives in trumpet/horn/vibraphone; tonic perfect fifth pedal (F-C); deceptive cadence into Coda (I64-V-bVII7)	mm. 77-84
Coda	strong deceptive arrival on bVII7; incipit motive of A section of melody in brass/upper woodwinds	mm. 85-92

Unit 8: Suggested Listening
Frank Ticheli, *Amazing Grace*
Ralph Vaughan Williams, *Rhosymedre, Linden Lea*
Welsh folksongs, *All through the Night, Hunting the Hare*
Haydn Wood, *Mannin Veen*

Unit 9: Additional References and Resources
Apel, Willi, ed. *Harvard Dictionary of Music.* Second edition. Cambridge, Massachusetts: Belknap Press, 1970.

Bantock, Granville, ed. *The One Hundred Folksongs of All Nations.* Boston: Oliver Ditson, 1911.

"The Basic Band Curriculum: Grades I, II, III." *BD Guide,* September/October 1989, 2-6.

Boni, Margaret Bradford, ed. *Fireside Book of Folk Songs.* New York: Simon & Schuster, 1947.

Brolga Music, Red Hill, Queensland, Australia

Duarte, Leonard P., Daniel S. Hiestand, Carol Ann Prater, Doy E. Prater. *Band Music That Works.* Volume 1. Burlingame, California: Contrapuntal Publications, 1987.

Duarte, Leonard P., Daniel S. Hiestand, Carol Ann Prater, Doy E. Prater. *Band Music That Works.* Volume 2. Burlingame, California: Contrapuntal Publications, 1988.

Dvorak, Thomas L., Cynthia Crump Taggart, and Peter Schmaltz. *Best Music for Young Band.* Edited by Bob Margolis. Brooklyn, New York: Manhattan Beach Music, 1986.

Farkas, Philip. *The Art of Musicianship.* Bloomington, Indiana: Musical Publications, 1976.

Garofalo, Robert J. *Instructional Designs for Middle/Junior High School Band.* Fort Lauderdale, Florida: Meredith Music Publications, 1995.

Kreines, Joseph. *Music for Concert Band.* Tampa, Florida: Florida Music Service, 1989.

Luboff, Norman and Win Strake, arr. Songs of Man: *The International Book of Folk Songs.* Englewood Cliffs, New Jersey: Prentice-Hall, 1969.

Rehrig, William H. *The Heritage Encyclopedia of Band Music.* Edited by Paul E. Bierley. Westerville, Ohio: Integrity Press, 1991.

Sadie, Stanley, ed. *New Grove Dictionary of Music and Musicians.* London: Macmillan Publishers Limited, 1980. S.v. "Wales," by Peter Crossley-Holland.

Stolba, K Marie. *The Development of Western Music.* Dubuque, Iowa: William C. Brown Publishers, 1990.

Teacher Resource Guide

"Mini Suite"
Morton Gould

(b. 1913–d. 1996)

Unit 1: Composer

Morton Gould was born in Richmond Hill, New York. A child prodigy, he played piano by the age of four and, at age six, published his first composition—a waltz aptly titled *Just Six*. At eighteen, Gould was appointed staff pianist at Radio City Music Hall at the time of its opening in 1932. At twenty-one, he landed his own radio program on the WOR-Mutual network, conducting a full symphony orchestra for which he composed many of his most notable works. By 1942, Gould's music had been conducted by Leopold Stokowski, Fritz Reiner, Sir John Barbirolli, and Artur Rodzinski. It was also during this time that Arturo Toscanini conducted *Lincoln Legend* with the NBC Symphony. Gould's pre-eminent stature as a composer of wind music is due not only to the excellence of his works, but to his early pioneering and promotion of the American band as a legitimate and viable performance medium. His *Ballad for Band* (1946) is perhaps the earliest example of a masterwork for band by an American composer. Mr. Gould was president of the American Society of Composers, Authors, and Publishers (ASCAP), a position he held since 1987. His other works for band include *West Point Symphony*, *Derivations for Clarinet and Band*, *St. Lawrence Suite*, *Prisms*, *American Salute*, *Jericho Rhapsody*, *Holiday Music*, and *Santa Fe Saga*.

Unit 2: Composition

Mini Suite is a set of three pieces "intended for the young player, the older player who still remembers being young, and the old player who would like to feel young again." Gould adapted the movements from a series of piano pieces he had written for his daughters on each of their birthdays. The three movements are entitled *Birthday March*, *A Tender Waltz*, and *Bell Carol*. The work is approximately four and one-half minutes in length.

Unit 3: Historical Perspective

As an active composer in the 1930's, Morton Gould had not written any works for band. In fact, few American composers had taken the medium seriously enough to devote any attention to producing band music. However, after having heard the University of Michigan Band under William Revelli, Gould "realized what a great music-making machine we had." His first works for winds included transcriptions of two of his own pieces: *Cowboy Rhapsody* and *Jericho*. After *Fanfare for Freedom* (one of eighteen fanfares commissioned by the Cincinnati Symphony), Gould was commissioned by the Goldman Band to write a piece for that group. The resulting work, *Ballad for Band*, was one of the first masterworks for band by an American composer. Following *Ballad*, many more American composers began contributing to the band's repertoire, including William Schuman (*George Washington Bridge*), Vincent Persichetti (*Pageant, Symphony for Band, Psalm for Band*), and H. Owen Reed (*La Fiesta Mexicana*).

Unit 4: Technical Considerations

The scales of Bb Major, Eb Major, G natural minor, along with their tonic, subdominant, and dominant arpeggios, are required for all players. Accidentals are used frequently in most parts. Rhythms are basic, with combinations of dotted half, half, dotted quarter, quarter, and eighth notes. Percussion parts also include rhythms consisting of combinations of sixteenth notes. Playing ranges are extended for trumpet I (G5) and trombone I (F4). Percussion requirements include snare drum, bass drum, suspended and crash cymbals, finger cymbals, triangle, chimes, and bells.

Unit 5: Stylistic Considerations

A wide variety of articulations are required throughout the work. The Trio theme in *Birthday March*, for example, indicates three types of articulation: slur, staccato dot, and tenuto mark (mm. 25-40). Brass accompaniment figures in *A Tender Waltz* (mm. 13-21) include tenuto marks, indicating that a light, legato tongue is needed for the front of the note with a rounded release at the next downbeat. The final movement, *Bell Carol*, requires an imitative bell sound from all instruments. This type of articulation should create a solid sound as a note is attacked and decays quickly. It would be helpful to request that players listen to, then imitate, the sound of chimes.

Unit 6: Musical Elements

The A theme of *Birthday Suite* incorporates "Happy Birthday" in its second phrase (mm. 16-21). The Trio theme (m. 25) provides contrast through changes in tonal center and articulation. The texture is chiefly melody versus accompaniment.

The second movement's two themes (mm. 5 & 22) highlight the relationship of relative major and minor keys (Bb Major/G minor). The harmonic structure of *A Tender Waltz* features chromatic harmony with the use of secondary dominant seventh chords (i.e., 13-21). A theme and variations form provides the structure for the final movement, *Bell Carol*.

Unit 7: Form and Structure

BIRTHDAY MARCH

	Introduction; snare drum solo; four-measure phrase, solo presentation of eventual accompaniment to A theme in solo cornet	mm. 1-4
A	Bb Major; primary theme (eight-measure phrase) in solo cornet; second phrase based on "Happy Birthday" tune (twelve-measure phrase); includes full ensemble with dia tonic harmonic accompaniment; cadence on tonic Bb	mm. 13-24
B	Eb Major; TRIO theme in clarinets and tenor saxophone; two eight-measure phrases, both end on tonic cadences; repeated TRIO with added flute/piccolo obbligato	mm. 25-42
A	Bb Major; return of primary theme, with "Happy Birthday" tune in second phrase; cadence in Bb; full ensemble	mm. 43-62
Coda	Based on first phrase of A section; IV-I6/4-V7-I	mm. 63-68

A TENDER WALTZ

	Introduction Bb Major; A theme motive presented in flute, clarinet, and horn; half cadence	mm. 1-4
A	A theme in flute and clarinet; first phrase—eight-measures, Bb pedal point; ends with half cadence; second phrase transitional harmony using secondary dominants; Bb pedal point; one-measure extension to phrase (elongation of tonic)	mm. 5-21
B	G minor tonal center (relative minor); B theme presented in low woodwinds and baritone; eight-measure phrase; cadence modulates back to relative major key	mm. 22-29

A	Bb Major; return of A theme—first phrase, with slight melodic variation and some chromatic harmony of the second phrase; full cadence on tonic Bb	mm. 30-37
B	G minor; B theme, with variation in accompanimental texture; modulatory shift to Bb	mm. 38-45
A	Bb Major; A theme—first phrase, with melodic variations; full cadence on tonic Bb	mm. 46-53
Coda	Dominant pedal below IV chord, leading to tonic; A theme motives presented in trombone/baritone	mm. 54-57

BELL CAROL

Main theme (bell theme);	Bb Major; presented in trombone and horn; six-measure phrase, used as a "groundbass" for subsequent variations	mm. 1-6
First variation;	dominant pedal point with three-octave range; fuller harmonic foundation; six-measure phrase	mm. 7-12
Second variation;	continued dominant pedal; bell theme in cornet I-II; syncopated rhythms add varied texture in accompaniment; six-measure phrase	mm. 13-18
Third variation;	bell theme in low woodwinds and brass; expanded use of syncopated accompaniment figure; six-measure phrase	mm. 19-24
Fourth variation;	similar presentation of bell theme; change in accompaniment to homorhythmic texture	mm. 25-30
Fifth variation;	portion of bell theme presented (first four measures) with change in texture; second four-measure phrase an extension of first	mm. 31-38
Sixth variation;	bell theme presented in eight-measure phrase through augmentation of theme's first four pitches	mm. 39-46
Coda	dominant V saturation with added vi chord (trombone/horn), leading to abrupt tonic pitch (ensemble unison)	mm. 47-59

Unit 8: Suggested Listening

Robert Russell Bennett, *Suite of Old American Dances*

Morton Gould, *West Point Symphony, American Salute, Santa Fe Saga, Ballad for Band*

Unit 9: Additional References and Resources

Apel, Willi, ed. *Harvard Dictionary of Music.* Second edition. Cambridge, Massachusetts: Belknap Press, 1970.

"The Basic Band Curriculum: Grades I, II, III." *BD Guide,* September/October 1989, 2-6.

Boosey & Hawkes Music Publishers, New York

Duarte, Leonard P., Daniel S. Hiestand, Carol Ann Prater, Doy E. Prater. *Band Music That Works.* Volume 1. Burlingame, California: Contrapuntal Publications, 1987.

Duarte, Leonard P., Daniel S. Hiestand, Carol Ann Prater, Doy E. Prater. *Band Music That Works.* Volume 2. Burlingame, California: Contrapuntal Publications, 1988.

Dvorak, Thomas L., Cynthia Crump Taggart, and Peter Schmaltz. *Best Music for Young Band.* Edited by Bob Margolis. Brooklyn, New York: Manhattan Beach Music, 1986.

Farkas, Philip. *The Art of Musicianship.* Bloomington, Indiana: Musical Publications, 1976.

Garofalo, Robert J. *Instructional Designs for Middle/Junior High School Band.* Fort Lauderdale, Florida: Meredith Music Publications, 1995.

Grout, Donald J. *A History of Western Music.* Third edition. New York: W. W. Norton, 1980.

Kreines, Joseph. *Music for Concert Band.* Tampa, Florida: Florida Music Service, 1989.

Rehrig, William H. *The Heritage Encyclopedia of Band Music.* Edited by Paul E. Bierley. Westerville, Ohio: Integrity Press, 1991.

Sadie, Stanley, ed. *New Grove Dictionary of Music and Musicians.* London: Macmillan Publishers Limited, 1980. S.v. "Morton Gould" by Ronald Byrnside.

Slonimsky, Nicholas, ed. *Baker's Biographical Dictionary of Musicians.* Fifth Edition. New York: G. Schirmer, 1958.

Stolba, K Marie. *The Development of Western Music.* Dubuque, Iowa: William C.

Brown Publishers, 1990.

Stone, Thomas. "Morton Gould—Champion of the Band." *BD Guide*, January/February 1995, 2-5.

Vinton, John, ed. *Dictionary of Contemporary Music*. New York: E.P. Dutton, 1974.

Watkins, Glenn. *Soundings*. New York: Schirmer Books, 1988.

Teacher Resource Guide

"Peace Song"
Timothy Broege
(b. 1947)

Unit 1: Composer

Timothy Broege was born in Belmar, New Jersey in 1947. He earned a Bachelor of Music degree in 1969 from Northwestern University and has held a number of teaching positions in the public schools and at the university level. A prolific composer for band, Broege has composed over 30 works for that medium, along with works for keyboard, guitar, and voice. His other works for band include a series of *Sinfonia*, *Three Pieces for American Band (Set 1 & Set 2)*, *Dreams and Fancies*, and *Serenata for Trumpet and Band*.

Unit 2: Composition

Peace Song is the third movement of another Broege work, *Three Pieces for Clavichord*. The work is intended to have the effect of a magical incantation—a prayer for an end to suffering, violence, and injustice. The work is approximately four minutes and forty-five seconds in length.

Unit 3: Historical Perspective

At times composers, through their music, have sought to express wishes for peace and reconcilitation, or to reflect on important social events or issues. Karel Husa, for example, in *Apotheosis of This Earth*, comments on the state of the Earth and its lack of care in the hands of humans. Mark Camphouse, in *A Movement for Rosa*, reflects upon the life of Rosa Parks, an unassuming person who single-handedly changed the direction and focus of the entire Civil Rights movement. These personal statements, along with works by Aaron Copland (*Lincoln Portrait*), David Gillingham (*Heroes, Lost and Fallen*), and Joseph Schwantner (*New Morning for the World (Daybreak of Freedom)*), are part of a small body of works inspired by the human condition and the human spirit—and all of their frailties. Through this body of music, including *Peace Song*, it is possible to encourage young musicians and listeners to experience the re-creation of feelings and emotions inherent in these works.

Unit 4: Technical Considerations

The scales of G and C natural minor are required from all players, although there are no key signatures provided in the work. A time signature of 4/4 is used throughout the piece. Harmonically, the texture is exposed with open fifths and unison voicings. The rhythmic challenges of the work are basic, with whole, half, dotted quarter, quarter, and eighth notes. Ties are also used to elongate note values. Playing ranges are extended for trumpet I (G5) and horn I-III (A5). Percussion requirements include timpani, vibraphone (with motor), chimes, xylophone, marimba, bass drum, suspended cymbals, crash cymbals, triangle, and gong.

Unit 5: Stylistic Considerations

With an atmosphere of great solemnity, *Peace Song* requires sustained legato playing throughtout. In fact, the composer requests that the resulting sonorities should resemble those of a cathedral organ. Therefore, a full-bodied tone quality is needed in all dynamics, particularly due to the stark quality of the parallel Perfect fifths that provide the total harmonic foundation. The work's single melody and primary moving line is to be played with thoughtful expression, requiring solid breath control and the patience to resist acceleration. Percussion metallophones (suspended cymbals, crash cymbals, and gong) highlight important arrivals in the work's musical structure. They should blend with the ensemble's sound, not dominate it.

Unit 6: Musical Elements

A four-measure harmonic progression composed of parallel Perfect fifths (mm. 1-4) provides a chaccone-like foundation to the melodic line and its motivic fragments. Colorful and varied orchestration provides interest and contrast between sections that contain similar melodic/harmonic material (mm. 18-24, for example), or in mini-development sections (mm. 34-41). Deceptively, the tonal center for the majority of the work is G minor. Only at the Coda is it revealed that G had been the dominant key, arriving on the true tonic of C. The final arrival, however, is unfulfilled with the open fifth voicing of C-G and a hint of the dominant seventh chord in the piccolo, Eb clarinet, and vibraphone.

Unit 7: Form and Structure

Introduction | Saturation of parallel Perfect fifths; four-measure chaccone-like progression played four times, final time with G-D and Eb-Bb intervals against each other, creating a quasi-harmony   mm. 1-17

A | Main theme presented twice: in A version twice; in B version once, (embellished) harmonically the same as introduction; fourth time in canon; eight measures parallel fifths alone, eight measures harmonized with G-D vs. Eb-Bb intervals   mm. 17-33

B | Theme fragment presented and briefly developed with harmonic accompaniment changed in content and texture; transitional in nature   mm. 34-44

C | New VII-i (G minor) unison B motive; dynamics and register expand together; initially accompanied by G-D/Eb-Bb fifths alternating with dominant seventh (d7), then harmonized with chaccone-like parallel fifths; climax of the work; two measure tutti rest   mm. 45-56

A | A theme material with chaccone-like progression (open fifths, then G-D/Eb-Bb juxtaposition); elision with next section   mm. 57-63

B | Diminution of original B motive centered on dominant, leading to tonic (G minor) added   mm. 64-69

Coda | Modal dominant preparation (lowered leading tone) for final tonic-C (third missing from final chord); eighth note motive in piccolo, Eb Clarinet, and vibraphone suggest dominant seventh chord on V; feeling of incompletion   mm. 70-75

Unit 8: Suggested Listening

Timothy Broege, *Sinfonias VI & IX, Three Pieces for American Band, Sets 1 & 2*
Mark Camphouse, *A Movement for Rosa*
Aaron Copland, *Lincoln Portrait*
David Gillingham, *Heroes, Lost and Fallen*
Morton Gould, *Hymnal*
Joseph Schwantner, *New Morning for the World (Daybreak of Freedom)*

Unit 9: Additional References and Resources

"The Basic Band Curriculum: Grades I, II, III." *BD Guide*, September/October 1989, 2-6.

Bourne Publishing Company, New York

Duarte, Leonard P., Daniel S. Hiestand, Carol Ann Prater, Doy E. Prater. *Band Music That Works*. Volume 1. Burlingame, California: Contrapuntal Publications, 1987.

Duarte, Leonard P., Daniel S. Hiestand, Carol Ann Prater, Doy E. Prater. *Band Music That Works*. Volume 2. Burlingame, California: Contrapuntal Publications, 1988.

Dvorak, Thomas L., Cynthia Crump Taggart, and Peter Schmaltz. *Best Music for Young Band*. Edited by Bob Margolis. Brooklyn, New York: Manhattan Beach Music, 1986.

Garofalo, Robert J. *Instructional Designs for Middle/Junior High School Band*. Fort Lauderdale, Florida: Meredith Music Publications, 1995.

Kreines, Joseph. *Music for Concert Band*. Tampa, Florida: Florida Music Service, 1989.

Manhattan Beach Music, Brooklyn, New York

Rehrig, William H. *The Heritage Encyclopedia of Band Music*. Edited by Paul E. Bierley. Westerville, Ohio: Integrity Press, 1991.

Teacher Resource Guide

"Portrait of a Clown"
Frank Ticheli

(b. 1958)

Unit 1: Composer

Frank Ticheli (b. 1958) is currently Composer-in-Residence of the Pacific Symphony Orchestra, and Assistant Professor of Music at the University of Southern California. A native of Louisiana, Ticheli received his doctoral and masters degrees in composition from the University of Michigan where he studied with William Albright, George Wilson, and Pulitzer Prize winners Leslie Bassett and Willian Bolcom. His compositions for wind ensemble and concert band have brought him numerous accolades, including the 1989 Walter Beeler Prize for Music for Winds and Percussion, and First Prize in the eleventh annual "Symposium for New Band Music" with Concertino for Trombone and Band. Other honors include a Charles Ives Scholarship and a Goddard Lieberson Fellowship, both from the American Academy and Institute of Arts and Letters, the Ross Lee Finney Award, and a residency at the McDowell Colony. Other Ticheli band works include *Postcard*, *Gaian Visions*, *Fortress*, and *Cajun Folk Songs*.

Unit 2: Composition

Portrait of a Clown, published in 1988, is a musical portrait of the comical and gentle sides of a clown. It was composed for, and first performed by the Murchison, Texas Middle School Matador Band, under Cheryl Floyd. The work, in ABA form, is scored to allow performances by bands lacking sufficient depth in low woodwinds and low brass. It is approximately two minutes and forty-five seconds in length.

Unit 3: Historical Perspective

Programmatic music has been an important part of music history for many years. Composers as varied as Hector Berlioz (*Symphonie Fantastique*), Modest Mussorgsky (*Pictures at an Exhibition*), Richard Wagner (use of *leitmotifs* throughout his opera cycle *Der Ring des Nibelungen*), Richard Strauss (*Till Eulenspiegel, Don Juan*), and Claude Debussy (*Prélude à l'après-midi d'un faune*) sought to portray characters, moods, and events through musical means. Late in the 20th century, composers such as John Adams (*Short Ride in a Fast Machine*) and Gunther Schuller (*Studies on Themes of Paul Klee*) still utilize aspects of programmatic music for their own works. In addition, today's motion pictures often rely on the creative and imaginative ideas of composers (John Williams, for example) to bring a complete and effective presentation to an audience. Some programmatic works that have been composed for band include: David Maslanka's *A Child's Garden of Dreams*, Michael Colgrass' *Winds of Nagual*, Cindy McTee's *Circuits*, and William Schuman's *George Washington Bridge*.

Unit 4: Technical Considerations

The scales of Bb Lydian, F Major, and F harmonic minor are required for all players. The instrumentation is suited for a young or incomplete band: flute/oboe, Bb clarinet I-II, Eb alto saxophone, Bb cornet I-II, F horn I-II/tenor saxophone, trombone/euphonium, low woodwinds/tuba, and percussion. The percussion requirements include snare drum, bass drum, crash cymbals, tambourine, and triangle. Accidentals occur frequently in most parts, mainly due to the modal forms of scales being used. Rhythms are basic, with combinations of whole, dotted half, half, quarter, and eighth notes.

Unit 5: Stylistic Considerations

Staccato, slurred legato, and legato-tongued articulations are required in this work. The staccato passages should have a "lifted" with a clean "tah" front to notes in this style, especially the A theme. The slurred legato and legato-tongued notes should have a lighter "dah" front to their notes for smoother, less percussive attacks. The B theme is marked *espressivo*, with legato articulation. The difference in style from the A section must be heard clearly, but at the same tempo as the A theme. Throughout the piece, either the A or B themes are always present. Balance of melody versus accompaniment should consistently be monitored, especially since the accompanimental texture changes often.

Unit 6: Musical Elements

Portrait of a Clown has three tonal centers: Bb Lydian (A-D), F harmonic minor (D-G), and F Major (G-H). The staccato A theme is initially presented in Bb Lydian above an active, playful accompanimental texture (letter A-B). Eight measures in length, it recurs five other times in the work, three times with one-measure

133

extensions (mm. 25, 76, 93), and once in inversion (mm. 77-84 in cornet I). A contrasting B1 theme distinguishes the larger B section with its smooth, legato style (letter D-E). This theme, also eight measures in length, is presented three times (letter D-F, G-H) and leads to a varied B2 theme (letter F-G). Accompanimental textures vary in both A and B sections. An interesting use of pedal points occur in several sections where an inverted pedal is passed through various registers and timbres on the syncopated fourth beat of measures (mm. 5-7, 26-29, 94-96).

Unit 7: Form and Structure

Introduction	Harmonic center is V, functioning as a dominant preparation for Bb Lydian; introductory theme primarily an extension of harmony; characterization of primary theme established	beginning-letter A
A letter A-D	Bb Lydian; A theme in flutes/oboes; light harmonic and rhythmic accompaniment	letter A-B
	A theme returns, doubled in alto saxophone and xylophone; varied texture in the accompaniment; one-measure extension to the theme	letter B-C
	transition, using material from Introduction(mm. 5-8); dominant preparation on C	letter C-D
B letter D-H	F harmonic minor; B theme in flutes; contrasting texture and articulation from A theme: legato, expressive; sustained chordal accompaniment	letter D-E
	B1 theme repeated, with oboe, alto saxophone, and cornet I added; varied accompanimental texture, more active with arpeggiated figures	letter E-F
	B2 theme, Ab Major, development of B1 theme; presented in middle register voices—low clarinets, horn, and tenor saxophone; preparation for second B1 presentation	letter F-G
	B1 theme, F Major; remains in F Major, with slight extension, as dominant preparation	letter G-H
A letter H-K	A theme returns, Bb Lydian; one-measure extension (echo)	letter H-m. 76

A theme repeated, similar accompaniment; added
thematic statement in inversion, incornet I

m. 77-letter J

third presentation of A theme, in brass and tenor
saxophone; one-measure extension; countermelody in
woodwinds   letter J-K

Coda letter   introductory material (mm. 5-8); dominant
      K-end   preparation for final two measures in Bb Lydian

letter K-end

Unit 8: Suggested Listening
Paul Dukas, *The Sorcerer's Apprentice*
Modest Mussorgsky, *Carnival of the Animals*
Dmitri Shostakovich, *Polka from "The Golden Age"*
Frank Ticheli, *Cajun Folk Songs, Fortress, Postcard*

Unit 9: Additional References and Resources
"The Basic Band Curriculum: Grades I, II, III." *BD Guide*, September/October
    1989, 2-6.

Duarte, Leonard P., Daniel S. Hiestand, Carol Ann Prater, Doy E. Prater.
    Band Music That Works. Volume 1. Burlingame, California: Contrapuntal
    Publications, 1987.

Duarte, Leonard P., Daniel S. Hiestand, Carol Ann Prater, Doy E. Prater.
    Band Music That Works. Volume 2. Burlingame, California: Contrapuntal
    Publications, 1988.

Dvorak, Thomas L., Cynthia Crump Taggart, and Peter Schmaltz. *Best Music for
    Young Band.* Edited by Bob Margolis. Brooklyn, New York: Manhattan
    Beach Music, 1986.

Garofalo, Robert J. *Instructional Designs for Middle/Junior High School
    Band.* Fort Lauderdale, Florida: Meredith Music Publications, 1995.

Kreines, Joseph. *Music for Concert Band.* Tampa, Florida: Florida Music
    Service, 1989.

Manhattan Beach Music, Brooklyn, New York

Rehrig, William H. *The Heritage Encyclopedia of Band Music.* Edited by Paul
    E. Bierley. Westerville, Ohio: Integrity Press, 1991.

Teacher Resource Guide

"Prospect"
Pierre La Plante

(b. 1943)

Unit 1: Composer
Pierre La Plante, of French-Canadian descent, was born in Milwaukee on September 25, 1943. He attended the University of Wisconsin at Madison, receiving his Bachelor and Master of Music degrees. His many years of teaching at the elementary through college levels include classroom, vocal and instrumental music. La Plante, a bassoonist, has been a member of the Dubuque Symphony, the Madison Theatre Guild Orchestra, and the Unitarian Society Orchestra. He performs with the Beloit-Janesville Symphony. La Plante, who teaches in the Pecatonica Area School District in Wisconsin, has written several works for band, including *American River Songs*, *A Little French Suite*, *A March on the King's Highway*, and *Triptych for Christmas*.

Unit 2: Composition
This composition is subtitled *Hymn for Band*. It is a setting of the folk song "Prospect" (also known as "The Seaman's Hymn"). This setting is simple, yet expressive. It builds slowly and steadily to a broad, quasi-fanfare finish. Most sections of the band have a chance to play the melody. The piece, composed in 1983, is 93 measures and three minutes and forty-five seconds long.

Unit 3: Historical Perspective
The melody that is set in this work comes from *The Southern Harmony and Musical Companion*, published in Philadelphia in 1835. This was one of the more popular "shaped note" tunebooks in 19th century America. Shaped notes were devised to make music reading easier for the novice. Each of the four pitches used had its own particular notehead shape. Tunebooks were, as a result, often used to teach

music by the traveling music teacher. The *Southern Harmony* is also a wealth of folk tunes, popular airs, and ballads as well as the expected hymn tunes. It is not only the source of *Prospect,* but of other well-known tunes such as *Amazing Grace* and *Rock of Ages.* Aaron Copland used the melody of *Amazing Grace* in his *Emblems.*

Unit 4: Technical Considerations

The scales of F Major and A-flat Major are required by the entire ensemble. This work is a simple hymn setting with no special rhythmic demands placed on any player. The ranges are appropriate with the cornet 1 part reaching A-flat2 at the Fine. The character of the music requires sustained playing from the ensemble members. There are many fully scored sections that will require players to listen for the melody and balance the lines with countermelody and harmony.

Unit 5: Stylistic Considerations

The lyrical quality of this music will demand good control and phrasing from all players. The melody lines are marked *sempre legato.* A full range of dynamics is used, from *piano* to *fortississimo,* with areas of crescendo and diminuendo. As the music builds in dynamics toward the end, the ensemble must take precautions not to reach its highest peak too soon.

Unit 6: Musical Elements

The tonal centers of F Major and A-flat Major are used. The harmony is very triadic and diatonic. The melody is very song-like and in clear phrases. The entire work is in a three meter with the eighth note the smallest division of the beat.

Unit 7: Form and Structure

Measure	Melodic Scoring
1	Introduction, full band (no as, ts)
10	Melody, phrases 1-2, fls, cls, as
18	Melody, phrase 3, fls, cl 1, hns
21	Melody, phrase 4, fls, cls, as
26	Interlude, Upper ww, hns, tuba
34	Melody, solo cor 1, fls countermelody
50	Interlude, key change, saxes, brass
58	Melody, phrases 1-2, fls, obs, cls, ts, tbns,countermelody in alto cl, hns, bar
66	Melody, phrase 3, as's, hns, tbns 1-2, (4-line polyphony)
70	Melody, phrase 4, fls, obs, cls, bar
74	Melody, phrase 3, fls, obs, cls, ts, cor 1, bar (3-line polyphony)
78	Melody, phrase 4, fls, obs, cl 1, ts, bar
83	Coda, phrase 3 motive

Unit 8: Suggested Listening
Aaron Copland, *Emblems*
Clare Grundman, *Fantasy on American Sailing Songs*
David Holsinger, *On a Hymn Song of Philip Bliss*
Pierre La Plante, *American Riversongs*
Dan Welcher, *Zion*

Unit 9: Additional References and Resources
Rehrig, William H. *The Heritage Encyclopedia of Band Music.* Westerville,
    OH: Integrity Press, 1991.

Teacher Resource Guide

"The Red Balloon"
Anne McGinty

(b. 1945)

Unit 1: Composer

Anne McGinty (b. 1945), a native of Findlay, Ohio, received her Bachelor of Music and Master of Music degrees from Duquesne University with emphases in flute performance and composition. Active throughout her career as a flutist, teacher, and clinician, McGinty is a well-known composer and arranger of music for young bands. She has composed over one hundred thirty works for band ranging from levels one through five. Along with her husband John Edmondson, McGinty operates Queenwood Publications which specializes in music for young musicians. Along with *The Red Balloon*, her other original band works include *Falling Branch, Clouds, American Folk Festival, Excelsior,* and *Divertissement.*

Unit 2: Composition

Composed in 1992, *The Red Balloon* is based on a painting which left an impression on the composer even though she viewed it only once. The painting depicts a small child and a grandfather facing away. The two people and the background were painted white-on-white. The only color in the painting is the red balloon, which is held by the child. This programmatic work is intended not only to suggest the flight of a balloon, but also to encourage the players to use their imaginations to visualize its journey in the air. The work is approximately two and one-half minutes in length.

Unit 3: Historical Perspective

Program music can be defined as referential music-instrumental music that describes, characterizes, suggests, interprets, or is inspired by a nonmusical subject or idea that the composer indicates through the title and/or any explanatory remarks. In the nineteenth century, program music became one of the prominent forms identified with the Romantic movement, with its free expression and frequent references to extramusical events, characters, or situations. Many important works have programmatic subjects, such as Berlioz', *Symphonie Fantastique* and *Romeo and Juliet*, Schumann's *Carnaval*, Tchaikovsky's *Overture 1812* and *Romeo and Juliet*, Mussorgsky's *Pictures at an Exhibition*, Paul Dukas' *The Sorcerer's Apprentice*, and Richard Strauss' *Don Juan* and *Till Eulenspiegel*. Works for band programmatic in nature include: Bassett's *Designs, Images and Textures*, *Colors and Contours*, Schuman's *George Washington Bridge*, Paulson's *Epinicion*, and Dello Joio's *Scenes from the Louvre*.

Unit 4: Technical Considerations

The instrumentation is suited for a young band: flutes and (optional) oboes, Bb clarinets I-II, Bb bass clarinet, alto saxophone, tenor and baritone saxophone, cornet/trumpet I-II, F horn (optional), trombone/baritone, tuba, bells, triangle, snare drum, suspended cymbal, claves, tambourine, and bass drum. Smooth legato playing is the primary requirement of all wind and brass players. In lieu of key signatures, accidentals (both sharps and flats) are used liberally in all parts. Rhythmic values are basic (dotted half, half, quarter, and eighth), with the dotted quarter being prominent in the melody. For young percussionists, the bell part will be challenging with its abundant accidentals and exposed writing.

Unit 5: Stylistic Considerations

In order to match the ideal of *The Red Balloon*, the melody must have an airy, ethereal quality in which the slurred phrases are sustained fully with a relaxed tone quality. Often the melody ends with one instrumental color and is immediately passed on to another, requiring a smooth connection of sound between the two phrases. Dynamic indications change often, with added diminuendos and cresendos. Consistent attention to balance, therefore, between the primary musical ideas and the accompaniment is important. The percussion section provides an array of color for variety, which should be subtle and not overpower the melodic ideas. The bells are used creatively to provide a complementary color to the melodic line, as well as to present melodic material alone.

Unit 6: Musical Elements

Following an initial presentation of the main melody (two phrases: an *A section* of four measures each, followed by the B section, an irregular eight-measure transitional portion), the music unfolds into a series of sections based on the melody. Some sections reiterate the melody in varied scoring, and some are developmental, utilizing a variety of compositional techniques (which include literal presentations of selected portions of phrases, transpositions into different modes, and prominent motives taken from the melody and developed independently).

In addition, phrases are presented in an irregular fashion—sometimes with a clear resting point, other times as an elision coinciding with the beginning of another musical idea. Interesting colors are created when the melody is shared by a variety of instruments (for example, in mm. 85-88, the melody is passed from trumpet I to the bells to the flutes and oboes). Percussion instruments are effectively used to add color to repetitions of the melody and, through the bell part, contribute to melodic presentations.

Unit 7: Form and Structure

SECTION 1

C Lydian tonality;	A section of melody presented in flutes/oboes; elision with B section of theme; mainly stepwise motion	
		mm. 1-16
B section of melody;	skips prominent in melodic line; harmonically unsettled: a dorian, Bb Lydian, Ab Lydian, Db Lydian (implied): tritone relationship to G Lydian arrival in m. 17	
		mm. 9-16

SECTION 2

Shift to G Lydian;	A section of melody presented in woodwinds, horn, bells	mm. 17-24
Shift to Db Lydian;	A section presented in trumpets; four-measure extension in D Major	mm. 25-36

TRANSITION

Eb Major;	first phrase of A section presented in low brass and woodwinds, followed by shift to G Lydian; repeated fragment from phrase used to slow forward motion	
		mm. 37-46

SECTION 3

A and B sections of melody return (similar to mm. 1-16); melodic line (A section) in alto saxophone with flute/oboe added in second phrase; Bb Lydian tonality, followed by transitional harmonic movement (B section)

mm. 47-62

SECTION 4

Varied form of A section's first two phrases; tonally unsettled, F Lydian   mm. 63-70

Second phrase of A section in Eb Lydian, followed by
B section of melody (similar to mm. 9-16), ending in Gb
Lydian; tritone relationship to C Lydian arrival in m. 81
(Gb-C)   mm. 71-80

CLOSING SECTION

Return to C Lydian, with harmonic movement through
F Lydian, Bb Lydian, and returning to C Lydian; literal
presentation of first phrase of A section of melody;
second phrase varied, with melodic line varied in pitch
and scoring as the theme is passed between trumpet I,
bells, flute/oboes; second phrase of A section recalled,
presented by bell solo; incomplete cadence in melodic
line   mm. 81-92

Unit 8: Suggested Listening

Lesslie Bassett, *Designs, Images and Textures*
Cassette recordings to *Queenwood Publications Beginning Band Books* 1 & 2
Michael Colgrass, *Winds of Nagual*
Norman Dello Joio, *Scenes from the Louvre*
David Maslanka, *A Child's Garden of Dreams*

Unit 9: Additional References and Resources

"The Basic Band Curriculum: Grades I, II, III." *BD Guide*, September/October
1989, 2-6.

Duarte, Leonard P., Daniel S. Hiestand, Carol Ann Prater, Doy E. Prater.
Band Music That Works. Volume 1. Burlingame, California: Contrapuntal
Publications, 1987.

Duarte, Leonard P., Daniel S. Hiestand, Carol Ann Prater, Doy E. Prater.
Band Music That Works. Volume 2. Burlingame, California: Contrapuntal
Publications, 1988.

Dvorak, Thomas L., Cynthia Crump Taggart, and Peter Schmaltz. *Best Music for
Young Band*. Edited by Bob Margolis. Brooklyn, New York: Manhattan
Beach Music, 1986.

Garofalo, Robert J. *Instructional Designs for Middle/Junior High School
Band*. Fort Lauderdale, Florida: Meredith Music Publications, 1995.

Kamien, Roger. *Music: An Appreciation*. New York: McGraw-Hill, 1988.

Kreines, Joseph. *Music for Concert Band*. Tampa, Florida: Florida Music
Service, 1989.

Queenwood Publications, Scottsdale, Arizona

Rehrig, William H. *The Heritage Encyclopedia of Band Music.* Edited by Paul
    E. Bierley. Westerville, Ohio: Integrity Press, 1991.

Teacher Resource Guide

"Snakes"
Thomas C. Duffy

(b. 1955)

Unit 1: Composer

Thomas C. Duffy received a Doctor of Musical Arts degree in composition from Cornell University, where he studied with Karel Husa and Steven Stucky. He is Director of Bands at Yale University and an Associate Professor of Music in the Yale School of Music. He is Editor of the College Band Directors National Association Journal and Past President of the New England College Band Association and the Connecticut Composers, Inc. In addition to *Snakes!*, Duffy has written one other work for band, *Crystals*.

Unit 2: Composition

Snakes! was commissioned by the Adams Middle School Band of Guilford, Connecticut. It was premiered by the Yale Concert Band in 1989 and first performed by a young ensemble in 1990 (the Nassau All-County Junior High School Honor Band). The work is a short piece of program music which explores different sounds one might associate with different snakes, including the cobra, python, and boa constrictor. Its use of contemporary compositional techniques (i.e., graphic/proportional notation (a brief section of the piece), a large array of percussion sounds, and speaking) make this a challenging work for young band.

Unit 3: Historical Perspective

The 20th century, by far, has seen the most experimentation and change in composition than any other century. Composers have experimented with a variety of new and traditional techniques and devices. The twelve-tone system, serialism, minimalism, atonality, unusual scoring, different ways of producing sounds on traditional instruments, and aleatoric music are only some of the vast array of developments in 20th-century composition. John Cage, Milton Babbitt, Barney Childs, Arnold Schoenberg, Anton Webern, and Edgard Varèse are just a few of the many composers who have stretched the traditional limits of composition.

Unit 4: Technical Considerations

Snakes! is based on a C harmonic minor scale, so a knowledge of at least C natural and harmonic minor scales would help students. Primarily using dotted half, quarter, and eighth notes, rhythmic considerations include groups of four sixteenths and some syncopated rhythms based on quarters and eighths. Percussionists also have triplet figures of three sixteenths/eighth in several parts. An early motive which creates a pyramid effect in the brass section is primarily made up of augmented fourths/diminished fifths. The brass instruments are required to play "1/2 valve (open) murmur" effect at letter E, while trombones have glissando figures. Six percussionists are needed for the piece, requiring them to play bongos, maracas, gong or tam tam, snare drum, sizzle cymbal, flex-atone, bass drum, timpani, bean shaker, and vibraslap.

Unit 5: Stylistic Considerations

As a programmatic piece, *Snakes!* encourages students to use their imaginations as performers. The more creative and personally involved the students are, the more vivid the interpretation will become. The wide variety of dynamics (from *pp* diminuendo to *niente*, up to *ff*) and sudden dynamic changes requires good tone quality in all ranges from all instruments and an attention to the balance of instrumental colors. Staccato and legato articulations also change suddenly and frequently. Speaking parts should be performed with enthusiasm and an understanding of the context in which they are used: for example, words are used to communicate (the names of snakes), or for their onomatopoeic effects ("snakes-s-s-s-s-s").

Unit 6: Musical Elements

The music is built primarily on a C harmonic minor foundation. Chromaticism occasionally "blurs" the tonality (the initial figures in the woodwinds in measure 1, for example), but C harmonic minor is clearly presented in a number of passages (i.e., in measure 18, the entire scale is present in the band). Motives are the rule, rather than melodies. Each section of the piece features its own distinctive motivic material, relating to the programmatic aspect of each "snake." The percussion writing provides energetic rhythmic accompaniment, which compliments the existing wind and brass textures. In addition, percussion adds color throughout, particularly in the aleatoric section.

Unit 7: Form and Structure

Section 1   Vertical sonorities; multiple percussion colors
                 accompanying; pyramids featuring augmented
                 fourths/diminished fifths, with imitative percussion
                 voices; ends with vertical sonorities, percussive;
                 presentation of entire C harmonic minor scale at once
                                                         mm. 1-21

Transition   E minor triad, through timbral modulation, changes to E
                 pedal in brass, then flutes and bassoons; percussion
                 introduces energetic accompaniment as introduction to
                 next section   mm. 22-28

Section 2   New motive in low winds and brass; continued rhythmic
                 pedal (moto perpetuo) in percussion; addition of melodic
                 figure based on harmonic minor scale with flatted second
                 scale degree; speaking, added chromatic lines to texture
                                                         mm. 29-55

Section 3   Abrupt release of forward motion and energy;
                 color/instrumental timbre most important element;
                 proportional notation in seconds; reitieration of
                 harmonic minor line   mm. 56-59

Coda   Return of energy with percussion rhythmic pedal;
                 remainder of ensemble speaks to the end   mm. 60-65

Unit 8: Suggested Listening

Daniel Bukvich, *Symphony No. 1*
Thomas Duffy, *Crystals*
Donald Erb, *Stargazing*
John Paulson, *Epinicion*
John Pennington, *Apollo*
Joseph Schwantner, *and the mountains rising nowhere*

Unit 9: Additional References and Resources

Apel, Willi, ed. *Harvard Dictionary of Music.* Second edition. Cambridge,
    Massachusetts: Belknap Press, 1970.

"The Basic Band Curriculum: Grades I, II, III." *BD Guide,* September/October
    1989, 2-6.

Duarte, Leonard P., Daniel S. Hiestand, Carol Ann Prater, Doy E. Prater.
    Band Music That Works. Volume 1. Burlingame, California: Contrapuntal
    Publications, 1987.

146

Duarte, Leonard P., Daniel S. Hiestand, Carol Ann Prater, Doy E. Prater. *Band Music That Works.* Volume 2. Burlingame, California: Contrapuntal Publications, 1988.

Dvorak, Thomas L., Cynthia Crump Taggart, and Peter Schmaltz. *Best Music for Young Band.* Edited by Bob Margolis. Brooklyn, New York: Manhattan Beach Music, 1986.

Farkas, Philip. *The Art of Musicianship.* Bloomington, Indiana: Musical Publications, 1976.

Garofalo, Robert J. *Instructional Designs for Middle/Junior High School Band.* Fort Lauderdale, Florida: Meredith Music Publications, 1995.

Grout, Donald J. *A History of Western Music.* Third edition. New York: W. W. Norton, 1980.

Kreines, Joseph. *Music for Concert Band.* Tampa, Florida: Florida Music Service, 1989.

Ludwig Music, Cleveland, Ohio

Machlis, Joseph. *Introduction to Contemporary Music.* New York: W. W. Norton, 1979

Rehrig, William H. *The Heritage Encyclopedia of Band Music.* Edited by Paul E. Bierley. Westerville, Ohio: Integrity Press, 1991.

Stolba, K Marie. *The Development of Western Music.* Dubuque, Iowa: William C. Brown Publishers, 1990.

Vinton, John, ed. *Dictionary of Contemporary Music.* New York: E.P. Dutton, 1974.

Watkins, Glenn. *Soundings.* New York: Schirmer Books, 1988.

Teacher Resource Guide

"Soldier Procession and Sword Dance" Bob Margolis

(b. 1949)

(after Tielman Susato, ca. 1500–1561-4)

Unit 1: Composer
Bob Margolis (b. 1949) was born in Staten Island, New York, and attended Brooklyn College and the University of California. In 1981, he founded Manhattan Beach Music, a publishing firm dedicated to producing quality band compositions and arrangements. Margolis has arranged many Renaissance works for band by composers such as Claude Gervaise, Michael Praetorius, and Tielman Susato. These pieces include *Color*, *Fanfare*, *Ode and Festival*, *Royal Coronation Dances*, and *Terpsichore*.

Unit 2: Composition
Based on music by Tielman Susato, *Soldiers' Procession and Sword Dance* are the titles of two works taken from Susato's *Danserye (Het derde musyck boexken)*, a collection of popular music published in 1551. Previously arranged for Renaissance instruments by Susato, Margolis has scored the two movements for contemporary concert band, specifically with a small ensemble in mind. The work is approximately two minutes and fifteen seconds in length.

Unit 3: Historical Perspective
Many Renaissance instruments were built in families or sets which incorporated graduated sizes. These families, known as *whole consorts*, covered the entire vocal range in use during the period. The family of instruments produced a homoge-

neous sound. Groups of instruments from a variety of families were known as *broken consorts*. Also, instruments of the period were categorized as loud (*haut*) or soft (*bas*). Generally, these instruments had fewer tonal colors and produced less intense sounds than instruments of today. When arrangements (usually adapted from either vocal or keyboard music) were performed, a variety in sound could be obtained through the alternation of consorts (haut or bas). Contemporary band arrangers often adhere to this principle in their scoring in order to approximate the effect of consorts in performance.

Unit 4: Technical Considerations
The scales of Eb Major, G natural minor, and G harmonic minor are required for the entire ensemble. The instrumentation is suited for a young or small band: flute I-II, oboe (optional), Bb clarinet I-II, low woodwinds, Eb alto saxophone I-II, trumpet I-II, F horn, trombone or euphonium, tuba, and percussion. Three percussionists are needed to play orchestra bells, medium and large tom toms, two "high drums", two woodblocks, two cymbals, triangle, and bass drum. Rhythms are basic, with combinations of half, dotted quarter, quarter, and eighth notes. Percussionists also perform four sixteenth, eighth/two sixteenth, and two sixteenth/eighth rhythmic combinations.

Unit 5: Stylistic Considerations
Transcribed from an original polyphonic four-part setting, doubled instrumental lines predominate the work, requiring careful decisions on balance and color. A "lifted" sound, with notes that are detached but have body, is necessary for proper ensemble sound. In addition, various hard and soft tonguing styles are needed for the range of articulation markings in the music. Uniform articulation, tonguing, and note lengths from all instruments are important for clarity within this style, especially in order to distinguish individual lines in the texture. Margolis has added rhythms and percussion instruments which are to be used in the Renaissance tradition of accompanying. Care should be taken to obtain sounds from each instrument that are characterisitic of the period, and not of the contemporary percussion section (i.e., too "sophisticated" in sound).

Unit 6: Musical Elements
Polyphonic in texture, both movements utilize several main ideas that are repeated, then passed on, yielding to a new idea. For example, in the first movement, *Soldiers' Procession*, the first four measures introduce a primary line (flute I, alto saxophone I) and three accompanying, yet independent, voices which end with a half cadence. This section is repeated in mm. 5-8 with no changes in pitch or harmony: the only variation is the orchestration, following the sound concept of the consort (see *Historical Perpective*). Phrases of three- and two-measures follow. In *Sword Dance*, three phrases of four measures are treated in a similar manner (i.e., mm 7-14). Margolis scores for a wide variety of consort sounds in the work:

entire ensemble, trumpet/trombone/low woodwind, and all woodwind. Percussion instruments are added for their traditional role of timekeeping, but also for color.

Unit 7: Form and Structure

SOLDIERS' PROCESSION

A   Eb Major, with primary line in flute I and alto saxophone
                    I; diatonic chords, phrase ends with half cadence;
                    repeated Section A, with variation in instrumentation;
                    identical lines and harmony; percussion added

                                                            mm. 1-8

B   New melodic material; three-measure phrase; repeated B
                    with variation in instrumentation only   mm. 9-14

C   Six-measure phrase with strong emphasis on IV chord in
                    third/fourth measures (m. 17-18); new thematic ideas

                                                            mm. 15-20

Coda   New material; establishes final cadence in Eb;
                    two-measure phrase, repeated with slight variation
                    in instrumentation; very active percussion
                    accompaniment   mm. 21-24

SWORD DANCE

Introduction   solo percussion establishes beat and primary rhythmic
                    pattern; texture provided by two drums (high/medium)

                                                            mm. 1-6

A   G minor; two-voice polyphony; four-measure phrase;
                    scored for trumpet/trombone-euphonium/low
                    woodwinds (continuous percussion accompaniment);
                    cadence in G minor with modal sound due to lack of
                    raised leading tone (F#); repeated A section with full
                    ensemble (minus trumpet II); two additional voices
                    provide harmonic depth; convincing cadence
                    in G minor with V-i   mm. 7-14

B   New scalar motives; return to two-voice polyphony;
                    four-measure phrase; begins in G minor, cadences in
                    relative key-Bb Major; repeated B section with
                    identical variations in scoring;   mm. 15-22

C   New arpeggiated motive in flute/trumpet, G minor;
                    four-measure phrase; full ensemble (minus alto
                    saxophone II); woodblock percussion accompaniment;

repeated C section; full ensemble with alto
saxophone II; staccato articulation; final cadence
in G minor   mm. 23-30

Unit 8: Suggested Listening

Thoinot Arbeau/arr. Margolis, *Belle Qui Tiens Ma Vie*
Pierre Attaignant/arr. Margolis, *Fanfare, Ode, and Festival*
Jan Bach, *Praetorius Suite*
Giovanni Gabrieli, any brass ensemble music: *Canzon, Sacrae Symphoniae*
David Munrow, recordings that accompany *Instruments of the Middle Ages and
    Renaissance* text
Michael Praetorius/arr. Margolis, *Terpsichore*
Tielman Susato/arr. Michael Walters, *Twelve Dances from the "Danserye"*

Unit 9: Additional References and Resources

Apel, Willi, ed. *Harvard Dictionary of Music.* Second Edition. Cambridge,
    Massachusetts: Belknap Press, 1970.

"The Basic Band Curriculum: Grades I, II, III." *BD Guide,* September/October
    1989, 2-6.

Duarte, Leonard P., Daniel S. Hiestand, Carol Ann Prater, Doy E. Prater.
    Band Music That Works. Volume 1. Burlingame, California: Contrapuntal
    Publications, 1987.

Duarte, Leonard P., Daniel S. Hiestand, Carol Ann Prater, Doy E. Prater.
    Band Music That Works. Volume 2. Burlingame, California: Contrapuntal
    Publications, 1988.

Dvorak, Thomas L., Cynthia Crump Taggart, and Peter Schmaltz. *Best Music for
    Young Band.* Edited by Bob Margolis. Brooklyn, New York: Manhattan
    Beach Music, 1986.

Farkas, Philip. *The Art of Musicianship.* Bloomington, Indiana: Musical
    Publications, 1976.

Garofalo, Robert J. *Instructional Designs for Middle/Junior High School
    Band.* Fort Lauderdale, Florida: Meredith Music Publications, 1995.

Kreines, Joseph. *Music for Concert Band.* Tampa, Florida: Florida Music
    Service, 1989.

Manhattan Beach Music, Brooklyn, New York

Munrow, David. *Instruments of the Middle Ages and Renaissance.* London:
    Oxford University Press, 1976.

Rehrig, William H. *The Heritage Encyclopedia of Band Music.* Edited by Paul E. Bierley. Westerville, Ohio: Integrity Press, 1991.

Sadie, Stanley, ed. *New Grove Dictionary of Music and Musicians.* London: Macmillan Publishers Limited, 1980. S.v. "Tielman Susato," by Susan Bain.

Slonimsky, Nicholas, ed. *Baker's Biographical Dictionary of Musicians.* Fifth Edition. New York: G. Schirmer, 1958.

Stolba, K Marie. *The Development of Western Music.* Dubuque, Iowa: William C. Brown Publishers, 1990.

Whitwell, David. *A Concise History of the Wind Band.* Northridge, California: WINDS, 1

Grade 3

Teacher Resource Guide

"Air for Band"
Frank Erickson

(b. 1923)

Unit 1: Composer

Frank Erickson was born on September 1, 1923, in Spokane, Washington. He began to study music—playing piano and trumpet—and compose while in high school. During World War II, he arranged for army bands and, following the war, worked as a dance band arranger while studying composition with Mario Castelnuovo-Tedesco. He received degrees from the University of Southern California, where he studied with Halsey Stevens. He taught at the University of California at Los Angeles and San Jose State College. Erickson has been music editor for several music publishers and he has more than 250 compositions and arrangements for band to his credit. Over 150 of his compositions have been published, including: *Balladair, Citadel March, Fantasy for Band, First Symphony for Band,* and *Second Symphony for Band.*

Unit 2: Composition

Since this work was first published in 1956, it has helped several generations of band musicians develop their ability to play a sustained line, to listen for the moving part, and to improve their intonation while playing. Revised in 1966, the work retains its wonderful melodic sense with graceful harmonic movement and skillful contrapuntal writing. The work is 53 measures and three minutes and fifteen seconds long.

Unit 3: Historical Perspective

The work was composed early in Erickson's career, in 1956, a period during which some composers were very mindful of writing tuneful works that had great educational value to young American bands. The term *Air* refers to a tuneful

154

melody, whether vocal or instrumental. The term, used to describe musical pieces for at least 400 years, aptly describes this 20th century work.

Unit 4: Technical Considerations

The tonality begins in C minor and moves to C Major. The scales of C Major and C minor are required for the entire ensemble. There should be no significant rhythmic concerns. In the last section there are entrances on the second eighth of the measure. The eighth note is the smallest division. Ranges are not extreme. Flutes go to f3, cornets to f2.

Unit 5: Stylistic Considerations

The slow tempo (quarter at 68-72) demands sustained playing by wind instrumentalists. There is ample opportunity to tune chords and intervals in both minor and major keys. The key center of C minor utilizes accidentals. Most dynamics are soft. There is a large, slow crescendo in the middle and also one at the end.

Unit 6: Musical Elements

The harmony is triadic with some seventh chords at cadence points. The tonality begins in C minor and shifts to C Major through a change in key signature. Melodic importance remains in the moving lines throughout. Attention to balance between the moving line and the harmonic accompaniment will help produce an effective performance.

Unit 7: Form and Structure

Measure:	1	9	17	28	36	44
Section:	a	a	b	a1	b1	a2
	C minor					C Major

Unit 8: Suggested Listening

J.S. Bach, *Air for the G String*
Frank Erickson, *Balladair*
Percy Grainger, *Colonial Song*
Percy Grainger, *Irish Tune from County Derry*

Unit 9: Additional References and Resources

Balent, Andrew. "Frank Erickson—The Composer's Point of View." *The Instrumentalist*, XL April 1986, 28-34.

Dvorak, Thomas L. *Best Music for Young Band*. Brooklyn, NY: Manhattan Beach Music, 1986.

Erickson, Frank. *"Frank Erickson: Air for Band and Toccata for Band."* BD Guide, January/February 1992, 27.

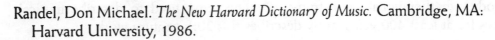

Randel, Don Michael. *The New Harvard Dictionary of Music.* Cambridge, MA: Harvard University, 1986.

Rehrig, William H. *The Heritage Encyclopedia of Band Music.* Westerville, OH: Integrity Press, 1991.

Smith, Norman and Albert Stoutamire. *Band Music Notes.* Lake Charles, LA: Program Note Press, 1989.

Teacher Resource Guide

"Australian Up-Country Tune"
Percy Grainger

(b. 1882–d. 1961)

arranged by Glenn Cliffe Bainum

(b. 1888–d. 1974)

Unit 1: Composer

George Percy Aldridge Grainger was born on July 8, 1882, in Melbourne, Australia. He studied piano, first with his mother, then with Louis Pabst. At age ten, he gave a series of recitals which financed his study in Germany. In 1900, he first started his career as a concert pianist, enjoying success all over the world. He was chosen by composer Edvard Grieg to appear as guest soloist in the premiere of Grieg's *Concerto in A* in 1907. He came to America in 1915. At the outbreak of World War I he enlisted as an Army bandsman, soon being promoted to the Army Music School. He became a US citizen in 1919, and again made many worldwide concert tours. For some time he was professor and head of the music department at New York University. A rugged individualist, Grainger was a remarkable innovator as a composer for orchestra and wind band. He was one of the first twentieth-century composers to embrace the wind band as a viable, expressive, artistic medium. His rhythmic inventiveness preceded Stravinsky; he was a pioneer in folk music collection at the same time as Bartok; his experiments with random and "free music" predated Varèse and other composers of electronic music. Grainger composed over thirty works for band, some of the most performed being *Children's March*, *Over the Hills and Far Away*, *Colonial Song*, *Country Gardens*, *Irish Tune from County Derry*, *Lincolnshire Posy*, *Shepherd's Hey*, and *Ye Banks and Braes O'Bonnie Doon*.

Unit 2: Composition

The original tune, written by Grainger in 1905, is called "Up-Country Song." It was arranged for a chorus of unaccompanied voices with wordless syllables in 1928. The choral version was first sung at Grainger's wedding to Ella Viola Strom at the Hollywood Bowl, California, August 9, 1928, by the Smallman a cappella Choir. Glenn Cliffe Bainum later arranged the work for concert band from the choral version. The 29-measure work is two minutes in length.

Unit 3: Historical Perspective

The composer has written that with his tune he "had wished to voice Australian up-country feeling as Stephen Foster had with American country-side feelings in his songs. I have used this same melody in my Australian *Colonial Song* and in my Australian *The Gumsuckers' March*."

Unit 4: Technical Considerations

The F Major scale is required for the entire ensemble. Eighth notes are the smallest division, but there are several occurrences of dotted-eighth and sixteenth notes. The biggest challenge will be the changing meters, several fermatas, and undulating dynamics. When the players are able to achieve a long, smooth line, a warm, rich, free, lyrical performance (typical of Grainger's writing) will result.

Unit 5: Stylistic Considerations

Careful attention to dynamic differences will provide a challenge for any ensemble. Unlike some of Grainger's other works for band, the dynamics written in this piece are unison dynamics, somewhat easing the challenge. The tempo is marked "Slowly", and the quarter note should probably equal around 60. The free feel of the lyrical line is expressed through the changing meters. The slow tempo will help facilitate the ensemble's travels through them, but great attention must be placed on accuracy of the different rhythms in the separate, simultaneous parts.

Unit 6: Musical Elements

The harmony, which fits in F Major, is very triadic. The melodic line is scored clearly throughout. A harmonized accompaniment creates non-complex polyphony. The melody is highly lyrical and very singable. Rhythmic challenges may be provided by the dotted-eighth and sixteenth patterns, the changing meters, and the fermatas.

Unit 7: Form and Structure

The work is a setting of three statements of the lyrical theme, with the texture increasing with each statement.

Unit 8: Suggested Listening

Stephen Foster, *Beautiful Dreamer; Jeannie with the Light Brown Hair; Swanee River*
Percy Grainger, *Colonial Song*
Percy Grainger, *Gum Suckers March*
Percy Grainger, *Lincolnshire Posy*

Unit 9: Additional References and Resources

Dvorak, Thomas L. *Best Music for Young Band.* Brooklyn, NY: Manhattan Beach Music, 1986.

Rehrig, William H. *The Heritage Encyclopedia of Band Music.* Westerville, OH: Integrity Press, 1991.

Smith, Norman and Albert Stoutamire. *Band Music Notes.* Lake Charles, LA: Program Note Press, 1989.

Uggen, Stuart. "Percy Grainger in Perspective." *The Instrumentalist,* XXIV June 1970, 38-41.

Wilson, Brian Scott. "Orchestrational Archetypes in Percy Grainger's Wind Band Music." Diss., The University of Arizona, 1992.

Teacher Resource Guide

"Belle Qui Tien Ma Vie"
Bob Margolis

(b. 1949)

after Thoinot Arbeau

(b. 1520–d. 1595)

Unit 1: Composer

Bob Margolis was born on April 30, 1949, on Staten Island, New York. He studied at Brooklyn College and the University of California. In 1981, he founded the publishing firm Manhattan Beach Music. Many of his works are modern settings of melodies and musical ideas from the Renaissance period. His works have been twice honored in composition contests by the American Bandmasters Association. He has over a dozen works written for band including: *Fanfare, Ode and Festival, Royal Coronation Dances,* and *Terpsichore.*

Unit 2: Composition

Belle Qui Tien Ma Vie (Beauty Who Has My Life) is a beautiful and stately pavane from the 16th century. The *pavane* is a grave and dignified dance whose musical form consists of a number of repeated sections. This pavane has two sections, and this arrangement plays the song three times. Phrasing, intonation and general sensitivity are crucial to the performance of this arrangement of the simple tune. The 55-measure work was composed in 1981 and is two minutes, forty-five seconds in length.

Unit 3: Historical Perspective

The music of this pavane comes from an important 16th century treatise on dancing, *Orchesography*, by Thoinot Arbeau (a 16th century French cleric). This particular pavane is the only music in this treatise that Arbeau arranged in four parts (the other music consists of tunes only). The seven stanzas of text (included in the score) are typical of the Renaissance songs, which deal with unrequited love. The arranger has retained the traditional percussion rhythm and Renaissance dance atmosphere.

Unit 4: Technical Considerations

The work is set in G minor. The half notes and quarter notes of this arrangement provide quiet and spacious sonorities and certainly no obvious technical challenges. The main challenges occur through the playing of tongued legato passages and long phrases. Good tone quality at the slow tempo as well as soft dynamics are imperative in this sustained music. The slow, sustained lines provide great opportunities for intonation correction and acute listening.

Unit 5: Stylistic Considerations

Care must be taken that the snare drum (with snares off) not be overbearing and monotonous. It should provide a subtle rhythmic background. The dynamics are mostly very soft with even "*ppp*" markings used. Care should be taken to maintain the subtle nature of the music. The tempo of a *pavane* can range from 80 to 100 for the quarter note. The arranger suggests a value of 80 for this work.

Unit 6: Musical Elements

The tonality of the work is G minor. The harmony is triadic and consonant. The melody is very clearly in four measure phrases, in a form of aabb. The rhythm is very even, mostly in quarter notes as each phrase starts with a half note.

Unit 7: Form and Structure

The 16 measure melody is in the form aabb. This melody is played three times in this arrangement. There is a continual evolving of texture and band color.

FORM

MEASURE	SECTION	SCORING
1	a	clarinet, trumpet, trombone, euphonium
6	a	Tutti
10	b	flute, trumpet, horn, trombone, euphonium
14	b	woodwinds
19	a	piccolo, flute, oboe, bassoon, clarinet 1, bass clarinet, trumpet, trombone, tuba
23	a	flute, oboe, clarinet, alto saxophone, trumpet
27	b	bassoon, clarinet, alto saxophone, trumpet, horn, trombone, euphonium
31	b	trumpet, trombone, euphonium, tuba

MEASURE	SECTION	SCORING
36	a	piccolo, flute, oboe, brass
40	a	trumpet, trombone, euphonium, tuba
44	b	flute, clarinet
48	b	saxophone, trumpet, trombone, tuba

Unit 8: Suggested Listening

Jan Bach, *Praetorious Suite*

Bob Margolis, *Terpsichore*

Unit 9: Additional References and Resources

Rehrig, William H. *The Heritage Encyclopedia of Band Music*. Westerville, OH: Integrity Press, 1991.

Teacher Resource Guide

"Blessed Are They"
Johannes Brahms

(b. 1833–d. 1987)

arranged by Barbara Buehlman

(b. 1936)

Unit 1: Composer

Johannes Brahms was born on May 7, 1833, in Hamburg, Germany. He showed a strong desire for music at an early age and began to study piano at age seven. Once studies of theory began in 1846, his life was devoted almost entirely to composition. Brahms was one of the great masters of the nineteenth century. Artistically, he was the successor of Beethoven, enriching the traditions of the Classical period. He was a staunch proponent of "absolute" music, eschewing the trend towards "program" music. He was the recipient of many honors in his lifetime. Brahms' four symphonies, the German *Requiem*, the *Academic Festival Overture*, and numerous songs are among his most famous works. Over sixty works have been transcribed for band, including several of his *Hungarian Dances*.

Unit 2: Composition

This work is a setting for band of the first movement of Brahms' *A German Requiem*, a magnificent work for chorus and orchestra. The opening chorus is "Blessed Are They That Mourn." It is well conceived for band, as the rich, sonorous textures of the band amply cover all the vocal and instrumental parts in the original version. The arrangement, published in 1970, is by Barbara Buehlman (a music educator in Chicago). The 87-measure piece is five minutes, fifteen seconds long.

Unit 3: Historical Perspective

Brahms composed his great choral work *A German Requiem* in 1867. It was first performed at Bremen Cathedral on Good Friday, 1868. The performance drew musicians from far and near. The Requiem Mass is the official service in the Catholic Church to honor the deceased; for centuries, composers have set the Latin text of the Mass to music. Compared to the text of the Mass Ordinary, the Requiem text offers many dramatic possibilities. Brahms employed a German text drawn from the Bible and chorales. Other 19th century composers who set a Requiem include Berlioz, Verdi, and Fauré.

Unit 4: Technical Considerations

The scale of F Major is required for the entire ensemble. The middle section becomes quite chromatic while moving to C Major and back to F Major. These measures utilize a number of accidentals (flats) in all parts. The sustained harmonies provide challenges for tone control and intonation. Legato articulation and expressive sensitivity are necessary skills for a most effective performance. There are no rhythms that should provide any technical difficulties; however, the repeated quarter notes in the low winds and timpani must be articulated clearly and match in style without rushing or falling behind. Woodwind and brass ranges are not excessive, but do reach higher limits. (Flutes at a3, Cornets at a flat2.)

Unit 5: Stylistic Considerations

This piece for winds incorporates the orchestral parts and the vocal parts written in the original composition. It is important that the lines played by wind instrumentalists reflect the smooth and sustained lines of singers. To ensure that original vocal lines are heard, the conductor should balance the ensemble so that the moving lines are always brought to the fore. The arranger has indicated rather rapid crescendo and diminuendo markings for expression. Wind players will face the challenge of making these dynamics heard without being overdone.

Unit 6: Musical Elements

The tonality is basically in F Major and mostly diatonic. The middle section of 25 measures involves chromatic modulations before moving back to F Major. The melodic line in the original moves around to different orchestral and choral voices. Generally, the moving lines in the winds should predominate in this arrangement.

Unit 7: Form and Structure

The form of the movement is rounded binary.

Section A: measures 1 - 47
> section a: measures 1 - 15
> section b: measures 15 - 37
> closing section: measures 37 - 47

Section B: measures 47 - 87
> section c: measures 47 - 63
> section a1:   measures 63 - 83
> final cadence: measures 83 - 87

Unit 8: Suggested Listening

Johannes Brahms, *A German Requiem*
Johannes Brahms, *Two Chorale Preludes, Op.* 122
Vincent Persichetti, *Chorale Preludes: O God Unseen*
Vincent Persichetti, *O Cool is the Valley*

Unit 9: Additional References and Resources

Dvorak, Thomas L., Robert Grechesky, and Gary Ciepluch. *Best Music for High School Band.* Brooklyn, NY: Manhattan Beach Music, 1993.

Randel, Don Michael. *The New Harvard Dictionary of Music.* Cambridge, MA: Harvard University, 1986.

Rehrig, William H. *The Heritage Encyclopedia of Band Music.* Westerville, OH: Integrity Press, 1991.

Smith, Norman and Albert Stoutamire. *Band Music Notes.* Lake Charles, LA: Program Note Press, 1989.

Whitwell, David. "Brahms—His Music for Winds." *The Instrumentalist,* XX February 1966, 59-60.

Teacher Resource Guide

"Cajun Folk Songs"
Frank Ticheli
(b. 1958)

Unit 1: Composer

Frank Ticheli was born on January 21, 1958, in Monroe, Louisiana. He was raised in Texas and holds degrees from Southern Methodist University and the University of Michigan. His principal composition teachers include William Bolcolm, Leslie Bassett, William Albright, and George Wilson. Ticheli is currently composer in residence of the Pacific Symphony Orchestra and Professor of Music at the University of Southern California. His many honors include a Charles Ives Scholarship and a Goddard Lieberson Fellowship, the Ross Lee Finny Award, the Walter Beeler Prize, and a residency at the MacDowell Colony. He has ten works that have been published for band, including: *Amazing Grace, Fortress, Gaian Visions, Pacific Fanfare,* and *Postcard.*

Unit 2: Composition

This is a very creative setting of two contrasting Cajun folk songs. The work was commissioned and premiered in 1990 by the Murchison Middle School Band, Austin, Texas. The first, *La Belle at le Capitaine,* is a flowing, plaintive song in the Dorian mode. The melody is stated three times starting with solo alto saxophone and continues to add textural thickness. The second movement, *Belle,* is in direct contrast to the first due to its much faster and brighter tempo and spirit. The dance-like character and frequent meter shifts of this second movement may provide a great challenge, but when properly performed, create a memorable impression. The two movements total 206 measures and six and one-half minutes long.

Unit 3: Historical Perspective

Basing compositions for wind band on folk songs is one of the most common compositional techniques. Most of Percy Grainger's tremendous output for bands are in that category. Clare Grundman, too, has composed dozens of works based on folk songs from around the world. Cajuns are descendants of the Acadians, a group of early French colonists who began settling in Nova Scotia around 1604. In 1755 they resettled in South Louisiana. Alan and John Lomax traveled to South Louisiana in 1934 to collect and record numerous Cajun folk songs in the field for the *Archive of Music* in the Library of Congress. The songs of these two movements are part of that collection.

Unit 4: Technical Considerations

The first movement uses the Dorian mode and scale on D. Sharp key signatures are used in the respective instruments. There are no rhythmic concerns except for the meter which occasionally shifts between 2 and 3. The melody is initially stated in a 16 measure alto saxophone solo. The challenges in this movement include the ability to play warmly, smoothly, and lyrically. In the third statement, the melody is scored for Clarinet 2, Alto Sax 1, Trumpet 2, Trombone 1, and Euphonium. Care must be take to avoid having the beautiful countermelody in the other voices predominate. The second movement is, no doubt, much more rhythmically challenging. The quarter note is marked at 152-160. The meter is 5/4, quarters grouped as three plus two. There is an occasional shift as 2/4 measures are added. As familiarity increases, the conductor may desire to indicate the 5/4 measures as 6/8 plus 2/4. The transparent scoring calls nearly every section and every player to task in confident and independent counting and playing. There are two spots of horn glissandos and one for trombones near the end of this movement.

Unit 5: Stylistic Considerations

The first movement requires sustained, warm, lyrical playing from every section. The initial alto saxophone solo should be played at least six measures without a break. The dynamic markings of the accompaniment line in the second statement are independent from the melody line and should be brought out. The second movement should begin with a Cabasa rather than Sand Blocks. The accents in the melody and accompaniment should not be overdone in this movement; however, it is often a challenge getting players to play any accent at all. With an emphasis on tempo and a dance-like style, this movement is exciting to play and pleasing to hear when the musical momentum is achieved.

Unit 6: Musical Elements

The Dorian mode of the first movement contributes to a genuine folk song character. Most of the harmonies are triadic and fit Dorian/D minor tonality. The second movement is in F Major. The pentatonic-like melody is stated in tonalities of F, A-flat, and C. The rhythmic element of the second movement gives this work its exciting spirit. It is written in 5/4 (with some shifts to 2/4 and 3/4), but "feels" like 6/8 plus 2/4.

Unit 7: Form and Structure

The first movement has three statements of the melody. The second movement has eleven statements of the melody (some incomplete) and nine statements of the composer's added original melody.

LA BELLE AT LE CAPITAINE

MEASURE	MELODIC SCORING
1	Solo Alto Sax
17	Cl 1, AS 1, Tpt 1, Ob 1
39	Flutes
50	Cl 2, AS 1, Tpt 2, Tbn 1, Euph

BELLE

MEASURE	MELODY	MELODIC SCORING
5	a	Tpt 1
12	b	Fl 1, Obs, Fl 2, Cls, AS 1
22	a	Fls, Cl 1, AS 1
28	b	Fls, Obs
31	a	Hns, Tbns, Euph
38	a	Fls, Obs, Cls, AS's, Tpts, Hns, Xylo
53	a	Tutti fragments
59	b	Fls, Xylo
65	a	fragments
74	a	fragments
88	a	TS, Hns, Euph
92	a	Tpt 1
96	a	Fls, AS's, Tpt 2
101	b	Fls, Ob 1
104	a	AS, TS, Hn 2, Tbn 1
120	a	Picc, Fls, Obs, Cls, Tpt 1, Xylo

Unit 8: Suggested Listening

Aaron Copland, *Rodeo Ballet*
Percy Grainger, *Irish Tune from County Derry, Shepherd's Hey*
Frank Ticheli, *Postcard*

Unit 9: Additional References and Resources

Dvorak, Thomas L., Robert Grechesky, and Gary Ciepluch. *Best Music for High School Band*. Brooklyn, NY: Manhattan Beach Music, 1993.

Teacher Resource Guide

"Chant and Jubilo"
W. Francis McBeth

(b. 1933)

Unit 1: Composer
William Francis McBeth was born in Ropesville, Texas, on March 9, 1933. He is professor of music, resident composer, and chairman (since 1957) of the theory-composition department at Ouachita University. He is the conductor emeritus of the Arkansas Symphony Orchestra and holds degrees from Hardin-Simmons University and the University of Texas. McBeth studied with Clifton Williams, Kent Kennan, Wayne Barlow, Bernard Rogers, Macon Summerlin, and Howard Hanson. He has composed works for many media, including choral, orchestral, chamber, and band. Among his many awards are the Presley Award, the Howard Hanson Prize, the Edwin Franco Goldman Award. In 1975, McBeth was appointed Composer Laureate of the state of Arkansas by the governor. Among his over 30 works for band are: *Beowulf, Cantique and Faranade, Canto, Kaddish, Masque, They Hung Their Harps in the Willows,* and *To Be Fed by Ravens.*

Unit 2: Composition
This work was commissioned by the Four States Bandmasters Convention in Texarkana, Texas, and was first performed by the Four States Bandmasters Band in 1962. It is a work in two connected contrasting movements. The Chant is a modal movement reminiscent of early church organum. The contrasting festive Jubilo uses faster tempos with explosive lower brass and percussion. The work is 136 measures and six minutes, forty-five seconds long.

Unit 3: Historical Perspective
Through the years, many very fine composers have written works for band with two contrasting movements. Often, the first movement is called *Hymn, Chorale,* or

170

Chant, and the contrasting movement is called *Alleluia, Toccata, Celebration,* or *Jubilo.* *Gregorian Chant* and *organum*-style singing in the Catholic Church date back almost 1500 years. We call the scales used *modes.* The performance of the musical line is very smooth and may even sound mystical to modern students' ears, although compact disc recordings of Gregorian Chants became popular in America during the 1990's. *Jubilante,* or *Jubilo,* refers to music, chants, and prayers that manifest the raising of one's voice in joy and exultation.

Unit 4: Technical Considerations

This work uses no key signatures; the tonal areas are indicated through accidentals. The Chant uses the Dorian mode on D and the D minor scale. The Jubilo uses the Mixolydian mode on F and the F Major scale. There are no major technical pitfalls, but the Chant requires sensitive playing of sustained lines. The Jubilo uses a fanfare motive of eighth and two sixteenths. The dotted-eighth and sixteenth pattern is also prevalent. The tempos of these rhythms range from quarter note at 96 to 108. When the tempo is at quarter equaling 144, eighths are then the fastest rhythm except at the climatic end where syncopated quarter notes drive to five sixteenth notes for the ensemble. There are several tempo changes that may challenge the ensemble in initial rehearsals.

Unit 5: Stylistic Considerations

The opening Chant section is marked with quarter equaling circa 72. The clarinets begin playing in unison with the baritones. This whole movement requires sensitive playing of the sustained line. Careful attention to tone and intonation are essential. The second movement requires clean articulation of the many fanfare-like figures. Several areas have ostinato patterns that must not become too heavy or out of tempo. The final Allegro section should have a feeling of driving to the rhythmic climax. The final Maestoso, following the Grand Pause, should sound as full as the climactic section that precedes it. Care should be taken so that the final "sfz-p *crescendo*" is not played too fast.

Unit 6: Musical Elements

The tonality of the melodies fit in modal scales and major and minor scales. The harmony is triadic. The Chant section uses mostly unison and homophonic textures with a number of chordal passages. The Jubilo section features half note-quarter note melodies with more rapid ostinato accompaniments.

Unit 7: Form and Structure

Measure	Scoring
1-12	Cls, Bar: phrases 1-3
13-19	Fls join: phrase 4
20-25	Fls, Glock: phrases 1-3
26-32	Fls, Obs, Cl 1, Bar: phrase 4

MEASURE	SCORING
33-45	Tutti: phrases 1-3
46-49	D Major cadence
50	sus cym: Jubilo begins
52-58	Tpts: fanfare
59-62	Tutti: fanfare
63-66	Low brass: fanfare
67-74	Fls: theme
74-77	Cls: theme
78-81	Fls, Obs, Cls: theme
81-89	Tpts: theme
90-97	Tutti: Extension
98-108	AS, TS, Hn, Bar: theme augmented/Fls motivic interval accomp.
108-113	Tpt: theme augmented
114-126	AS, TS, Tpt, Tbn: theme motive imitated driving to rhythmic climax
127	G.P.
128-136	Tutti: Maestoso F Major Coda

Unit 8: Suggested Listening

Howard Hanson, *Chorale and Alleluia*

Robert Jager, *Chorale and Toccata*

W.Francis McBeth, *Cantique and Faranade; Kaddish; They Hung Their Harps in the Willows*

Unit 9: Additional References and Resources

Dvorak, Thomas L. *Best Music for Young Band.* Brooklyn, NY: Manhattan Beach Music, 1986.

McBeth, W. Francis. "W. Francis McBeth: Chant and Jubilo." *BD Guide,* September/October 1991, 25.

Rehrig, William H. *The Heritage Encyclopedia of Band Music.* Westerville, OH: Integrity Press, 1991.

Smith, Richard James. "Theoretical Analyses and Practical Applications to the Rehearsal and Performance of Selected Wind Band Compositions by W. Francis McBeth (Volumes I-IV)." Ph.D. diss., The Louisiana State University and Agricultural and Mechanical College, 1986.

Smith, Norman and Albert Stoutamire. *Band Music Notes.* Lake Charles, LA: Program Note Press, 1989.

Teacher Resource Guide

"Come Sweet Death"
J. S. Bach

(b. 1685–d. 1750)

setting by Alfred Reed

(b. 1921)

Unit 1: Composer

Johann Sebastian Bach was born in Eisenach, Germany, on March 21, 1685, and died in Leipzig in 1750. With a background which boasted approximately 200 musical ancestors, it is not surprising that Bach developed a keen interest in music at a young age. Left an orphan at the age of ten, Johann began to teach himself music. At fifteen Johann was engaged as a singer at St. Michael's Church, where he continued his study of music. Having mastered the violin and clavier, he devoted himself to the study and mastery of the organ. Offered a position as organist in the town of Arnstadt at the age of eighteen, he accepted, and proceeded to dedicate himself to the art of composition. As a court organist and violinist under Duke Wilhelm Ernst of Weimar, and as director of chamber music to young Prince Leopold of Anhalt-Cöthen, he took advantage of every free moment to perfect himself in composition. For his last 27 years, Bach was director of music in the churches of St. Thomas and St. Nicholas and choirmaster at St. Thomas School in Leipzig. Many of his greatest works were composed during this period. The great polyphonic style of the Baroque period culminated with the compositions of J.S. Bach. Bach's only known work for a large wind ensemble is the *Cantata No. 18, O Jesu Christ, Mein Lebens Licht*, written in 1737 as a funeral cantata. However, over 140 of Bach's compositions have been arranged for band.

Unit 2: Composition

The German title is, *Komm', Süsser Tod*. It is one of a group of 69 so-called "Sacred Songs and Airs" attributed to J.S. Bach, each of which exists in the form of a single melodic line with figured bass. These pieces were first published in 1736, some 14 years before Bach's death, as the musical settings for a huge collection of 954 sacred songs and hymns assembled by Georg Christian Schemelli and edited by Bach himself. This setting is a realization for winds from the original figured bass. Set by composer Alfred Reed, Bach's harmonic intentions have been faithfully adhered to throughout. This setting was published in 1976. The work, only 46 measures, is three and one-half minutes in length.

Unit 3: Historical Perspective

This sacred song was composed during Bach's years at Leipzig. It was first published in 954-song collection edited by Bach. In 1832, Bach's so-called "Sacred Songs and Airs" appeared as an addendum to the 371 four-part, fully harmonized chorales in an edition published by C.F. Becker. Subsequent published editions of Bach's sacred songs have also included this melody, *Komm', Süsser Tod*. Alfred Reed has set this melody as a *Chorale Prelude* for band. The chorale prelude, a very common type of composition in Bach's day, is a short polyphonic setting of a chorale melody, usually performed by the church organist as preparation for congregational singing of the chorale. Bach wrote at least 375 chorales and a great number of chorale preludes. Alfred Reed has arranged eight of Bach's chorales for band.

Unit 4: Technical Considerations

The scale of C minor is required for the entire ensemble. The indicated tempo is "eighth note equals circa 76" creating a challenge to not hurry the moving eighths and to sustain the held notes. With "molto ritenuto al fine" indicated for the last three measures, the conductor must explain the subdivided conducting gestures needed to control the held harmonic suspensions and anticipations. As in other scores by Reed, he asks for a proportion of two trumpets on each of the three trumpet parts to one cornet on each of the two cornet parts.

Unit 5: Stylistic Considerations

Like other Chorale Prelude settings for winds, this requires a very sustained singing legato line to be maintained in every part throughout the performance of the music. There are many crescendi and diminuendi that require careful control of instrumental color and tone. A relaxed, unhurried, yet not dragging rhythmic flow is vital to a successful performance.

Unit 6: Musical Elements

The harmony of C minor is maintained throughout the work. The harmonic rhythm and chord changes are vitally important. In performance, a tempo must be maintained that allows the richness of the harmony to be heard yet still provides a sense of movement. The melody is clearly stated in six phrases.

Unit 7: Form and Structure

The melody is in 6 phrases and is stated 2 times.

MEASURE	PHRASE	MELODY VOICING
1	A	Ob 1, Eb Cl, Cl 1, cued in Cor 1
5	B	OB 1, Eb CL, Cl 1, cued in Cor 1
9	C	Fls, Cl 1, As 1
13	D	Ob 1, Cl 1
16	E	Fls, Ob 1, Eb Cl, Cl 1, As 1
19	F	Fls, Ob 1, Eng Hn, Eb Cl, Cls, As's, Hn 1-2
24	A	Fl 1, Tpt 1, Bar 1
28	B	Fl 1, Tpts, Cors
32	C	Fls, Ob 1, Eng Hn, As's, Ts
35	D	Cl 1, Tpt 1
38	E	Obs, Eng Hn, Eb Cl, Cls, A Cl, Ts
41	F	Picc, Fls, Obs, Eng Hn, Eb Cl, Cls, A Cl, As's, Ts, Hns, Cors

Unit 8: Suggested Listening

J.S. Bach, *Chorale Preludes* performed on organ

J.S. Bach (arr. Alfred Reed), *My Heart is Filled with Longing; My Jesus! Oh, What Anguish; Thus Do You Fare, My Jesus*

Unit 9: Additional References and Resources

Dvorak, Thomas L., Robert Grechesky, and Gary Ciepluch. *Best Music for High School Band.* Brooklyn, NY: Manhattan Beach Music, 1993.

Rehrig, William H. *The Heritage Encyclopedia of Band Music.* Westerville, OH: Integrity Press, 1991.

Smith, Norman and Albert Stoutamire. *Band Music Notes.* Lake Charles, LA: Program Note Press, 1989.

Stolba, K. Marie. *Development of Western Music.* Dubuque, IA: Brown and Benchmark, 1990.

Whitwell, David. "Bach—Wind Music." *The Instrumentalist,* XXI November 1966, 39.

Teacher Resource Guide

"Court Festival"
William P. Latham

(b. 1917)

Unit 1: Composer

William Peters Latham was born in Shreveport, Louisiana, on January 4, 1917. His music training included degrees from the Cincinnati Conservatory of Music, where he studied with Sydney Durst and Eugene Goosens, and the Eastman School of Music. At Eastman, he earned a Ph.D. degree studying with Herbert Elwell and Howard Hanson. Latham taught composition and music at North Texas State Teachers College, Eastern Illinois Teachers College, the University of Northern Iowa, and at the University of North Texas, where he was Director of Graduate Studies and honored as a Distinguished Professor in 1978. He has composed over 100 works for orchestra, band, choir and chamber groups. Included in his over 32 works for band are: *Brighton Beach, Dodecaphonic Set, March Three by Four,* and *Three Chorale Preludes.*

Unit 2: Composition

This work is a four-movement suite in the style of instrumental dance music of the late sixteenth and seventeenth centuries. The music evokes the Renaissance style of dances used at various European court festivals and other ceremonies. The four movements are *Intrada, Pavan, Galliard,* and *The Horses Branle.* All thematic material is original with the exception of *The Horses Branle,* which appeared in Arbeau's "Orchésographie," first published in 1588. The four movements are 149 measures and five and one-half minutes in length.

Unit 3: Historical Perspective

During the Renaissance period, composers began to write music for wind bands that played to accompany dancing. Those musicians who made a living playing wind instruments usually worked either for a church or a court. An *Intrada* (literally "entrance") is an opening piece of festive or march-like character. It first appeared in the music of Spanish composers in the mid-16th century, and was later extensively used by North German composers. The *Pavan* and *Galliard* were both known throughout Europe from the early part of the 16th century. Both are believed to be of Italian origin. Toward the end of the century they were invariably coupled, and this linking of dances led to the highly stylized Baroque dance suite. The pavane is a stately dance in duple meter, the galliard a gay dance in triple meter. The *Branle* was very popular in the 16th century. It was danced everywhere, in the country and at the courts, and included singing, swaying movements of the body and hands, and pantomime.

Unit 4: Technical Considerations

The keys and scales of G minor, D Major, B flat Major, and G Major are used by the entire ensemble. The first, second, and fourth movements are marked *alla breve*, the third is in 3/4. The only rhythm that may challenge some players is in the first movement. In *alla breve*, a primary motive is quarter-rest, dotted-quarter-note, eighth-note, quarter-note. The tempo of the fourth movement is *Vivace* with half marked at 132. Clarity and precision may be challenging for some bands at this tempo. The fourth movement begins with an extended piccolo solo.

Unit 5: Stylistic Considerations

An effective performance of this work depends heavily on achieving the proper style of the dances. The first movement effectively contrasts brass and woodwind choirs as well as terraced dynamics. The primary motive should be played by all with a matching accent and "sparkle." The second movement is a simple melody with both legato notes and staccato notes that should be realized with care. The third movement, which is neither a waltz nor a minuet, should not be played too fast. The fourth movement, marked *Vivace*, should be played with brilliance, but also with clarity and precision. The percussion should not be overdone.

Unit 6: Musical Elements

The primary tonal centers are G minor, D Major, B-flat Major, C Major, and G Major. The harmony is consonant and the chords are triadic. The melody is repeated in sections, but with changes in color and dynamics. The rhythms should be played steadily, with precision, to reflect the spirit and style of these dances.

Unit 7: Form and Structure

Intrada: This movement is in two sections, each repeated, that use the same melodic/rhythmic motive.

Pavan: This movement is in three sections, each repeated. The second section is similar to the first, the third is similar to the second.

Galliard: This movement is in three sections, each repeated. Each section is, again, related to the previous section.

"The Horses"   This movement is in three similar sections. Each section is
Branle: in two parts.

Unit 8: Suggested Listening
Jan Bach, *Praetorious Suite*
Bob Margolis, *Terpsichorie*
Michael Praetorious, *Terpsichorie*
Tielman Susato, *Danseyre Suite*

Unit 9: Additional References and Resources

Kreines, Joseph. *Music for Concert Band.* Tampa, FL: Florida Music Service, 1989.

Latham, William P. "Meet the Composer: William P. Latham." *The Instrumentalist,* XXVI September 1971, 88-89.

Rehrig, William H. *The Heritage Encyclopedia of Band Music.* Westerville, OH: Integrity Press, 1991.

Teacher Resource Guide

"Flourish for Wind Band"
Ralph Vaughan Williams

(b. 1872–d. 1958)

Unit 1: Composer

Ralph Vaughan Williams was born on October 12, 1872, in Down Ampney, Gloucestershire, England. He received his education at Charterhouse (London), Trinity College, Cambridge and the Royal College of Music. One of the most respected of English composers, he found inspiration in the study of the folk music and works of early English composers. Vaughan Williams (along with Gustav Holst) provided some of the earliest music for the twentieth century concert band. Several of his works written for orchestra are standards in the repertoire. His compositions for winds are pillars of band compositions. There are almost 20 published works for band including: *English Folk Song Suite*, *Sea Songs*, and *Toccata Marziale*.

Unit 2: Composition

This work was composed as an overture to the pageant *Music and the People* and was first performed in the Royal Albert Hall, London, in 1939. This work, a *flourish*, has the character of a fanfare with a legato middle section. The 63 measure work is one and a half minutes long.

Unit 3: Historical Perspective

This work followed on the heels of Vaughan Williams' great works for wind band, *English Folk Song Suite* and *Toccata Marziale*. It is a relatively easy work for band by a composer of high stature and skill. Although written in the 1930's, it was not made available to American bands until published in 1972.

Unit 4: Technical Considerations

The scales of B-flat Major and F Major are required for the entire ensemble. There are no technical demands placed on any section. The performance should have a fanfare-like, majestic quality. This requires players to sustain the musical lines with a full sound. Ranges are not excessive, although Cornet 1 goes to a g2. In some editions the first and second trombones are in the tenor clef.

Unit 5: Stylistic Considerations

The *flourish*, being a fanfare, should be played in a well-articulated style. The held notes should be performed with a full, supported sound. The middle section is more flowing and legato. It is also at a much softer dynamic. This dynamic contrast should be attended to for an effective performance.

Unit 6: Musical Elements

The harmony is triadic and diatonic, fitting in the key areas of B-flat Major and F Major. The melody has the triadic character of a fanfare, historically meaningful since early fanfares were performed on natural instruments. The rhythms used are mostly quarter notes with half notes and some eighths in 3/4 meter.

Unit 7: Form and Structure

The work is in ABA form.

MEASURES	EVENTS
1-10	Brass fanfare motive a in imitation
11-19	Tutti fanfare motive b
20-27	Woodwinds, Horns, Cornet 1 legato motive a
28-35	Woodwinds, Horns, Cornet 1 legato motive b
36-44	Tutti legato motive a
45-53	Brass fanfare motive a in imitation
54-63	Tutti fanfare motive b

Unit 8: Suggested Listening

Gustav Holst, *Second Suite in F*
Gustav Holst, *Hammersmith*
Gustav Holst, *The Planets*
Ralph Vaughan Williams, *Folk Song Suite*
Edward Elgar, *"Enigma" Variations*

Unit 9: Additional References and Resources

Dvorak, Thomas L. *Best Music for Young Band*. Brooklyn, NY: Manhattan Beach Music, 1986.

Randel, Don Michael. *The New Harvard Dictionary of Music*. Cambridge, MA: Harvard University, 1986.

Rehrig, William H. *The Heritage Encyclopedia of Band Music*. Westerville, OH: Integrity Press, 1991.

Smith, Norman and Albert Stoutamire. *Band Music Notes*. Lake Charles, LA: Program Note Press, 1989.

Teacher Resource Guide

"Ginger Marmalade"
Warren Benson

(b. 1924)

Unit 1: Composer

Warren Frank Benson was born on January 26, 1924, in Detroit, Michigan. He received bachelor's and master's degrees in music from the University of Michigan, then played timpani with the Detroit Symphony Orchestra in 1945. Self-taught in composition, he is a graduate in theory from the University of Michigan. He was awarded successive Fulbright Teacher Grants to Greece, where he organized the first co-educational choral group in that country. Later his Ithaca Percussion Ensemble was the first such group in the Eastern United States. After serving as music professor and composer in residence at Ithaca College from 1953 to 1967, he joined the faculty of the Eastman School of Music as Professor of Composition. Benson has composed works in every medium. His works are varied and non-doctrinaire in their technique. He has composed over 20 important works for band, including *Dawn's Early Light, The Leaves are Falling, The Passing Bell,* and *The Solitary Dancer.*

Unit 2: Composition

The piece is a double canon, light in texture, emphasizing crisply articulated accents and staccatos. The percussion writing is for non-keyboard instruments, and moments of hand clapping and heel rapping provide some interesting timbres. The composer has written, that for inspiration, "It must be the ginger marmalade and ricotta cheese on pumpernickel toast every morning—and coffee, lots of coffee—but, mostly, ginger marmalade." The 64-measure work is three minutes in length.

Unit 3: Historical Perspective

The work, published in 1978, was part of a commission for contemporary works for school bands. Most of this composer's works have been written for mature and advanced bands. The ideas of hand clapping and heel rapping were relatively new techniques of player performance at the time of composition.

Unit 4: Technical Considerations

The primary tonal center is G minor. The rhythms involve dotted eighths with sixteenths and eighths with eighth rests. Careful counting is required of all players. All players (except tuba and percussion) are involved with clapping rhythms, the woodwinds add a stomp (heel rap). The range is not challenging. There are two short glissandi for trombones.

Unit 5: Stylistic Considerations

Articulations are very specific, and the composer has marked every note. There are many accents and staccato notes that must be played crisply and in the dynamic that is written for the instrument. The hand claps and foot stomps should be spirited and playful, yet firm and accurate with accents preserved. The main challenge is maintaining a steady, consistent tempo with only very subtle shifts of dynamics and line. Musical independence and control, without overblowing, are keys in performance.

Unit 6: Musical Elements

The harmony and melody lines fall mostly in G minor. There are two sections that are quite polyphonic when the double canon has everyone playing. The meter, common time, is unchanging throughout. It is marked "Accented, spirited, quarter note equals 96."

Unit 7: Form and Structure

The work is a double canon. Trumpets and flutes imitate motives in measures 4 and 7. Clarinets, flutes amd oboes play in measures 8 and 11. Bass clarinet, bassoon, bari sax, trombone and clarinet 3, alto sax, tenor sax, and horn play in measures 16 and 19. Trumpets, flutes, and clarinets play in measures 15 and 18. This first section concludes with clarinets and flutes in measures 27 and 29. After the hand-clapping, foot-stomping interlude, imitative entries begin to appear again in measure 44 in the trumpets.

Unit 8: Suggested Listening

Warren Benson, *Danzon-Memory*
Warren Benson, *The Solitary Dancer*
Steve Reich, *Drumming*

Unit 9: Additional References and Resources

Dvorak, Thomas L. *Best Music for Young Band*. Brooklyn, NY: Manhattan Beach Music, 1986.

Rehrig, William H. *The Heritage Encyclopedia of Band Music*. Westerville, OH: Integrity Press, 1991.

Smith, Norman and Albert Stoutamire. *Band Music Notes*. Lake Charles, LA: Program Note Press, 1989.

Teacher Resource Guide

"Little English Suite"
Clare Grundman

(b. 1913–d. 1996)

Unit 1: Composer

Clare Ewing Grundman was born on May 11, 1913, in Cleveland, Ohio. He received bachelors and masters degrees from Ohio State University. After three years as an instrumental music teacher he returned to Ohio State as an instructor of orchestration, bands, and woodwinds. During World War II he served as a chief musician in the U.S. Coast Guard. Grundman credits Manley R. Whitcomb with first encouraging him-to write for bands and Paul Hindemith with providing practical techniques for composition. He has written scores and arrangements for radio, television, motion pictures, ballet, and Broadway musicals. His many honors and awards include the Edwin Franco Goldman Memorial Citation, the Academy of Wind and Percussion Arts Award, and the Mid-West International Band and Orchestra Clinic Medal of Honor. Grundman's many works for band range in difficulty from music suitable for inexperienced instrumentalists to that which demands the technical and musical maturity of professional performers. Notable among his band works are those which draw on folk and popular melodies for their substance. Among the over 65 works for band are: 4 *American Folk Rhapsodies*, *The Blue and the Gray*, *Concord*, *Fantasy on American Sailing Songs*, *Hebrides Suite*, and *Two Moods Overture*.

Unit 2: Composition

This work is a suite of four old English folk songs: *The Leather Bottle*, *Roving*, *We Met*, and *The Vicar of Bray*. The composer's most notable and popular compositions draw on folk and popular melodies for their substance. This suite belongs to that genre. This group of settings was published in 1968. The four movements, totaling 206 measures, are seven minutes in length.

Unit 3: Historical Perspective

Like the works of Percy Grainger, Clare Grundman's *Little English Suite* uses tuneful old English folk songs. Players who are familiar with Grainger's music will find Grundman's settings much simpler in style and texture. Grundman's *Little English Suite* was published in the same year as this composer's larger work for band, *English Suite for Band*.

Unit 4: Technical Considerations

The Leather Bottle uses the E-flat Major scale for the entire ensemble. *Roving* uses the F Major scale for the entire ensemble. *We Met* uses the B-flat Major scale for the entire ensemble. *The Vicar of Bray* uses the E-flat Major scale for the entire ensemble. There are no technical problems throughout the work. The greatest challenge will be giving life and a singing quality to the melodies.

Unit 5: Stylistic Considerations

Achieving the proper style of each movement will bring about an effective performance. The first movement, *The Leather Bottle*, is in 6/8 compound time, marked "Allegro moderato", and should bounce without being heavy. *Roving*, the second movement, is in common time and is marked "Freely, with motion." A fine, singing tone quality is called for here. The third movement, *We Met*, is marked "Moderato" and begins in triple meter, switches to common time, then returns to triple meter. The eighth note accompaniment should remain steady throughout. The final melody, *The Vicar of Bray*, is set in an *alla breve* meter, and is the only movement with an indicated metronome marking (half equals 92). Care must be taken to distinguish between the alternating marcato and legato phrases.

Unit 6: Musical Elements

The harmony is tonal and triadic throughout all four movements. The folk song melodies are clearly scored and in regular phrases. The melodies are written in quarter notes and eighth notes, with the first movement written in compound time, the second and third in common and triple time, and the fourth movement in an *alla breve* meter.

Unit 7: Form and Structure

The Leather Bottle:	After an eight-measure introduction, the melody is stated three times, each scored more fully. The movement ends with an eleven-measure Coda that relaxes the mood before the second movement.
Roving:	The mood is set with a nine-measure introduction. After the several phrases are stated the movement ends similarly to as it began.

We Met:	The eight-measure melody is played twice. After an eight-measure chorus, the sixteen measures of the first section are restated in a different scoring.
The Vicar of Bray:	The sixteen measure melody is stated two times. After eight bars of big brass chords the melody returns one final time, with the last four measures extended through an "Allargando" and 3/2 meter signature.

Unit 8: Suggested Listening

Percy Grainger, *Lincolnshire Posy*
Clare Grundman, *American Folk Rhapsody; An Irish Rhapsody*
Robert Jager, *Colonial Airs and Dances*

Unit 9: Additional References and Resources

Rehrig, William H. *The Heritage Encyclopedia of Band Music.* Westerville, OH: Integrity Press, 1991.

Smith, Norman and Albert Stoutamire. *Band Music Notes.* Lake Charles, LA: Program Note Press, 1989.

Teacher Resource Guide

"On a Hymn Song of Philip Bliss"
David Holsinger

(b. 1945)

Unit 1: Composer
David Holsinger was born on December 26, 1945, in Hardin, Missouri. He studied at Central Methodist College, Central Missouri State University, and at the University of Kansas, where he was arranger for university bands and the swing choir. He has written extensively for band. His compositions have received commendations in numerous competitions including winning two Ostwald Awards. Currently, he is Chief Musician at Shady Grove Church in Grand Prairie, Texas. Much of his music is known for its high energy and driving rhythms. He has written over fifteen band compositions and continues to publish new works. Some of his large works include *HavenDance, On Ancient Hymns and Festal Dances,* and *To Tame the Perilous Skies.*

Unit 2: Composition
Those familiar with the music of Holsinger will find this music to be a radical departure of his style. The frantic tempos and ebullient rhythms associated with Holsinger are replaced by a restful, gentle, and reflective composition. The work is based on the 1876 Philip Bliss - Horatio Spafford hymn, "It is Well with my Soul." This setting states the tune two times, the first statement shared by brass and woodwinds, the second as a majestic brass chorale. This piece was written to honor the retiring Principal of Shady Grove Christian Academy in 1989. The work, 70 measures, is three minutes, forty-five seconds in length.

Unit 3: Historical Perspective
As common as folk songs have been for stimulating the imagination of composers of band pieces, so, too, have various hymns seen widespread use in

188

numerous settings. There are hundreds of band works with the word "hymn" in their titles, and there are undoubtedly hundreds more inspired by hymn songs.

Unit 4: Technical Considerations

The D-flat Major scale is required for the entire ensemble. There are no extremes in range and no particular technical difficulties. The first statement of the hymn-song begins in the soli horn 1, but is cued by the trumpets. The eighth note accompaniment alternates between groups between beat 1-2 and 3-4. Attention to balance will be required here. The greatest challenge to players will be the expressive, smooth and sustained playing of melodic and harmonic accompaniment lines necessary for an effective performance.

Unit 5: Stylistic Considerations

The beginning of the work is marked "Freely, with expression" and a suggested tempo of quarter equals 76-80 is given. The subsequent tempo changes are clearly indicated to enhance an expressive performance. There are no major dynamic shifts that should pose any challenges. With a handful of accents as the only articulation markings throughout the work, players should interpret and play their lines smoothly and lyrically.

Unit 6: Musical Elements

The tonality of the work is D-flat Major. The piece is triadic and diatonic with some suspensions and sevenths used in the harmony. The melody is very clearly scored in half notes and quarter notes.

Unit 7: Form and Structure

The work has two statements of the hymn song, the first shared by brass and woodwinds, the second as a brass chorale. The eight-measure introductory material is also used as an interlude between statements and also as an ending.

MEASURE	MELODIC SCORING
1	Cls, AS's, Moving eighth-note introduction motive
8	Soli Hn 1, First phrase of hymnsong
13	Fl, Second phrase of hymnsong
17	Hns, Tbn 1, Third phrase of hymnsong
20	Low WW, All Brass, Fourth phrase of hymnsong
24	Cls, TS, Bar, hymnsong ending
31	Cls, AS's, introduction motive as interlude
42	Tpts, Hns, Tbns, Bar, First phrase of hymnsong in chorale style
46	Tpts, Hns, Tbns, Bar, Second phrase of hymnsong in chorale style
50	AS's, Tpts, Hns, Tbn 1, Third phrase of hymnsong

MEASURE	MELODIC SCORING
54	Tutti ensemble, Fourth phrase of hymnsong
57	Cls, TS, Bar, hymnsong ending
64	Introduction motive as ending

Unit 8: Suggested Listening

Alan Hovhaness, *Hymn to Yerevan*
Vincent Persichetti, *Chorale Prelude: O God Unseen*
William Schuman, *Chester*
William Schuman, *When Jesus Wept*

Unit 9: Additional References and Resources

Rehrig, William H. *The Heritage Encyclopedia of Band Music.* Westerville, OH: Integrity Press, 1991.

Teacher Resource Guide

"Overture for Winds"
Charles Carter
(b. 1926)

Unit 1: Composer

Charles Edward Carter was born in Ponca City, Oklahoma, on July 10, 1926. He grew up in Worthington, Ohio, and attended Ohio State University, the Eastman School of Music, and Florida State University. He taught low brass and was arranger for the Ohio State University Marching Band. Later, he went to Florida State University as an arranger for its bands and was also a Professor of Theory and Composition. Along with numerous marching band arrangements, he has over thirty works for concert band. Well known pieces include: *Chorale and Variations*, *Dance and Intermezzo*, *Sonata for Winds*, and *Symphonic Overture*.

Unit 2: Composition

This tuneful overture is in the familiar ABA form. The opening section's theme is robust and rhythmic. The second theme, slightly slower and expressive, is a free-form based on the original idea. The last section is a repetition of the opening thematic ideas, building to a final climax. The work was composed in 1959. The piece, 188 measures long, lasts five and a half minutes.

Unit 3: Historical Perspective

The overture has always been a popular form and style for band compositions. French composers C. Catel, H. Jadin, and L. Jadin wrote overtures for the 18th century military concert bands. F. Mendelssohn wrote overtures for 19th century German and European bands. N. Miaskovsky wrote overtures for Russian concert bands. Many contemporary composers around the world continue to publish overtures for concert bands in various styles.

Unit 4: Technical Considerations

The key centers include Eb Major, C minor, Bb Major, and their scales are required for the entire ensemble. The tempo of the outer sections is marked "Allegro con moto" and the quarter note equals 152. Rhythmic vitality is essential to an effective performance. The main motive and a short sixteenth-note run in low woodwinds and baritone start on the upbeat of beat 1. Clean entrances with these rhythms may challenge some players. There is a Baritone solo of two measures prior to the middle section. There are short sixteenth-note figures for woodwinds, Cornet 1 and Baritone in a middle development section.

Unit 5: Stylistic Considerations

Rhythmic preciseness is required for the robust theme of the fast outer sections. The slower middle section provides opportunities for instrumentalists to perform in a sustained, lyrical, and expressive style. The tempo marking of "Allegro con moto" demands a fast and steady tempo. There should be no balance difficulties, but the several changes in dynamics are fundamental to effective performance.

Unit 6: Musical Elements

The harmony is traditionally triadic and the melodies tuneful. The fast sections feature imitative entries. Player counting is vital. The slower middle section is more polyphonic with flowing melody and countermelody lines. The rhythm is steady throughout, but entrances on the upbeats are part of the motive and may challenge some players.

Unit 7: Form and Structure

The overture is one movement in ABA form with a short development section before the return of the A section.

Measure	Section
1	Section A
1	Theme a
9	Theme a
17	Theme b
39	Theme a
50	Transition (baritone solo)
52	Section B
52	Theme c
64	Theme c
79	Development of a
100	Transition - 4-stage sequence with crescendo allargando
116	Section A
116	Theme a
124	Theme a

132	Theme b
156	Theme a
164	Coda

Unit 8: Suggested Listening

Charles Carter, *Symphonic Overture*
Elliot Del Borgo, *Overture for Winds*
Felix Mendelssohn, *Overture for Winds Op.24*
W.A. Mozart, *Overture to the Marriage of Figaro*

Unit 9: Additional References and Resources

Dvorak, Thomas L. *Best Music for Young Band.* Brooklyn, NY: Manhattan Beach Music, 1986.

Rehrig, William H. *The Heritage Encyclopedia of Band Music.* Westerville, OH: Integrity Press, 1991.

Smith, Norman and Albert Stoutamire. *Band Music Notes.* Lake Charles, LA: Program Note Press, 1989.

Teacher Resource Guide

"Plymouth Trilogy"
Anthony Iannaccone

(b. 1943)

Unit 1: Composer

Anthony Joseph Iannaccone was born in Brooklyn, New York, on October 14, 1943. He began the study of violin, piano, and theory at an early age and later graduated from the Manhattan School of Music and the Eastman School of Music. He studied privately with Vittorio Giannini, David Diamond, and Aaron Copland. After teaching briefly at Manhattan, he was appointed Professor at Eastern Michigan University, where he established an electronic music studio. Iannaccone has composed music for voice, chamber groups, and orchestra with tape, but some of his best music is for concert band. In 1988 he won the National Band Association's annual composition contest with *Apparitions*. He has over a dozen works for band. Others include *After a Gentle Rain, Images of Song and Dance, No. 1: Orpheus,* and *Images of Song and Dance, No. 2: Terpsichore.*

Unit 2: Composition

This three-movement work was commissioned by the Michigan Council of the Arts and the Plymouth Arts Council in 1982. It is tuneful throughout the course of its three contrasting movements. The *Overture* is a basic march in 6/8 time which presents its melodic material in fragments before assembling them into into a complete theme. *Reflection* transforms thematic material from the *Overture* into a contemplative movement. The third movement, *Carousel*, also utilizes first movement material to create a sprightly, spirited, syncopated rag. The composition, totaling 279 measures, is eight minutes in length.

Unit 3: Historical Perspective

Through the performance of this work students may gain an exposure to and an understanding of the syncopated rag style. This style of highly syncopated music developed in the United States in the late 19th century through the influences of West African and African-American music.

Unit 4: Technical Considerations

No key signatures are used in the three movements. The first movement centers around E-flat Major, the second movement around C minor, and the third movement around B-flat Major. Ranges are not excessive. The most technical demands are the result of the rhythms. The first movement is in a march style with the quarter note equal to a range of 112-120. Except for a middle passage of 11 measures in 2/4 time, the movement is in 6/8 time. Items that may challenge players include playing only one, two, or three beats of an eighth note melodic fragment, starting the melodic line on the second eighth of the bar, and playing the last and first eighth notes tied over the bar line. The second movement begins with markings of "Cantabile" and quarter equal to 40. It may behoove the ensemble to rehearse and perform this section with the eighth note as the pulse. The tempo soon changes to quarter at 60 and then to 76. The middle section of the second movement features a sustained melody for the brass while the woodwinds play an accompaniment in eighth notes that will require some restraint. The melodic motives of the third movement, the Rag, are predominantly syncopated in sixteenth notes with eighth notes articulated as "long-short." An understanding of syncopation and an ability to play "terraced" dynamics are needed to bring the finale to life.

Unit 5: Stylistic Considerations

Performing this composition in the correct styles is its greatest challenge. No matter what tempo is taken in the first movement, the challenge is to keep the 6/8 melody and accompaniment light and spirited. The second movement makes demands on the entire ensemble to properly perform the many forte-piano markings. It is important that the third movement not be performed too fast. The quarter note is marked in the range of 69-84. If played any faster, the ragtime feel is lost.

Unit 6: Musical Elements

The work is mostly triadic and tonal. There are no key signatures. The first movement centers around E-flat Major, the second movement around C minor, and the third movement around B-flat Major. There are full statements of each melody in each movement, but the composer's style utilizes melodic fragments and motives that may get lost or hidden in the areas of thick texture. The element of rhythm plays a substantial role in this composition. The first movement depends on the lilting 6/8 meter. The second movement opens and closes with an eighth-note pulse in common time. The third movement is based on the fundamental rhythm of ragtime—syncopation.

Unit 7: Form and Structure

OVERTURE

MEASURE	EVENT
1	Introduction featuring eighth note melodic fragments and sustained quarter note melody fragments
24	Solo Cor motive
26	Solo AS Melody
31	Cl 1 Melody
35	Expansion of motives
46	Fl 1, TS quarter note melody
50	AS quarter note melody
55	Cor, AS, Fl, Cl eighth note motives
65	Hns quarter note melody in simple time
76	Tutti expansion of eighth note motives
93	Fl quarter note melody
108	WW eighth note melody
118	Brass quarter note melody

REFLECTION

MEASURE	EVENT
1	Introduction in eighths with melodic shape
5	Solo Cor quarter note melody
12	Low Brass begin quarter note melody
13	Melody in fragments, building leading to:
29	Brass quarter note melody
46	Climax
47	Ending with quarter note fragments and introduction material

CAROUSEL (RAG)

MEASURE	EVENT
1	Theme
10	Theme in fragments and changing instrumentation
28	Theme
37	Theme extended
45	Low Brass quarter note melody added
53	Solo AS Theme in new rhythm
37	(D.S.) theme extended
45	low brass quarter note melody added

Unit 8: Suggested Listening
Anthony Iannaccone, *After a Gentle Rain; Apparitions*
Scott Joplin, *The Red Back Book*

Unit 9: Additional References and Resources
Dvorak, Thomas L. *Best Music for Young Band.* Brooklyn, NY: Manhattan Beach
   Music, 1986.

Plank, Max. *"Anthony Iannaccone, An Introduction to His Work."* Journal
   of Band Research XXVI (Fall 1989): 65-67.

Rehrig, William H. *The Heritage Encyclopedia of Band Music.* Westerville,
   OH: Integrity Press, 1991.

Teacher Resource Guide

"Prelude and Fugue in B-flat"
J. S. Bach

(b. 1685–d. 1750)

transcribed by Roland L. Moehlmann

(b. 1907–d. 1972)

Unit 1: Composer

Johann Sebastian Bach was born in Eisenach, Germany, on March 21, 1685, and died in Leipzig in 1750. With a background which boasted approximately 200 musical ancestors, it is not surprising that Bach developed a keen interest in music at a young age. Left an orphan at the age of ten, Johann began to teach himself music. At fifteen Johann was engaged as a singer at St. Michael's Church where he continued his study of music. Having mastered the violin and clavier, he devoted himself to the study and mastery of the organ. Offered a position as organist in the town of Arnstadt at the age of eighteen, he accepted, and proceeded to dedicate himself to the art of composition. As a court organist and violinist under Duke Wilhelm Ernst of Weimar, and as director of chamber music to young Prince Leopold of Anhalt-Cöthen, he took advantage of every leisure moment to perfect himself in composition. In his last position, which he held for twenty-seven years, Bach was director of music in the churches of St. Thomas and St. Nicholas and choirmaster at St. Thomas School in Leipzig. Many of his greatest works were composed during this period. The great polyphonic style of the Baroque period culminated with the compositions of J.S. Bach. Bach's only known work for a large wind ensemble is the *Cantata No. 18, O Jesu Christ, Mein Lebens Licht*, written in 1737 as a funeral cantata. Over 140 of Bach's compositions have been arranged for band.

Unit 2: Composition

This composition is a setting of Bach's keyboard music. It is in two movements played together without much of a break between them. Both the Prelude and the Fugue are polyphonic compositions, reflecting the typical style of the Baroque period in J.S. Bach's day. Transcribed by Roland L. Moehlmann in 1955, it is inscribed to Dr. Raymond F. Dvorak, a former Director of Bands at the University Of Wisconsin. The work has 110 measures and is five minutes, thirty seconds in length.

Unit 3: Historical Perspective

A Prelude is a work (usually for keyboard) most often paired with a subsequent work (such as a Mass movement, motet, hymn, ricercar, fugue, set of dances, etc.). Its purpose is primarily to establish the pitch or key of the following work. The Fugue, which became fully developed in the Baroque period, is based upon the procedure of imitative counterpoint. J.S. Bach considered the different parts (voices) of a fugue "as if they were persons who conversed together like a select company." Bach's *Well-Tempered Clavier* and *The Art of the Fugue* have come to be regarded as the supreme examples of fugal composition.

Unit 4: Technical Considerations

The scales of Bb Major and F Major are required for the entire ensemble. The meter is marked "alla breve", and there is much eighth note figuration that is typical of the genre. In the Prelude, the eighth note motive begins on the second eighth of the measure. In both the Prelude and the Fugue there are series of expanding and contracting intervals in eighth notes, but none are written across the break for clarinets.

Unit 5: Stylistic Considerations

Both the Prelude and the Fugue feature motives that are stated in alternating voices. The challenge is to balance the voices in both dynamics and style. Sections with repeated eighth notes should remain light. Rhythmic and harmonic accompaniment sections with repeated quarter notes should remain separated (but not too short). The half notes should be held full value. The tempo (Moderato) remains constant throughout except for the ritardandi marked at the end of both the Prelude and the Fugue. The marked dynamics range from *piano* to *forte* throughout, but without many changes. There is a crescendo to *fortissimo* at the end of the Fugue.

Unit 6: Musical Elements

The tonality of the work is Bb Major with some modulation to F Major indicated by accidentals in the parts. Typical of keyboard works of the Baroque period are the repeated rhythmic and melodic figures. They often appear stated in alternating voices and are often sequenced. The challenge is to maintain a consistent style in all instruments throughout.

Unit 7: Form and Structure
The Prelude is in two sections (24 measures and 32 measures), both repeated, and both based upon the same melodic/rhythmic motive. The Fugue typically alternates statements of subject and answer with episodic areas.

MEASURE	SECTION
1	Subject
5	Answer
9	Episode 1
12	Subject
16	Answer
20	Episode 2
26	Answer
30	Episode 3
32	Subject
36	Episode 4
41	False Entry
44	Subject
45	Answer in "stretto"

Unit 8: Suggested Listening
J.S. Bach, *Preludes and Fugues from the "Well Tempered Clavier"*
J.S. Bach, (arr. Donald Hunsberger), *Passacaglia and Fugue in C minor*
J.S. Bach, (arr. Donald Hunsberger), *Toccata and Fugue in D minor*

Unit 9: Additional References and Resources
Randel, Don Michael. *The New Harvard Dictionary of Music.* Cambridge, MA: Harvard University, 1986.

Rehrig, William H. *The Heritage Encyclopedia of Band Music.* Westerville, OH: Integrity Press, 1991.

Smith, Norman and Albert Stoutamire. *Band Music Notes.* Lake Charles, LA: Program Note Press, 1989.

Whitwell, David. "Bach—Wind Music." *The Instrumentalist*, XXI November 1966, 39.

Teacher Resource Guide

"Symphonie for Band"
Louis E. Jadin
(b. 1768–d. 1853)

Unit 1: Composer

Louis Emmanuel Jadin was born in Versailles, France, on September 21, 1768. He was taught violin by his father, Jean B. Jadin. Louis became chief accompanist at the Theatre de Monsieur in 1791. In 1792, he joined the Band of the National Guard, which was being organized to perform at the Revolutionary Festivals. For these occasions, he composed many pieces for band and for chorus with wind band accompaniment. Jadin taught piano at the Paris Conservatory from 1796-1816, succeeding his brother, Hyacinthe Jadin. At that time Louis was regarded as one of the finest accompanists in Paris. His first operas appeared in the 1790's. He was a prolific composer, composing for a wide variety of performing media. Several of his works have been arranged for 20th century bands, including *March of the Bands of the Revolution, Overture in C,* and *Symphony in One Movement.*

Unit 2: Composition

This is an original band work from the French Revolution. This single-movement work captures perfectly the classical style. In a lively *Allegro* throughout, it follows the form of an overture. Written in 1794, it was rescored for modern band by William Schaeffer in 1963. The 200-measure work is five minutes long.

Unit 3: Historical Perspective

During the French Revolution, and in the period immediately following, the many outdoor ceremonial functions led to a concentration of works for band. This work, like many composed in the genre at that time, was written in F due to the use of natural trumpets in that key. The instrumentation included the serpent in addition to the more familiar instruments. The work was found in the archives of the National Library of Paris.

Unit 4: Technical Considerations

The major tonal centers include F Major, C Major, and A-flat Major. The several areas of modulation use accidentals. The meter is 3/4 and the feeling should be 1 per bar. The main rhythmic concern may be the matching of style of the dotted-eighth and sixteenth rhythms. The style may provide a challenge, but technical aspects will not.

Unit 5: Stylistic Considerations

This work does not place highly technical demands on the players; the greatest challenge will be to perform in the proper style—light and crisp. The articulation must be light and fluent. Players and conductor must discipline themselves to avoid excessive levels of sound. The quarter notes followed by rests should be held full value. The dotted-eighth and sixteenth rhythms should be played crisply with some space between them (as in eighth, sixteenth rest, sixteenth note).

Unit 6: Musical Elements

The harmony is very tonal and chords are triadic. The primary tonal area is F Major with modulatory passages to C Major and A-flat Major. The melody is generally in the upper instruments, much of the allegro motive section is homorhythmic. The main rhythmic feature is the dotted-eighth and sixteenth rhythm.

Unit 7: Form and Structure

The work is in an early sonata form. There is a first theme area, second theme area, short development and contrasting section, and recapitulatory section.

MEASURE	SECTION
1	A motive F Major
24	B motive C Major
40	Closing Section modulatory around C
78	Middle section A and B motives
137	B motive F Major
153	Closing Section mostly F Major

Unit 8: Suggested Listening

Hector Berlioz, *Symphonie funèbre et triomphale*
Francois J Gossec, *Symphonie Militaire*
Franz Joseph Haydn, early symphonies
Hyacinthe Jadin, *Overture in F*
Louis Jadin, *Overture in C*

Unit 9: Additional References and Resources

Dvorak, Thomas L. *Best Music for Young Band*. Brooklyn, NY: Manhattan Beach Music, 1986.

Kreines, Joseph. *Music for Concert Band*. Tampa, FL: Florida Music Service, 1989.

Rehrig, William H. *The Heritage Encyclopedia of Band Music*. Westerville, OH: Integrity Press, 1991.

Swanzy, David Paul. *"The Wind Ensemble and Its Music During the French Revolution (1789-1795)"*. Ph.D. diss., Michigan State University, 1966.

Teacher Resource Guide

"Three Airs from Gloucester"
Hugh Stuart

(b. 1917)

Unit 1: Composer

Hugh M. Stuart was born in Harrisburg, Pennsylvania, on February 5, 1917. He studied at the Oberlin Conservatory of Music, the University of Michigan, Columbia University, and Rutgers University. He had a long and distinguished career as a public school music teacher and supervisor in New Jersey schools. 18 of his works for band have been published, including *Derby Day*, *Queen's Regiment*, and *Variations on a Theme by Prokofief*.

Unit 2: Composition

This work, composed in 1969, is in 3 short movements. It was the result of the composer's fascination with an old 10th century Couplet:

"There's no one quite so comely
As the Jolly Earl of Cholmondeley."

The resulting movements, in early English folk song style, are designed to capture the mood of the peasants and their life on the fiefs of Wembley castle. The first movement, *The Jolly Earl of Cholmondeley*, is an *Allegretto* march-like movement, and 66 measures and one and a quarter minutes long. The second movement, *Ayre for Eventide*, marked *Andante* with a slow, flowing melody, is 62 measures and two minutes long. The third movement, *The Fiefs of Wembley*, is in a lilting *Allegro* 6/8, and 58 measures and one minute in length.

Unit 3: Historical Perspective

This suite is in the style of early English folk songs. Basing compositions for wind band on folk songs is one of the most common compositional techniques. Most of Percy Grainger's tremendous output for bands are in that category. Clare

Grundman, too, has composed dozens of works based on folk songs from around the world. The important early work for 20th-century band, Vaughan Williams' *Folk Song Suite*, is based on English folk songs.

Unit 4: Technical Considerations

This work uses the keys and scales of F Major, B-flat Major, E-flat Major, and D minor. The first movement is marked *alla breve* with the half note equal to 96. There are short solos for clarinet and cornet, but nothing in this movement should prove to be technically demanding. The second movement is marked *Andante* with the quarter equal to 63. Here, the theme is a gracious melody set over a rich accompaniment. The challenge will be for players to perform in a smooth *cantabile* style. The initial melody is scored for the horns (but cued in the alto saxophone) and reaches a c2. The third movement is a lilting 6/8 *Allegro* with the dotted quarter equal to 108. The only challenge here may be performing in a light and spirited style.

Unit 5: Stylistic Considerations

The ensemble must be cautious to let the melody predominate throughout; depending on its instrumentation, the accompaniment may be too thickly scored. The first movement requires precise articulation in the *alla breve* style. Quarter notes marked tenuto should not be clipped short. The second movement calls for sustained lyrical playing. The middle statement of the theme, to be played a little faster, invites rich, full sounds from the entire ensemble. The third movement, in 6/8 time, demands a light and spirited style. Care must be taken so that the accompanying quarter notes are not played too short; they should provide both a rhythmic and harmonic accompaniment.

Unit 6: Musical Elements

The tonality of the works centers in the keys of F Major, B-flat Major, E-flat Major, and D minor. The harmony is very triadic and diatonic with some occasional chromaticism. The melodies, inspired by old English folk songs, are very tuneful, singable, and playable. The rhythms of the three movements are very basic as they fit into *alla breve*, triple meter, and compound meter.

Unit 7: Form and Structure

Measure	Melodic scoring
1	Cors: phrases 1,2
9	Solo Cl: phrase 3
13	Fls, Obs, Cls, Cors: phrase 4
17-24	repeat of 9-16
25,29	Fls: phrase 5

MEASURE	MELODIC SCORING
33	Cors, Hns, Bar: phrase 6
37	Fls, Obs: phrase 5
43	Solo Cor: phrase 3
47	Fls, Obs, Cls, Cors: phrase 4
51-58	repeat of 43-50
59	Cors: phrases 1,2
67	Hns: Ayre theme
83	Fls, Cls, Hns: modified theme
99	Fls, Obs, Cl 1, Cor 1: theme
115	Fls: theme ending
119	Hns, Solo Fl, Solo Hn: ending
129	Tutti: introduction
133	Fl: theme
149	Cors: theme
167	Fls, Obs, Cls, AS's: theme

Unit 8: Suggested Listening

Percy Grainger, *Lincolnshire Posy*
Robert Jager, *Colonial Airs and Dances*
Ralph Vaughan Williams, *English Folk Song Suite*

Unit 9: Additional References and Resources

Dvorak, Thomas L. *Best Music for Young Band*. Brooklyn, NY: Manhattan Beach Music, 1986.

Rehrig, William H. *The Heritage Encyclopedia of Band Music*. Westerville, OH: Integrity Press, 1991.

Teacher Resource Guide

"Toccata for Band"
Frank Erickson
(b. 1923)

Unit 1: Composer

Frank Erickson was born on September 1, 1923, in Spokane, Washington. He began to study music, playing piano and trumpet, and started to compose while in high school. During World War II, he arranged for army bands and, following the war, worked as a dance band arranger while studying composition with Mario Castelnuovo-Tedesco. He received degrees from the University of Southern California where he studied with Halsey Stevens. He taught at the University of California at Los Angeles and San Jose State College. Erickson has been music editor for several music publishers and he has more than 250 compositions and arrangements for band to his credit. Over 150 compositions have been published, including: *Balladair, Citadel March, Fantasy for Band, First Symphony for Band*, and *Second Symphony for Band*.

Unit 2: Composition

This very popular work has become a well-established part of band repertoire since its publication in 1957. The one movement piece is in ABA form, with a quick and rhythmic motive in the "Allegro non troppo" section and a more slow and lyrical theme in the "Andante con moto" section. The 204-measure work is five minutes, 15 seconds in length.

Unit 3: Historical Perspective

The three-part form has always been a popular and effective form for band compositions. The idea of a *Toccata* has also been a common style for winds. There are over 25 band works titled *Toccata*. The term *toccata* refers to a fanfare-like piece. As early as the 14th century, a brass piece written for a royal or courtly processional would have been referred to as a *toccata*. The opening of the most famous early opera (Monteverdi's "Orpheo" of 1607) is labeled *Toccata*. The best known toccata for band may be *Toccata Marziale* (1924) by Ralph Vaughan Williams.

Unit 4: Technical Considerations

This piece uses a modal sound. There are no key signatures, as accidentals are used in all parts throughout. The Dorian on D and on C are used along with major keys of D and C. Sixteenth notes are used often in the Allegro sections, but they are scalar and in groups of 4. The main motive enters on the second half of beat one. The accompaniment plays eighths on beat one and the second half of beat two. Some bands may have to work for clarity and precision with this opening motto. The last part of the initial Allegro has syncopation and short change from duple to triple meter. This will catch some players, but the rhythms are unison. Ranges are not extreme, but cornet 1 goes to G2, trombones 1, 2 to F#1.

Unit 5: Stylistic Considerations

The Allegro sections are marked at quarter note equal to 124. Rhythmic precision and clarity will be enhanced by maintaining a tempo that does not rush much beyond this suggested speed. The rests written in the opening accompaniment line may challenge some players not to rush. The composer has indicated specific articulations. Great care should be taken to observe lengths of quarter notes and eighth notes with markings. Dynamics in the cornet line in measures 47-48/140-141 are often misread. Attention to these dynamics and the "forte-piano" markings will greatly enhance any performance. In the Andante section (marked "quarter at 72"), the alto sax/horn countermelody line should be deliberately brought out for an effective performance.

Unit 6: Musical Elements

Melodies are modal, with Dorian on D and C used. Cadences and chords used are D Major, C Major and their dominants, A Major and G Major. No key signatures are used, and all chromatic pitches are indicated with accidentals. The tuneful, rhythmic first theme forms the motivic basis for the second, smoother theme. The occurrence of sixteenth notes is only as a short fragment of the first Allegro theme. Other themes rely on eighth notes, and these themes begin on the second eighth of the first beat of the measure. There are several short areas of syncopation.

Unit 7: Form and Structure

The three-part form is clearly delineated by its themes.

MEASURE	SECTION	TONALITY	MELODIC SCORING
1	a	D	Fl, Ob, Cl, As, Cor
9	b	C	Cl
30	a	D	Fl, Ob, Cl, As, Cor
38	b	C	Cor
55	a	C	Fl, Ob, Cl
73	c	C	Fl, Ob, Cl/As, Hn
81	c	C	Hn, Cor
91	b1	G	Cl 1
123	a	D	Fl, Ob, Cl, As, Cor
131	b	C	Cor
148	a1	A	Bs, Bcl, Bsn, Tbn, Bar, Tba/Cor
171	a	D	Fl, Ob, Cl/Cor
184	c1	D	Fl, Ob, Cl/As, Cor, Hn
196	c1	D	As, Cor, Hn/Fl, Ob, Cl (canon)

Unit 8: Suggested Listening

Frank Erickson, *First Symphony for Band; Second Symphony for Band*
Ralph Vaughan Williams, *Toccata Marziale*

Unit 9: Additional References and Resources

Arwood, Pamela Joy. *"Frank Erickson and his Music: A Biography, Analysis of Selected Compositions, and Catalogue."* MA thesis, Central Missouri State University, 1990.

Erickson, Frank. "Frank Erickson: Air for Band and Toccata for Band." *BD Guide*, January/February 1992, 27.

Randel, Don Michael. *The New Harvard Dictionary of Music.* Cambridge, MA: Harvard University, 1986.

Rehrig, William H. *The Heritage Encyclopedia of Band Music.* Westerville, OH: Integrity Press, 1991.

Smith, Norman and Albert Stoutamire. *Band Music Notes.* Lake Charles, LA: Program Note Press, 1989.

Teacher Resource Guide

"Two Grainger Melodies"
Percy Grainger

(b. 1882–d. 1961)

arranged by Joseph Kreines
(b. 1936)

Unit 1: Composer

Percy Aldridge Grainger was born on July 8, 1882, in Melbourne, Australia. He studied piano, first with his mother, then with Louis Pabst. At the age of ten he gave a series of recital which financed his study in Germany. In 1900 he first started his career as a concert pianist, with successes all over the world. He was chosen by composer Edvard Grieg to appear as guest soloist in the premiere of Grieg's *Concerto in A* in 1907. He came to America in 1915. At the outbreak of World War I he enlisted as an Army bandsman, soon being promoted to the Army Music School. He became a U.S. citizen in 1919, and again made many worldwide concert tours. For some time he was professor and head of the music department at New York University. A rugged individualist, Grainger was a remarkable innovator as a composer for orchestra and wind band. He was one of the first twentieth-century composers to embrace the wind band as a viable, expressive, artistic medium. His rhythmic inventiveness preceded Stravinsky; he was a pioneer in folk music collection at the same time as Bartok; his experiments with random and "free music" predated Varèse and other composers of electronic music. Grainger composed over thirty works for band, some of the most performed being: *Children's March, Over the Hills and Far Away, Colonial Song, Country Gardens, Irish Tune from County Derry, Lincolnshire Posy, Shepherd's Hey,* and *Ye Banks and Braes O'Bonnie Doon.*

Unit 2: Composition

This publication contains settings of *Six Dukes Went A-Fishin'* and *Early One Morning*. The lyrical first setting reflects the sad and poignant quality of the text of the folk song, which is about six dukes on a fishing party who found the body of another duke (who had disappeared) floating in the sea. They removed the body to London and buried him where he had been born. This transcription follows the setting for voice and piano which Grainger completed in 1912. The setting of the second folk song is also lyrical, but scored in thin textures of accompanied solo instruments. This transcription uses a 1950 version as its basis. Joseph Kreines (a Grainger scholar and arranger) arranged these two melodies in 1988. The two melodies, played as two movements, are 41 and 42 measures and four and one-half minutes in length.

Unit 3: Historical Perspective

Grainger settled in England in 1901 as a concert pianist. Through his developing contacts with other British musicians, he became interested in folk music and spent a good deal of time during the years 1905-09 collecting folk songs throughout the English countryside. Grainger collected *Six Dukes Went A-Fishin'* from the singing of George Gould Thorpe during his first trip to Lincolnshire in 1905. Grainger began the setting of the better known folk song, *Early One Morning*, in 1901, but did not complete it until 1939-40, when he made three different scorings. In 1950, he made yet another version, which differs in several respects from the earlier ones. Over half of Grainger's immense output uses folk song as its basis.

Unit 4: Technical Considerations

The first melody, *Six Dukes Went A-Fishin'*, is modal, mixolydian on B-flat. The key signature of E-flat is used. The changing meters between quadruple and triple meter should not pose problems at the indicated tempo of quarter equals 76. Both the dotted-eighth and sixteenth rhythm and sixteenth and dotted-eighth rhythm are part of the melody. There are a few spots of even eighths against a quarter-eighth triplet figure. The solo Trumpet goes up to an A-flat2. There is a part for soprano sax, but its line is either covered or cued in other parts. The second melody, *Early One Morning*, begins in F minor and changes to F Major. The piece moves chromatically, using accidentals five measures prior to the final chord. Two groups of 32nd notes appear before the end for the entire ensemble (in contrary motion) that may present a challenge to players. The foremost challenge is the scoring, involving thin textures of accompanied solo instruments.

Unit 5: Stylistic Considerations

There are no particular technical problems in these arrangements, but the lyrical quality of the music demands good control and phrasing from all players. There are no major shifts in dynamics in *Six Dukes Went A-Fishin'*. The areas of undulating dynamics in *Early One Morning* are performed mostly in unison. The arranger has indicated specific tempos that, when followed, present a satisfying musical flow that will enhance any performance.

Unit 6: Musical Elements

The harmony of both movements is basically triadic with some extended chords which produce mild dissonance. A chromatic twist precedes the final chord of *Early One Morning*, but the final F Major is very satisfying. The melodies, two folk songs, are obviously tuneful, and the old English song, *Early One Morning*, is probably familiar to most players and audience members. *Six Dukes Went A-Fishin'* is basically in a three meter. There are 22 changes between triple and quadruple meters in its 41 measures. The meters of four represent a stretching at phrase endings, characteristic of a folk singing style.

Unit 7: Form and Structure

SIX DUKES WENT A-FISHIN'

MEASURE	MELODY SCORING
1	Fls, Cl 1
9	Cl 1, B Cl, Tbn 1, Euph
17	Ob solo
25	Fls, Cl 1, Tpt 1, Vibes
33	Sop Sax, Vibes

EARLY ONE MORNING

MEASURE	MELODY SCORING
	Phrase 1
2	Euph solo
7	Bssn solo
	Phrase 2
14	Fl solo
18	Ob solo
19	Cl solo
20	Fl solo
21	Hn solo
	Phrase 3
23	Tpt solo
27	Fls, Obs, Cls 1
28	Tpts 1
29	Fls, Obs, Cls 1
	Phrase 4
31	Fls, Cls 1, Tpts 1
35	Fls, Cls 1, Tpts 2
39	Coda

Unit 8: Suggested Listening

Percy Grainger, *Australian Up-Country Tune; Colonial Song; Lincolnshire Posy*

Unit 9: Additional References and Resources

Rehrig, William H. *The Heritage Encyclopedia of Band Music.* Westerville, OH: Integrity Press, 1991.

Smith, Norman and Albert Stoutamire. *Band Music Notes.* Lake Charles, LA: Program Note Press, 1989.

Uggen, Stuart. "Percy Grainger in Perspective." *The Instrumentalist,* XXIV June 1970, 38-41.

Wilson, Brian Scott. *"Orchestrational Archetypes in Percy Grainger's Wind Band Music."* Diss., The University of Arizona, 1992.

Teacher Resource Guide

"Yorkshire Ballad"
James Barnes
(b. 1949)

Unit 1: Composer

James Charles Barnes was born on September 9, 1949, in Hobart, Oklahoma. He received bachelor's and master's degrees in theory and composition from the University of Kansas in 1974 and 1975 and studied conducting privately with Zuohuang Chen. Since 1977, he has been affiliated with the University of Kansas and is presently an Associate Professor of Theory and Composition and Assistant Conductor of Bands. He is also a tubist and has performed with numerous professional organizations. He has received many awards, grants and commissions and was twice recipient of the Ostwald Composition Award. He has written over 45 works for band, most notably *Brookshire Suite*, *Centennial Celebration Overture*, *Fantasy Variations on a Theme by Nicolo Pagannini*, *Heatherwood Portrait*, and *Invocation and Toccata*.

Unit 2: Composition

This work was composed in 1985. It is a rather uncomplicated three-statement setting of a four-phrase melody with an effective climax at the last phrase of the third statement. The work is very diatonic with a phrase modulation up a Perfect fourth at the third statement. The 59-measure work is three minutes, 45 seconds long.

Unit 3: Historical Perspective

Settings of song-like melodies have always been popular compositions for bands. The ballad, as a compositional form, is a traditional narrative song. The melodies are typically cast in four phrases. Research has shown that ballad-style songs have been sung from as early as the Middle Ages. The ballad of American popular music from the late 19th century and into the twentieth century became a song with sentimental text, in a slow tempo, with a phrase arrangement of AABA.

Unit 4: Technical Considerations

The scales of Bb Major and Eb Major are required for the entire ensemble. The eighth note is the smallest unit and there are some dotted notes; there is no syncopation. The score is marked "Adagio - Legato e sostenuto." A challenge will be to keep the eighth notes flowing without rushing in time. The longer notes of the harmonic accompaniment should be held with careful attention to tone, intonation, and balance.

Unit 5: Stylistic Considerations

The ballad style should be performed at a rather slow tempo, while remaining smooth and sustained. There are not many dynamic fluctuations in individual parts throughout. The last 15 measures progress from *fortissimo* to *morendo al niente*.

Unit 6: Musical Elements

The tonality of the work begins in Bb Major and changes to Eb Major half way through. The four-phrase melody is diatonic. It is clearly stated three times with changes in countermelody and accompaniment.

Unit 7: Form and Structure

MEASURE	SECTION	MELODY VOICING
1	a1	Cls, AS's, Hns
5	a2	Cl 1, AS 1, Hn 1
9	b	Cls, AS's, Hns
13	a3	Cl 1, AS 1, Hn 1
17	a1	Fl 1
21	a2	Fl 1
25	b	Fl 1, Ob 1, Cl 1
29	a3	Fl 1, Ob 1, Cl 1, Hn 1
33	a1	Ts, Tpt 1, Bar (modulates to Eb)
37	a2	TS, Tpt 1, Bar
41	b	Fl 1, Cl 1, Tpt 1, Tbn 1
45	a4	Fl 1, Cl 1, Tpt 1 / Bsn 1, TS, Tbns, Bar
49	Coda	

Unit 8: Suggested Listening

James Barnes, *Brookshire Suite*
Percy Grainger, *Colonial Song*
Percy Grainger, *Irish Tune from County Derry*

Unit 9: Additional References and Resources

Randel, Don Michael. *The New Harvard Dictionary of Music.* Cambridge, MA: Harvard University, 1986.

Rehrig, William H. *The Heritage Encyclopedia of Band Music.* Westerville, OH: Integrity Press, 19

Grade 4

Teacher Resource Guide

"Allerseelen"
Richard Strauss

(b. 1864–d. 1949)

transcribed by Albert O. Davis

(b. 1920)

Unit 1: Composer

Richard Strauss was one of the major transitional composers from the Romantic era of music to modern music. Well known as a conductor and composer of operas, symphonic tone poems, chamber music, and art songs, he is considered a post-Romantic composer in his expansive forms. In the area of harmony and subject matter, however, he was a great innovator. His advanced harmonic vocabulary went well beyond the compositions of his contemporaries, and his innovations served as examples for Schoenberg and Ravel. Although his subject matter could be quite shocking at times (e.g. the opera *Salome*), he had great successes in spite of being labeled a "modernist." In fact, he was a composer of great melodic genius from an early age, and his long career serves testament to the fact that he was a major influence on most composers in the first half of the 20th century. His greatest contributions to opera are in harmonic language and in tackling risqué subject matter. In instrumental literature, he is best remembered for his tone poems that serve as both program music and (somewhat) as personal narration. Most of his career was spent in Munich and Berlin. At the height of his fame, the only living composer considered an equal was Debussy. He is still revered today as a genius who personified Wagner's vision of *Zukunftmusik*, or music of the future.

Unit 2: Composition

Allerseelen, or "All Souls (Day)," written in 1885, belongs to a collection of songs from Strauss' Op. 10. Note that Strauss was only 21 years old when he wrote this opus. The original composition was 43 measures in length and first scored for voice and piano. It has been arranged several times for orchestra, including an arrangement by Strauss himself. In the original version, there were two verses. In the orchestral version and the transcription by Albert Davis, a longer introduction was added, along with a lengthy development and a third verse. In the arrangement for band, Davis has retained the original key and form from the orchestra version. Extremely Romantic in compositional style, Strauss' love of transitory modulations make this work a delight to analyze, since several keys are explored, albeit briefly. Typical of Strauss, these short changes of tonal center involve modulations a third from the primary tonal center and use motivic fragments as a unifying device. It is of medium difficulty and has a length of five to six minutes, depending on tempo and use of *rubato*. A companion selection much in the same style is *Zueignung*, another transcription of a Strauss song from the same opus number.

Unit 3: Historical Perspective

Although transcribed in 1950 by Davis, *Allerseelen* rightfully belongs in the era of the late Romantic era of music, before Strauss began his avant-garde period of composition. Much of the composition is reminiscent of Richard Wagner or Hugo Wolf, and care should be taken to interpret the music as it would have been performed in the late 19th century. The use of *rubato* would be expected, and it would be expected to perform the *fortissimo* and *pianissimo* passages with an extreme of dynamic range. Articulation during this period in music history and for this genre would be very broad at all times.

Unit 4: Technical Considerations

Most of the technical considerations in *Allerseelen* come from making the melody the most prominent voice. The composition as a whole is in E-flat Major, but there are several short key changes that are explored without a change of key signature. These are located at measures 35-36 (G Major), measures 41-43 (C minor), measures 65-68 (C minor), measures 73-76 (G Major), measures 77-82 (B-flat minor), measures 83-86 (D Major), and measures 87-90 (B-flat Major). The prominent rhythmic motive is in measure 3. There are solos for oboe, cornet, horn, and euphonium, with the brass soloists carrying the bulk of the melody. Range demands are moderate, with cornet 1 playing high B-flat once in measure 98 during the work's climax. The entire composition is in common time, with no difficult rhythms. The clarinet and flute sections have two instances where sixteenth notes and triplets must be played as accompaniment; those technical passages are in moderate tempo and not very difficult.

Unit 5: Stylistic Considerations
The major stylistic challenges in this work are to have a base tempo consistent with Strauss' original intent, to use *rubato* tastefully near cadences and emotional peaks, and to keep the melody prominent by reducing accompanimental voices. Regarding the tempo, the Davis arrangement has a tempo of 120 beats per minute. This is wrong, of course, as Strauss' original song clearly states *Tranquillo* as the tempo indication. A more suitable range would be from 72 to 80 beats per minute. Rhythmic exactness is not a high priority in this composition. The use of *rubato* should be evident, especially at major cadences such as measures 17, 20, 23, 30, 38, 49, 62, 64, 90 (a *ritard molto* is a common and justified interpretation here), 103, and 107. The articulation throughout should be *legato* and *cantabile* in the extreme. What few *staccato* notes are written should be performed as lightly separated tones. Since the original song is clearly marked "for high voice" while the band transcription frequently has the euphonium and horn with the melody, it is imperative that trumpets, flutes, clarinets, and oboe play very lightly in these circumstances. Excessive doubling of these parts will lead to a lack of clarity. Please note that the theme begins in measure 24, but in the original song, the voice began (in the band transcription) at measure 30, with the first cornet having the melody.

Unit 6: Musical Elements
The primary tonality is E-flat Major with brief excursions into C minor and other keys. The term "third relationship" should be used to explain Strauss' fascination with key changes a minor or major third from the base tonal center. Although the melody is fairly chromatic, the harmony is still triadic with some seventh chords. Melodically, the verses and theme are built around the E-flat scale. The *leitmotif*, or primary musical motive, is an arpeggio that first appears in measures 3-4 and is the primary means of unification for the development section. The texture is usually thick, but the melodic and accompanimental roles are usually well separated. The use of sequence figures strongly from measures 41-49. Rhythmic pulse is strictly in simple meter with strong emphasis on beats 1 and 3.

Unit 7: Form and Structure
Overall form: Introduction, A B A codetta

Introduction	measures 1-23	E-flat Major

primary motive introduced with some development

A (verses 1 and 2)	measures 24-64	E-flat Major and C minor
verse 1	measures 24-34	E-flat Major
bridge	measures 35-49	G Major, E-flat Major, and C minor
verse 2	measures 50-64	E-flat Major

B (development)
C minor, E-flat Major, G Major, B-flat minor, G minor, D Major, and
   B-flat Major

A	(recap)	measures 91-105	E-flat Major
	verse 3	measures 91-105	

Codetta		measures 106-108	E-flat Major

Unit 8: Suggested Listening
Richard Strauss, *Zueignung*
Richard Strauss, *Four Last Songs*
Richard Strauss, *Suite in B-flat*
Richard Wagner, *Trauersinfonie*

Unit 9: Additional References and Resources
Dvorak, Thomas L., Robert Grechesky, and Gary Ciepluch. *Best Music for High
   School Band.* Brooklyn, NY: Manhattan Beach Music, 1993.

Smith, Norman and Albert Stoutamire. *Band Music Notes.* Lake Charles, LA:
   Program Note Press, 1989.

Watkins, Glenn. *Soundings.* New York: Schirmer Books, 1988.

Teacher Resource Guide

"Amazing Grace"
Frank Ticheli

(b. 1958)

Unit 1: Composer
Frank Ticheli, a native of Louisiana, received his masters and doctoral degrees in composition from the University of Michigan, where he studied with William Albright, George Wilson, and Pulitzer-Prize winners Leslie Bassett and William Bolcom. His many compositions for wind ensemble/concert band have brought him numerous accolades, including the 1989 Walter Beeler Prize (Music for Winds and Percussion) and First Prize in the 11th Annual Symposium for New Band Music (Concertino for Trombone and Band). Other honors include a Charles Ives scholarship and a Goddard Lieberson Fellowship, the Ross Lee Finney Award, and a residency at the MacDowell Colony.

Unit 2: Composition
Amazing Grace was composed in 1994 and is Ticheli's seventh work for wind ensemble/concert band. It was commissioned by John Whitwell, currently Director of Bands at Michigan State University, in loving memory of his father, John Harvey Whitwell.

Unit 3: Historical Perspective
Ticheli's *Amazing Grace* is based on the well-known spiritual by the same name. Ticheli states: "The spiritual *Amazing Grace* was written by John Newton (1725-1807), a slaveship captain who, after years of transporting slaves across the Atlantic Ocean to the New World, suddenly saw through divine grace the evilness of his acts."

Unit 4: Technical Considerations

The work is in Eb Major and 3/4 meter, with sections of modulation to Bb Major, and brief tonicizations to Db and F. The Eb Major and Bb Major scales are required for all parts. Rhythmic demands are not severe. Tempo is quarter equal to 72-80, and there are only brief passages of sixteenth notes. The texture is polyphonic throughout; Ticheli skillfully weaves contrapuntal lines around the hymn-melody. Ticheli's sense of pacing and his keen understanding of the phrasing capabilities of winds are strong features of this work.

Unit 5: Stylistic Considerations

This music requires expressive playing and sonorous tone production, and should be as legato as possible. Because of the polyphonic scoring of the work, care must be taken to achieve balance and to bring out the inner voices. The *Amazing Grace* theme and its derivative perfect-fourth motif, which recur throughout the work, must be performed in a consistently uniform style. For an effective performance of this work, it is important to pace the building of intensity throughout; an expressive approach to rhythm and dynamics is crucial to the dramatic pacing. The final statement of the chorale should be a magnificent climax.

Unit 6: Musical Elements

The harmonic construction of this work is quite triadic and tonal. Polyphonic texture prevails. Exceptional orchestration and wonderful lines combine in this wonderfully rewarding, accessible piece of music. The form is A-B-A, with introduction and coda.

Unit 7: Form and Structure

MEASURES	SECTION	KEY	MUSICAL EVENTS
1-8	Intro	Eb Major	Flowing introductory statement
9-24	First Statement	Eb Major	First statement of *Amazing Grace*; chamber setting, melody in alto sax solo
25-38	Second Statement	Eb Major	Second statement of *Amazing Grace*; tutti
39-46	Episode	Modulating	Episode serving as an extension and transition to the development
47-69	Development	Bb...Db...F	Development of theme and perfect fourth motif
70-82	Transition	Bb (pedal)	Long, building transition over Bb pedal

| 83-98 | Final Statement | Eb Major | Climactic statement of theme |
| 99-106 | Coda | Eb Major | Quiet coda, piece ends ppp |

Unit 8: Suggested Listening

Frank Ticheli, *Concerto for Winds and Percussion, Concertino for Trombone and Band, Cajun Folk Songs*

Unit 9: Additional References and Resources

Dvorak, Thomas L., Robert Grechesky, and Gary Ciepluch. *Best Music for High School Band*. Brooklyn, NY: Manhattan Beach Music, 1993.

Teacher Resource Guide

"Caccia and Chorale"
Clifton Williams

(b. 1923–d. 1976)

Unit 1: Composer

Clifton Williams was a native of Arkansas and received his first music education in the public schools of Little Rock and Malvern. He received his Bachelor's degree in composition from Louisiana State University, where he studied with Helen Gunderson, and a Master of Music degree from the Eastman School, where he studied with Bernard Rogers and Howard Hanson. He was on the composition faculty at the University of Texas (Austin) from 1949 to 1966. He then moved to the University of Miami, where he was chair of Theory and Composition until his untimely death. He was best known as one of the first serious composers of the 1950s to write frequently for wind band, especially for music performable by school groups. He was the first winner of the ABA Ostwald Award in 1956, a prize (still awarded) for the outstanding composition for wind band. He, along with Persichetti, was known for his challenging writing for percussion. The major difference between Williams and Persichetti is that Williams wrote less pointillistically and melodically for percussion, although the percussion parts in his music were by far more challenging than found in earlier band music. His formal structures are less traditional than Persichetti's, but his writing was more aligned towards melodic expression.

Unit 2: Composition

Caccia and Chorale, Clifton Williams' last composition, was written in 1975. It was commissioned by Williams' friend, Donald E. Green, Director of Bands at the University of Wisconsin (Stevens Point). Since 1969, his health had been failing, and shortly before he began the composition, Williams was diagnosed with cancer. An operation was advised quickly to excise the cancer. Feeling that he might not survive the operation, Williams intended to write only a *Caccia*, an ancient musical name dating back to the 14th and 15th centuries that literally means "chase." After the surgery, the *Chorale* was written as both a prayer of thanks and for his own programmatic purposes. The composer wrote:

> While it remains open to question whether music can convey any message other than a purely musical one, composers often tend to attempt philosophical, pictorial, or other aspects within a musical framework. Such is the case with *Caccia and Chorale*, two title words borrowed from Italian because of their allegorical significance. The first, *Caccia*, means hunt or chase, and is intended to reflect the preoccupation of most people in the world with a constant pursuit of materialism. The *Chorale* is, by contrast, an urgent and insistent plea for greater humanity, a return to religious or ethical regeneration by all mankind.

Unfortunately, Williams died soon after completing this composition.

Unit 3: Historical Perspective

Caccia and *Chorale* was composed in 1975 during a time when wind band compositions were becoming more available to school bands. The composition was scored in a contemporary style yet conservative within the the simple framework of tonality and techniques of composition. Other innovative composers outside the wind band medium during the 70's utilized different compositional techniques in a more experimental approach. Some of those included: George Crumb, John Cage, György Ligeti, Steve Reich, and John Adams.

Unit 4: Technical Considerations

There are a number of complexities in this composition dealing with meter. The 3/2 and 2/2 meter involve some mild syncopations and eighth-note runs at 126 beats/minute. These woodwind runs involve non-scalar material and are moderately difficult. In the *Caccia*, the scales of B-flat minor, E-flat minor, and D-flat Major should be very familiar to the ensemble. The 6/8 section at H is really an easy introduction to 6/8 time and could be treated as such. The first cornet carries the brunt of the range demands, but rarely ascends above the staff; there is only one high C in the *Caccia*. The 9/4 time signature at letter L poses some moderate problems of execution. The brass play a chorale while the woodwinds play a very syncopated figure, conducted in 3 to the measure. Explaining the morse code significance of the rhythm (D-E-G, for Donald E. Greene) and rehearsing very slowly will help solidify this concept. The chorale has some half-step dissonances in the brass that require careful listening for balance. There is an English horn solo played in the upper register; cues for oboe work very well.

Unit 5: Stylistic Considerations

The primary considerations for style are found in the title and its significance in music history. Since *Caccia* means "hunt" in Italian, the programmatic significance should be explained to students. The snare drum sets this frantic, pursuing idea almost throughout. In combination with the fanfares, the *Caccia* sets a *marcato* and *bravura* style throughout, mainly in the area of crisp articulation. At letter L, crisp articulation is necessary to imitate the morse code idea. The *Chorale* should provide as many opportunities for contrast as possible. *Legato* playing and long phrases, regardless of the level of dissonance, should be the rule. The English horn (or oboe) solo should be very expressive with phrasing and dynamics linked to the rise and fall of the melodic line.

Unit 6: Musical Elements

Compound meter and division of half-note as the pulse must be covered in detail in this composition. The relation of dissonance to consonance is important in recognizing phrase structure and form. The minor and phrygian modes make up the melodic material for the *Caccia*. Comparing and contrasting these scalar constructions will help to explain Williams' desire to use modal construction with reference to an ancient genre. In the *Chorale*, the melody moves diatonically, and this contrast with earlier sections should also be explained. The changing meters are directly related to the formal structure of the composition. Students should be able to identify the large sections of the form through this alone.

Unit 7: Form and Structure

Caccia—modified sonata form

Section	Measures	Tonal Center	Rehearsal Letter
Fanfare	measures 1-16	E-flat	
transition	measures 17-20	transitory	A
A	measures 21-44	B-flat minor	9 after A
Fanfare	measures 45-64	E-flat	C
transition	measures 65-66	transitory	2 before E
A	measures 67-86	F minor	E
transition	measures 87-94	C minor	G
B (devel.)	measures 95-106	G-flat Major; melody in B-flat phrygian mode	H
B′	measures 107-118	A Major with melody in C# phrygian mode	I
transition A	measures 119-130	B-flat	J
transition B	measures 131-140	transitory; fanfare added	K
C	measures 141-164	C Major, B-flat Major, and F Major	L

fanfare treated as chorale; both cyclical and anticipatory

Chorale—A B A coda form

A	measures 165-172	D-flat Major	8 before N
B	measures 173-189	D-flat Major	N
A	measures 190-197	D-flat Major	6 after O
Coda	measures 198-202	D-flat Major	6 after P

Unit 8: Suggested Listening

Clifton Williams, *Fanfare and Allegro*
Clifton Williams, *Concertino for Percussion and Band*
Clifton Williams, *Symphonic Dance #3, "Fiesta"*
Vincent Persichetti, *Pageant*

Unit 9: Additional References and Resources

Daniel, Joe Rayford. "The Band Works of James Clifton Williams." Ph.D. diss., The University of Southern Mississippi, 1981.

Siler, John Robert. "The Non-formalized Pitch-Rhythm Ostinato in Band Works of Clifton Williams: A Categorization of Patterns." Ph.D. diss., University of South Carolina, 1985.

Smith, Norman and Albert Stoutamire. *Band Music Notes.* Lake Charles, LA: Program Note Press, 1989.

Teacher Resource Guide

"Chorale and Alleluia"
Howard Hanson

(b. 1896–d. 1981)

Unit 1: Composer

Howard Hanson was born in Wahoo, Nebraska in 1896, and died in Rochester, New York in 1981. He exerted widespread influence as a composer, conductor, and educator. He studied music at Luther College, the Institute of Musical Art (which later became the Juilliard School), and at Northwestern University. In 1924 he became the director of the Eastman School of Music, a position he held until 1964. In 1944 he received the Pulitzer Prize for his Symphony No. 4, and he also received the Ditson and Peabody Awards, in addition to honorary doctorates from 32 universities and colleges. As the teacher of two generations of American composers, he contributed greatly to the national standards of musical excellence in the United States. Hanson believed that romantic ideals should be the animating force of all music. He was primarily a symphonist, and found his natural language in instrumental composition. His music was always rooted firmly in tonality, and asymmetrical rhythms and compound meters are characteristic. His major works include an opera, six symphonies, many choral and chamber works, and five works for band; *Dies Natalis, Young Person's Guide to the Six-Tone Scale, Laude, March Carillon,* and *Chorale and Alleluia.*

Unit 2: Composition

Chorale and Alleluia, composed in January 1954, was Hanson's first work for symphonic band. It was commissioned by Edwin Franko Goldman for the American Bandmasters Association, and was premiered that year at the ABA conference at West Point. It is a single movement work, approximately five minutes in length.

Unit 3: Historical Perspective

Chorale and Alleluia is another of the many works commissioned from leading American composers by Edwin Franko Goldman. This was an important commission, for it added a piece to the repertoire by a composer who had received both the Prix de Rome and the Pulitzer Prize. Goldman and his son Richard also commissioned works from William Schuman, Virgil Thomson, Roy Harris, Samuel Barber, Vincent Persichetti, Peter Mennin, and many other composers active mainly in the mid-20th century. Their works added significant depth to the band repertoire.

Unit 4: Technical Considerations

The work covers a multitude of keys, including C Major, Bb Major, Ab Major, F Major, A Major, E Major, C minor, D minor, and Eb Major. Rhythmic demands are minimal. The tempo never exceeds quarter equal to 120 and there are no rhythms containing consecutive sixteenth notes. What is most difficult to achieve is the legato, sustained style required in the chorale sections; a full, rich sonority is required without forcing or overblowing. The woodwind and brass writing is consistent for full sections, without any significant solos. A good timpanist is required for the many tuning changes, as well as the important dramatic role that the part requires. Other percussion parts are well-written, but not overly demanding.

Unit 5: Stylistic Considerations

The opening chorale requires expressive playing and sonorous tone production, and should be as legato as possible. Because of the generally thick scoring of the work, care must be taken to achieve balance and to bring out the inner voices. The "Alleluia" motif that recurs throughout the work must be performed in a consistently uniform style. For an effective performance of this work, it is important to pace the building of intensity throughout. The final statement of the chorale should be a magnificent climax.

Unit 6: Musical Elements

The harmonic construction of this work is quite triadic and tonal. Occasional instances of polymodality are quite consonant, and usually result in an 11th or 13th-chord type. Functional harmony is non-existent; a harmony may remain static for long periods, then suddenly shift to a new, seemingly unrelated pitch center. The application of pedal points and motivic ostinato is frequent. Three main themes comprise the entire work: the "Chorale" theme in the opening, the "Alleluia" theme (actually a short motif), and a bold third theme introduced by horns and euphonium in the "Alleluia" section. The work is unified by the "Alleluia" theme, a one-measure rhythmic and melodic motif which is first heard at the phrase endings of the opening chorale (Section A) and which serves as a

rhythmic ostinato for the entire B section. Section C consists of alternating statements of the "Chorale" and "Alleluia", with each section gaining in intensity until
all three themes are heard in an impressive, resounding climax.

Unit 7: Form and Structure

MEASURES	SECTION	KEY	MUSICAL EVENTS
1-3	A	C Major	Opening chorale, brass choir
4-6		Bb Major	Second chorale statement, brass choir w/ low ww
7-9			First statement of Alleluia theme, flutes and clarinets, over sustained Bb chord
10-13		Ab Major	Chorale statement, clarinets, trumpets, horns
14-16			Alleluia theme, flutes and clarinets over sustained Ab Major chord
17-26		F Major	Two phrases of chorale; first tutti, second brass choir, A Major
27-30	B	A	Faster tempo, 3/4 time, quarter equal to 100; Alleluia section begins w/ theme in upper woodwinds
31-39		D Major over C Major (C13)	Alleluia theme continues as ostinato over pedal C in bass; Theme III enters in m. 32 in horns and euph.
40-44		E Major over C pedal	Theme III and ostinato presented in new key, w/same pedal
45-48		A minor/ D Major	Ostinato in 1 measure antiphonal statements between woodwind families in A minor, then D Major
49-52		Ab7/ D Major	Antiphonal statements of ostinato and Theme III between Ab7 and D Major
53-58	B	F Major	Ostinato over sustained chords
59-66		F Major over Eb Major (Eb13)	Faster tempo, 3/4 time, quarter equal to 120; pedal Eb, with ostinato and theme III in F Major

MEASURES	SECTION	KEY	MUSICAL EVENTS
67-72		G Major over Eb pedal	Pedal Eb, with ostinato and theme III in G Major
72-75		C minor	Pedal Eb, with ostinato and theme III in C minor
76-79		Bb minor/ E Major	Ostinato and theme III continue in alternating harmonies; Bb minor-E Major
80-87		G Major over C Major (Cmaj9)	Climactic statement of Section B; ostinato in G Major, theme III in canon in G Major
88-89	A	E Major	Chorale returns, *Largamente Molto*, 4/2 meter
90		F Major	Interjection of Alleluia theme
91-92		D minor	Chorale statement
93		Eb Major	Interjection of Alleluia theme
94-96		Eb Major	Chorale statement
90		Db Major	Interjection of Alleluia theme
91-92		D minor	Chorale statement, builds dramatically toward final climactic Alleluia statement
93		A Major	Climactic alleluia statement, theme III enters m. 113; final two measures, "Amen" figure

Unit 8: Suggested Listening

Howard Hanson, *Symphony No. 4, Dies Natalis, Laude*

Unit 9: Additional References and Resources

Dvorak, Thomas L., Robert Grechesky, and Gary Ciepluch. *Best Music for High School Band.* Brooklyn, NY: Manhattan Beach Music, 1993.

Fennell, Frederick. "Howard Hanson: Chorale and Alleluia." *BD Guide,* September/October 1990, 20.

Johnson, Barry Wayne. "An Analytical Study of the Band Compositions of Howard Hanson." Diss., University of Houston, 1986.

Prindl, Frank Joseph. "A Study of Ten Original Compositions for Band Published in America Since 1946." Diss., The Florida State University, 1956.

Sadie, Stanley. *The New Grove Dictionary of Music and Musicians.* London: Macmillan, 1980.

Smith, Norman and Albert Stoutamire. *Band Music Notes.* Lake Charles, LA: Program Note Press, 1989.

Teacher Resource Guide

"Chorale and Shaker Dance"
John Zdechlik

(b. 1937)

Unit 1: Composer

John Zdechlik is a trumpeter whose music education began in the public schools of Minnesota. Since high school, he has had an interest in jazz, both as a performer and as a composer. He received the Bachelor of Music Education degree from the University of Minnesota in 1957. After a few years as a music teacher, Zdechlik returned to the University of Minnesota, where he received the masters degree in theory and composition. He was a faculty member both during and after his graduate work, but decided to pursue a Ph.D. in composition and theory, which he completed in 1970. He then accepted a position at Lakewood Community College, where today he is Chair of the Department of Music and Band Director. Zdechlik is best known as a composer of music suitable for school bands, with *Chorale and Shaker Dance* his most famous work. Other well known compositions by Zdechlik include *Faces of Kum Ba Yah, Lyric Statement, Psalm 46,* and *Dance Variations*. He is best known for composing in theme and variation form.

Unit 2: Composition

The title, *Chorale and Shaker Dance*, refers to the principal sections of the composition, the opening chorale, and the set of variations on the Shaker hymn, *"Tis a Gift to be Simple."* Written in 1972, it was commissioned by the Jefferson High School Band of Bloomington, Minnesota. The premiere took place at the National MENC convention in 1972. Composed in a theme and variation form, the sectional structure is straightforward, making it a good introduction to variation form for any ensemble. Zdechlik's love of jazz is shown in the contrapuntal intricacies and use of syncopated rhythms typical of big bands. It is nine minutes in duration, and the complexity makes it moderately challenging for high school and some college bands. This composition could probably be viewed as a companion to *Dance Variations*, another work for band set entirely in variation form.

Unit 3: Historical Perspective

Chorale and Shaker Dance was composed in 1972 at a time when compositions for school bands were at a peak. Composers such as Claude T. Smith, Francis McBeth, and Robert Jager were among the best-known composers of music for school bands, while Warren Benson was leading composition for winds in a completely different direction with *The Solitary Dancer*. During the early 1970s, there was a schism among composers as to the direction that composition for band should take. Many composers were writing music for bands on the premise that school bands would perform more of their music, while composers such as Donald Erb and Karel Husa were viewing the band and wind ensemble as a yet-unexplored artistic medium. This dichotomy in compositional intent continued through the 1970s. The general trend among the composers of school band music was a majority of writing for tutti ensemble with little emphasis on solo or chamber music writing.

Unit 4: Technical Considerations

The tonal centers of D, E-flat, F, A-flat, and B-flat are all present in this work. At one time or another, these tonal centers are supported by scalar constructions, some more subtle than others. Woodwinds have more technically demanding passages in the D Major sections, while the brasses have the melodic material more often in the keys of E-flat, F, and B-flat. Rhythmic considerations are moderate, with some mild syncopation and use of eighth-note runs (usually scalar or repetitive) in the woodwinds. There is quite a bit of writing in 2/2 and 3/2 meters, but the rhythmic demands there are light and very accessible. Range demands are moderate with the exception of trumpets, where trumpet 1 must play a $C\#^3$, trumpet 2 an A^2, and trumpet 3 an E^2 one measure before H; its approach by sequence makes it playable by most high school bands. Repeated tonguing is expected of trumpets and other brasses occasionally. Solos exist for flute, oboe, clarinet 1 and 2, alto sax, and timpani, although the technical demands are moderate. There is much of what appears to be chromatic writing, but most lines are actually diatonic within changing tonal centers (no key signatures are used).

Unit 5: Stylistic Considerations

The opening chorale and the Shaker hymn answer must be performed with attention to balance. The upper woodwinds must not dominate the texture. Zdechlik frequently enlivens the repeated notes of the Shaker hymn with changes of chords underneath; the effect is that of common tones acting as a pedal. These common tones should just be heard above the chord changes. Stagger breathing may be necessary through much of the introduction; the concept is to imitate the sustaining of an organ. At letter C, the soloists should play all eighth notes lightly. The ensemble should not play very aggressively in articulation or volume until 8 before F. Four measures after G, explanation of jazz syncopation in regards to articulation (alternation of "off" and "on" the beat), will help. Letters I, J, and K are elaborated chorales and should be performed as such. Letter Q requires a light articulation. The low brass at letter R should enter with "bell tones," a firm attack and immediate *diminuendo*. The woodwinds at T should not interfere with the brass chorale. A successful performance relies on contrasting the light, fast, articulated passages against the chorales.

Unit 6: Musical Elements

Zdechlik switches tonal centers with each phrase, though the melody moves diatonically. This is similar to Shostakovich's treatment of melody. Zdechlik develops each variation as it unfolds. The use of canon at C and O should be explained, along with possible cyclical connections. Zdechlik frequently uses pedal as a tonal anchor, especially in woodwinds and horns. These uses are important to unifying those phrases (horns in letter G, for example). The return of the chorale at later points is a strong unifying device in the composition. After its initial entrance, the chorale is usually rhythmically augmented as a counter-melody or harmonic support, especially at T. The peak of the *andante* between M and N is related to both these chromatic alterations of the motives and the interplay of major and minor thirds; these elements establish the section's peak. The use of pedal is greatest in the last five measures of the timpani, where D is affirmed as the primary tonal center.

Unit 7: Form and Structure

SECTION	TONAL CENTER	LOCATION	LEADING VOICES/COMMENTS
Theme (intro)	B-flat to D	m.1-C	woodwind choir
Var. 1	F	C	alto sax, flute, solo clarinet 1 and 2
Var. 2	D to A-flat	F	tutti (trumpets, upper woodwinds)
Var. 3	A-flat	I	trombones, brass choir
Var. 4	B to F# to D	L	interplay in thirds-unclear tonality (development)
Var. 5	D to A to E-flat	O	similar to letter C but developed further
Var. 6	E-flat to D	S	woodwinds with trumpets and horns in augmentation

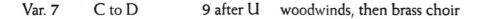

Var. 7   C to D   9 after U   woodwinds, then brass choir

Unit 8: Suggested Listening
John Zdechlik, *Dance Variations*
John Zdechlik, *Psalm 46*
John Zdechlik, *Lyric Statement*
Aaron Copland, *Appalachian Spring*
Dimitri Shostakovich, *Symphony #5, Movement 2*

Unit 9: Additional References and Resources

Dvorak, Thomas L., Robert Grechesky, and Gary Ciepluch. *Best Music for High School Band.* Brooklyn, NY: Manhattan Beach Music, 1993.

Rehrig, William H. *The Heritage Encyclopedia of Band Music.* Westerville, OH: Integrity Press, 1991.

Smith, Norman and Albert Stoutamire. *Band Music Notes.* Lake Charles, LA: Program Note Press, 1989.

Teacher Resource Guide

"Chorale and Toccata"
Jack Stamp

(b. 1954)

Unit 1: Composer

Jack Stamp was born on March 5, 1954. He is Conductor of Bands at Indiana University of Pennsylvania, directing the Wind Ensemble, Symphony Band, and Concert Band, and teaches courses in conducting and percussion. Prior to his appointment at Indiana University of Pennsylvania, Stamp was Chair of the Division of Fine Arts at Campbell University in North Carolina. He also taught for several years in the public schools of North Carolina. In addition to these posts, he served as conductor of the Duke University Wind Symphony and was musical director of the Triangle British Brass Band, leading them to a national brass band championship in 1989. He holds degrees from Indiana University of Pennsylvania, East Carolina University, and Michigan State University. Stamp's primary composition teachers have been Robert Washburn and Fisher Tull. He has also studied with noted American composers David Diamond and Joan Tower. As the recipient of numerous commissions, he has over twenty compositions which appear frequently on programs throughout the country. Many have been recorded on compact disc, including *Aubrey Fanfare, Divertimento in "F", Gavorkna Fanfare,* and *Past the Equinox.*

Unit 2: Composition

This work was commissioned by the Ohio Private College Instrumental Conductors Association for their 1992 Honor Band. Stamp writes, "The request was to write a challenging, yet accessible, work suited for small colleges or advanced high school bands. With this challenge, I called upon my days of study with Robert Washburn, using many of the classic 20th century compositional techniques he taught me. Therefore, the work is written in a traditional style with a main chorale melody, a toccata theme, and a recurring chordal motif which binds the Toccata. During the Toccata, the main theme is used in inversion and appears in a double canon with its inversion. The chorale then returns toward the end of the Toccata to complete the work with a cyclic idea." The 167 measure work is five minutes, fifteen seconds in length.

Unit 3: Historical Perspective

Many works for band with two contrasting movements have been written through the years by fine composers. Often the first movement is called *Hymn*, *Chorale*, or *Chant* and the contrasting movement is called *Alleluia*, *Toccata*, *Celebration* or *Jubilo*. The term, *Toccata*, refers to a fanfare-like piece. As early as the 14th century, a brass piece written for a royal or courtly processional would have been referred to as a *toccata*. The opening of the most famous early opera (Monteverdi's "*Orfeo*" of 1607) is labeled *Toccata*. The best known toccata for band may be *Toccata Marziale* (1924) by Ralph Vaughan Williams.

Unit 4: Technical Considerations

This work uses the tonal centers of F minor and C Major and requires those scales from the entire ensemble. Key signatures are not used. All flats and sharps are written in as accidentals. Several rhythmic aspects of the work require close examination. The initial four-note motif is introduced at one-beat intervals in the mallet percussion and woodwinds. The four measures of transition into the Toccata feature the timpani and percussion in a 5/8 rhythm over a four meter. The recurring toccata motif is highly syncopated and uses changing meters. The range is not extensive for this level. The Trumpet 1 part reaches a B flat2 in the recurring toccata motif. A piano, sizzle cymbal, and wind chimes are scored for the Chorale and provide valuable timbres. The first appearance of the Chorale theme is scored for English Horn.

Unit 5: Stylistic Considerations

The introduction to the Chorale is marked "Dreamlike." The challenge will be for the band to play this section clearly and smoothly and to maintain this atmosphere of sound for 18 measures. The rhythms of the Toccata movement must be performed cleanly, crisply and precisely. The recurring toccata motifs are scored for the entire ensemble and require this accurate playing.

Unit 6: Musical Elements

The harmony of the work is in F minor and C Major and the chords are triadic. At the beginning of the Chorale and at places in the Toccata are instances of imitative or canonic entries. These polyphonic sections should be rehearsed so that all lines are equal and matching in sound and style. The melodies of the Chorale and Toccata are clearly defined and shaped. The work, especially in the

Toccata, is very rhythmic. Shifting meters and syncopated rhythms prevail, although they should not overly challenge groups at this level.

Unit 7: Form and Structure

FORM

MEASURE	SECTION
1	4-note motive, first in piano, repeated in mallets and wood-winds obscuring the bar lines
19	Chorale theme in English Horn
28	Chorale theme in Trumpets, now harmonized
37	Transition, in percussion
41	First appearance of recurring Toccata motif
53	Toccata theme in Trumpets
57	Toccata theme in Woodwinds
62	Recurring Toccata motif
72	Toccata theme in inversion
81	Recurring Toccata motif
90	Toccata theme in canon at 2-bar entries
94	Toccata theme in canon at 1-bar entries
98	Inverted Toccata theme in canon at 1-bar entries
104	Recurring Toccata motif with change in harmonization
112	Opening 4-note motive returns in woodwinds
113	Recurring Toccata motif in Trumpets
114	Toccata theme in Trombones metrically displaced
120	Repeated Toccata fragment
128	Chorale in augmentation in brass
138	Toccata theme in inversion (from measure 101)
143	Recurring Toccata motif
155	Opening motive, harmonized
159	Cadence to C Major

Unit 8: Suggested Listening

Howard Hanson, *Chorale and Alleluia*
Robert Jager, *Chorale and Toccata*
Jack Stamp, *Divertimento in "F", Elegy and Affirmation, Past the Equinox*
Ralph Vaughan Williams, *Toccata Marziale*

Unit 9: Additional References and Resources

Rehrig, William H. *The Heritage Encyclopedia of Band Music.* Westerville, OH: Integrity Press, 1991.

Teacher Resource Guide

"English Folk Song Suite"
(Movement I–March–Seventeen Come Sunday)
(Movement II–Intermezzo–My Bonny Boy)
(Movement III–March–Folk Songs from Somerset)
Ralph Vaughan Williams
(b. 1872–d. 1958)

Unit 1: Composer

Ralph Vaughan Williams was born in Down, Ampney, England in 1872, and died in London in 1958. He was acknowledged as Britain's leading composer after the death of Sir Edward Elgar in 1934, and he was the leader of the 20th-century English national school. From 1938 until his death, his time was devoted to composition, folk song research and publication, church music, and music for amateur use. His main contributions include nine symphonies and other orchestral works, including *Variations on a Theme by Thomas Tallis*, solo works such as the *Tuba Concerto*, choral works, operas, and several works for band, including *Sea Songs*, *Toccata Marziale*, *Flourish for Wind Band*, and *Rhosymedre* (arr. Beeler). His *Symphony No. 8* contains *Scherzo alla Marcia*, a movement composed entirely for wind section and often performed as an individual work by wind ensembles.

Unit 2: Composition

English Folk Song Suite was composed for British military band in 1924. It is in three movements (March—Seventeen Come Sunday, Intermezzo—My Bonny Boy, and March—Folk Songs from Somerset). Based entirely on folk music sources, the work is approximately nine and one-half minutes long.

Unit 3: Historical Perspective

English Folk Song Suite, along with the two Suites by Gustav Holst, was one of the first works in this century's repertoire of compositions specifically composed for wind band. Vaughan Williams's use of folk music materials can be attributed to his nearly life-long interest and research in English folk songs. Folk sources can be found in many of his other works from this period, as Nationalism in music flourished during the years between the two world wars.

Unit 4: Technical Considerations

The tonal center for the first movement is F dorian, with modulation to Ab Major for the entire B section. The meter is 2/4, and the tempo c. 116-120 equal to quarter-note. Vaughan Williams superimposes a technically challenging 6/8 woodwind obligato over 2/4 in section C.

The tonal center for the second movement is F dorian. The meter is 3/4, and the tempo c. 72 equal to quarter-note. There is an interlude "Poco Allegro Scherzando" where the meter remains 3/4, but the tempo increases to c. 72 equal to dotted half-note. All players will need to be fluent with the F dorian (Eb Major) scale and arpeggio. A mature sense of phrasing and tone quality is required. Piccolo and cornet solos are very exposed, and require musically sensitive playing.

The tonal centers for the third movement include Bb Major, C aeolian (C natural minor), and Eb Major. The meter for this march is 2/4, with a trio in 6/8 (much like the first movement). Low brass are required to execute fast sixteenth-note passages with accuracy. There is a technically challenging upper woodwind unison melody in the trio that requires fluent performance of the C natural minor scale. Facility in the extreme upper range is demanded in the flute parts here, and all clarinets must play up to a unison high D above the staff—all this at a dynamic level of piano.

Unit 5: Stylistic Considerations

FIRST MOVEMENT

The melodies of the three songs in the work, "I'm Seventeen Come Sunday", "Pretty Caroline", and "Dives and Lazarus", must be performed with folk-like lyricism. Large sections of the work are delineated by textural and dynamic contrast; a light articulate style is required for the A section, a lyrical legato for B, and a heavy marcato style for C. The graceful cornet solo of "Pretty Caroline" (section B) requires a warm tone and confident playing.

SECOND MOVEMENT

The dark, brooding character of the "My Bonny Boy" theme in the outer sections of this movement requires a richness of tone and warmth of expression. The scherzando of the interlude, which contains the folk tune "Green Bushes" demands lightness and facility of technique. Like the other movements, the lyricism and cantabile qualities of the folk music must sing through. The phrases of My Bonny Boy are simple, but their intensity and contour must be carefully shaped. This plaintive, mournful song has many opportunities for *rubato* and expressive dynamic nuance. The accompaniment must remain subtly quiet and flowing. All entrances must be tenuto, all releases unhurried.

THIRD MOVEMENT

The bright, joyful character of the outer sections of this march requires a light and clearly articulated style, as well as careful attention to dynamics and stylistic markings. The woodwind melody in the trio is very exposed, and must remain light even though the technical demands are severe. The brass fanfare in the second half of the trio must be marcato and forte, but with characteristic British pomp and reserve. Like in the other movements, the lyricism and cantabile qualities of the folk music must sing through.

Unit 6: Musical Elements

FIRST MOVEMENT

The form of this movement is standard British march form (ABCBA). Sections are clearly defined by textural and timbral contrast. The texture is mainly homophonic, often with a theme set against a repetitive, syncopated accompaniment and simple bass line. Compositional techniques include the use of modal harmonies and melodies and superimposing 6/8 meter over 2/4.

SECOND MOVEMENT

The form of this movement is ABA. Large sections are clearly delineated by textural, timbral, and rhythmic contrast. The texture is mainly homophonic, with some phrases containing simple countermelodies with chordal accompaniment. Compositional techniques include the use of modal harmonies and melodies, basic rhythmic modulation, and rhythmic augmentation of the theme.

THIRD MOVEMENT

The form of this movement is A-B(trio)-A. Large sections are clearly delineated by textural, dynamic, and rhythmic contrast. The texture is homophonic throughout. Compositional techniques include the use of modal harmonies and melodies, basic rhythmic modulation, and rhythmic augmentation of the theme. The folk tunes used are "Morning Dew", played by the cornet solo at the beginning; "High Germany", played by the low brass in the second strain; "The Tree So High", heard in the woodwinds at the trio; and "John Barleycorn", sung out by the brass in the last strain on the trio.

Unit 7: Form and Structure

1ST MOVEMENT

MEASURES	SECTION	TONAL CENTER	MUSICAL EVENTS
1-30	A	F dorian	4-bar intro, followed by two phrases of "I'm Seventeen", first time by woodwind w/ lightly-textured accomp., 2nd time tutti
31-64	B	Ab Major	2-measure transition, followed by four 8-measure phrases of "Pretty Caroline" (32-bar song form, aaba); light, legato, cantabile style
65-96	C	F Dorian	C section (Trio); melody in low brass, ww obbligato in 6/8; heavy marcato style throughout
97-128	B	G minor	Restatement of "Pretty Caroline"
129-161	A	F Dorian	Restatement of "I'm Seventeen" following a 4-bar transition; 3-bar codetta concludes

2ND MOVEMENT

MEASURES	SECTION	SUB-SECTION	TONAL CENTER	MUSICAL EVENTS
1-2	A	Introduction	F dorian	F minor chord
3-19		Theme I- "My Bonny Boy"		Oboe/Cornet solos
20-22		transition		3-bar fl/Eb clar. transition into restatement; line continues on as counter-melody
23-40		Theme I		Restatement in low brass and low woodwinds
41-43		transition		3-bar cantabile clarinet solo
44-60	B	Theme II- "Green Bushes"		New tempo marking *poco allegro scherzando*; Theme II stated in piccolo/oboe/Eb clarinet soli

| 61-78 | | Theme II | | Theme stated in cornet, euph, alto clar. and alto sax soli; Eb and Bb clar's play eighth-note arpeggios; section concludes with 2-bar rit. and transition back to Tempo I |
| 79-98 | A | Theme I | | Restatement of Theme I in antiphonal 4-bar statements between low brass/low woodwinds and cornets/clarinets; rhythmic augmentation of theme in final four measures |

3RD MOVEMENT

MEASURES	SECTION	SUB-SECTION	TONAL CENTER	MUSICAL EVENTS
1-4	A	Introduction	Bb Major	Intro based on last 4 measures of "Morning Dew"
5-28		Theme I		Cornet solo, 1st statement of "Morning Dew"
29-44		Theme II	G Aeolian	Low brass play "High Germany"
23-40		Theme I	Bb Major	Cornet solo, restatement of "Morning Dew"
41-42		transition		2-bar 6/8 transition into trio
43-60	B	Theme III	C Aeolian	"The Tree So High" stated in the woodwinds; p dynamic level, 6/8 meter
61-78		Theme IV	Eb Major	"John Barleycorn" played in low brass; contrast to previous section—forte, marcato march-style
79-98	A	Theme I		Complete Restatement of Introduction and A Section

Unit 8: Suggested Listening

Ralph Vaughan Williams, *Toccata Marziale, Sea Songs, Symphony No. 8, Variations on a Theme by Thomas Tallis, Overture to The Wasps*
Gustav Holst, *Second Suite in F*

Unit 9: Additional References and Resources

Dvorak, Thomas L., Robert Grechesky, and Gary Ciepluch. *Best Music for High School Band.* Brooklyn, NY: Manhattan Beach Music, 1993.

Fennell, Frederick. "Vaughan Williams' Folk Song Suite." *The Instrumentalist*, XXX June 1976, 45-48.

Pittman, Daniel Sayle, Jr. "Percy Grainger, Gustav Holst, and Ralph Vaughan Williams: A Comparative Analysis of Selected Wind Compositions." Diss., Memphis State University, 1979.

Sadie, Stanley. *The New Grove Dictionary of Music and Musicians.* London: Macmillan, 1980.

Smith, Norman and Albert Stoutamire. *Band Music Notes.* Lake Charles, LA: Program Note Press, 1989.

Teacher Resource Guide

"Fantasia in G Major"
Johann Sebastian Bach

(b. 1685–d. 1750)

transcribed by Richard Franko Goldman

(b. 1910–d. 1980) and Robert L. Leist (b. 1921)

Unit 1: Composer

Johann Sebastian Bach was born in Eisenach, Germany on March 21, 1685. He was a renowned organist, composer and violinist in Germany during his lifetime. He held positions in Weimar as court organist and Concert Master under Duke Wilhelm Ernst (1708-1717), in Cöthen as *Kapellmeister* to Prince Leopold (1717-1723), and in Leipzig as director of music in the churches of Saint Thomas and Saint Nicholas and cantor of the Thomasschule (1723-1750). He wrote extensively for keyboard, including works for harpsichord, clavichord, and organ.

Unit 2: Composition

The great G Major Fantasia for organ is the middle portion of a three-part Fantasia for organ, listed as #572, Volume XXXVIII in the Bach *Gesellschaft* edition of the complete works. Date and place of composition are listed as "...1705/6 Arnstadt (or Weimar?)". It was here, at the beginning of his career, that his music was found by the Consistory to be too full of "wonderful variations and foreign tones," and certainly the Fantasia is strikingly dissonant in its constant texture of suspensions. But, the breadth of the five-part polyphonic writing and the richness of the harmonic sonority make the Fantasia one of the grandest of all Bach's compositions for organ. It is also one that lends itself well to the sound and sonority of the modern wind band. The piece is one movement, is a Grade 4 difficulty and lasts about six and a half minutes.

Unit 3: Historical Perspective

The transcription by Richard Franko Goldman and Robert L. Leist was undertaken as a memorial to Edwin Franko Goldman, who was the first bandmaster to include the works of Bach regularly in the band's concert repertoire, and who did so much to introduce the music of this great master to wide popular audiences. In the transcription, an attempt is made to recapture the sound of the Baroque organ through the medium of the modern band. The first performance of the transcription was given by The Goldman Band, Richard Franko Goldman conducting, on July 1, 1957.

Unit 4: Technical Considerations

The scales of G Major and its related keys are required for the entire ensemble. The rhythmic demands are very basic, with the use of whole, half, quarter, eighth, and sixteenth notes. Some ornaments (such as inverted mordents) are written out in thirty-second notes. Accuracy in ensemble to achieve organ style is essential. There are no tempo changes, and special care must be given to ensure that while the tempo does not rush, the piece does push forward consistently. Ranges and scaler passages are not difficult (cornet I plays a high C at the end). The clarinet parts should be of approximately equal strength, and flutes and oboes should be as strong as possible.

Unit 5: Stylistic Considerations

Dynamics encompass a wide variety with several crescendos and diminuendos. Rich and full tone quality is required, as well as ensemble blend, to achieve the organ style. This music is ideally suited to the sonority and performance resources of today's large wind band—a sort of living organ from which the necessary continuous outpouring of sound is limited only by the skill with which the players provide the breath that produces it. The chief problem in performance is that of maintaining a smooth and sustained tone, with full note values at all times. Phrasing should be consistent, and phrases should not be too markedly separated.

Unit 6: Musical Elements

The piece is in the concert key of G Major and several related keys and consists of a single movement with a single, but driving, tempo (Grave h equal to 48/50). The original time signature, preserved in this transcription, is 2/2, but there is no reason why the conductor may not perform the work as 4/4 since many will feel a more comfortable pulse in four—especially if a relatively broad movement is kept. The harmony is typical of late-Baroque music and Bach in particular. Special care should be taken to ensure that tied notes, especially those resulting in dissonances to be resolved, are carried through without loss of tone or volume, and not released prematurely. The breadth, sonorities, and magnificence of this music originally written for organ makes it ideal for transcription as a band number but also makes it challenging for an ensemble to maintain a uniform blend and sound throughout the entire work.

Unit 7: Form and Structure

Phrase 1	Beginning to A; G Major, false movement to D Major
Phrase 2	A to B; G Major
Phrase 3	B to C; E minor
Phrase 4	C to D; G Major
Phrase 5	D to E; A minor
Phrase 6	E to F; G Major, all woodwinds only
Phrase 7	F to G; A minor, brass only
Phrase 8	G to H; G Major, restatement of Phrase 1
Phrase 9	H to I; A minor, restatement of Phrase 1
Phrase 10	I to K; G minor, C Major, A minor
Coda	K cadence to G Major for closing, crescendo to end

Unit 8: Suggested Listening

J.S. Bach, *Toccata and Fugue in D minor, BWV565*

J.S. Bach/arr. Stokowski, *Toccata and Fugue in D minor, BWV565*

J.S. Bach/arr. Hindsley, *Toccata and Fugue in D minor, BWV565*

J.S. Bach/arr. Hunsberger, *Toccata and Fugue in D minor, BWV565*

J.S. Bach/trans. Erik Leidzen, *Toccata and Fugue in D minor, BWV565*

J.S. Bach, *Passacaglia and Fugue in C minor, BWV582*

J.S. Bach/arr. Hunsberger, *Passacaglia and Fugue in C minor, BWV582*

Unit 9: Additional References and Resources

Baker, Theodore. "Bach, Johann Sebastian," *Baker's Biographical Dictionary of Musicians*. 6th ed., revised by Nicolas Slonimsky. New York: Schirmer Books, 1984.

Grout, Donald. *A History of Western Music*. 3rd edition. New York: W. W. Norton & Company, Ltd, 1980.

Kopetz, Barry. "Bach's Fantasia in G." The Instrumentalist, XLVIII August 1993, 25-34.

National Band Association Selective Music List for Bands

Rehrig, William H. *The Heritage Encyclopedia of Band Music*. Westerville, OH: Integrity Press, 1991.

Westrup, J. A. and F. Ll. Harrison. *The New College Encyclopedia of Music*. Revised by Conrad Wilson. New York: W. W. Norton & Company, Ltd, 1981.

Whitwell, David. "Bach—Wind Music." *The Instrumentalist*, XXI November 1966, 39.

Teacher Resource Guide

"First Suite in E-flat"
(Chaconne, Intermezzo, March)
Gustav Holst
(b. 1874–d. 1934)

Unit 1: Composer

Gustav Holst, along with Ralph Vaughan Williams, served as the models of British composition in the first half of the twentieth century. Holst used the traditions of Elizabethan folk music, infused with early 20th-century compositional techniques, to form a new British style based on melody. Characteristically, his compositions are guided by melody, prominent at all levels of hearing. The companion work to the *Suite in E-flat* is the *Second Suite in F*, composed two years later.

Unit 2: Composition

The *First Suite* was composed in 1909, and for the most part the only known wind bands of the era were either military, like the Guard Republicaine of Paris, or touring bands such as Sousa's or Gilmore's. Holst would have been most familiar with the military band, and his original instrumentation (including bass saxophone, cornets, trumpets, and flugel horns) indicates the brass-heavy writing typical of military bands. The suite uses traditional forms in all three movements, but the first movement is mislabeled as a chaconne; it is really a passacaglia in form. It is usually considered a medium-difficulty work, primarily due to length (about eleven minutes), the stamina required for the brasses, and the woodwind and cornet solos.

Unit 3: Historical Perspective

Since *Suite in E-flat* was composed in 1909, it is generally considered to be the first significant composition approximating what is today's standard band instrumentation. It utilizes classical forms with an occasional modern variation—for example, the use of simultaneous recapitulation in the last movement. The trend of writing for wind bands during the early years of this century favored imitating the military literature and major genre, the march, and that is used here as the concluding movement. What sets this work apart, however, is its treatment of the band as potential soloists. Many instruments have solos, and there is frequent use of small groups of instruments being treated as chamber ensembles. There is a strong parallel in Vaughan Williams' *Folk Song Suite*, written fourteen years later (and probably the only parallel in these early years of modern band composition).

Unit 4: Technical Considerations

Most of the First Suite is in the key of E-flat Major, but the scales of C minor, C Major, and A-flat Major should be familiar to the ensemble as well. There are no strenuous rhythmic considerations other than mildly syncopated figures in the last movement. The second movement features a number of solos: piccolo, oboe, clarinet, cornet. There are also solos in the first movement featuring the aforementioned instruments and alto sax (letter C). The most challenging technical demands are on the woodwinds, who must negotiate a unison sixteenth note passage in the first movement for eight measures. This is mostly diatonic material, however. Solo cornet has several solos and must play high 'C' on a few occasions. Otherwise, the brass demands are moderate. Percussion scoring uses snare, bass, cymbal, triangle, and timpani; these parts are not very challenging.

Unit 5: Stylistic Considerations

First Suite in E-flat requires careful control of articulation and balance. Classical in format and construction, each movement has a set tempo; there are only three tempo changes in the entire composition. In the first movement, the prevailing style of all parts should be horizontal and broad. Regular eight-measure phrases make shaping of line easier. In the second movement, articulation should be approached as in chamber music: light and not too short in *staccato* passages. The third movement must be thought of as British march style, not as fast as American marches and with no heavy tonguing.

Unit 6: Musical Elements

This composition is a delightful introduction to the passacaglia form; it would even be fitting to study in a composition seminar. Each statement of the passacaglia theme is, in effect, a variation. In rehearsal, stressing what is retained and what is new in each phrase is helpful. The section containing the inverted theme (in the ninth variation) is a good place to compare and contrast key, melodic structure, and scoring. In the second movement, there is good opportunity to discuss sequence and pointillism in melody. Fragmentation occurs in the A sections of the second movement, while the B section is very contrasting. Students could be asked to list the number of ways the A and B sections differ.

Unit 7: Form and Structure

I. CHACONNE (ACTUALLY PASSACAGLIA)

A

theme	Var.1	Var.2	Var.3	Var.4	Var.5	Var.6	Var.7	Var.8

E-flat Major

theme and variations 8 measures each except Var.13

B			A			(recap)		coda
Var.9	Var.10	Var.11	Var.12	Var.13	Var.14	Var.15	Var.16	
C minor			E-flat Major					

II. Intermezzo (ABA form)

A

a	b	a
mm. 1-24	25-42	43-66

C minor

B antecedent and consequent

a	a'	transition
mm. 67-82	83-98	99-108

C Major

A (greatly shortened)
mm. 119-122

Coda (using A and B material juxtaposed)
mm. 123-142

III. MARCH (MARCH FORM)

intro	first strain	trio	false recap and devel.	recap+trio	coda
m.1-4	5-36	37-88	89-122	123-168	169-179
E-flat		A-flat	transition to E-flat	E-flat	E-flat
Major		Major	Major	Major	Major

Unit 8: Suggested Listening

Gustav Holst, *Second Suite in F*
Gustav Holst, *Hammersmith*
Gustav Holst, *The Planets*
Ralph Vaughan Williams, *Folk Song Suite*
Edward Elgar, *"Enigma" Variations*

Unit 9: Additional References and Resources

Dvorak, Thomas L., Robert Grechesky, and Gary Ciepluch. *Best Music for High School Band*. Brooklyn, NY: Manhattan Beach Music, 1993.

Mitchell, Jon C. "Early Performances of the Holst Suites for Military Band." *Journal of Band Research* XVII/2 (Spring 1982): 44-50.

Mitchell, Jon Cleander. "Gustav Holst: The Works for Military Band." Diss., University of Illinois, 1980.

Rehrig, William H. *The Heritage Encyclopedia of Band Music*. Westerville, OH: Integrity Press, 1991.

Smith, Norman and Albert Stoutamire. *Band Music Notes*. Lake Charles, LA: Program Note Press, 1989.

Tarwater, William Harmon. "Analyses of Seven Major Band Compositions of the Twentieth Century." Diss., George Peabody College for Teachers, 1958.

Watkins, Glenn. *Soundings*. New York: Schirmer Books, 1988.

Teacher Resource Guide

"Irish Tune from County Derry"
Percy Grainger

(b. 1882–d. 1961)

Unit 1: Composer

Percy Grainger, a composer and pianist, was born in Australia. His first musical experiences were from his mother, who taught him piano. At age ten, he performed his first recital, and his recognizable talent earned him the opportunity to study in Europe. By age eighteen, he had performed on three continents of the eastern hemisphere and was a recognized authority on the interpretation of Bach. During his travels, he became friends with Edvard Grieg, and the two promoted each other's music before Grieg's death in 1907. His interpretation of Grieg's *Concerto* earned him great acclaim. During these years, Grainger became an expert in the collection of folk songs in the British Isles. He began experiments in random music, electronics, and irregular meter long before Cage, Varèse, and Bartok. After a stint as an army bandsman (where his love for the soprano sax was established), Grainger moved to America, where he became famous in spite of his extremely eccentric behavior and reputation as a (mere) folk-song collector and arranger. It is only in recent years that his foresight as an *avant-garde* composer and troubled genius has been recognized.

Unit 2: Composition

The composition originates from the famous Irish folk song "O Danny Boy", first published in Ireland in 1885. Grainger wrote four settings of this song, all for differing instrumentation and all between the years 1902-1918. Many sources list the date of composition as 1909, but this may be in error. The second arrangement, for piano, is dated July 1911 and labeled "British Folk-Music Setting Nr. 6." The band arrangement, published in 1918, bears the inscription, "British Folk-Music Setting Nr. 20." It thus seems very unlikely that 1909 would be the date

255

of composition. This was not his first writing for band; the two *Hill Songs* were written between 1901 and 1907. The title page bears the inscription, "Lovingly and reverently dedicated to the memory of Edvard Grieg." This is understandable since Grieg had died a few years earlier and was friends with Grainger. The composition itself is only 64 bars long and all in the key of F, but features Grainger's love of counterpoint and technique of burying the melody occasionally within the texture. The compositional technique is reminiscent of Grieg's late Romantic style and the overall form is a simple two-verse form. Although moderate from a technical standpoint, this five minute composition requires a high degree of phrasing ability and a mature tone from all performers.

Unit 3: Historical Perspective

Grainger had already written his *Hill Song #1 and #2* for winds after reaching an agreement with Boosey and Hawkes in which he could borrow different instruments for a short time to learn their capabilities. His fascination with folk song could be traced to both his friendship with Grieg and his belief in the superiority of folk music, with its rhythm dependent upon the particular singer. At the time of these arrangements, only Holst and Vaughan Williams had written for modern band and their compositions of the period were also based upon folk song. It is noteworthy that this was the start of modern writing for band. Since the work was probably written in 1918, or shortly before, Grainger's instrumentation was probably influenced by the size of the military band at Fort Hamilton in Brooklyn, where Grainger served.

Unit 4: Technical Considerations

The tonality of *Irish Tune* is in F Major throughout, with no modulations. In terms of rhythm, this work poses no challenges whatsoever. From the standpoint of sustained playing, exposure of tone quality, and intonation challenges, however, the music is moderately difficult in all respects. Euphonium, cornet 1, and trombone 1 must play high concert A on their instruments. There are short cornet and horn solos. The (solo) flute and oboe must be able to match pitches exactly and are exposed throughout the music. The (solo) horn has an eight-measure solo beginning at m. 41 and must play a high A. The exposed parts in soprano sax and cornet 1 also provide a formidable challenge in tuning. The conductor will find it challenging to keep the melody prominent in the thickly contrapuntal writing.

Unit 5: Stylistic Considerations

The major interpretive considerations are the use of *rubato* and the playing of sustained, shaped phrases by the ensemble. The regularity of phrases helps to place appropriate rising and falling of volume within the phrases. The melody is not always in the highest voice, though, and in these cases overlapping voices, especially cornet 1, must be hidden within the texture. Grainger wrote only a condensed score and parts, but he gave many generalities of dynamic and tempo changes. For the conductor, standardizing where the ensemble breathes will greatly help ensemble phrasing. The tempo is marked "Flowingly, quarter note equal to about 80," but in the three earlier editions the word "slowly" or "slowish" is included. In this light, a speed of 56 to 69 beats per minute is recommended. In measures 58-63, the countermelody should be equal in volume to the melody.

Unit 6: Musical Elements

There are no complex harmonies in the composition; this reflects Grainger's view of the melody as unadorned and simplistic. There is a considerable amount of counterpoint in which the suspension is the prominent non-harmonic tone. A thick polyphonic texture permeates the entire composition, and one can easily view the influences of Bach and Grieg. The melody moves mostly stepwise, only two leaps of a sixth throughout; the melody remains in the major mode with no chromatic alterations. In fact, there are extremely few accidentals in any of the parts. A natural rise and fall to the melody regulates the phrases to four measures each. The entire composition is in common time, evident even in the thick contrapuntal style.

Unit 7: Form and Structure

A		measures 0-32	
	verse 1a	measures 0-16	alto clarinet, baritone sax, horn 4, trombones 1-2, euphonium with melody
	verse 1b	measures 17-32	tenor sax, horns 1-4, trombones 1-2 with melody mm.17-24 horns 1-4, trombone 1, euphonium with melody mm.25-28 alto clarinet, baritone sax, horns 3-4, trombones 1-2, euphonium with melody mm.29-32
A'		measures 33-64	
	verse 2a	measures 33-48	flute with melody mm.33-40 flute, alto saxophone, horn 1 with melody mm.41-48
	verse 2b	measures 49-64	flute, E-flat clarinet, clarinet 2, soprano sax, cornet 1, cornet 3 (only to m.57) with melody

Unit 8: Suggested Listening
Percy Grainger, *Hill Song #2*
Percy Grainger, *Lincolnshire Posy*
Ralph Vaughan Williams, *Folk Song Suite*
Gustav Holst, *Suite No. 2 in F*

Unit 9: Additional References and Resources

Dvorak, Thomas L., Robert Grechesky, and Gary Ciepluch. *Best Music for High School Band*. Brooklyn, NY: Manhattan Beach Music, 1993.

Fennell, Frederick. "Percy Grainger's Irish Tune From County Derry and Shepherd's Hey." The Instrumentalist, XXXIII September 1978, 18-25.

Grainger, Percy. Ed. R. Mark Rogers. *Irish Tune from County Derry*. San Antonio: Southern Music, 1994.

Rehrig, William H. *The Heritage Encyclopedia of Band Music*. Westerville, OH: Integrity Press, 1991.

Smith, Norman and Albert Stoutamire. *Band Music Notes*. Lake Charles, LA: Program Note Press, 1989.

Uggen, Stuart. "Percy Grainger in Perspective." *The Instrumentalist*, XXIV June 1970, 38-41.

Wilson, Brian Scott. "Orchestrational Archetypes in Percy Grainger's Wind Band Music." Diss., The University of Arizona, 1992.

Teacher Resource Guide

"Liturgical Music for Band, Op. 33"
Martin Mailman

(b. 1932)

Unit 1: Composer

Martin Mailman was born in New York City on June 30, 1932. He received his B.M., M.M. and Ph.D. from the Eastman School of Music where he studied composition with Louis Mennini, Wayne Barlow, Bernard Rogers and Howard Hanson. Dr. Mailman is the recipient of many awards and commissions including the Edward Benjamin Award (1955), prizes from the Birmingham Arts Festival (1966), Willamette University (1966), and the Walla Walla Symphony (1967), an NEA grant (1982), the Queen Marie-Jose Prize (1982), the Shelton Excellence in Teaching Award (1982), the Annual ASCAP Award, the American Bandmasters Association/NABIM award (1983), the National Band Association/Band Mans Award and the American Bandmasters Association/Ostwald Award (1989). He has been a guest conductor, composer, lecturer and clinician at numerous international, national, regional and state meetings as well as universities, high schools and festivals. He has over ninety compositions to his credit, involving genres such as chamber music, band, choral, orchestra, film scores, television music and opera. Some of his other works for band include *Geometrics for Band, Op. 22; Exaltations, Op. 67;* and *For precious friends hid in death's dateless night, Op. 80.*

Unit 2: Composition

Liturgical Music for Band, Op. 33, completed in 1963 in Greenville, North Carolina, was commissioned by the Greenville County High School Band, Emporia, Virginia (John Savage, director) and was premiered by that group in 1963. The piece is in four movements, is of Grade four difficulty, and lasts about ten minutes.

Unit 3: Historical Perspective

Mailman belongs to a generation of late-twentieth-century composers that includes Ron Nelson and Fisher Tull. He was one of the composers selected to participate in the Ford Foundation Project, an important vehicle for several aspiring musicians. He is currently in demand as composer, conductor and clinician, and his works are already highly-respected, as is evidenced by his *For precious friends hid in death's dateless night* becoming the first piece to ever win both the ABA/Ostwald Prize and the NBA/Band Mans Award in the same year.

Unit 4: Technical Considerations

The piece has no key signatures, so accidentals abound. There are changes of meter within movements, but only on the quarter-note level. The tempos remain consistent within the movements. There are both staccato and legato articulations, so contrast is important. Instruments rarely have exposed sections or solos, but the percussion section is featured prominently, especially in the third movement. Ranges and scalar passages are not difficult. The E-flat clarinet has some difficult parts, and the clarinet section is required to sustain several sections softly.

Unit 5: Stylistic Considerations

Articulations should be as accurate as possible. All markings in the score support this. Each section has its own style but a certain drive should propel the work throughout. The intensity and movement of the music should be equal to the phrasing, articulation, rhythms and principles of the line. This is a twentieth-century work with twentieth-century sounds; it should be approached with a twentieth-century interpretation.

Unit 6: Musical Elements

The piece is based on four movements selected from the Mass Proper and Ordinary. The ensemble has the opportunity to learn about the parts of the Mass. There are times when the band must play in a chime-like style to sound like bells. There is also a fugue in the fourth movement which would require some instruction. The theme of the second movement is the same rhythm as the word "Kyrie", and the theme of the third movement is the same rhythm as the word "Gloria". The second movement also has the same three sections as the Kyrie from the Mass. Key areas are sometimes difficult to identify, but solid cadences occur at the ends of the movements.

Unit 7: Form and Structure

MOVEMENT I: *INTROIT*	G Major, C Major, other related keys
ALLEGRO MODERATO	Mm. 1-22, opening, chime-like fanfare, tutti
	Mm. 23-51, call and answer between WW's and low brass

	Mm. 52-58, transition to fanfare theme
A little broader	Mm. 59-71, return of opening, chime-like fanfare, tutti
MOVEMENT II: *KYRIE* ADAGIO A TEMPO	G minor & other related keys
	Mm. 1-25, "Kyrie eleison", clarinets featured
	Mm. 26-44, "Christe eleison", brass alternating with WW
	Mm. 45-60, "Kyrie eleison", clarinets featured
MOVEMENT III: *ALLELUIA* GIOCOSO	F Major & other related keys
	Mm. 1-19, introduction
	Mm. 20-29, fugato
	Mm. 30-60, underlying drive in low brass and reeds
	Mm. 61-69, transition
	Mm. 70-79, theme augmentation with fragmentation
	Mm. 80-85, tutti, closing
MOVEMENT IV: *GLORIA* ALLEGRO ENERGICO	C Major & other related keys
	Mm. 1-22, fugato, four different instrument entrances
	Mm. 23-38, chorale theme, tutti
	Mm. 39-57, theme fragmentation throughout ensemble
	Mm. 58-67, chorale theme, tutti
	Mm. 68-73, tutti, material based on countersubject
	Mm. 74-81, tutti, chordal, closing, ending in C Major

Unit 8: Suggested Listening

Howard Hanson, *Chorale and Alleluia*
Martin Mailman, *For precious friends hid in death's dateless night*, Op. 80
Martin Mailman, *Liturgical Music for Band*, Op. 33
Martin Mailman, *Secular Litanies for Band*, Op. 90
Matthew Mailman, *Effects for Symphonic Band*
Ron Nelson, *Rocky Point Holiday*

Unit 9: Additional References and Resources

Baker, Theodore. "Mailman, Martin," *Baker's Biographical Dictionary of Musicians.* 6th ed., revised by Nicolas Slonimsky. New York: Schirmer Books, 1984.

National Band Association Selective Music List for Bands

Rehrig, William H. *The Heritage Encyclopedia of Band Music.* Westerville, OH: Integrity Press, 1991.

Teacher Resource Guide

"Night Dances"
Bruce Yurko

(b. 1951)

Unit 1: Composer

Bruce Yurko, born in 1951, received his music degrees from Wilkes College and Ithaca College. His composition studies at Ithaca included work with Karel Husa. Yurko is currently the Director of Wind Ensembles at both Cherry Hill (New Jersey) East and West High Schools. As a composer, Yurko has written a number of works for band and wind ensemble and published them himself. These works include *Divertimento for Wind Ensemble*, *Chant and Toccata*, *Rituals*, and *Sinfonia No. 3*. His compositions also include several concerti, including *Concerto for Wind Ensemble*, *Concerto for Horn*, and *Concerto for Trombone*.

Unit 2: Composition

Night Dances, first published by the composer in 1994, was commissioned by the Dover Middle School Concert Band. The work is dedicated to that ensemble and its director, Albert Muccilli. Composed with middle school technical capabilities in mind, *Night Dances* is a richly-scored piece that was titled after completion. Its moods and rhythmic vitality suggested "dances" to the composer, particularly of a twentieth-century flavor. The work is approximately six minutes in length.

Unit 3: Historical Perspective

A general trend in band literature for young musicians, particularly middle school instrumentalists, has been to concentrate on "block scoring", where instrumental parts are consistently doubled throughout a work, or on the musical elements that make popular music so well-known (bland, syncopated melodies with predictable harmonic and rhythmic accompaniment). As a result, less attention has been placed on the elements that young students (through lack of playing technique and experience) rarely encounter: motivic development and transformation, unique and advanced harmonic progressions, lighter scoring with attention to unique instrumental combinations, and a role for the percussion section other than timekeeping. Yurko is one of a number of innovative composers that are helping young band musicians experience a variety of interesting compositional techniques at an easier level. In turn, the students' experience in making music is ultimately more rewarding.

Unit 4: Technical Considerations

The work is not based in a specific tonal key, but it is easy to hear because motives are consistently repeated at the same pitch level or include sequential repetitions. The instrumentation is extended for a young band: piccolo, flute I-II-III, oboe, Bb clarinet I-II-III, Bb bass clarinet, bassoon, alto saxophone I-II, tenor saxophone, baritone saxophone, trumpet I-II-III, horn I-II-III-IV, trombone I-II-III, baritone, tuba, and an extensive percussion section (timpani, bass drum, five tom-toms, chimes, tenor drum, orchestra bells, gong, claves, crash cymbals, and vibraphone-with motor). The time signature of 4/4 is used throughout. The rhythmic structure is composed of whole, half, quarter, and eighth note combinations. The percussion parts include a variety of sixteenth-note combinations. The keyboard mallet parts are exposed but not technically demanding.

Unit 5: Stylistic Considerations

A sustained, legato style is required from the entire ensemble (i.e., mm. 17-34), with solid breath control. Crisp articulations with staccato note lengths dominate the texture in the *con spirito* sections of the work (mm. 99-109). The percussion instruments are used consistently throughout, for motivic presentations and for color. The scoring calls for clear, distinct sounds from the keyboard instruments, requiring that a variety of mallet choices be available. The tom toms, particularly in the percussion ostinato (mm. 19-49), must be tuned carefully and be played with timpani mallets that will still convey a clean, articulate sound. The dynamic contrast ranges from *piano* to *fortissimo*, with sudden changes, forte-piano attacks, crescendos, and diminuendos. Motives are presented in distinct instrumental colors, indicating important balance and listening considerations.

Unit 6: Musical Elements

A variety of motives are presented throughout the work that are identified with specific instrumental families. The percussion section, for example, presents one motive that is built on sequential tritone intervals (mm. 8-16, 53-56) and another that features a leap of a ninth (mm. 2-16). The latter is the foundation of a new motive that is initially introduced by the clarinets in the following section of the piece (mm. 23-25). This motive is subsequently passed to the lower woodwinds and brass (mm. 27-34). An energetic minor third brass motive introduces the *con spirito* section of the work (m. 57), leading to a prominent trumpet fanfare motive which is presented in unison (mm. 73-80). The entire ensemble, in turn, echoes this motive, with a final presentation in the timpani (mm. 89-116).

Unit 7: Form and Structure

Introduction	percussion section soli; motives presented in chimes and vibraphone/bells (tritones); early presentation of flute motive	mm. 1-18
Section A	percussion provides rhythmic ostinato as accompaniment texture below flute motive; clarinets answer with transformed chime motive; brass state similar answer in unison; build in texture and dynamics, followed by gradual decrease, with augmentation of motives in flute and clarinet;Introductory percussion material returns, with complementary colors in flutes and clarinets	mm. 19-56
Section B	trumpets and trombones introduce minor third motive; accompaniment consists of sustained pedal Bb, spread throughout seven octaves; added pitch "F" outlines Bb minor triad	mm. 57-70
Section C	con spirito; unison trumpet fanfare motive, features intervals of perfect fourth and fifth harmonic series on open valves; major second added to complete the motive; horns and trombones included in motive presentation; return to unison trumpets, accompanied by Bb sound mass in woodwinds and remaining brass; entire ensemble presents motive or fragments, leading to a sustained chord built on motivic pitches Bb, F, C, G; timpani reiterate motivic fragment as intensity and sound subside	mm. 71-115
Section D	Andante; clarinet thematic area derived from inverted minor third motive as timpani accompanies with fanfare motive; flutes, saxophones, and horns added to clarinet theme, as trumpets, trombones, baritone, and tuba join timpani in fanfare presentation	mm. 116-136
Section C	con spirito; return to full ensemble presentation of fanfare motive	mm. 137-144
Section B	return of minor third motive, with added F to form Bb minor triad	mm. 145-157

Coda   sound mass, consisting of superimposed Bb Major,
                    D Major, and D minor seventh chords, accompanies solo
                    timpani presentation of fanfare motive
                                        mm. 158-164

Unit 8: Suggested Listening
Bruce Yurko, *Divertimento for Wind Ensemble, Concerto for Horn, Concerto for Wind Ensemble*

Unit 9: Additional References and Resources
"Basic Band Curriculum: Grades I, II, III." *BD Guide*, September/October 1989, 2-6.

Duarte, Leonard P., Daniel S. Hiestand, Carol Ann Prater, Doy E. Prater. *Band Music That Works*. Volume 1. Burlingame, California: Contrapuntal Publications, 1987.

Duarte, Leonard P., Daniel S. Hiestand, Carol Ann Prater, Doy E. Prater. Band Music That Works. Volume 2. Burlingame, California: Contrapuntal Publications, 1988.

Dvorak, Thomas L., Cynthia Crump Taggart, and Peter Schmaltz. *Best Music for Young Band*. Edited by Bob Margolis. Brooklyn, New York: Manhattan Beach Music, 1986.

Garofalo, Robert J. *Instructional Designs for Middle/Junior High School Band*. Fort Lauderdale, Florida: Meredith Music Publications, 1995.

Kreines, Joseph. *Music for Concert Band*. Tampa, Florida: Florida Music Service, 1989.

Ludwig Music Publishing Company, Cleveland, Ohio

Rehrig, William H. *The Heritage Encyclopedia of Band Music*. Edited by Paul E. Bierley. Westerville, Ohio: Integrity Press, 1991.

Teacher Resource Guide

"Old Home Days (Suite for Band)"
(Waltz, The Opera House and Old Home Day,
The Collection, Slow March,
London Bridge is Fallen Down)
Charles Ives
(b. 1874–d. 1954)

arranged by Jonathan Elkus
(b. 1931)

Unit 1: Composer

Charles Ives was born in Danbury, Connecticut and lived in New England all of his life. His father, George, a famous Civil War bandmaster, was Charles' first and most influential teacher. From his father, Charles learned both traditional and unorthodox ways of creating and looking at music. Although Charles was an extremely prolific composer, he was virtually unknown during his lifetime for musical accomplishments. Instead, he was quite famous for his pioneering work in the insurance industry. Ives' own theories and publications about life insurance were used by other insurance firms for many years. His business successes allowed Charles to publish his compositions, which were, by and large, considered unperformable due to their difficulty. His experiments in polytonality, sound masses, microtonality, and new formal structures were at least twenty years ahead of their time; it could be said that he foreshadowed Copland, Schuman, Cowell, and Berio in these techniques. Typical of the musical *cognoscenti*'s tardiness in finding his music, his *Symphony No. 3* received the Pulitzer Prize in 1947, although it was composed at least twenty years prior. Ives disliked and never quite understood all the attention given his music, but he had a fierce belief in composing from recollections and surrounding events, regardless of what anyone

267

else thought. Ives is considered today a very individualistic composer of visionary genius.

Unit 2: Composition

Although Charles Ives wrote all of the music for *Old Home Days*, it should be noted that four of the six movements (two songs are combined in movement 2) were originally written for voice and/or keyboard. Elkus transcribed these for band and arranged them into a suite. All of the music was written early among Ives' compositions. The first movement, *Waltz*, is an adaptation of the early popular song "Little Annie Rooney". The second movement begins with Ives' song "Memories". The first line of the song, "We're waiting at the opera house", describes the expectancy of the opening curtain. When the curtain does open, however, the "narrator" (Ives/Elkus) has a flashback of a drum roll, town bands, and the ringing of bells. This song is "Old Home Day" which features quotations of popular tunes of Ives' boyhood. "The Collection" was from an organ setting of *Tappan* featuring the church offertory, a soprano soloist, and the choral response. "Slow March" was possibly Ives' first song, written for the death of the family dog. It should be noted that Ives quotes from Handel's oratorio *Saul* and combines this skillfully with his own lyrics and original music. The last movement is Ives' variations (he used the term "take-off" for this treatment) on *London Bridge is Fallen Down!* Several well known compositional techniques of Ives are prominent in the last movement. The total length of the composition is nine minutes.

Unit 3: Historical Perspective

Since most of the music in *Old Home Days* was written prior to 1920 and for organ or voice and piano, there arises the question as for suitability for arrangement. Ives was very interested, however, in bands and their music, even incorporating early 20th-century band music into his compositions for orchestra. Since the vast majority of works being performed by bands in the early part of this century were marches and transcriptions, it seems suitable to include this suite as both a tribute to that era and as an introduction to Ives' music. When rehearsing this work, mention should be made to the popular tunes quoted within and their significance in American music history circa, 1900. Original band music written at the turn of the century was scarce, but includes significant works such as Grainger's *Ye Banks and Braes O' Bonnie Doon* and the Holst *Suite No. 1 in E-flat*.

Unit 4: Technical Considerations

The keys of C, E-flat, F, G-flat, A-flat, and B-flat Major should be known to the ensemble. The ensemble should be familiar with playing triple meter with one beat per measure conducted (movement 1) as well as some knowledge of compound meter (movement 2). In the last half of movement 2, woodwinds must tongue triplets and sixteenths at 126 beats per minute. The third movement features a cornet solo and an exposed countermelody in flute and E-flat clarinet. A short oboe duet occurs in the same movement, but it is not technically difficult. The fourth movement features short alto sax, clarinet, and trumpet solos; the fifth movement has a bi-tonal section starting at rehearsal 32 and offset rhythmic patterns at rehearsal 35 that is intended to make the ensemble sound "lost." The last twelve measures are composed to deliberately sound cacophonous. Third and fourth horns flutter tongue in the last measure. There are no extremes of tessituras, and the overall technical demands are moderate.

Unit 5: Stylistic Considerations

All styles of articulation are utilized in the suite, and Elkus is very specific about the notation markings. The carat is used frequently with an added accent. Melodies are indicative of the early 20th century; accompanimental figures are more difficult since many are written to purposely clash with the melody in both key and rhythm. A light tonguing style is necessary for woodwinds in the second and last movements, while soloists must play in a *cantabile* style in the third and fourth movements.

Unit 6: Musical Elements

In the first movement, chromatic countermelodies are present in a tonal framework. Traditional band forms (verse and refrain, "roll off") are found in the second movement. The third and fourth movements are quite simple tonally, while polyrhythms and polytonality must be explained and rehearsed in the last movement. Separate tonal centers and rhythmic patterns from rehearsal number 32 until the ending should be rehearsed separately.

Unit 7: Form and Structure

Movement 1	intro.	A^1	A^2	codetta	A^1	A^2	codetta
	m.1	#1	#2	#3	#5	#6	#7

Movement 2a	A^1	A^2	B^1	B^2	A^1	A^2
	#8	#9	#10	#11	#12	#13

Movement 2b	intro	A	B	A	B
	#15	#16	#17	#18	#19

Movement 3	intro	verse1	refrain	intro		verse2	refrain
	m.1	#21	#22	#23		#25	#26

Movement 4	intro	A	B+truncated A	codetta (using intro material)
	m.1	#27	#28	#29

Movement 5	intro	verse1	bridge	verse2	verse3	verse4	verse5	verse6
	m.1	#30	#31	#32	#33	#34	#35	#36

Unit 8: Suggested Listening

Henry Cowell, *The Tides of Manaunaun*

Charles Ives, *114 Songs* (especially *Flanders Field*)

Charles Ives, *Variations on 'America'*

Charles Ives, *Piano Sonata #2, "Concord, Mass., 1840-1860"*

Charles Ives, *Old Home Days*

   (Cincinnati College-Conservatory of Music, Eugene Corporon, Conductor;
   KCD-11042)

   (University of Miami, OH, Wind Ensemble, Gary Speck, Conductor; KCD-
   11042)

Unit 9: Additional References and Resources

Burk, James. "The Wind Music of Charles Ives." *The Instrumentalist*, XXIV
   October 1969, 36-40.

Cowell, Henry, and S. Cowell. *Charles Ives and His Music.* New York: 1955.

Hitchcock, H. Wiley. *Ives.* London: 1977.

Milligan, Terence. "Charles Ives: A Survey of the Works for Chamber Ensemble
   which Utilize Wind Instruments (1898-1908)." *Journal of Band Research* XVIII/I
   (Fall 1984): 60-68

Perlis, Vivian. *Charles Ives Remembered: An Oral History.* New York, NY:
   Da Capo Press, 1974.

Teacher Resource Guide

"Pageant"
Vincent Persichetti
(b. 1915–d. 1987)

Unit 1: Composer

Vincent Persichetti studied composition with Roy Harris and conducting with Fritz Reiner, and was a graduate of The Philadelphia Conservatory and the Curtis Institute. In 1947, Persichetti joined the faculty at the Juilliard School of Music, where he served as chair of the department of composition for many years. His works in virtually every form and media have been performed by premiere ensembles all over the world. Persichetti always had a special relationship with the concert band medium, contributing many works to the repertoire including *Symphony No. 6*, as well as *Masquerade, Divertimento for Band, Psalm for Band*, and several original chorale preludes.

Unit 2: Composition

Pageant, composed in 1953, was Persichetti's third work for band. It is in two-part form; the piece opens in a slow tempo with solo horn playing a three-note motif that recurs throughout the work, followed by a slow chorale section. The second part of the form is quick and lively (likened to a parade by the composer), with Persichetti's characteristic stylings, including concise sections of articulate counterpoint, abrupt contrasts of texture, and timbral juxtaposition between phrases.

Unit 3: Historical Perspective

Pageant was commissioned by Edwin Franko Goldman for the American Bandmasters Association in 1953. The first performance was by the University of Miami Band, with Persichetti conducting, at the ABA Convention in Miami. This was one of Persichetti's earliest works for band, preceding his *Symphony No. 6*, whose fourth movement shares many compositional characteristics with *Pageant* (most notably thematic writing for percussion and the technique of simultaneous recapitulation of themes).

Unit 4: Technical Considerations

The writing throughout the work is idiomatic, without extremes in range, making this one of Persichetti's more technically accessible works for high school or college band. The playing must be strong in all sections of the band in order to effectively perform rapidly alternating antiphonal soli statements. There are important solos for horn, trumpet, piccolo, and important soli sections for all instruments. The chorale section requires a mature control of tone and pitch; phrases are brief, and endurance is not as difficult an issue as control of pitch within the frequently polytonal harmonies. The allegro section requires facility of technique, but challenges are rudimentary. The execution of frequent accidentals and rapidly changing harmonies will present challenges.

Unit 5: Stylistic Considerations

The first, chorale-like section of this music requires expressive playing and sonorous tone production and should be as legato as possible. Because of the polyphonic scoring of the work, care must be taken to achieve balance and bring out the inner voices. The motif heard in the first two measures of the piece is important throughout the work, and an understanding of the work's themes and formal construction are crucial to an effective interpretation. Care must be taken to enhance the flow of one section into another, particularly in the fast music, in order to prevent harsh, block-like phrasing. Careful attention to releases, and a unified interpretation of the various themes and motives are important ways to avoid this "choppy" effect. A strong sense of direction and contour of the music is vital for the performers to effectively control the work's energy flow toward its dramatic conclusion.

Unit 6: Musical Elements

Melodic ideas in the work are largely based upon two brief motives. Motive 1 is a three-note figure that moves by leap, containing either a perfect fourth or perfect fifth. Motive 2 is a step wise tetrachord spanning the interval of a perfect fourth. Thematic and sub-thematic materials are constructed based on the motives. The harmonic idiom is polytonal and polyphonic, with contrapuntal writing prevalent throughout.

Unit 7: Form and Structure

MEASURES	SECTION	TONAL CENTER	MUSICAL EVENTS
1-2	Intro	Bb	Horn solo; three-note Motive 1
3-10	A		First chorale statement in three-voice harmony by clar.s;

			contains motives 1 & 2
11-18			8 bar phrase of counterpoint, ww dominated texture; begins on motive 2
18-27			Brass antecedent (mm. 18-21); ww consequent (mm. 22-27) statements based on Motive 1
27-29			transition - motive 2
30-34	B	C	Counterpoint in upper ww, sim. to mm. 11-18
35-42		G	WW antecedent (mm. 35-38); brass consequent (mm 39-42) statements based on motive 1
43-50	A1	Bb	Recap. of first chorale theme clar.s; picc. obliggato based on motive 2
51-58			Rich, developmental counterpoint, omitting straight-bore brass timbre
58-66		C	Antecedent (tpts/tbns); consequent (ww/conical brass)
67-72		Bb	Codetta; fragmented statements of motives 1 and 2 serve as transition to fast section
73-76	A		Perc. intro of Allegro, based on Theme I
77-81		Bb	First melodic statement of Theme I
82-92			Development of Theme I
93-101			transition
101-107		C	First Statement of Theme II
108-121		G	Development/fragmentation of Theme II
122-129			transition
130-151	B	Bb	Four bar sections of Theme III alternate with sections of Theme II set in counterpoint; timbral and textural juxtaposition between themes
152-159		Eb	Theme II
160-177			Development of motive 1

178-185		Bb	transition, with materials from previous transition sections developed
186-189	**B1**	Ab	Theme I
190-213		C	Theme II presented twice, each time followed by sections of material developed from motive 2
214-221		Eb	Theme II
222-229			Development of motive 1
230-243			transition, with materials developed
245-251	**A**	Bb/Eb	Simultaneous recap. of Themes I and II
252-255			Percussion break based on Theme I
256-262		Bb/Eb	Theme II
263-279			transition
280-289	**Coda**	Bb/Eb	Simultaneous recap. of Theme I and II
290-293		Bb	Closing brass fanfare
294-295			Final chord cluster containing all 12 pitches except B, C# and F#; missing three pitches have same interval content as opening motive 1

Unit 8: Suggested Listening

Persichetti, *Symphony No.6 for Band, Masquerade, Divertimento, Bagatelles, Psalm for Band*

Unit 9: Additional References and Resources

Dvorak, Thomas L., Robert Grechesky, and Gary Ciepluch. *Best Music for High School Band*. Brooklyn, NY: Manhattan Beach Music, 1993.

Hilfiger, John Jay. "A Comparison of Some Aspects of Style in the Band and Orchestra Music of Vincent Persichetti." Ph.D. diss., The University of Iowa, 1985.

Morris, Donald Alan. "The Life of Vincent Persichetti, with Emphasis on his Works for Band." Ph.D. diss., The Florida State University, 1991.

Morris, Donald and Jean Oelrich. "Vincent Persichetti Remembered: Music from Gracious to Gritty." *The Instrumentalist*, XLVII/4 November 1992, 30-38.

Morris, Donald. "Persichetti Rediscovered: The Manuscripts of Vincent Persichetti's Band-Works - Part One: Pageant and the Symphony for Band (Symphony No. 6)." Journal of Band Research XXVIII/1 (Fall 92), 1-20.

Prindl, Frank Joseph. "A Study of Ten Original Compositions for Band Published in America Since 1946." Diss., The Florida State University, 1956.

Workinger, William Colvin. "Some Aspects of Scoring in the Band Works of Vincent Persichetti." Diss., New York University, 1970.

Teacher Resource Guide

"Prelude, Siciliano, and Rondo"
(Movement I, Prelude)
(Movement II, Siciliano)
(Movement III, Rondo)
Malcolm Arnold
(b. 1921)
arranged by John Paynter
(b. 1928–d. 1996)

Unit 1: Composer
Born on October 21, 1921 at Northampton, England, Malcolm Arnold is today one of England's most recognized and successful composers. An accomplished composer of symphonies, concertos, chamber music, and a variety of film scores (including "The Bridge Over the River Kwai"), his music is characterized by an immodest freedom of spirit and an unusually humorous, lighthearted style. He was educated at the Royal College of Music, where he studied composition with Gordon Jacob. As a performer, he played trumpet professionally with the London Philharmonic and BBC Symphony, and since 1948 has devoted much of his time to conducting.

Unit 2: Composition
Prelude, Siciliano and Rondo was originally composed as a brass band work entitled *Little Suite for Brass*. John Paynter, Director of Bands at Northwestern University, completed this arrangement for band, expanding the piece to include woodwinds and additional percussion, but faithfully retaining the light, sparkling character of the original work.

Unit 3: Historical Perspective

Prelude, Siciliano and Rondo is a contemporary work in the tradition of fine English music for wind band by Holst, Vaughan Williams, and Jacob. The work's tuneful, almost folk-like melodies are characteristic of the British band tradition, as is the composite, multi-movement form of a suite. Arnold's other works for band (which are also arrangements), *Four Scottish Dances*, *English Dances*, and *Four Cornish Dances* are in this same tradition.

Unit 4: Technical Considerations

FIRST MOVEMENT

Rhythmic demands are basic. There are frequent entrances on weak beats, and syncopation is a factor. Tonal centers vary and include Bb Major, Ab Major, G Lydian, Eb Lydian, D minor, and D Major. However, the technical demands in these keys are not severe. Low Brass and low woodwinds must execute Db Major, and F Major scales in eighth notes at quarter equal to 112. Flutes and xylophone must play a brief ascending Bm7 arpeggio in sixteenth notes at quarter equal to 112.

SECOND MOVEMENT

The tonal center for the movement is Eb Major, with brief moments of modulation and some altered chords. The meter is 6/8, and the suggested tempo is dotted-quarter equal to 60, although this music is often taken at a slower tempo, c. 52 beats per minute. Rhythmic demands are basic, except for a difficult eight-bar, sixteenth-note obbligato passage in the clarinets. They must be able to arpeggiate the following chords in sextuplets at 60 beats per minute: Eb Major, Bb minor, Ab augmented, C dominant 7, F minor 7, Ab half-diminished 7, and Bb dominant 7. Harp, vibraphone, English horn, contrabass clarinet, contrabassoon and string bass parts add much to the score, but are frequently cross-cued, and can be substituted without loss of essential musical material. For example, the harp/celeste part that is mostly cross-cued could be performed on piano, marimba, or vibraphone. Lyrical and sensitive playing is required, particularly from solo cornet.

THIRD MOVEMENT

The tonal center for the movement is Bb mixolydian, with brief moments of modulation and some altered chords. The meter is 3/4, and the suggested tempo is quarter equal to 152. Rhythmic demands are more demanding here than in the other movements, particularly with regard to syncopated accompaniment patterns. Good double-tonguing skills are required from the brass in order to achieve required tempo and exciting style. Solid technique is required from all players. Harp, vibraphone, English horn, contrabass clarinet, contrabassoon and string bass parts add much to the score, but are frequently cross-cued, and can be substituted without loss of essential musical material. Piccolo, flutes, Eb and

Bb clarinets, alto clarinet, bass clarinet, bassoon, baritone, tuba and xylophone must execute a Bb melodic minor scale in sixteenth notes.

Unit 5: Stylistic Considerations

FIRST MOVEMENT

The Prelude, beginning much like a fanfare, is an exciting opener to the work. A detached style of articulation is important in order to enhance the exciting rhythms, especially the eighth- and sixteenth-note figures. Special attention must be given to stress the differences between the various articulation markings, especially staccato and marcato. The texture is polyphonic, and contrasting textures and sonorities must be well-balanced. The snare drum plays an important thematic role in the music of the first six measures, and must not be covered by the tutti chords in the ensemble.

SECOND MOVEMENT

Achieving the desired lilting quality of the 6/8 siciliano is a necessary, though often difficult, task. The quarter-note of the quarter-eighth ostinato pattern that exists as an accompaniment throughout most of the movement should be tenuto, and the eighth-note very light. Releases should be gently tapered and reluctant. The sixteenth note that follows the dotted-eighth in the melody should be played almost like an upper-neighbor grace note. An expressive singing style is desirable throughout. Expressive dynamic nuances should be added to the melodic contours of this beautiful melody.

THIRD MOVEMENT

A quick tempo, light style and excellent technique are required for this movement to be most effective. Contrasting styles of articulation are utilized throughout the movement, and dynamics encompass a wide range of expression. Sudden textural and dynamic shifts create contrast between sections. The syncopated rhythmic accompaniment must be performed with a light, staccato articulation. Proper execution of written accents are required to achieve the proper rhythmic style.

Unit 6: Musical Elements

FIRST MOVEMENT

The form of this movement is five-part song form (ABACA), with introduction and coda. The movement begins strongly in a fanfare style, recedes, then reaches a middle climax before winding down to a quiet return of the opening theme that fades to silence. Sections B and C are developmental. Compositional techniques include simple polyphony (two-part counterpoint) and the use of complementary themes, or *countermelodies*.

SECOND MOVEMENT

The form of this movement is five-part song form (ABACA), with introduction and coda. The texture is mainly homophonic. Compositional techniques include borrowed chords, chromatic harmonies, and brief moments of tonicization. Most of this harmonic activity occurs in parts B and C, which are transient development sections. Simple, four-bar phrases pervade the movement, and contour and linear direction are important for an effective interpretation.

THIRD MOVEMENT

The form of this movement is five-part song form (ABACA) with coda. Sections are clearly defined by textural and timbral contrast. The texture is mainly homophonic, often with a theme set against a repetitive, syncopated accompaniment and simple bass line. Compositional techniques include the use of modal harmonies and melodies, borrowed chords, chromatic harmonies and brief moments of tonicization, and moments of antiphonal statements between instrumental groups.

Unit 7: Form and Structure

MOVEMENT I, PRELUDE

MEASURES	SECTION	TONAL CENTER	MUSICAL EVENTS
1-8	Intro	Bb Major Ab Major	Three-measure fanfare theme (theme 1) presented three times in different keys; root movement of harmonies by perfect fourth (Bb-Eb-Ab-Db); complementary theme A played by Tenor and Bari sax, horn 3, 4, baritone and trombone III
9-18	A	G Lydian Eb Lydian	Theme 2 set in canon in brass, upper woodwinds and saxes introduce complementary theme B; after four bars, harmony modulates to Eb Lydian from G Lydian
19-23	B	D minor	Development of complementary theme A, set as a brass fanfare in canon between trumpets and horns/trombones/ baritone/ snare drum
24-29	A	D Major	Two brief restatement of main themes 1 and 2 as they are juxtaposed in counterpoint
30-38	C	D Major Bb Major	Development of complementary themes A and B in two-part counterpoint, woodwinds, horns and xylophone

MEASURES	SECTION	TONAL CENTER	MUSICAL EVENTS
39-47	A	Bb Major	Final statement of theme 2 and complimentary theme B
48-55	coda	Bb Major	Fanfare theme A restated in quiet setting without complementary theme

MOVEMENT II, SICILIANO

MEASURES	SECTION	TONAL CENTER	MUSICAL EVENTS
1-4	Intro	Eb Major	Introduction of rhythmic ostinato that accompanies the main theme in each statement
5-20	A	Eb Major	Eight-bar main theme introduced in cornet solo, second statement in cornet, flutes, and E. horn
21-28	B	Eb Major w/tonic-ization to V/V	Brief development based on ostinato material; increased harmonic activity: tonicization, chromatic harmony
29-44	A	Eb Major	Two restatements of main theme; first time with clarinet obbligato, second time with tutti, homophonic texture
45-53	C	B minor, Bb Major	Brief development based on ostinato material; antiphonal statements between brass/woodwind groups; increased harmonic activity: borrowed chords, chromatic harmony
54-69	A	Eb Major	Final two statements of main theme in woodwinds and solo cornet
70-75	Coda	Eb Major	Quiet six-measure conclusion based on ostinato

MOVEMENT III, RONDO

MEASURES	SECTION	TONAL CENTER	MUSICAL EVENTS
1-24	A	Bb	Opening statement of 12-bar rondo theme, Mixolydian tutti-forza, followed by second statement by smaller forces

25-32	B	Alternates between D Major and Bb melodic minor	Brief eight-bar development based on piece of rondo theme. Entire section repeated without alteration of musical materials
33-44	A	Eb Major	Restatements of rondo theme; first time with flute/oboe/bells soli and harp obbligato, second time with tutti, homophonic texture
45-60	C	G minor	New, contrasting legato theme introduced; simplified, "waltz-like" accompaniment in contrast to syncopated rhythms of other sections; minor harmony
61-81	A	Bb Mixolydian	Two statements of rondo theme; first time in low brass and low woodwinds, second time in climactic final statement
82-95	coda	Bb Mixolydian	Coda in two parts; first part slowly building Fm7 chord, *presto* second part in Bb drives to exciting conclusion

Unit 8: Suggested Listening

Malcolm Arnold, *Four Scottish Dances, English Dances, Four Cornish Dances*

Unit 9: Additional References and Resources

Dvorak, Thomas L. *Best Music for Young Band*. Brooklyn, NY: Manhattan Beach Music, 1986.

Dvorak, Thomas L., Robert Grechesky, and Gary Ciepluch. *Best Music for High School Band*. Brooklyn, NY: Manhattan Beach Music, 1993.

Sadie, Stanley. *The New Grove Dictionary of Music and Musicians*. London: Macmillan, 1980.

Smith, Norman and Albert Stoutamire. *Band Music Notes*. Lake Charles, LA: Program Note Press, 1989.

Teacher Resource Guide

"Scenes from 'The Louvre'"
(The Portals, Children's Gallery, The Kings of France, The Nativity Paintings, Finale)
Norman Dello Joio
(b. 1913)

Unit 1: Composer

Norman Dello Joio was born in New York City and descended from three generations of organists; he himself was a church organist and choir director at age fourteen. He attended the Juilliard School for three years, then transferred to Yale, where he studied with Paul Hindemith. He held positions at Sarah Lawrence College (NY) and at the Mannes College of Music in New York City, where he was Professor of Composition. In 1972, he moved to Boston, and from 1972 to 1979, was Dean of the School of Arts at Boston University. Dello Joio has composed for virtually every medium, including television. In addition to winning an Emmy in 1965 for the original version of this score and the New York Music Critics Circle Award, he won the Pulitzer Prize in 1957 for *Meditations on Ecclesiastes*. Another notable and well-known work for band is *Variants on a Medieval Tune*.

Unit 2: Composition

Scenes from "The Louvre" was originally written for orchestra to accompany an NBC television special on the Louvre gallery. Broadcast in November 1964, the version for band was commissioned by Baldwin-Wallace College for its Symphonic Band, conducted by Kenneth Snapp. The transcription was completed and premiered in 1966 with the composer conducting. The composition is a suite of the television music, portraying the museum's development during its construction. Cast in five movements, classical forms are used such as binary, strophic, and theme with variations. The composition does not have a particularly modernistic sound due to its original purpose as descriptive music, but Dello Joio uses a liberal dash of chromaticism, adding spice to his accompaniments. Parallels to *Variants on a Medieval Tune* are apparent, especially in the fourth movement. A chorale and *cantus firmus* treatment of development figure prominently in the third movement.

Unit 3: Historical Perspective

Since 1950, more and more "serious" composers had been paying attention to the band as a viable medium for composition. Spurred on by the acceptance and quality of such works as Piston's *Tunbridge Fair*, Schuman's *George Washington Bridge*, and Morton Gould's *West Point Symphony*, the 1950s were the germinal decade for growth in American bands and composers. By the 1960s, there was a veritable explosion of compositions for bands of all musical levels. Dello Joio, as a composer of band music, was extremely important because he was known both to popular culture (as a writer for television) and to academic circles (as the 1957 Pulitzer Prize winner). *Scenes from "The Louvre"* served to combine the fascination with bands and with television at the same time. A parallel may be seen in David Amram's *King Lear Variations*, originally written for BBC television.

Unit 4: Technical Considerations

Most of the composition is built around the keys of C, G, and F Major. However, much of the music has chromatic alterations, which may prove a challenge for sight-reading. Much of the technical challenge comes from rhythmic independence, which is prominent in every movement. Movement two has the most pointillistic passages, with sixteenth note figures broken up among ten different instruments for four measures. There are no extreme demands on the performer from the standpoint of tessitura. The only solos are for clarinet and oboe; extended solos exist for the trumpets, horns, and woodwinds. The oboe's technical demands require a high 'D' and sustained upper register playing for several measures. As for meter, the first, second, and fourth movements are written in compound meter and have some difficult, non-syncopated rhythms. The independence of parts in these places should be considered carefully.

Unit 5: Stylistic Considerations

In general, this composition uses music meant to imitate *Renaissance* styles in the middle three movements; this is surrounded by two outer movements deliberately composed to give a feeling of grandeur and of entrancing and exiting. This should be a consideration in rehearsing this music. The middle movement, in particular, is set apart by its use of chorale and canon. This movement should stand apart as the most *legato* and *espressivo* playing. In movements two and four, articulation throughout should be in the *Classical* manner; e.g. lightly tongued and detached (rather than short) *staccato* notes. In the outer movements, the fanfare concept should predominate.

Unit 6: Musical Elements

Although major tonalities are prevalent, modality is frequently used as descriptive of the *Renaissance* period. The use of actual Elizabethan melodies (*in dulce jubilo*, for example) serves to enhance this long-ago feeling. The outer movements contain the greatest degrees of dissonance; the inner movements rely on either major keys or mixolydian modes. Melodic structure is achieved mostly through diatonic means or arpeggios; wide leaps are rare. In the first and third movements, contrast between sections of the movement is achieved through changes in meter, specifically to compound meter. This gives the impression of variation form rather than sectional.

Unit 7: Form and Structure

Within the five movements, arch form: ABCBA

MOVEMENT 1   EXTENDED FANFARE AND PROCESSIONAL

intro	A	A developed	B	B′	codetta
m.1	m.12	m.20	m.26	m.35	m.45

MOVEMENT 2   THEME AND VARIATIONS

intro	theme	var. 1	var.2	var. 3
m.1	m.10	m.17	m.23	m.39

MOVEMENT 3   CHORALE AND DEVELOPMENT

A	B (canon)	C (canon)
m.1	m.19	m.40

MOVEMENT 4   STROPHIC

intro	A	A′ (embellished)
m.1	m.6	m.22

MOVEMENT 5   STROPHIC-RONDO

4 fanfares	A	A′	trans.	A″ codetta
m.1	m.17	m.25	m.32	m.35 m.43

Unit 8: Suggested Listening

Norman Dello Joio, *Variants on a Medieval Tune*
Norman Dello Joio, *A Jubilant Song*
Norman Dello Joio, *Meditations on Ecclesiastes*
Fisher Tull, *Sketches on a Tudor Psalm*

Unit 9: Additional References and Resources

Baker, William Elmer, Jr. "Developing Musicality Through the Junior High School Band Program." Diss., Columbia University, 1974. (background, genesis, analysis)

Dvorak, Thomas L., Robert Grechesky, and Gary Ciepluch. *Best Music for High School Band.* Brooklyn, NY: Manhattan Beach Music, 1993.

Rehrig, William H. *The Heritage Encyclopedia of Band Music.* Westerville, OH: Integrity Press, 1991.

Smith, Norman and Albert Stoutamire. *Band Music Notes.* Lake Charles, LA: Program Note Press, 1989.

Teacher Resource Guide

"Second Suite in F (Op. 28 No.2)"
(First Movement "March")
(Second Movement "Song Without Words")
(Third Movement "Song of the Blacksmith)
(Fourth Movement "Fantasia on the Dargason)
Gustav Holst
(b. 1874–d. 1934)

Unit 1: Composer
Gustav Holst was born in Chettenham, England in 1874, and died in London in 1934. After graduating from the Royal College of Music, Holst earned a living as a professional trombonist. From 1904, Holst focused his musical pursuits on composing and teaching. In addition to his duties as music director of St. Paul's Girls School in London, Holst held teaching positions at Morley College, the Royal College of Music, and for a short time at Harvard University. His compositional output includes operas, symphonies, ballets, chamber music, solo songs, choral works, and several works for wind band, including *First Suite in E-Flat*, *Second Suite in F*, and *Hammersmith, Prelude and Scherzo* (op. 52).

Unit 2: Composition
Second Suite in F was composed in 1911, but was not performed until 1922. Unlike the *First Suite in E-Flat*, the Second Suite is based entirely on material from folk songs and morris dances. The work is approximately ten and a half minutes in length and is in four movements (I: March, II: Song Without Words, III: Song of the Blacksmith, and IV: Fantasia on the Dargason).

Unit 3: Historical Perspective

The *Second Suite in F* was one of the first works in this century's repertoire of compositions specifically for wind band. Holst's use of folk music materials can be attributed to his rediscovery of English folk songs. Nationalism in music flourished during the years between the two World Wars and composers' interest in folk music was indeed an important element in that movement. But Holst was also attracted to the economy of means and directness of expression in folk songs. His concern for clarity of expression in his music was also influenced by his study of Eastern philosophy.

Unit 4: Technical Considerations

FIRST MOVEMENT

Tonal centers include F Major and B-flat Dorian mode. Performance challenges begin in the first measure, where Holst requires the euphonium and basses to execute the first five notes of an ascending F Major scale as staccato eighths. The euphonium has a substantial solo later in the movement that requires maturity of tone and expression. Rhythmic demands are relatively light in the outer sections of the movement, which are in cut-time. The middle section, in 6/8, requires a fluid execution of D-Flat pentatonic scale patterns (eighth notes) by woodwinds and first cornet.

SECOND MOVEMENT

Tonal center for the entire movement is F Dorian. The piece demands a mature concept of expressive, legato style from the soloists (clarinet, cornet, alto saxophone, euphonium, bass) and accompanists. Contour and shaping of the phrase are crucial to unlocking this movement's expressive potential. Rhythms are basic, but flowing eighth-note lines in the accompaniment require constant attention to subdivision, and a concerted effort to avoid rushing. Pitch challenges are pervasive, particularly between flutes, oboe, E-flat clarinet and trumpet at mm. 19-32.

THIRD MOVEMENT

The majority of the technical demands in this movement are rhythmic. Mixed meters are prevalent throughout (usually 4/4 & 3/4). A syncopated but repeating ostinato-accompaniment figure pervades most of the movement in the brass and low woodwinds. The Blacksmith tune, performed at various times by upper woodwinds, alto/tenor saxophones, first cornet, and/or horns, requires exacting execution of somewhat challenging dotted-sixteenth/32nd-note rhythms. Euphonium and first and second trombone must to be able to articulate brief sixteenth-note patterns in the range of fourth space G up to F. The final chord requires an A above the staff from trombone I. An anvil, or a suitable substitute, is an integral part of the percussion section.

FOURTH MOVEMENT

Tonal center throughout the movement is F Major. The F Major and chromatic scales are required for all instruments. Rhythmic demands include playing eighth-note patterns in 6/8 (dotted quarter equal to 160), and superimposing 3/4 against 6/8. Important solo playing is required of cornet I, euphonium, clarinet, alto saxophone, piccolo, and tuba. The antiphonal piccolo/tuba duet that closes the movement can be rhythmically challenging, and will require special attention in rehearsal.

Unit 5: Stylistic Considerations

FIRST MOVEMENT

The interpretation of this movement should be guided by the phrasing, contour and characteristic style of the three folk melodies it contains: "Morris Dance", a traditional dance tune from English rural areas;" Swansea Town", a sprightly sea chantey named for a Welsh coastal town; and "Claudy Banks", a Hampshire folk song. These folk melodies should be interpreted in a direct, singing style; a clarity and economy of style is most appropriate, without exaggeration. It is important to maintain the pulse and drive of a march throughout the various sections.

SECOND MOVEMENT

The interpretation of this movement should be guided by the phrasing and contour of this romantic setting of a beautiful English folk song. "I'll Love My Love" is a Cornish song about a woman driven to insanity by her grief over the loss of her lover. This plaintive, mournful love song is appropriately set in the dark key of F minor (dorian). The melody should always be *cantabile*, and, unlike the first movement, there are opportunities here for *rubato* and expressive dynamic nuance. The accompaniment must remain subtly quiet and flowing; all entrances must be tenuto, all releases unhurried. Proper treatment of apoggiaturas is crucial; tension and weight should be added, then released on the resolution. As written, the final chord has a tendency to end abruptly. Frequently, the final chord is held slightly longer than written to avoid this.

THIRD MOVEMENT

Consistency and unity of articulation are especially crucial to an effective performance of this work. The ostinato pattern must be executed in a uniformly marcato style. Holst's articulation markings are especially clear to the melodic instruments, and should be followed with precision. Perhaps most important is the setting of a proper tempo; *Moderato e Maestoso* does not mean fast or rushed—this music should be allowed to have weight. The dynamic contrast at m. 19 is especially important. Pace the dynamic volume throughout the work so that a fff can be achieved with control at the final statement of the tune at m. 24.

FOURTH MOVEMENT

The eight-measure "Dargason" tune, an old English folk tune known to exist since the 16th century, is stated consecutively 25 times over 200 measures in a series of constant-melody variations. Every member of the ensemble is called upon to perform this tune at least once. Therefore it is important for all players to consistently match their styles of articulation and rhythmic interpretation of the tune. Frederick Fennell suggests that players should "make the quarter vibrant, tenuto, and long" and "toss off the eighth" in this iambic rhythm. He also suggests whistling the tune as a means of discovering its proper, "light but incessant" style. The tempo should remain fixed throughout, at dotted-quarter equal to c.160. The tempo is frequently challenged at both entrances of the second folk tune "Greensleaves," which is in 3/4 time superimposed over the 6/8 Dargason. The conductor should conduct in one, but everyone involved needs to diligently subdivide to avoid slowing.

Unit 6: Musical Elements

FIRST MOVEMENT

Although the prevailing texture is homophonic, Holst creates textural contrast between major sections by changing styles of articulation, subdivision of pulse, and harmonic rhythm. The most striking contrast occurs at the trio, where the subdivision abruptly changes from simple time to compound, and the key area modulates to the minor subdominant mode (Bb dorian). Within sections, contrast is enhanced by antiphonal effects between brass and woodwinds.

SECOND MOVEMENT

As in every movement of this work, the melodic line and its attributes must predominate all other elements. The entire movement is in the dorian mode, reflecting the music's folk origins. The absence of a leading-tone seventh enhances the movement's dark, brooding character. It also challenges the performers to enhance harmonic tension and provide a sense of linear direction without the convention of functional harmony.

THIRD MOVEMENT

The chord progression of the two-measure ostinato pervading most of the movement is harmonically interesting and structurally important. The progression centers around G dorian, and the chords contain open-fifth sonorities. An interesting aspect of its use as an accompaniment is that it remains harmonically static, even while the melody is being performed in different keys (the first and third statements are in D aeolian, the second in G aeolian). At the third and final statement, Holst alters the first chord of the two-measure ostinato (F replaces G dorian) which serves to enhance the brilliant affect of the climactic statement. The final D Major chord is derived from the key of the final statement of the tune, D aeolian, but with a raised, or "Picardy," third.

FOURTH MOVEMENT

As with all types of variation forms, it is important for the interpreter to recognize contrasting elements between sections, as well as those elements which remain constant. This fantasia is a set of 25 constant-melody variations, where the melody remains essentially unchanged in each variation. Holst creates variation of timbre (orchestration), rhythm, dynamics, and harmonic accompaniment. The prevailing texture throughout the Suite is homophony, but each entrance of "Greensleeves" results in a heterophonic texture—two-part polyphony with homophonic accompaniment. These entrances are also examples of phrase elision between the two melodies. The final eleven measures of the piece, a tuba/piccolo duet based on fragments of the "Dargason" tune, recall the antiphonal effects of the opening of the first movement.

Unit 7: Form and Structure

FIRST MOVEMENT

MEASURES	SECTION	SUB-SECTION	KEY	MUSICAL EVENTS
1-2	A	Introduction	F Major	Antiphonal statements between euph/bass and upper woodwinds
3-18		Theme I; "Morris Dance"		Cornet melody/homophonic brass accomp
19-26		Interlude		Brief development of Theme I by woodwinds
27-42		Theme I		Restatement
43-46		Transition		Gradual dynamic and rhythmic decay
47-110		Theme II; "Swansea Town"		Textural contrast; legato Euphonium solo, followed by tutti statement in warm, sonorous style
111	B	Transition	Bb dorian	Sudden one-measure transition
112-159	B	Theme III; "Claudy Banks"		Theme stated first by upper ww, against homophonic chords in brass and low ww
1-110	A	Theme I, II	F Major	da capo repetition

SECOND MOVEMENT

MEASURES	SECTION			MUSICAL EVENTS
1-2	Introduction			Quiet accompaniment

3-18	Theme Statement	Melody: clarinet solo
19-34	Theme Restatement	Melody: fl, ob, eb cl, cornet Accomp: flowing eighth-note lines
35-37	Coda	Quiet ending: clar.,a. sax, euphonium, bass solos

THIRD MOVEMENT

MEASURES	SECTION	MUSICAL EVENTS
1-6	Introduction	Two-measure syncopated ostinato accompaniment, Brass
7-14	First Statement	Blacksmith Tune: oboe, clarinets, alto sax,tenor sax, horns (ostinato continues in brass)
15-23	Second Statement	Melody in cornet I; ostinato in low brass Subito piano and anvil entrance in m. 19; mm. 19-23, brief canonic treatment of theme and gradual crescendo toward final statement
24-31	Third Statement	Final climactic statement; tutti *fff*
32-33	Codetta	Brief rhythmic extension of ostinato, final chord: D Major

FOURTH MOVEMENT

MEASURES	SECTION	KEY	MUSICAL EVENTS
1-56	A	F Major	Seven statements of "Dargason" set in constant-melody variations; begins with solo woodwinds, gradual adding of forces to first climactic statement at 41; last statement diminishes. into Section B

FOURTH MOVEMENT

MEASURES	SECTION	KEY	MUSICAL EVENTS
57-88	B	G minor	1st entrance of "Greensleaves" in 3/4; euph. solo, joined by clarinet and trumpet solos; juxtaposed against four statements of Dargason by woodwinds in 6/8
89-144	A	F Major	Seven statements of "Dargason" in constant-melody variations; somewhat more elaborate treatment than opening section, containing chromatic harmonies and more intricate timbral and rhythmic variation
145-176	B	G minor	Restatement of "Greensleaves" by brass, set against four "Dargason" statements in woodwinds
177-200	A	F Major	Extension of "Greensleaves" material in fragmentation with three statements of "Dargason"
201-211	Coda	F Major	Tuba/Piccolo duet on fragments of "Dargason;" tutti F Major chord on last beat

Unit 8: Suggested Listening

Gustav Holst, *Suite in E-Flat, Hammersmith; Prelude and Scherzo, St. Paul's Suite*

Unit 9: Additional References and Resources

Fennell, Frederick. *Basic Band Repertory.* Evanston, IL: The Instrumentalist Co., 1980.

Fennell, Frederick. "Gustav Holst's Second Suite in F for Military Band." *The Instrumentalist,* XXXII November 1977, 42-52.

Garofalo, Robert J. *Guides to Band Masterworks*. Ft. Lauderdale, FL: Meredith Music Publications, 1992.

Holst, Imogen. *The Music of Gustav Holst and Holst's Music Reconsidered.* Third edition revised. Oxford: Oxford University Press, 1986.

Mitchell, Jon C. "Early Performances of the Holst Suites for Military Band." *Journal of Band Research* XVII/2 (Spring 1982): 44-50.

Mitchell, Jon C. "Gustav Holst's Three Folk Tunes: A Source for the Second Suite in F." Journal of Band Research XIX/1 (Fall 1983): 1-4.

Mitchell, Jon Cleander. "Gustav Holst: The Works for Military Band." Diss., University of Illinois, 1980.

Pittman, Daniel Sayle, Jr. "Percy Grainger, Gustav Holst, and Ralph Vaughan Williams: A Comparative Analysis of Selected Wind Compositions." Diss., Memphis State University, 1979.

Teacher Resource Guide

"Shadows of Eternity"
Thomas Stone

(b. 1957)

(This study guide was contributed by the composer)

Unit 1: Composer

Thomas Stone received his Bachelor's degree from Lawrence University, where he studied composition with Steven Stucky, and his Master's degree from DePaul University. He received his Doctor of Musical Arts Degree in wind conducting from the University of Cincinnati College Conservatory of Music, where he was a student of Eugene Corporon. For six years, he was Director of Instrumental Music at The Latin School of Chicago. Mr. Stone served as Composer/Conductor-in-Residence at the Saskatchewan School for the Arts during the summer of 1988, and in 1989, he was appointed Director of Bands at The Bolles School in Jacksonville, Florida. His first two published works for band, *Shadows of Eternity* and *Mentor*, were selected by the Yamaha Corporation of Japan for its list of "100 Best Compositions for Bands" in 1992 and 1993, respectively. His article, "Morton Gould: Champion of the Band," was published in the January 1995 issue of *BD Guide*. He is currently Conductor of the Wind Ensemble and Assistant Professor of Music at Centenary College, a post he assumed in the fall of 1995.

Unit 2: Composition

Shadows of Eternity is Thomas Stone's first publication. Written originally for chorus and chamber orchestra, the work was completed in December of 1985 and was premiered by the Student-Faculty Chorale at the Latin School of Chicago in April of 1986. *Shadows of Eternity* was transcribed for concert band by the composer at the request of publisher Larry Daehn in 1989. This version was first performed by the Faculty Wind Ensemble at the Saskatchewan School for the Arts in July of 1989, Dr. Peter Demos conducting.

Unit 3: Historical Perspective

The original choral version of the work used as its text *The Retreat*, by 17th-century English poet Henry Vaughan. Portions of the poem used as text are in boldface type below. Rehearsal letters indicate musical passages corresponding to the text:

(C)	**Happy those early days, when I**
	Shin'd in my Angel-infancy!
	Before I understood this place
	Appointed for my second race,
	Or taught my soul to fancy aught
	But a white celestial thought:
	When yet I had not walked above
	A mile or two from my first Love,
	And looking back-at that short space-
	Could see a glimpse of His bright face:
(K)	**When on some gilded cloud, or flow'r**
	My gazing soul would dwell an hour,
	And in those weaker glories spy
	Some shadows of eternity:
	Before I taught my tongue to wound
	My Conscience with a sinful sound,
	Or had the black art to dispense
	A several sin to ev'ry sense,
	But felt through all this fleshly dress
	Bright shoots of everlastingness.
(2 before L)	**O how I long to travel back,**
	And tread again that ancient track!
	That I might once more reach that plain
	Where first I left my glorious train;
	From whence th'enlightened spirit sees
	That shady City of Palm-trees.
	But ah! my soul with too much stay
	Is drunk, and staggers in the way!
(O)	**Some men a forward motion love [know],**
	But I by backward steps would move [go],
	And when this dust falls to the urn,
	In that state I came, return.

295

Unit 4: Technical Considerations

The trumpet parts are by far the most difficult; there are few rests and many demands. Three types of mutes are needed: straight, cup, and Harmon. The trumpet/horn figure two bars before Letter B is not nearly as difficult as it appears. The conductor should subdivide these measures and at corresponding points later. In teaching these rhythms to younger players, I begin with the last beat of activity (beat 2, one bar before B), then I teach each individual beat working backward to the beginning of the figure, all on Concert Bb. Then, I ask them to read the rhythms while playing the written pitches. Coach the percussionists to place their entrance on the two 32nds that conclude the brass figure. The quick mute changes in the trumpets often cause errors in preparation for the next entrance. Strategic platooning of muted and unmuted players (where enough players are available) can help. The *marcato* brass pyramids after F are a chronic source of technical miscues. The interval sequence seems to be the culprit in the trumpets and trombones. The trumpet triplet figure three bars before I is the type of spot that may cause some conductors to opt for a slower tempo throughout the entire fast section. An intelligent simplification of this rhythm is preferable to a reduction in tempo.

Unit 5: Stylistic Considerations

The opening measure should start almost subliminally, with one person singing as softly as possible. A tuning pitch "A" can provide a reference for the singers. Singers should be coached to "sneak in", using aspirant initiations rather than glottal attacks. The vocal tone should be very indirect, incandescent. The audience should be virtually unaware that the music has begun. The conductor should beat time beginning with measure 2. Use bowed crotales rather than vibraphone to achieve the ethereal effect in measures 3 and 6 (and later after M). Remove the a2 designation from the bassoon part in measure 5; use only one player. If Eb contralto clarinet is not used, be certain to have the tuba play the cues. Otherwise, the lowest sounding pitch is F, with no Bb below. Having the tuba (or string bass reading a tuba or contralto clarinet part) play the cue is a good idea regardless. Ask the bell player to use hard plastic mallets rather than brass on all parts. Remove the divisi designation from all three clarinet parts one measure before A. All players should play the bottom octave notes, omitting the upper octave entirely. Use only bells and crotales two measures before B, not bowed vibraphone. Have each player strike octave E's. The effect should be stunning and very metallic. These changes should be applied to ensuing statements of the same material as well. The section at Letter B employs cross-rhythms of African origin in the accompaniment. I discovered these rhythms at a demonstration of music of the black slaves in Colonial Williamsburg. The rhythms demonstrated were:

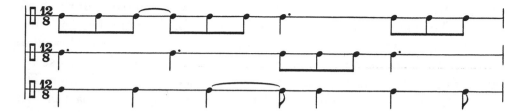

Consider having three or more percussionists substitute these rhythms for the castanet/tambourine part, playing them softly by clicking snare drum sticks together. Different size sticks could be used for each rhythm, producing a multi-level effect. The horn and baritone collaborate in a loose rendition of rhythm 3 above. The horn must remain within the texture. There are many opportunities in the work for sensitive musicians to create "moments." Maximizing these opportunities, creating the poetic atmospherics they demand, is one way to bring the music to its fullest voice. Another is finding the best tempo for each section. The text arrayed above, where it applies, can help the conductor to find the most natural pace. I like a free tempo within the framework of MM equal to 52 at the beginning. Mutes are used in Shadows of Eternity not to effect reduced dynamics, but to add color. Always ask players with mutes to project through the mute's resistance. Be careful not to over-romanticize letter C. Keep the texture light and elevated, not too emotional. I like MM equal to 80 here. Please consider performing this section with staggered breathing. Play through the slur breaks, especially four bars after C. Place the ritard before D one measure earlier so that the two eighths at the end of the second measure before D begin to pull back the tempo. Rehearse the clarinets and horns together two measures before E. The trumpets have a quick mute change here. Experimenting, some players with mutes, some without, may bring strength to the three eighths leading to E. I never hear enough timpani at letter F! There is a printed mistake in the score one bar before G; remove the snare drum part and replace it with one measure of rest. The snare drummer should resume the part one measure after G at piano. The horns should dominate at H. Their articulations are marcato beneath the woodwind slurs. They must not be lured into playing what they hear above. Trumpet I dominates at the third measure of H. The most often-asked question about this composition refers to the triplets three before I.

The key to understanding this measure lies in the eighth-note pattern in the low brass. Three beats are squeezed into the space of what were previously two (as in Bernstein's "America"). The triplets above must be imprinted into that concept. The 3/4 bar, then, occupies the identical amount of real time as the individual measures that surround it. The melody at J was the first music that I came up with in April of 1985. It led me to conceptualize the opening measures (the major second from D to C became A to G). Play this melody with much expression, not in a metronomic or monotonous fashion. Stretch the "D" in the fourth bar, the "D" in the eighth bar, and the "F" in the ninth bar. Play with as much imagination as possible within the constraints of the accompanying rhythmic structure. The brass/saxophone entrance four bars before I should start "mf", then crescendo into K. All tempo markings between K and the end are calibrated to the quarter note, not because the quarter should be conducted, but only so the relativity of these tempi can be gauged. Please conduct all meters as written. The passage at letter K is often conducted in four as a relaxed, gentle 4/4 passage, but this interpretation is off the mark. K is a point of very high energy. Strive for tension in the timpani sound; work toward a grandioso effect with lots of sonority and sweeping melodic lines. Trumpet 1 should dominate the texture upon its entrance in the seventh bar. Keep the horns within the texture and beneath the trumpet. The cadence four before L is very fragile. Coach the low brass to arrive gently. Take lots of time with the ritard and fermati before proceeding into L. The 3/2 section should be conducted in three until the ritard, where it can be subdivided. Vocalists encounter difficulty picking out the "A" two measures before M. The "A" is in third clarinet only and is difficult to isolate. Instruct the players to listen to clarinet 1, then sing a whole step higher. If this doesn't work, ask one trumpet player to gently "suggest" the "A" as subtly as possible. Again, let the vocal tone arise seemingly from nowhere and ask the singers to carry the musical motion into M. Allow the flutist to "conduct" the ritard into M. I often visualize the ending section at letter O as one thousand people singing as softly as possible. Experimentation with dynamics might create some wondrous effects. I like the texture to be full, but as soft as possible until the crescendo. The comma should be a luftpause only. The tag section, "In that state I came, return," works best when the text gauges the tempo. It actually begins at a faster tempo than the music preceding it, although most conductors ignore this. I like motion in the first measure, then a grand ritard, taking lots of time on the two fermati. Wait three or four seconds for the chord to settle before cueing the bells, which should be spaced strategically for effect.

Unit 6: Musical Elements

I used no system in composing *Shadows*, other than to employ cross-rhythms. These rhythms led to the creation of the middle section in fast 6/8 meter. There is a perfect-fifth-based chant motif stated in its purest form two bars before E in the alto saxophones, supported by the tenor saxophone and euphonium. This pattern is inserted into the texture in various forms, but should always maintain a quality of otherworldliness. Melodic material always emerges from my harmonic thinking, as I am primarily an architect of harmonies. Seventh chords must have been primary in my thoughts, perhaps because there were four choral parts to work with. The chord progressions at letter O are, I believe, the most interesting in the entire work. Somehow it all ends up in D Major.

298

Unit 7: Form and Structure

A   Lyrical Exposition

B   Energetic Diversion (D)

A1   Lyrical Resolution (2 bars before L)

Unit 8: Suggested Listening

Stone, Thomas. *Mentor: A Musical Portrait of Albert Einstein.*
Stone, Thomas. *Ancient Visions*

Unit 9: Bibliography

The Instrumentalist, "Music Review: Shadows of Eternity by Thomas Stone."
   October, 1990.

Stone, Thomas. Mentor: *A Musical Portrait of Albert Einstein.* New Glarus:
   Daehn Publications, 1992.

Stone, Thomas. *Shadows of Eternity.* New Glarus: Daehn Publications, 1990.

This study guide was contributed by the composer in June, 1995.

Teacher Resource Guide

"Sinfonia V"
(Symphonia Sacra et Profana)
Prelude, Rag, Alla Turca, Chorale, Rag, Ragtime Alla Turca, Chant and Pavanne
Timothy Broege
(b. 1947)

Unit 1: Composer

Timothy Broege was born in New Jersey and received the Bachelor of Music degree from Northwestern University. He taught twelve years for the public schools in Chicago, Illinois and New Jersey. He is currently Director of Music at First Presbyterian Church in Belmar, New Jersey and resides in Oceanport, New Jersey. For his compositions for school bands, Broege received the Goldman Award at the 1994 ASBDA Convention. The series of compositions for wind band titled *Sinfonia* and his *Concerto for Piano and Wind Orchestra* are noteworthy and indicative of his compositional style, which shows a fascination with jazz.

Unit 2: Composition

Sinfonia V could be thought of as a divertimento in that the composition is made up of short sections of varying character. Broege changes this form by using seven sections connected together without pause. This may cause the composition to appear through-composed, although traditional formal structures are present and later sections of the composition are actually developmental sections of earlier movements. Composed in 1990 and commissioned by the University City, Missouri Wind Ensemble, the composition is seven minutes in length and should be considered difficult in its technical and musical demands (improvisation requirements, use of piano and electric piano, high difficulty of percussion parts). Overall, it can be said that this composition is influenced heavily by jazz rhythms and formal freedom.

Unit 3: Historical Perspective

Sinfonia V is one of a series of Broege's compositions for band. The compositions in this series with odd numbers (1, 3, 5) are considered more difficult than the ones with even numbers (2, 4, 6). This composition is quite contemporary in its approach to overall form, use of percussion, and unusual instrumental effects. There may be a parallel in these techniques and their level of difficulty in the music of Bruce Yurko. Interestingly, one section involves a chorale patterned after the antiphonal instrumental works of the Baroque composer Samuel Scheidt, while the final section begins with a sung chant. Both of these "retro" sections are composed and developed by contemporary means. Since 1970, composers have generally tended to write more technically challenging parts for all instruments, and this is reflected here. Compositions written during the same year include *Arctic Dreams* by Colgrass and *Heroes, Lost and Fallen* by Gillingham.

Unit 4: Technical Considerations

The very challenging percussion parts must be played by a minimum of four musicians, who must deal with complex divisions of the beat, singing, and a small amount of improvisation. It should be noted, however, that most of the composition is to be performed at a speed of 84 beats per minute. There are only 18 measures at a faster tempo (Pavanne), and this section contains the easiest technical passages. Woodwinds must frequently play syncopated passages and require a great deal of independence. All woodwind instruments have solos at some point. Bassoons must play up to high A-flat during an exposed duet in unison (measures 7-14). Four trumpet soloists are needed in measures 33-38, and trombone and euphonium range must be considered (high A-flat and B-flat, respectively). Brass parts show a great deal of independence, but there are not as many solos as in the woodwind parts. For the ensemble, measures 41-43 will present a challenge in rhythm; there are nine eight notes per measure, but it is conducted in four beats (2+2+2+3). In general, rhythm and meter are the greatest technical challenges; the necessity of complete instrumentation, especially regarding the woodwinds, make this composition a formidable challenge.

Unit 5: Stylistic Considerations

Most of the syncopated rhythms in brass and woodwinds germinate from the ragtime ideas. The concept of ragtime should be introduced before detailed rehearsal begins. The concept of *legato* melody above syncopated and/or *staccato* accompaniment is also important and appears (almost) entirely throughout the composition. Demonstration of ragtime style and its emphasis on light *staccato* is necessary. A wide variety of dynamics must be employed by all members of the ensemble. Since many parts of the composition utilize "sound layering", or the concept of superimposing contrasting ideas, much time will be needed for performers to understand their musical role as it changes. There is a short chorale ("after Scheidt"); Baroque antiphonal style will need to be explained, and the concept of alternating choirs of voices will be helpful.

Unit 6: Musical Elements

The concept of "poly-genre" is important in this composition, where two or more different style periods of music are often explored simultaneously. Later in the composition, these contrasting styles (rag, chorale, jazz) are even developed simultaneously. These are frequently presented as sound layers and are mostly separated into woodwind, brass, and percussion choirs. The subtitle, "Sacra et Profana", is especially significant in that the chorale and chant (sacred) seems to be treated as a central element of, and responsorial to, the jazz elements (profane). Students must be familiar with *canon* and its terminology (*dux, comes,* etc.) as much material is presented in this manner (see measures 21-24, 28-32, 33-38). In general, the composition moves from a state of rhythmic activity to non-activity, and this sense of direction is in itself a type of form.

Unit 7: Form and Structure

PRELUDE	intro m.1	A m.6	A' m.12
			transition m.17
RAG	A m.19	B m.26	A' m.33
			transition m.41
ALLA TURCA	A m.46	B m.52	transition m.60
CHORALE	in fugato style with free improvisation m.63		
RAG	intro m.79	jazz treatment of E-flat clarinet figure (m.75) m.83	
RAGTIME ALLA TURCA	free improvisation plus part 6 theme plus mouthpiece effects m.91		
CHANT AND PAVANNE	A m.102	A' m.106	Pavanne m.115 Codetta m.134

Unit 8: Suggested Listening
Timothy Broege, *No Sun, No Shadow* (Elegy for Charles Mingus)
Charles Ives, *The Fourth of July*
Scott Joplin, *The Entertainer*
Bob Margolis, *Terpsichore* (after Michael Praetorius)
Alec Wilder, *Entertainment #5*
Bruce Yurko, *Incantations*

Unit 9: Additional References and Resources
Dvorak, Thomas L., Robert Grechesky, and Gary Ciepluch. *Best Music for High School Band*. Brooklyn, NY: Manhattan Beach Music, 1993.

Teacher Resource Guide

"Variations on a Korean Folk Song"
John Barnes Chance
(b. 1932–d. 1972)

Unit 1: Composer

John Barnes Chance was born in Beaumont, Texas, on November 20, 1932. He began his formal musical training at age 9, studying piano with Jewell Harned. He began studying composition at 15 and received both his Bachelor and Master of Music degrees from the University of Texas. Chance's primary composition teachers were Kent Kennan and Clifton Williams. He performed as timpanist with the Austin Symphony and was an arranger for the Fourth and Eighth United States Army Bands. Chance was a composer-in-residence at Greensboro, North Carolina, from 1960-1962, under the auspices of the Ford Foundation Young Composers Project. From Fall 1966 until his early death, he was professor of composition at the University of Kentucky and was made head of Theory and Composition in 1971. Chance won the American Bandmasters Association Ostwald Award in 1966 for *Variations on a Korean Folk Song*. Of the 20 compositions Chance wrote, five for band have been published: *Blue Lake Overture, Elegy, Incantation and Dance, Symphony No. 2,* and *Variations on a Korean Folk Song*.

Unit 2: Composition

This work is based on the Korean Folk song, "Arrirang." The composer wrote: "I became acquainted with the folk song while serving in Seoul, Korea, as a member of the Eighth U.S. Army Band in 1958-59. The tune is not as simple as it sounds, and my fascination with it during the intervening years led to its eventual use as the theme for this set of variations." The pentatonic theme is stated two times before five distinct variations and a coda. The work, composed in 1965, won the Ostwald Award for composition in 1966. It is 262 measures and six and one-half minutes in length.

Unit 3: Historical Perspective

Over the many years that composers have been writing original works for band, the theme and variations setting has been a favored form. William Schuman's *Chester* (1957) and Norman Dello Joio's *Variants on a Medieval Tune* (1963) are two well known outstanding works for band that use theme and variations style. The song "Arrirang" has historically been most popular in Korea when the country has been in a state of crisis. The song has many verses with a constant refrain and refers to a man about to leave his girl with pain in her heart. As he leaves for a long journey to the capital, she is upset that he will not let her accompany him.

Unit 4: Technical Considerations

The work is tonal, but uses the pentatonic scale, Eb-F-Ab-Bb-C, and five transpositions. Percussion instruments required include: Timpani, Vibraphone, Xylophone, Bells, Temple Blocks, Gong, along with Snare and Bass Drums, Cymbals and Triangle. A minimum of six players are needed to cover the ten percussion instruments scored. The first variation has long sixteenth-note passages for woodwinds and melodic percussion. The final variation needs careful accuracy by the conductor to maintain the polymetric (sesquialtera) rhythms. The second variation demands expressive and lyrical playing by the solo oboe and solo trumpet.

Unit 5: Stylistic Considerations

One of the strengths of this work is that it requires both very expressive playing and attention to technical and rhythmic detail. The theme is marked *"semplice e cantabile."* The initial section of the theme is scored for soli unison clarinets. The tempo of the first variation is marked quarter equal to 132. Rhythmic stability is very important as ensembles prepare and perform this section. The three slow sections that contain most of the duration of the composition should be treated with freshness and in a singing style. A controlled *rubato* should be used between and within the regularly occurring phrases to prevent these sections from losing listener interest. The 6/8 meter of the third variation, the march, should dance along. Ensembles should be careful not to allow the accompaniment to become too ponderous in this section.

Unit 6: Musical Elements

The harmony used throughout is basically triadic in a Western tonal function. The melody uses six transpositions of a pentatonic scale. The initial statement may be viewed as in A flat Major. The variations use canon, imitation, inversion, augmentation, ostinato and polymeter.

Unit 7: Form and Structure

MEASURES	SECTION	SCORING

STATEMENT OF THEME (CON MOTO)

1	A	unison clarinets
9	B	picc, fls, cls
17	A′	as, ts, bar
25	B′	cls, hns
32	Codetta	tutti

VARIATION I (VIVACE)

38	A	rhythmic variation in canon in woodwinds
48	B	sustained in tpts, tbns under rhythmic variation ostinato
53	A′	rhythmic variations in canon
63	B′	sustained in cls, hns, bar, vibr
68	Codetta	

VARIATION II (LARGHETTO)

78	Intro	
82	A	oboe solo inversion
90	B	fl, cl and oboe
98	A′	fl, as, hn inversion
108	Codetta	tpt solo

VARIATION III (ALLEGRO CON BRIO) (6/8 TIME)

116	Intro	brass, timp march beat
124	A	unison tpts
132	B	
140	A′	woodwinds
147	Extension	
150	A″	tpts, accompanied by two rhythms
158	B′	
166	Codetta	
173	Transition	snare drum

VARIATION IV (SOSTENUTO) (3/2 TIME)

183	A	woodwinds sustained
191	B	tutti

VARIATION V (CON ISLANCIO)

199	Intro	multi percussion set up canon
208	A	temple blocks
211	A-B	vibes and woodwinds
223	A′-B′	brass in elongation, sesquialtera rhythm
241	Coda	ends with Bb Major

Unit 8: Suggested Listening

John Barnes Chance, *Incantation and Dance; Elegy; Blue Lake Overture;*
   Symphony No. 2
Norman Dello Joio, *Variants on a Mediaeval Tune*
William Schuman, *Chester*

Unit 9: Additional References and Resources

Anthony, Donald Allen. "Published Band Compositions of John Barnes
   Chance." DME diss., University of Southern Mississippi, 1981.

Chance, John Barnes. "Variations on a Korean Folk Song." *Journal of Band
   Research* 3 (Fall 1966): 13-16.

Dvorak, Thomas L., Robert Grechesky, and Gary Ciepluch. *Best Music for High
   School Band.* Brooklyn, NY: Manhattan Beach Music, 1993.

Fennell, Frederick. "John Barnes Chance: Variations on A Korean Folk Song."
   BD Guide, September/October 1989, 15.

Randel, Don Michael. *The New Harvard Dictionary of Music.* Cambridge, MA:
   Harvard University, 1986.

Rehrig, William H. *The Heritage Encyclopedia of Band Music.* Westerville,
   OH: Integrity Press, 1991.

Smith, Norman and Albert Stoutamire. *Band Music Notes.* Lake Charles, LA:
   Program Note Press, 198

Grade 5

Teacher Resource Guide

"Canzona"
Peter Mennin
(b. 1923–d. 1983)

Unit 1: Composer
Peter Mennin was born Peter Mennini in Erie, Pennsylvania in 1923, and died in New York in 1983. He attended the Oberlin Conservatory and the Eastman School of Music, where he studied composition with Bernard Rogers and Howard Hanson. He taught composition at the Juilliard School of Music (1947-58) and was director of the Peabody Conservatory (1958-62). From 1962 until his retirement, he served as president of Juilliard. Mennin was one of the important New York-school American composers of the mid-20th century that included Copland, Harris, Persichetti, Thomson, and Schuman. Generally acknowledged as musically conservative, he was primarily a symphonist, and a composer of concertos, string quartets and sonatas.

Unit 2: Composition
Canzona was composed in 1951 on a commission from Edwin Franko Goldman and the League of Composers. This single-movement work is Mennin's only work for band. Like the many other works commissioned by the League of Composers, *Canzona* was given its premiere by the Goldman Band. The work is approximately five minutes in length.

Unit 3: Historical Perspective
The concept of the "canzona" in this piece is based on the late-renaissance canzoni of Giovanni Gabrieli (1555-1612), which exploited the acoustics of the Cathedral of St. Mark in Venice with contrasting, antiphonal statements by opposing forces of brass. In this setting, Mennin alternates blocks of woodwind and brass sonorities while applying 20th-century concepts of harmony, polypho-

ny, and rhythm. Since its creation, the work has been a standard in the wind band repertoire.

Unit 4: Technical Considerations

The work is frequently polymodal. Technical demands are considerable. Execution of rapid sixteenth-note rhythms is required of all woodwinds and trumpets. Varied articulation adds varying degrees of difficulty to these sixteenth-note patterns. Percussion parts are limited, but exacting rhythmic execution is vital. Flute and oboe solos occur in the middle section. "B" above the staff is required in first trumpet. The polyphonic textures of the work require confident, independent playing from everyone in the ensemble. The polymodal harmonies also require a non-traditional understanding of the intonation of vertical sonorities.

Unit 5: Stylistic Considerations

The scoring of *Canzona* is traditional English military band scoring with substantial doublings; the polyphonic and antiphonal lines are sometimes difficult to balance, depending on the configuration of the ensemble. The middle register of the band is particularly heavy, with many doublings. Conductors may desire to thin these textures. There is substantial fugal writing throughout, with the subject frequently in the bass voice. The brevity of phrases and sections can make the work sound very "sectional", but one may prevent this by always maintaining a *cantabile* approach to thc lincs. Unlike many band works, this piece is inherently *linear*, rather than *vertical*. Placing an emphasis on breadth of sound, rather than on the attack, is desirable. Articulation markings are plentiful, and should be followed exactly; staccato markings should have tone, and accents should have stress rather than sharp attack.

Unit 6: Musical Elements

Except for the first eleven measures, the prevailing texture is contrapuntal. Fugal writing exists, with the usual techniques associated: augmentation, diminution, stretto, subject in different voices. Contrasting textures exist within sections; legato lines are frequently contrasted with staccato motives. Harmonic techniques include triadic parallelism and polymodality.

Unit 7: Form and Structure

Canzona is in rounded-binary form (A-B,A1).

SECTION	MEASURES	MUSICAL EVENTS
A	1-6	Theme I presented by brass, saxes; parallelism and bimodal sonorities
	7-11	Theme I; Tutti, rhythmic variation

	12-25	Theme II introduced in upper woodwinds against staccato background figures and bass line; fugal entrance (by P5) of theme II in m. 21 by low ww/brass
	26-30	Theme III introduced in parallel major triads in ww's
	31-36	Theme IV introduced; pointallistic accompaniment; counter melody enters at m. 34
	37-41	Tutti variation of mm. 26-30
	42-44	Tutti variation of mm. 31-33
	45-55	Theme II in canon at the fifth between low and high voices
	56-63	Tutti; theme I in augmentation, brings section to close B
	64-71	Theme V in fl/oboe; lighter texture, feeling of repose
	72-75	Theme VI, tpts/trombones
	76-88	Theme V returns in picc/ob; fugal statement in clar/fl at 81
	89-96	Development of Theme VI
	97-112	Fugue of Theme II in rhythmic augmentation, beginning in bass voice; New Theme VII in upper woodwinds; Theme IV added in m. 108
	113-117	Tutti ww; Theme III
	118-120	Theme IV in ww, with new countermelody in horns
	121-135	Theme V in upper ww in rhythmic augmentation; brass/low ww play pointallistic accomp.
B (cont.)	136-146	Theme II in low voices; set in counterpoint w/ derivative upper ww line, and brass ostinato patterns
A1	136-146	Tutti; canon between brass/low ww and upper ww on Theme I
Codetta	153-156	Brief fanfare in D Major

Unit 8: Suggested Listening

Gustav Holst, *Suite in E-Flat, Hammersmith, Prelude and Scherzo, St. Paul's Suite*

Unit 9: Additional References and Resources

Dvorak, Thomas L. *Best Music for Young Band.* Brooklyn, NY: Manhattan Beach Music, 1986.

Dvorak, Thomas L., Robert Grechesky, and Gary Ciepluch. *Best Music for High School Band.* Brooklyn, NY: Manhattan Beach Music, 1993.

Hunsberger, Donald. "Score Study and Preparation, Part II." *The Instrumentalist,* September 1980, 34-39.

Kopetz, Barry E. "Peter Mennin's Canzona: An Interpretive Analysis." *The Instrumentalist,* XVIII January 1989, 17-22.

Sadie, Stanley. *The New Grove Dictionary of Music and Musicians.* London: Macmillan, 1980.

Smith, Norman and Albert Stoutamire. *Band Music Notes.* Lake Charles, LA: Program Note Press, 1989.

Teacher Resource Guide

Children's March
"Over the Hills and Far Away"
Percy Aldridge Grainger

(b. 1882–d. 1961)

Revised by Frank Erickson (b. 1923)

Unit 1: Composer

Percy Aldridge Grainger was born at Brighton in Melbourne, Australia on July 8, 1882. He spent time living in England, where he collected folk songs, and then lived in the United States until his death on February 20, 1961 at White Plains, New York. He used irregular rhythms before Stravinsky, pioneered in folk music collections at the same time as Bartok, and predated Varése in experimentation with electronic music. Some of his other works transcribed for band include *Lincolnshire Posy*, *Molly on the Shore*, *Hill-Song No. II*, and *Irish Tune from County Derry*.

Unit 2: Composition

Children's March is one of many works for band composed by Grainger. The piece was composed as a piano solo while Granger was in the Coast Artillery Band in the U.S. Army as a "musician, second class" between July 1917 and January 1919. It is an original work for band, even though its tunes may sound like folk songs. The scoring for band was completed in February 1919. Grainger said it was "especially written to use all the forces of the Coast Artillery Band in which I was serving in 1918." The work was dedicated to "my playmate beyond the hills." This playmate is believed to be a Scandinavian beauty with whom the composer corresponded for eight years but did not marry because of his mother's jealousy. The piece is one movement, is a Grade 5 difficulty and lasts about seven minutes.

Unit 3: Historical Perspective

Grainger was one of the first 20th-century composers to embrace the band as a viable, expressive artistic medium. His innovative scoring led to techniques which were to be emulated and admired by future generations of composers. Grainger wrote for families of instruments, was an advocate of what he called "Free Music", and used piano and "tuneful" percussion regularly. The deeply personal approach of Grainger's musical commitment is only beginning to be studied and appreciated.

Unit 4: Technical Considerations

The piece is in the concert keys of F Major, Bb Major, Eb Major, and Ab Major. There are no meter changes and the tempo remains consistent and fairly fast (dotted quarter note equal to about 126). There are no tempo changes. There are both staccato and legato articulations, so contrast is important. Upper wood-winds have several exposed sections and several solos as does the percussion section at the end. Woodwinds have to play 16th-note F Major scales over an octave and a half. French horn(s) has a difficult solo staccato ostinato.

Unit 5: Stylistic Considerations

Articulations should be crisp, uniform and march-like. All markings in the score support this. Even during slurred passages the music must push forward. The interpretation is quite straightforward in this regard. An effort should be made to perform at or slightly above the indicated metronome markings. The intensity and movement of the music should be equal to the phrasing, articulation, rhythms and principles of the line.

Unit 6: Musical Elements

The main theme is first stated in F Major, and the piece progresses through B-flat, E-flat and A-flat Major. Tonicizations and chord movements are clear. There are several meter changes but the main pulse stays the same. The piano has a very important part, but thanks to Grainger's "elastic scoring," the piece can be performed without a piano.

Unit 7: Form and Structure

OPENING   F Major, mm. 1-16, Introduction

THEME 1   Mm. 17-84 stated mostly in woodwinds
                 Theme 1 repeated mm. 85-116 in brass

THEME 2   B-flat Major, mm. 117-132 stated in upper/middle woodwinds
                 Mm. 133-152 quasi-development of Theme 1

TRANSITION   Mm. 153-164 low WW and brass; French horn soloist

THEME 1	Mm. 165-196 tutti
	Theme I repeated mm. 197-252 tutti (E-flat)
TRANSITION	A-flat Major, mm. 252-267
THEME 1	Mm. 268-282 stated emphatically tutti
THEME 2	Mm. 283-305 quasi-development of Theme 1
THEME 1	Mm. 306-370 starting large and gradually fading
OPENING	B-flat Major, mm. 371-402, introduction theme
CODA	Mm. 403-413 fading more & percussion solos

Unit 8: Suggested Listening
Percy Aldridge Grainger, *Lincolnshire Posy*
Percy Aldridge Grainger, *Hill-Song No. II*
Percy Aldridge Grainger, *The Lads of Wamphray March*

Unit 9: Additional References and Resources

Baker, Theodore. "Grainger, Percy Aldridge," *Baker's Biographical Dictionary   of Musicians.* 6th ed., revised by Nicolas Slonimsky. New York: Schirmer Books, 1984.

Fennell, Frederick. "Basic Band Repertory: 'Children's March' by Percy Grainger." *The Instrumentalist,* XXXVII December 1982, 20-26.

National Band Association Selective Music List for Bands

Rehrig, William H. *The Heritage Encyclopedia of Band Music.* Westerville, OH: Integrity Press, 1991.

Uggen, Stuart. "Percy Grainger in Perspective." *The Instrumentalist,* XXIV June 1970, 38-41.

Westrup, J. A. and F. Ll. Harrison. *The New College Encyclopedia of Music.* Revised by Conrad Wilson. New York: W. W. Norton & Company, Ltd, 1981.

Teacher Resource Guide

"Colonial Song"
Percy Aldridge Grainger
(b. 1882–d. 1961)

Unit 1: Composer

Percy Aldridge Grainger was born at Brighton in Melbourne, Australia on July 8, 1882. He spent time living in England, where he collected folk songs, and then lived in the United States until his death on February 20, 1961 at White Plains, New York. He used irregular rhythms before Stravinsky, pioneered in folk music collections at the same time as Bartok, and predated Varése in experimentation with electronic music. Some of his other works transcribed for band include *Lincolnshire Posy*, *Molly on the Shore*, *Hill-Song No. II*, *Children's March "Over the Hills and Far Away"*, and *Irish Tune from County Derry*.

Unit 2: Composition

Colonial Song is one of many works for band composed by Grainger. The piece was composed as a piano piece given to his mother as a 1911 "Yule gift". Listed in his own files as first of a series called "Sentimentals", it remains the lone contribution to that category. *Colonial Song* was premiered in a series of concerts in February and March of 1913, conducted by Grainger and scored for soprano, tenor, harp and orchestra. Grainger prepared the band version in 1918. The piece is one movement, is a Grade 5 difficulty and lasts about five and a half minutes.

Unit 3: Historical Perspective

Grainger was one of the first 20th-century composers to embrace the band as a viable, expressive artistic medium. His innovative scoring led to techniques which were to be emulated and admired by future generations of composers. Grainger wrote for families of instruments, was an advocate of what he called

"Free Music", and used piano and "tuneful" percussion regularly. *Colonial Song* was Grainger's attempt to write a melody as typical of the Australian countryside as Stephen Foster's songs are of rural America.

Unit 4: Technical Considerations

The piece is in the concert key of E-flat Major. Wind and brass players are required to sustain uncharacteristically *legato* phrases in the high register, as well as play very slow repeated *staccato* notes. There are several meter changes which demonstrate Granger's "free music" concept. There are both staccato and legato articulations, so contrast is important. Upper woodwinds and brass have to play difficult, improvised-sounding ornament figures together. There are two important trumpet I solos. In the closing measures, starting from *pp*, instruments are added to the *crescendo* until a *fff* level is reached.

Unit 5: Stylistic Considerations

Articulations should be crisp, uniform and march-like. There is a feeling of *rubato* throughout to match the style of a singer singing the song in a free manner. The intensity and movement of the music should be equal to the phrasing, articulation, rhythms and principles of the line; there must be a feeling of tension and release throughout to mark high points of the piece.

Unit 6: Musical Elements

The main theme is first stated in E-flat Major, and the piece stays in E-flat Major. Tonicizations and chord movements are clear, but accidentals abound. There are several meter changes, most of them not difficult. Balance is a crucial issue since the scoring is, at times, very thickly-textured; *crescendos* and *decrescendos* occur frequently at the same time in different instruments. There are also several fermatas of differing length.

Unit 7: Form and Structure

OPENING	E-flat Major	
Introduction	Mm. 1-11, slurred throughout, theme in low reeds	
THEME 1	E-flat Major	
A Tempo	Mm. 12-20, alto sax solo	
THEME 2	E-flat Major	
A Tempo	Mm. 21-36, trumpet I solo, staccato accompaniment	
THEME 3	E-flat Major	
A Tempo	Mm. 37-55, theme expanded, tutti	
(poco meno)		
THEME 1	E-flat Major	
A Tempo	Mm. 56-65, trumpet I solo, staccato accompaniment	

CODA E-flat Major
  A Tempo Mm. 66-72, long-building cresc. & dim. through
      instrumentation

Unit 8: Suggested Listening

Percy Aldridge Grainger, *Lincolnshire Posy*
Percy Aldridge Grainger, *Hill-Song No. II*
Percy Aldridge Grainger, *The Lads of Wamphray March*

Unit 9: Additional References and Resources

Baker, Theodore. "Grainger, Percy Aldridge," *Baker's Biographical Dictionary of Musicians.* 6th ed., revised by Nicolas Slonimsky. New York: Schirmer Books, 1984.

Fennell, Frederick. "Basic Band Repertory: 'Colonial Song' by Percy Grainger." *The Instrumentalist,* XXXVII March 1983, 14-19.

National Band Association Selective Music List for Bands

Rehrig, William H. *The Heritage Encyclopedia of Band Music.* Westerville, OH: Integrity Press, 1991.

Uggen, Stuart. "Percy Grainger in Perspective." *The Instrumentalist,* XXIV June 1970, 38-41.

Westrup, J. A. and F. Ll. Harrison. *The New College Encyclopedia of Music.* Revised by Conrad Wilson. New York: W. W. Norton & Company, Ltd, 1981.

Wilson, Brian Scott. "Orchestrational Archetypes in Percy Grainger's Wind Band Music." Diss., The University of Arizona, 1992.

Teacher Resource Guide

"Divertimento for Band"
(Prologue, Song, Dance, Burlesque, Soliloquy, March)
Vincent Persichetti
(b. 1915–d. 1987)

Unit 1: Composer

Vincent Persichetti was born in Philadelphia and lived in the Northeast all of his life. He received the Bachelor of Music degree from Combs College and studied conducting with Fritz Reiner at the Curtis Institute. His Master of Music and Doctor of Music Administration were from the Philadelphia Conservatory, and he was head of the Composition and Theory Department for six years. In 1963, he was named head of the Juilliard Schools' Literature and Materials Department. In addition to nine symphonies, twenty "parables" for solo instruments, and three cantatas, he wrote *Hymns and Responses for the Church Year* and "Twentieth-Century Harmony". Some of his well-known works for band include *Symphony No. 6*, Op. 69 and *Masquerade*, Op. 102. In his own words, his compositional style could best be characterized as alternations and combinations of "gracious and gritty." Formally, Persichetti used classical forms with clever idiosyncratic deviations.

Unit 2: Composition

The title "divertimento" refers to a genre originating in the Classical period of music history to designate a composition in several movements of a lighter nature. Five movements was the usual length, and Persichetti kept this tradition while incorporating his own descriptive titles for each movement. Composed in 1950, the work began as an orchestral sketch with brass and woodwind alternations; he stated, "I realized that the strings were not going to enter." Thus, his first composition for band began. It was premiered by and dedicated to the Goldman

Band. In the first movement (Prologue), the conductor can receive a quick introduction to Persichetti's general compositional style; the movement is clearly tonal, but the accompaniment features poly-chordal punctuations under a tonal melody. Brass and woodwind choirs are alternated frequently. The total length of the composition is eleven minutes. This composition is generally indicative of Persichetti's overall style, but a more mature writing can be seen in *Symphony No. 6*.

Unit 3: Historical Perspective

Since the *Divertimento* was composed in 1950, it may be said that this composition represents one of the first of many new works by respected composers to emerge during this era. Other major works to emerge at about the same time are: *La Fiesta Mexicana* (1949), *George Washington Bridge* (1950), and *Tunbridge Fair* (1950). Since the 1950s were the decade that first showed significant numbers of original works for band (especially by well-known composers), it should be noted that none of the compositions listed above are similar in material or compositional form. These years saw the first attention given to the band regularly by established, "serious" composers.

Unit 4: Technical Considerations

Piccolo, flute, oboe, English horn, E-flat clarinet, trumpet, and horn solos are present, although none are very technically difficult. Flutes must be proficient in piccolo (third movement). The most difficult technical consideration is the clarinet parts in the third movement, where tongued and slurred sixteenth notes must be played at 132 beats per minute. A challenging bass clarinet solo in sixteenth note triplets at 132 beats per minute (notation misprinted in score) must be performed at the end of the movement. The fourth movement features a trumpet solo throughout; the trumpet must be able to play *dolce* in medium and high registers (up to A#). At the end of the movement, trumpet and flute solo must play octave E-flats by themselves. Percussion is featured throughout as melodic, as well as rhythmic components. Throughout, rhythmic demands are modest.

Unit 5: Stylistic Considerations

Movements 1, 3, and 5 feature mostly *marcato/staccato* styles; movements 2 and 4 feature *legato* and *cantabile* styles. A wide range of dynamics is expected, especially in sudden changes of volume. The principal melodic line is usually obvious and mostly in upper woodwind or upper brass voices. A warm and lyrical quality must be matched from the solo cornet and flute in movement 5.

Unit 6: Musical Elements

Poly-chordal accompaniment under a tonal melody is commonplace. The first movement uses tonal centers of G, A, and E. The second movement has a loose tonal center of D, while the third moves from B-flat to E-flat tonally. The fourth movement has whole-tone elements while based on C. The fourth movement is based on E-flat with a whole-tone influenced melody; it features canonic writing throughout. The fifth movement is the most traditional in harmony and melody. The last movement continues the fourth movement's whole-tone influence in a polychordal march using B-flat, C, and D Major triads. The harmonic writing can be compared to Schuman's (he co-authored a book, *William Schuman*, in 1954). Most lines are diatonic or whole-tone; very little chromatic writing can be found in the melodies.

Unit 7: Form and Structure

Movement 1	A	B	A	devel. A (ext.)		codetta
	m.1	m.13	m.35	m.44 m.62		m.71
Movement 2	intro	A	B	A		
	m.1	m.3	m.13	m.21		
Movement 3	intro	A	A'	B and devel.	A	codetta
	m.1	m.3	m.11	m.19 m.45	m.55	
Movement 4	A	B	A (canon)	codetta (using B material)		
	m.1	m.19	m.50	m.86		
Movement 5	A	B	A (shortened and used as codetta)			
	m.1	m.13	m.29			
Movement 6	Intro	A	B	bridge A	B	coda
	m.1	m.9	m.35	m.51 m.9	m.35	m.68
				(2x)	(2x)	

Unit 8: Suggested Listening

Vincent Persichetti, *Divertimento for Band*
   (ACC Heritage of America Band, Lt. Col. Lowell Graham, Conductor; promotional only)
Vincent Persichetti, *Divertimento for Band*
   Tokyo Kosei Wind Ensemble, Frederick Fennell, Conductor
Vincent Persichetti, *Symphony No. 6*
William Schuman, *George Washington Bridge*

Unit 9: Additional References and Resources

Dvorak, Thomas L., Robert Grechesky, and Gary Ciepluch. *Best Music for High School Band*. Brooklyn, NY: Manhattan Beach Music, 1993.

Fennell, Frederick. "Vincent Persichetti: Divertimento for Band." *BD Guide*, September/October 1984, 1.

Fraschillo, Thomas. "Conducting Persichetti's Divertimento." *The Instrumentalist*, XLVIII July 1994, 16.

Hilfiger, John Jay. "A Comparison of Some Aspects of Style in the Band and Orchestra Music of Vincent Persichetti." Ph.D. diss., The University of Iowa, 1985.

Morris, Donald Alan. "The Life of Vincent Persichetti, with Emphasis on his Works for Band." Ph.D. diss., The Florida State University, 1991.

Rehrig, William H. *The Heritage Encyclopedia of Band Music*. Westerville, OH: Integrity Press, 1991.

Smith, Norman and Albert Stoutamire. *Band Music Notes*. Lake Charles, LA: Program Note Press, 1989.

Tarwater, William Harmon. "Analyses of Seven Major Band Compositions of the Twentieth Century." Diss., George Peadody College for Teachers, 1958.

Workinger, William Colvin. "Some Aspects of Scoring in the Band Works of Vincent Persichetti." Diss., New York University, 1970.

Teacher Resource Guide

"Fantasies on Theme by Haydn" Norman Dello Joio

(b. 1913)

Unit 1: Composer

Norman Dello Joio was born in New York City on January 24, 1913. He quickly showed remarkable aptitude and facility for playing the organ. At 14, he already was organist and choir director of the Star of the Sea Church in City Island. He attended Juilliard and studied at Yale University with Paul Hindemith. He won a number of awards for composition in the United States. He has written for virtually every medium including operas, incidental music, ballets, chamber music, and choral music. Dello Joio served on the faculties of Sarah Lawrence College and the Mannes College of Music. Notable works by Dello Joio include *Fantasies on a Theme by Haydn*, *From Every Horizon*, and *Scenes from "The Louvre"*.

Unit 2: Composition

Fantasies on a Theme by Haydn was commissioned by the Michigan School Band and Orchestra Association. It was dedicated to Mr. Leonard Falcone, Director of Bands at Michigan State University, upon his retirement, in recognition of devoted service to music, to education, and to his colleagues. It was first published in 1968 by Edward B. Marks Music Corp. The piece is in one movement, is a Grade 5 difficulty, and lasts about fourteen minutes.

Unit 3: Historical Perspective

This piece for band is based on a theme from a composition for piano by Franz Josef Haydn. The subtly-conceived theme offered Dello Joio the opportunity to "fantasize in the musical language of today." The three movements are a constantly-varied examination of Haydn's basic idea. The bubbling humor of the first and third fantasies flank a second which is very lyrical. "In the final sense, it is my homage to a composer who will always remain contemporary."

Unit 4: Technical Considerations

The piece requires the keys of F Major and some related keys for the full ensemble. The meters are straightforward, and the few meter changes that do occur happen only on the quarter-note level. There are no tempo changes except between sections. The rhythmic demands are very basic with the use of quarter, eighth, and sixteenth notes. Scalar passages and ranges are not difficult; the highest trumpet note is an A concert. There are no key signatures, but several accidentals.

Unit 5: Stylistic Considerations

Each large section has its own style. The intensity and movement of the music should be equal to the phrasing, articulation, rhythms and principles of the line. This is a piece inspired by a work from the Classic period and scored for modern wind band. There are no solos, and the lines are not very exposed. All melodies should be played in singing style. Balances are important between melody and accompaniment. A blend of sound is essential. Rhythm and dance-style must have contrast between sections. Tempos should match the styles and the articulations.

Unit 6: Musical Elements

The main theme is stated in F. Compositional devices used include call-and-answer ostinatos, the use of countermelodic material, and inserted 2/4 measures of silence. Dello Joio adds the element of instrumental texture to show Haydn's implied dynamic contrasts. It is a decidedly tonal piece using harmonies which demonstrate not only the clarity and pureness of Haydn's 18th-century style but also Dello Joio's imaginative creativity in this setting. The traditional British Brass Band sonority is embellished and enhanced with the use of woodwinds and percussion.

Unit 7: Form and Structure

THEME	F Major
Theme statement	Mm. 1-38
Fugato	Mm. 39-75
Closing	Mm. 76-103

FANTASY I	F Major
Lo stesso tempo	Mm. 104-124
2nd statement	Mm. 125-144
3rd statement	Mm. 145-159
Closing	Mm. 160-179

FANTASY II	A-flat and other related keys, ends on A Major
Adagio	Mm. 180-189
2nd phrase	Mm. 190-204, woodwinds & horns
march-like	Mm. 205-214, dotted rhythms
Closing	Mm. 215-250, tutti
FANTASY III	F Major with several related keys
Allegro, molto spiritoso	
	Mm. 251-266, tutti, very staccato & rhythmical
2nd phrase	Mm. 267-305, constant staccato eighth notes with accomp
rhythmical	Mm. 306-331, alternating large instrument groups
slurs	Mm. 332-343, tutti piano and slurred
staccato	Mm. 344-375, tutti staccato
Coda	Mm. 376-384, tutti closing

Unit 8: Suggested Listening

Norman Dello Joio, *Scenes from "The Louvre"*
Norman Dello Joio, *Variants on a Medieval Tune*
Norman Dello Joio, *From Every Horizon*
Gordon Jacob, *William Byrd Suite*
Martin Mailman, *Concerto for Wind Orchestra (Variations), Op. 89*
Jan Pieterszoon Sweelinck/arr. Walters, *Ballo del granduca*

Unit 9: Additional References and Resources

Baker, Theodore. "Dello Joio, Norman," *Baker's Biographical Dictionary of Musicians.* 6th ed., revised by Nicolas Slonimsky. New York: Schirmer Books, 1984.

National Band Association Selective Music List for Bands

Rehrig, William H. *The Heritage Encyclopedia of Band Music.* Westerville, OH: Integrity Press, 1991.

Westrup, J. A. and F. Ll. Harrison. "Dello Joio, Norman," *The New College Encyclopedia of Music.* Revised by Conrad Wilson. New York: W. W. Norton & Company, Ltd, 1981.

Teacher Resource Guide

"George Washington Bridge: An Impression for Band" William Schuman

(b. 1910–d. 1992)

Unit 1: Composer

William Schuman, eminent American composer, educator and music administrator, was born in New York City on August 4, 1910. His early musical training was with Max Persin and Charles Housiel. He graduated from Columbia University and privately studied composition with Roy Harris from 1936 to 1938. He taught at Sarah Lawrence College from 1935 to 1945 and was president of the Julliard School from 1945 to 1962. He attracted the attention of conductor Serge Koussevitsky who premiered many of his works. Schuman has composed for virtually all genres, including orchestra, chorus and symphonic band. Schuman was the first recipient of the Pulitzer Prize for music in 1943 for his composition "A Free Song". Some of his other works for band include *New England Triptych*, *Circus Overture*, and *American Hymn*.

Unit 2: Composition

Schuman completed *George Washington Bridge* on April 17, 1950 while living in New Rochelle, New York. It was written for the Michigan School Band and Orchestra Association and first performed on July 31, 1951 at Interlochen, Michigan by the Michigan All-State Band, conducted by Dale Harris. The piece makes use of 20th-century compositional elements such as bi-chordal tonalities, explosions of sound, and modal mixtures. The piece is one movement, is of Grade 5 difficulty and lasts about nine minutes.

Unit 3: Historical Perspective

Schuman wrote: "There are few days in the year when I do not see George Washington Bridge. I pass it on my way to work as I drive along the Henry Hudson Parkway on the New York shore. Ever since my student days, when I watched the progress of its construction, this bridge has had for me an almost human personality, and this personally is astonishingly varied, assuming different moods depending on the time of day or night, the weather, the traffic and, of course, my own mood as I pass by. I have walked across it late at night when it was shrouded in fog, and during the brilliant sunshine hours of midday. I have driven over it countless times and passed under it on boats. Coming to New York City by air, sometimes I have been lucky enough to fly right over it. It is difficult to imagine a more gracious welcome or dramatic entry to the great metropolis." This piece was among the pieces selected for the first University of Rochester/Eastman School of Music/Mercury Records Longplay recording made by the Eastman Wind Ensemble on May 14, 1953. The entire album was recorded in a single two-hour session.

Unit 4: Technical Considerations

There are no key signatures but many accidentals and chromatic gestures. The tonality shifts frequently and is predominantly bi-tonal. Ranges and tempos are not too difficult. Instead, great effort must be spent to achieve a uniformity of articulation and blend. Schuman uses simple rhythms in half, quarter and eighth notes.

Unit 5: Stylistic Considerations

The sections each require their own style differences to create the proper contrasts. Dynamics in the piece range from *fff* to *pp*. Articulations are specific. The *sostenuto molto* section must be sustained uniformly. An expert percussion section is required. One must be careful not to overdot any figures but rather play them accurately in a 20th-century style.

Unit 6: Musical Elements

Most of Schuman's ideas were conceived in terms of a large sonic arsenal, capable of infinite variety and producing huge blocks of sounds. Everything about the piece, like the structure it portrays, is engineered and proportionally distributed for the balanced achievement of its purpose. The bi-chordal statement beginning in m. 1 with the C Major triad in soprano brass and horns over the one in B-flat of all low brass establishes a bi-tonal harmonic pattern that is Schuman's resource throughout the score. Most of the material moves vertically; there is little counterpoint.

Unit 7: Form and Structure

A
                                  Opens on F Major, but quickly moves away
    MAESTOSO MODERATO   Mm. 1-41, features theme 1

B
    ALLEGRETTO   Mm. 42-96, features theme 2, WW vs. brass groups

C
    PIÙ MOSSO FLOWING (CANTABILE)
                                    Mm. 97-163, features theme 3
    CANTABILE E DOLCE   Mm. 164-186, second section

B1
    ALLEGRETTO   Mm. 187-229, features theme 2, tutti, staccato

A1
    SLOWER THAN BEGINNING Mm. 230-263, features theme 1, longer note values

Coda
                                   ends on C Major
    FLOWING   Mm. 263-278, chordal, tutti driving to end

Unit 8: Suggested Listening

Ingolf Dahl, *Sinfonietta*
Martin Mailman, *Geometrics No. 1 for Band, Op. 22*
Martin Mailman, *Geometrics No. 5 for Band, Op. 58*
Peter Mennin, *Canzona*
Vincent Persichetti, *Masquerade for Band*
Gunther Schuller, *Meditation*
William Schuman, *New England Triptych*

Unit 9: Additional References and Resources

Baker, Theodore. "Schuman, William," *Baker's Biographical Dictionary of Musicians.* 6th ed., revised by Nicolas Slonimsky. New York: Schirmer Books, 1984.

Brown, Michael. "Enduring Wisdom from William Schuman, An Unpublished 1986 Interview." *The Instrumentalist,* XLVIII November 1993, 26-29.

Brown, Michael Ray. "The Band Music of William Schuman: A Study of Form, Content and Style." Diss., University of Georgia, 1989.

Fennell, Frederick. "William Schuman: George Washington Bridge - an Impression for Band". *BDGuide,* VII/4 March/April 1993, 28-36.

Grimes, Ev. "Conversations with American Composers: Ev Grimes Interviews William Schuman." *Music Educators Journal*, 72/8 (April 1986), 46, 47, 50-54.

National Band Association Selective Music List for Bands

Prindl, Frank Joseph. "A Study of Ten Original Compositions for Band Published in America Since 1946." Diss., The Florida State University, 1956.

Rehrig, William H. *The Heritage Encyclopedia of Band Music*. Westerville, OH: Integrity Press, 1991.

Rhodes, Stephen L. "A Comparative Analysis of the Band Compositions of William Schuman." Diss., University of Colorado, 1987.

Westrup, J. A. and F. Ll. Harrison. "Schuman, William," *The New College Encyclopedia of Music*. Revised by Conrad Wilson. New York: W. W. Norton & Company, Ltd, 1981.

Whitwell, David. "Schuman—His Music for Winds." *The Instrumentalist*, XXI January 1967, 40-41.

Teacher Resource Guide

"La Fiesta Mexicana"
H. Owen Reed
(b. 1910)

Unit 1: Composer

H. Owen Reed was born in Odessa, Missouri in June 1910. He earned a Bachelor of Music (1934), Master of Music (1936), and A.B. degrees from Louisiana State University. He was a pupil of Howard Hanson and Bernard Rogers at the University of Rochester's Eastman School of Music where he earned his Ph.D. in 1939 and subsequently studied privately with Roy Harris. He taught at the University of Michigan from 1939 to 1976 and wrote several books on theory and composition. In 1948-49, he was awarded a Guggenheim Fellowship for study and composing in Mexico. He was a member of ASCAP and the Music Teachers National Association. Some of his other works include *For the Unfortunate* for band, the ballet *The Masque of the Red Death*, the opera *Peter Homan's Dream*, three works classified as "Chamber dance-operas", a symphony, a violin concerto, and a cello concerto.

Unit 2: Composition

La Fiesta Mexicana is one of many works for band composed by H. Owen Reed. The piece was composed in 1949 for full wind ensemble with a harp (in the *mariachi* tradition) and a large assortment of percussion instruments. The premiere was given that year by the U.S. Marine Band under Lt. Colonel William F. Santelman. Fifteen years later, Reed prepared an orchestral version, but it has never begun to challenge the popularity of the original. The Work's designation as "A Mexican Folk-Song Symphony" suggests certain parallels with the aforementioned *Latin-American Symphonette* of Morton Gould, but there are stronger ones, in terms of both the three-movement structure and the programmatic substance, with Debussy's masterwork in the Hispanic idiom, *Ibéria*. The piece has three movements, is a Grade 5 difficulty (NBA lists it as a Grade 6) and lasts about twenty-two minutes.

Unit 3: Historical Perspective

In his thirties, Reed traveled a good deal in the Americas and Europe, and responded warmly to the folk music he heard in such diverse settings as Scandinavia and the Caribbean islands. It was during a five-month 1949 sojourn in Mexico, on a Guggenheim Fellowship, that he found his inspiration and materials for *La Fiesta Mexicana*. He did not confine himself to the capital, but spent about two months in Cuernavaca, a similar period in Chapala, and only a few weeks visiting such spots as Mexico City and Acapulco. The authentic folk tunes he used in this work were found for the most part in Chapala, Jalisco and Guadalajara. Other themes were borrowed from published collections of Gregorian motifs and Aztec dances.

Unit 4: Technical Considerations

The piece has no key signatures, so accidentals abound; the score is in C, and there are no octave transpositions. There are a few basic meter changes, and the tempos remain consistent within the movements. There are both staccato and legato articulations, so contrast is important. All instruments have several exposed sections and several solos as does the percussion section. Ranges and scalar passages are not difficult.

Unit 5: Stylistic Considerations

Each movement has its own style (fast, slow, meditative, etc.). The intensity and movement of the music should be equal to the phrasing, articulation, rhythms and principles of the line. This is a 20th-century work with 20th-century sounds, and it should be approached with a 20th-century interpretation. The *mariachi* style is desirable from the band.

Unit 6: Musical Elements

The Mexican, as a result of his religious heritage, feels an inner desire to express love and honor for his Virgin. The Mexican "Fiesta", an integral part of this social structure, is a study in contrasts: it is both serious and comical, festive and solemn, devout and pagan, boisterous and tender. *La Fiesta Mexicana*, which attempts to portray musically one of these "Fiestas", is divided into three movements. The first movement, "Prelude and Aztec Dance", contains the opening of the festival, announced by church bells and fireworks. After the quiet interlude of night, the church bells announce the new day with a parade complete with band and Aztec dances. The second movement, "Mass", is a reminder that the festival is a religious celebration as the celebrants gather for worship. The final movement, "Carnival", contains a myriad of entertainments, all an integral part of the fiesta: a circus, the market, the bullfight, the town band, and the cantinas with their bands of mariachis. The score includes program notes and possible choreographic notes for each movement. The score is "generously" cued so that smaller bands can perform it.

Unit 7: Form and Structure

MVMT I: PRELUDE AND AZTEC DANCE	F, B-flat, other related keys
Allegro maestoso (church bells & procession)	Beginning to **1**
"...celebrators settle down..."	**1** to **4**
"...church bells & fireworks..."	**4** to **5**
"...parade announcement..."	**5** to **6**
"...band in the distance..."	**6** to **7**
"...Aztec Dancers..."	**7** to end
MVMT II: MASS	G Major & other related keys
Largo	Beginning to **16**
Meno mosso	**16** to end
MVMT III: CARNIVAL	C, B-flat, A-flat, other related keys
Allegro con brio (2/4)	Beginning to **22**
Allegro con spirito (3/4)	**22** to **28**
Tempo I	**28** to end

Unit 8: Suggested Listening

Aaron Copland, *El Salon Mexico*
Claude Debussy, *Ibéria*
Morton Gould, *Latin-American Symphonette*
Morton Gould, *Santa Fé Saga*
Roger Nixon, *Fiesta del Pacifico*
Frank Perkins/arr. Werle, *Fandango*
H. Owen Reed, *For the Unfortunate*
Clifton Williams, *Symphonic Dance No. 3, "Fiesta"*

Unit 9: Additional References and Resources

Baker, Theodore. "Reed, H. Owen," *Baker's Biographical Dictionary of Musicians*. 6th ed., revised by Nicolas Slonimsky. New York: Schirmer Books, 1984.

Bruning, Earl Henry Jr. "A Survey and Handbook of Analysis for the Conducting and Interpretation of Seven Selected Works in the Standard Repertoire for Wind Band." Diss., Ball State University, 1980.

National Band Association Selective Music List for Bands

Rehrig, William H. *The Heritage Encyclopedia of Band Music.* Westerville, OH: Integrity Press, 1991.

Westrup, J. A. and F. Ll. Harrison. *The New College Encyclopedia of Music.* Revised by Conrad Wilson. New York: W. W. Norton & Company, Ltd, 1981.

Teacher Resource Guide

"Overture in C"
Charles Simon Catel

(b. 1773–d. 1830)

edited by Richard Franko Goldman (b. 1910–d. 1980)

and Roger Smith

Unit 1: Composer

Charles Catel was born in 1773. He was a French composer and held his first professional post at the age of 14, and in 1790 became the director of the Band of the National Guard. During the French Revolution he was active as a composer of military music and works in celebration of the new regime. He was appointed Professor of Harmony at the Paris Conservatoire when it was founded in 1795. Of his ten operas, *Les Bayadères* (1810) was the most successful. His *Traitè d'harmonie* (1802) was a standard textbook for many years. Another of his works for band is *Symphonic Militaire*.

Unit 2: Composition

Overture in C was composed in 1792 for the Band of the National Guard. The work was rediscovered by Richard Franko Goldman and edited for present-day performance by Goldman and Roger Smith. The first American performance was by the Goldman Band, Richard Franko Goldman conducting, on June 19, 1953. The piece has one movement, is a Grade 5 difficulty (NBA lists it as a Grade 3) and lasts about six minutes.

Unit 3: Historical Perspective

Along with Cherubini, Paer, Gossec, Jadin and Mehul, Catel is one of the very first important composers whose names are associated with the development of large bands in the 19th century (following the *Harmoniemusik* period). The elegance and clarity of the *Overture in C* is characteristic of the perfection of late 18th-century style. The influence of Mozart can be heard, and the straightforward sonata form is comparable to those similar works of his contemporaries.

Unit 4: Technical Considerations

The scales of C Major and its related keys are required for the entire ensemble. The rhythmic demands are very basic with the use of quarter, eighth, and sixteenth notes. There is one meter change from 4/4 in the opening *Larghetto* to cut time for the *Allegro vivace.* The *Allegro* section is fast (quarter note equal to 144-152) and requires some rapid *staccato* accompaniments from clarinets. Accuracy of articulations and sustaining of lines is necessary. Ranges and scale passages are not difficult.

Unit 5: Stylistic Considerations

The piece should be performed in an "overture" style, that is, in a light, fast, energetic style. Articulations should be crisp and uniform. The interpretation is quite straightforward in this regard. An effort should be made to perform at or slightly above the indicated metronome markings. The intensity and movement of the music should be equal to the phrasing, articulation, rhythms and principles of the line.

Unit 6: Musical Elements

The piece is in the concert key of C Major and several related keys and consists of a slow introduction, followed by the *Allegro*. The harmony is typical of French Classical music. Tonicizations and chord movements are clear. Contrasts of dynamics during statements and restatements of themes is essential to style, but not always indicated in the score. There are many grace notes requiring an interpretive decision for uniformity.

Unit 7: Form and Structure

INTRODUCTION	C minor, C Major
LARGHETTO	Mm. 1-30
EXPOSITION	C Major and other related keys
ALLEGRO VIVACE	Mm. 31-54, first theme
	Mm. 55-78, first theme second time
	Mm. 79-123, E minor, first theme with chordal interjections
DEVELOPMENT	G Major
	Mm. 124-152
	Mm. 153-183, E-flat Major
	Mm. 184-220, E Major, progression to G dominant

RECAPITULATION   C Major
   TEMPO I   Mm. 221-249
                                  Mm. 250-262, first theme second time
                                  Mm. 263-289
                                  Mm. 290-325, C minor, A-flat Major, C Major
                                  Mm. 326-330, A-flat Major

CODA
   CLOSING   Mm. 331-357, use of theme I, development theme,
                                  ending in C Major

Unit 8: Suggested Listening

Charles Catel, *Symphonic Militaire*
François Joseph Gossec, *Classic Overture in C*
François Joseph Gossec, *Military Symphony in F*
François Joseph Gossec, *Victor March*
Jadin, *Overture in F*
Etienne Henri Nicolas Mehul, *Overture in F*

Unit 9: Additional References and Resources

Baker, Theodore. "Catel, Charles Simon," *Baker's Biographical Dictionary of
   Musicians.* 6th ed., revised by Nicolas Slonimsky. New York: Schirmer
   Books, 1984.

Dudley, Walter Sherwood, Jr. "Orchestration in the Musique D'harmonie
   of The French Revolution" (Volumes I and II). Ph.D. diss., University
   of California, Berkeley, 1968.

National Band Association Selective Music List for Bands

Rehrig, William H. *The Heritage Encyclopedia of Band Music.* Westerville, OH:
   Integrity Press, 1991.

Swanzy, David Paul. "The Wind Ensemble and Its Music During the French
   Revolution (1789-1795)." Ph.D. diss., Michigan State University, 1966.

Westrup, J. A. and F. Ll. Harrison. *The New College Encyclopedia of Music.*
   Revised by Conrad Wilson. New York: W. W. Norton & Company, Ltd,
   1981.

Teacher Resource Guide

"Overture for Winds, Op. 24"
Felix Mendelssohn-Bartholdy

(b. 1809–d. 1847)

arranged by John Boyd

(b. 1944)

Unit 1: Composer
Felix Mendelssohn-Bartholdy was born in Hamburg, Germany. He studied piano with his mother, Marie Bigot, Ludwig Berger, and Moscheles, and composition with Zelter. He was a prolific composer starting at an early age, writing his first piano quartet at age 12. He also worked on behalf of other composers, in particular J. S. Bach, whose cause he championed by conducting (at the age of twenty) the first public performance of the *St. Matthew Passion* since Bach's death. He conducted the Philharmonic Society in London and was music director at Düsseldorf. In 1835, he became conductor of the famous *Gewandhaus* concerts in Leipzig. He knew other composers such as Berlioz, Schumann, Liszt and Chopin. In 1842 he co-founded the Leipzig Conservatorium. He composed five symphonies, four oratorios, seven operas, choral music, chamber music, concertos, piano works, organ sonatas and songs.

Unit 2: Composition
Mendelssohn composed the Opus 24 in July 1824 for the court orchestra of Bad Doberan, near Rostock, where the composer was accompanying his father. The original score was lost but recopied by Mendelssohn in July of 1826. These two scores were entitled *Nocturno* and were written for flute, two clarinets, two oboes, two bassoons, two horns, trumpet and English bass horn. The piece follows the model of the French overture by having two sections: slow, fast. The piece is one movement, is a Grade 5 difficulty and lasts about ten minutes.

Unit 3: Historical Perspective

On November 30, 1838, Mendelssohn sent the publisher, Simrock, an *Ouvertüre für Harmoniemusik* scored for 23 winds and percussion along with a four-hand piano score. The 1838 composition is a rescoring of the *Nocturno* for German Band of that era and was not published until 1852 following his death. It is possible that the rescoring was an attempt to acquire greater performance opportunities for his work by making it available in settings for British and German bands along with a proposed edition for orchestra. The *Harmoniemusik* was a very popular ensemble of the day with virtually all composers writing and/or arranging for it.

Unit 4: Technical Considerations

The scales of C Major and its related keys are required for the entire ensemble. The rhythmic demands are very basic with the use of quarter, eighth, and sixteenth notes. Phrasing and articulations are uniform. There are fast ostinato rhythms in the "Allegro vivace". Everyone must be able to play light with staccatos and accents as well as legato with tenutos and slurs. Rapid rhythmic figures will require double-tonguing from brass players.

Unit 5: Stylistic Considerations

The first section requires smoothness and controlled separations between notes. Slurs with staccato notes underneath necessitate interpretive decisions on the part of the conductor. A rich, sonorous tone should be employed in this section. Some overdotting of dotted eighth notes would be appropriate. The second section requires a lightness and energy to maintain its rapid tempo (quarter note equal to 152-160) as well as a feeling of "bounce" to the pulse. The tone should be brighter, and the rhythmic accompaniments must be precise and light. Flutes, saxophones and clarinets must play sixteenth-note C Major scales in this tempo.

Unit 6: Musical Elements

The piece is in the concert key of C Major and several related keys and consists of a opening section and an "Allegro vivace" section. Some counterpoint is used between voices, but the texture remains mostly four-voice. The harmony is typical of early Romantic music, and Mendelssohn in particular. There are a couple of very tricky fermatas for several players at a time. The second section is a typical overture style of rhythmic intensity and drive of pulse. Chords move very vertically.

Unit 7: Form and Structure

ANDANTE   C Major
    Introduction   Beginning to m. 26
    Section 2   Mm. 27-40
    Section 3   Mm. 41-48

Section 4	Mm. 49-67 begins some French overture rhythmic figures
ALLEGRO VIVACE	C Major & related keys
Section 1	Mm. 68-85 tutti large statement to open new section
Section 2	Mm. 85-97 thinning texture & softer dynamic
Section 3	Mm. 98-112 tutti
Section 4	Mm. 112-150 semi-development
Section 1	Mm. 150-168 tutti large statement to signal return
Section 2	Mm. 168-180 thinning texture & softer dynamic
Coda	Mm. 180-226 tutti closing

Unit 8: Suggested Listening

Ludwig van Beethoven, *Lenore III*

Leonard Bernstein, *Overture to "Candide"*

Felix Mendelssohn-Bartholdy/arr. Griessle, *Overture for Winds*, Op. 24

Carl Maria von Weber, *Preciosa Overture*

Unit 9: Additional References and Resources

Baker, Theodore. "Mendelssohn-Bartholdy, Felix," *Baker's Biographical Dictionary of Musicians*. 6th ed., revised by Nicolas Slonimsky. New   York: Schirmer Books, 1984.

Boyd, John Pretz. "Ouverture fur Harmoniemusik Op. 24 by Felix Mendelssohn-Bartholdy: An Edition for Contemporary Wind Band." Diss., University of Missouri-Kansas City, 1981.

Gambill, Tommie G. "Contemporary Editions of Nineteenth Century Wind Band Literature." Diss., Florida State University, 1979.

Garofalo, Robert J. "Mendelssohln Overture for Band." *BD Guide*, January/ February 1991, 22.

Grout, Donald. *A History of Western Music*, 3rd edition. New York: W. W. Norton & Company, Ltd, 1980.

National Band Association Selective Music List for Bands

Reed, David R. "The Original Version of the Overture for Wind Band of Felix Mendelssohn-Bartholdy." *Journal of Band Research* XVIII/1 (Fall 1982): 3-10.

Rehrig, William H. *The Heritage Encyclopedia of Band Music*. Westerville, OH: Integrity Press, 1991.

Westrup, J. A. and F. Ll. Harrison. *The New College Encyclopedia of Music.* Revised by Conrad Wilson. New York: W. W. Norton & Company, Ltd, 1981.

Whitwell, David. "Mendelssohn—His Music for Winds." *The Instrumentalist,* XXI February 1967, 40-41.

Teacher Resource Guide

Overture to "Candide"
Leonard Bernstein

(b. 1918–d. 1990)

arranged by Clare Grundman

(b. 1913–d. 1996)

Unit 1: Composer

Leonard Bernstein was born in Lawrence, Massachusetts in 1918 and died in New York City in 1990. He is considered to be the first internationally-known musician to be entirely the product of American schooling and was one of the few composers equally at home in the popular theater and concert hall. He studied at Harvard University and the Curtis Institute of Music in Philadelphia. His teachers included Walter Piston for composition and Serge Koussevitsky and Fritz Reiner for conducting. In 1942 he became Koussevitsky's assistant at the Berkshire Music Center, and in 1957 he became assistant conductor of the New York Philharmonic. In 1959 he succeeded Dmitri Mitropoulos as music director. Bernstein wrote music for orchestra, chorus, music theater, movies, and television. He was also well known for his many recordings and his tireless efforts on the behalf of young conductors and composers around the world. Some of his other works transcribed for band include *Slava!*, *Symphony No. 1: Jeremiah* (1942), *Symphonic Dance Music from "West Side Story"*, *Divertimento*, *A Musical Toast*, *Selections from "West Side Story"*, and *Three Dance Episodes from "On the Town"*.

Unit 2: Composition

Although his adaptation of Voltaire's *Candide* would prove to be one of Bernstein's most successful works for the musical stage (along with *On the Town* (1944) and *West Side Story* (1957)), it actually ran fewer than eighty performances when it opened on Broadway on December 1, 1956. The piece is an overture-style work that states several of the main themes of the songs found in *Candide*. It received its first concert performance in 1957 by the New York Philharmonic with Bernstein conducting and has been a favorite of American audiences ever since. It is performed often in both its original orchestra version and in this band arrangement. The piece is one movement, is a Grade 5 difficulty and lasts about five minutes.

Unit 3: Historical Perspective

Bernstein composed *Candide* in 1956. Candide was a collaboration between Bernstein and Lillian Hellman. Hellman's concept was to adapt Voltaire's original work to modernity, satirizing the McCarthy anti-communism of the early 1950's, which she experienced firsthand. The first edition of this arrangement was published in 1986; there is also an arrangement by Walter Beeler.

Unit 4: Technical Considerations

The piece is in the concert key of E-flat Major. There are several meter changes and the tempo is fast (Allegro molto con brio (quarter note equal to 132)), so there are many rapid articulations. There are tempo changes including a *rallantando*, a grand pause, and a *più mosso*. There are both staccato and legato articulations, so contrast is important. Upper woodwinds have several exposed sections and some solos.

Unit 5: Stylistic Considerations

The piece should be performed in an Overture style; that is, in a light, fast, energetic style. Articulations should be crisp and uniform. All tempo indications in the score support this. The interpretation is quite straight-forward in this regard. An effort should be made to perform at or slightly above the indicated metronome markings. The intensity and movement of the music should be equal to the phrasing, articulation, rhythms and principles of the line.

Unit 6: Musical Elements

The piece features some meter changes and trans-meter rhythms and ostinatos found frequently in twentieth-century music; however, the piece is firmly rooted in tonality and is easy to listen to, much in the style of an overture by Mozart, Rossini or Suppé. The piece alternates sections between the concert keys of E-flat Major and B-flat Major. There are elements of polytonality and clusters; however, the entire piece is "listenable" from a harmonic point of view. The first and third sections contain three themes and an opening announcement theme. One main theme is used in the second and fourth sections. The coda features two new themes (from the song "Glitter and Be Gay") as well as previous themes. Tonicizations and chord movements are clear. There are several meter changes but the main pulse stays the same. Compound as well as simple meters are used.

Unit 7: Form and Structure

SECTION 1   E-flat Major
  Opening   Mm. 1-6, introduction
  Theme 1   Mm. 7-18, theme stated in upper woodwinds
                            Mm. 19-23, introduction repeated
                            Mm. 24-31, theme 1 repeated in upper woodwinds
  Theme 2   Mm. 32-46, stated in upper woodwinds
  Theme 3   Mm. 47-63, stated in brass and low woodwinds
  Transition   Mm. 64-82, use of upper woodwinds

SECTION 2   B-flat Major
  Theme 4   Mm. 83-133

SECTION 3   E-flat Major
  Opening   Mm. 134-140, introduction repeated
  Theme 1   Mm. 141-153, stated in upper woodwinds
  Theme 2   Mm. 154-160, stated in upper woodwinds
  Theme 3   Mm. 161-177, stated in brass and low woodwinds

SECTION 4   B-flat Major
  Theme 4   Mm. 178-205
  Coda   E-flat Major
  Theme 5   Mm. 206-230, "Glitter and Be Gay" I
  Theme 6   Mm. 231-254, "Glitter and Be Gay" II
  Opening   Mm. 255-270, introduction theme fragmented
  Theme 3   Mm. 271-276
  Theme 4   Mm. 276-287, tutti close

Unit 8: Suggested Listening

Leonard Bernstein/arr. Grundman, *Slava!*
Leonard Bernstein/arr. Grundman, *A Musical Toast*
Leonard Bernstein/arr. Polster, *Symphonic Dance Music from "West Side Story"*
Martin Mailman, *Exaltations, Op. 67*
Wolfgang Amadeus Mozart, *Overture to Le Nozze di Figaro*
Gioacchino Rossini, *Overture to Il barbiere di Siviglia*

Unit 9: Additional References and Resources

Baker, Theodore. "Bernstein, Leonard," *Baker's Biographical Dictionary of Musicians.*
    6th ed., revised by Nicolas Slonimsky. New York: Schirmer Books, 1984.

Peyser, Joan. *Bernstein: A Biography.* New York: Ballantine Books, 1987.

Rehrig, William H. *The Heritage Encyclopedia of Band Music.* Westerville, OH:
    Integrity Press, 1991.

Westrup, J. A. and F. Ll. Harrison. *The New College Encyclopedia of Music.* Revised by Conrad Wilson. New York: W. W. Norton & Company, Ltd, 1981.

Teacher Resource Guide

"Sketches On A Tudor Psalm"
Fisher Tull

(b. 1934–d. 1994)

Unit 1: Composer

Fisher Aubrey Tull was born in Waco, Texas, on September 24, 1934. He earned all of his degrees at the University of North Texas. Tull's principal composition teacher was Samuel Adler. He was Distinguished Professor of Music at Sam Houston State University where he taught theory and composition from 1957. Among the many awards his works have won are the Ostwald Award for *Toccata*, the Arthur Fraser Memorial Award for *Three Episodes for Orchestra*, and the Walter Beeler Award. Tull's career encompassed a broad range of musical achievements as a trumpet performer, arranger, composer, conductor, educator, and administrator. Throughout his life he fulfilled over forty commissions and earned a reputation as one of the premiere composers of music for winds and percussion. He wrote over twenty works for band. Some of his major works include *Concerto Grosso for Brass Quintet and Band, Cryptic Essay, The Final Covenant, Prelude and Double Fugue,* and *Toccata.*

Unit 2: Composition

This work is based on a 1567 setting of the second psalm by Thomas Tallis. The original was in the Phrygian mode with the melody in the tenor voice. A modern adaptation is still used today in Anglican services. After an introduction that sets the harmonic character, the theme is first presented by the solo alto saxophone. The Allegro section contains a continuous set of variations on rhythmic and melodic fragments of the theme before the theme returns in augmentation leading to a fully scored climax. The composer wrote, "encouraged by the acceptance of my *Toccata*, I was motivated to try my hand at another band work in theme-and-variation form similar to my *Variations on an Advent Hymn for Brass*

Ensemble. I considered using a number of themes found in the Episcopal Hymnal but always seemed to gravitate to Thomas Tallis' setting of the second psalm. My reluctance to finalize this choice was caused by the awareness that Ralph Vaughan Williams had used the same material for his *Fantasia for Double String Orchestra* (1910), a work with which I was quite familiar; nonetheless, against the advice of some of my colleagues, I decided to take the plunge. After locking away my Vaughan Williams recording and score, my first step was to consult Tallis' original setting which is found in *Musica Disciplina, Vol. II,* pp. 198-199." The work, composed in 1971, is 335 measures and eleven minutes in length.

Unit 3: Historical Perspective

Over the many years that composers have been writing original works for band, the theme and variations setting has been a favored form. William Schuman's *Chester* (1957) and Norman Dello Joio's *Variants on a Mediaeval Tune* (1963) are two well-known, outstanding works for band that use theme and variations style. *Musica Disciplina* is part of ancient Greek writings concerning music as an explained science. Thomas Tallis (ca.1505-85) was a leading English composer from the Renaissance period whose musical production bridges early and late 16th-century English styles and whose career reflects the religious and political changes that affected English Church music in this period.

Unit 4: Technical Considerations

This composition juxtaposes the keys of F minor, F Major, and A Major, and uses the phrygian mode on A. The original Tallis setting alternates between meters of three and five. This is reflected in Tull's composition. The opening *Andante* accommodates the melody with shifts between 5/4, 4/4, and 3/4. The *Allegro* shifts between 5/8, 6/8, 2/4, 3/4, and 4/4. The polyphonic accompaniment in the introduction sets eighth-note triplets against even eighths, quarters and syncopated quarters. Dotted eighth-sixteenth-eighth triplet patterns along with sixteenth-note triplets appear throughout. There is a 34-measure passage of sixteenth-note tonguing for the Trumpets in the *Allegro.* There is an extended Alto Saxophone solo that is the initial statement of the theme. There are also solos for almost all woodwind sections. There are important parts for Alto Clarinet (that may be played on Bass Clarinet or Basset Horns) and for Celesta.

Unit 5: Stylistic Considerations

The opening *Andante* requires attentive control and balance from the ensemble. The melody, whether scored for solo instruments or in full band should be played lyrically, singingly, and expressively. The initial appearance in the Alto Saxophone should be performed with a clarity of articulation as though the player were singing the text. A full range of dynamics is used and must be observed for a truly effective performance. The full scoring of the melody at measure 56 is only *forte*, while at measure 299, the climax, is *fortissimo*. Many performances have the timpanist double measure 333 with an *allargando* for a truly triumphal closing on the A Major chord.

Unit 6: Musical Elements

The harmonic construction of the work juxtaposes F minor and F Major. The melody is in the Phrygian mode on A. The music is basically tonal. The uneven measuring of the phrases in the original setting inspired the composer to use multimeters throughout the work.

Unit 7: Form and Structure

The composition is based on a harmonic motif stated at the beginning (the F Min. and F Maj.7 chords), and on 8 thematic motifs from the phrases of the melody (1, 2, 1a, 2a, 3, 4, 5, and 6).

INTRODUCTION (1-10)
1-5	Harmonic motif (brass) followed by motif 2
6-10	Harmonic motif (woodwinds) followed by motif 2

THEME (11-87)
12-33	Theme (sax, horns, oboes)
34-40	Harmonic motif followed by motif 2
41-67	Restatement of theme
67-87	Harmonic motif, development of motif 5

DEVELOPMENT BY CONTINUOUS VARIATIONS (88-226)
88-100	Ostinato (percussion, trombone)
101-104	Motif 1 (horns, cornets)
111-150	Melody derived from retrograde of theme
151-176	Development of motifs 1,1a,2
177-199	Development of motif 6
200-212	Development of motifs 4,2
213-242	Combination of motifs 5, 1
243-261	Conclusion of development with harmonic motif and motifs 2, 6

RECAPITULATION AND CODA (262-335)
262-268	Harmonic motif (woodwinds) motif 6 (chimes)
269-298	Theme in augmentation followed by motif 2
299-310	Last half of theme (tutti)
311-335	Coda based on motifs 3,1

Unit 8: Suggested Listening

Norman Dello Joio, *Variants on a Mediaeval Tune*
William Schuman, *Chester*
Claude T. Smith, *Variations on an English Folk Song*
Fisher Tull, *The Final Covenant; Prelude and Double Fugue; Toccata*
Ralph Vaughan Williams, *Variations on a Theme of Thomas Tallis for Orchestra*

Unit 9: Additional References and Resources

Grout, Donald and Claude Palisca. *History of Western Music.* 4th ed., New York, NY: Norton & Co., 1988.

Randel, Don Michael. *The New Harvard Dictionary of Music.* Cambridge, MA: Harvard University, 1986.

Rehrig, William H. *The Heritage Encyclopedia of Band Music.* Westerville, OH: Integrity Press, 1991.

Smith, Norman and Albert Stoutamire. *Band Music Notes.* Lake Charles, LA: Program Note Press, 1989.

Tull, Fisher. "Analysis of Sketches on a Tudor Psalm," *The Instrumentalist,* XXXV February 1981: 36-40.

Tull, Fisher. "Sketches On A Tudor Psalm." *Journal of Band Research* XIII/1 (Fall 1977): 20-26.

Teacher Resource Guide

"Suite Francaise"
I–Normandie, II–Bretagne, III–Ile-de-France
IV–Alsace-Lorraine, V–Provence
Darius Milhaud
(b. 1892–d. 1974)

Unit 1: Composer

Milhaud was born in Aix-en-Provence, France in 1892. He died in Oakland, California in 1974, where he was composer-in-residence at Mills College. In 1920 Milhaud became known as one of Les Six, a group of French composers that included, most notably, Poulenc and Honneger. This group rejected the impressionist style, and believed that a simpler approach to form and style was needed. Les Six had a profound influence on French music in the 20th century, and Milhaud and Poulenc are recognized as France's most important composers of the period. In 1940 Milhaud emigrated to the United States. After WW II he alternated years between Mills College and the Paris Conservatory, where he taught until the age of seventy. His music was frequently influenced by American jazz and Brazilian rhythms, and Milhaud used polytonal and polyharmonic devices extensively. Other works for band/wind ensemble include: *Suite Francaise*, *Symphony No. 5* (composed for chamber wind ensemble of ten winds), *Introduction et Marche Frnebre, Op. 153*, *Two Marches, Op. 260: In Memoriam; Gloria Victoribus*, and *West Point Suite*.

Unit 2: Composition

Suite Francaise was composed in 1945, and was commissioned by the Leeds Music Company as part of a proposed series of new works by contemporary composers. It was first performed by the Goldman Band in 1945, and was later premiered in its orchestral form by the New York Philharmonic. It is in five movements;

Normandy, Brittany, Ile-de-France, Alsace-Lorraine, and Provence, and is approximately sixteen minutes long.

Unit 3: Historical Perspective

The composer provided the following program note:

> The five parts of this suite are named after French provinces, the very ones in which the American and Allied armies fought together with the French underground for the liberation of my country. I used some folk tunes of the provinces. I wanted the young Americans to hear the popular melodies of those parts of France where their fathers and brothers fought.

Suite Francaise is truly a significant, historical work for the medium from one of the twentieth century's foremost composers.

Unit 4: Technical Considerations

An extensive variety of tonal centers exist throughout the work, including all major keys except E, Ab, and B, and the minor keys of G, E, B, A, and F#. The movement I is in 6/8 time, dotted-quarter equal to 144. Rhythmic demands are minimal, with little syncopation; occasional layering of themes results in uneven phrasing and off-setting of the downbeat. Occasional grace-note figures are challenging. Movement II is in a very slow 6/8, and requires mature control. Movement III is very quick and light (half-note equal to 112) and requires facility of technique and articulation in all instruments in the keys of F, Db, G, and C Major. Movement IV is slow and very expressive and, like II, requires maturity of tone and control. An important piccolo and alto sax soli will require significant attention to pitch. Movement V requires dexterous technique and advanced articulation skills, especially from flutes, all reeds, and cornets.

Unit 5: Stylistic Considerations

The odd-numbered movements are light and cheerful sounding; lightness of articulation and approach to tone and dynamics is necessary. Movements II and IV are dark and brooding, with significantly more depth than the other movements; the character of the music must be reflected in the timbres of the ensemble—dark and heavy. Dissonance, as it occurs in the slow movements, must be interpreted as an expressive device. As with all music based on folk melodies, the lyrical and expressive qualities of the melody must sing and project above all other elements.

Unit 6: Musical Elements

The prevailing texture is homophonic, but a common technique is the layering of themes to create a heterophonic texture. Harmonic modulations occur between nearly every phrase, and dissonant chromatic harmonies are common in the slow movements. Harmonies are tonal and triadic, but its function is at times non-conventional, and many of the folk songs that comprise the melodic material of the work frequently have modal qualities. Phrases are consistently divided into regular two, four, or eight-measure segments.

Unit 7: Form and Structure

MOVEMENT I (ABA)

SECTION	MEASURES	SUB-SECTION	KEY	MUSICAL EVENTS
A	1-19	Theme I	Bb Major	Theme I stated; two part theme (mm. 1-8; mm. 9-19).
	19-22	Bridge		Transition into next period; saxophones, horns
	23-34	Theme II	G minor	Theme II stated in ww
B	35-42	Development	F minor	Theme I in brass, countermelody in ww
	43-52		F# Major	
	53-58		F# Major	Dev. of motive from Theme I (m 9)
	59-62		B Major	Dev. of material from Theme II
	63-66		G Major/ B Major	Dev. of material Themes I and II, polytonal harmonies created by layered themes
	67-74		G Major in theme w/ chrom. chordal accomp	Segment of Theme I in ww, segment of Theme II layered into mm. 71-74
	75-78		Bb Major w/chrom. accomp	Segment of Theme I
	79-82		Bb Major	Transition back to Recap; tutti

Section	Measures	Sub-section	Key	Musical Events
A	83-101	Recap.	Bb Major	Recap of Theme I
	102-108	Coda	Bb Major	Coda on Theme I

MOVEMENT II (ABCBA) ARCH FORM

Section	Measures	Sub-section	Key	Musical Events
A	1-11	Theme I	D Major	Opening Bb contrasts w/ tune in D Major; contrasts here forebodes harmonic tension which occurs later; in mm. 10-11, theme which bridges all sections in the movement is first heard
B	12-26	Theme II	E minor	Theme II played by oboe w/sustained accompaniment, against repeating dissonant chords in flute/trombones
C	27-37	Theme III	B minor	Theme III stated in flutes/clarinets against dissonant, chromatic chords in lowbrass, horns, bassoons
B	38-53	Theme II	E minor	Theme II played by oboe again, w/counter-melody in euph, against repeating dissonant chords in flute/trombones
A	54-66	Theme I	D Major	Final statement of Theme I; concluding D Major chord, first movement of harmonic relaxation in the movement

MOVEMENT III (ABA) MODIFIED SONATA-ALLEGRO

SECTION	MEASURES	SUB-SECTION	KEY	MUSICAL EVENTS
A	1-13	Theme I, Ia	F Major	2 bar intro, Theme I stated cornet, upper ww; m. 8 theme Ia introduced by clarinets, flutes, and alto sax
	14-19	Theme II	Db Major	Theme II in upper ww, Theme I in low brass
	20-24		A Major	Theme Ia in canon between euph, horns in A Major, woodwinds in D Major
	25-36	Theme III	G Major	Theme III introduced by alto sax, alto clarinet, joined by flutes, clar.s; legato theme contrasts with previous sections
B	36-70	Development	G Major-C Major-F Major	Dev. of themes
A	71-75	Recap.	F Major	Recap of Theme I
	76-79	Coda	F Major	Coda on Theme III

MOVEMENT IV (ABACBA)

SECTION	MEASURES	SUB-SECTION	PITCH CENTER	MUSICAL EVENTS
A	1-8	Theme I	A minor	Theme I introduced in saxophones; glissando in m. 4 is an important recurring motif throughout the movement
	9-16	Theme Ia		Theme Ia introduced by flutes and alto sax

	17-24	Theme II		Theme II in upper ww; countermelody based on glissando motif
B	25-32	Theme III	C	Theme III in solo cornet; melody in G Major; bass line outlines D dim7 chord, C as pitch center
	33-36	Theme IIIa		Theme IIIa, which recurs frequently throughout the movement, is introduced in cornet I
A	37-52	Themes I, Ia	A minor	Return of Theme I, Ia, layered with statements of Theme IIIa and glissando motif
C	53-67	Interlude	F Major	New material, similar in character and style to themes, set in a development-like interlude
B	68-80	Return of B		Theme III in canon fl/ob and cornet I in mm. 68-76; mm. 76-80 has Theme IIIa in 3-part canon
A	81-102	Return of A	A Major	Climactic return of Themes I, Ia, and II, juxtaposed with layers of Theme IIIa and glissando motif
	103-109	Coda	A Major	Coda on Theme IIIa in rhythmic augmentation

MOVEMENT V (ABACABA) RITURNELLO FORM

SECTION	MEASURES	SUB-SECTION	KEY	MUSICAL EVENTS
A	1-14	Theme I	C Major	Theme I in upper ww

B	15-28	Theme II	F Major	"Fife and drum" section between flutes/percussion; 2 bar retransition into restatement of Theme I
A	29-35	Theme I, II	C Major	Theme I restated in upper ww; Theme II in euphonium as countermelody; 1 bar trumpet Fanfare theme serves as transition into next section
C	36-49	Theme III and Fanfare motif	Ab Major	Theme III in flutes, alto saxes, and alto clarinet, accomp. line in alto sax 2 and horn based on Fanfare motif
A	50-57	Restatement of Theme I w/ new Theme IV	F# minor	Theme IV in upper woodwinds over variation on Theme I in cornets, euph, clarinets; trumpet Fanfare motif segues into next section
	58-68	Restatement of Theme I w/ melody based on Fanfare motif	G Major	Melody based on Fanfare motif in flutes, picc, and Eb clar; Theme I in clarinets, alto sax, and cornet I
B	69-78	Return of Theme II	C Major	"Fifes and Drums"
A	79-84	Return of Themes I, II	G Major	Simultaneous final statement of Themes I and II
	85-89	Coda	G Major	Brief coda on Fanfare motif in rhythmic augmentation

Unit 8: Suggested Listening

Darius Milhaud, *La Creation du Monde, Symphony No. 5 for Winds*

Unit 9: Additional References and Resources

Dvorak, Thomas L. *Best Music for Young Band.* Brooklyn, NY: Manhattan Beach Music, 1986.

Dvorak, Thomas L., Robert Grechesky, and Gary Ciepluch. *Best Music for High School Band.* Brooklyn, NY: Manhattan Beach Music, 1993.

Prindl, Frank Joseph. "A Study of Ten Original Compositions for Band Published in America Since 1946." Diss., The Florida State University, 1956.

Sadie, Stanley. *The New Grove Dictionary of Music and Musicians.* London: Macmillan, 1980.

Smith, Norman and Albert Stoutamire. *Band Music Notes.* Lake Charles, LA: Program Note Press, 1989.

Teacher Resource Guide

"Suite of Old American Dances"
Robert Russell Bennett

(b. 1894–d. 1981)

Unit 1: Composer

Robert Russell Bennett was born in 1894. He enjoyed a brilliant career in musical arranging, orchestrating over 200 Broadway shows. He studied composition with Carl Busch and with Nadia Boulanger during which time he knew Aaron Copland and Roger Sessions. Later, he was associated with Richard Rogers and Jermoe Kern among many others. He wrote music for films, the opera *Maria Malibran*, the *Abraham Lincoln Symphony*, a *Symphony in D for Dodgers* (referring to the Brooklyn baseball team), chamber music, and choral works. He also wrote *Symphonic Songs for Band* (1957).

Unit 2: Composition

Bennett attended a concert honoring the 70th birthday of Edwin Franko Goldman on January 3, 1948. He became aware of "all the beautiful sounds the American concert band could make that it hadn't yet made". He wrote the suite and showed it to Goldman under the original name of "Electric Park" referring to Electric park in Kansas City which was "a place of magic to us kids". One could hear in the dance hall all afternoon and evening the pieces the crowd danced to, and the five movements of the suite are samples of the dances of the day. The piece is five movements, is a Grade 5 difficulty and lasts about fifteen minutes and thirty seconds.

Unit 3: Historical Perspective

The seemingly endless stream of orchestral magic which Robert Russell Bennett conjured up for each successive hit of the Broadway musical theater attested to his firm position as the dean of America's arrangers. *Suite of Old American Dances* was his first major work for the wind band; the title "Electric Park" was never used after it was published. He also wrote an orchestral version of the piece published by Chappell in 1950. The movements are reflective of the dance styles they seek to portray; Bennett decribes them as "dance moods of my youth".

Unit 4: Technical Considerations

Ranges and tempos are not too difficult. Instead, great effort must be spent to achieve a uniformity of articulation and blend. Bennett uses simple rhythms in half, quarter, eighth and sixteenth notes. There are very few exposed sections, so ensemble blend is important. There are no meter changes within movements, and execution of the given tempos is not difficult.

Unit 5: Stylistic Considerations

Each movement has its own style (fast, slow, meditative, etc.) and requires its own style to create the proper contrasts and recreate the proper dance style. The intensity and movement of the music should be equal to the phrasing, articulation, rhythms and principles of the line. Dynamics in the piece range from $f\!f$ to $p\!p$. Articulations are specified.

Unit 6: Musical Elements

It is important to execute the proper dance styles with crispness or length of rhythms as well as energy. Syncopations abound. There are several jazz-style chords with sevenths and ninths, but the harmony mostly is very tonal. Melodies are pronounced clearly and are almost always given full statements by whatever instrument begins the melody.

Unit 7: Form and Structure

MVMT 1 - "CAKE WALK"	"C BLUES"
Introduction	Beginning to 1
Theme	1 to 3 stated by cornets, trombones, euphoniums
Theme	3 to 7
Transition	7 to 9 tutti
Coda	9 to end closing tutti
MVMT 2 - "SCHOTTISCHE"	G MAJOR
A	Beginning to 2 stated by clarinets and saxes
B	2 to 3 stated by clarinets
C	3 to 4 stated by woodwinds & low brass
B (transition)	4 to 5 stated by clarinets, woodwinds & trumpets
A	5 to end stated by clarinets and saxes

MVMT 3 - "WESTERN ONE-STEP" "C BLUES"

Introduction	Beginning to 1
A	1 to 2
B	2 to 3
C	3 to 4
D	4 to 6
E	6 to 9
B	9 to 10
Coda	10 to end

MVMT 4 - "WALLFLOWER WALTZ" F MAJOR

Introduction	Beginning to 1 stated by flutes and English horn
Waltz theme	1 to 4 stated by clarinets
theme 2	4 to 6 flutes & oboes; clarinet solo
Introduction	6 to end stated by flutes and English horn with accompaniment

MVMT 5 - "RAG"   "B-FLAT BLUES"

Introduction	Beginning to 1
A	1 to 2
B	2 to 3
C	3 to 6
A	6 to 7
D	7 to 11
A	11 to end

Unit 8: Suggested Listening

Robert Russell Bennett, *Suite of Old American Dances (orchestral version)*
Robert Russell Bennett, *Symphony Songs*
Vincent Persichetti, *Divertimento for Band, Op.* 42
Robert Jager, *Third Suite for Band*

Unit 9: Additional References and Resources

Baker, Theodore. "Bennett, Robert Russell," *Baker's Biographical Dictionary of Musicians.* 6th ed., revised by Nicolas Slonimsky. New York: Schirmer Books, 1984.

Fennell, Frederick. "Basic Band Repertory: Suite of Old American Dances." *The Instrumentalist,* XXXIV September 1979, 28-40.

Ferencz, George J. *Robert Russell Bennett: A Bio-Bibliography (Bio-Bibliographies in Music, No. 29).* ISBN 0-313-26472-4, December 1990.

Huitink, Susan. The Wallflower Waltz (based on the fourth movement of Suite of Old American Dances by Bennett).

Johnson, Charles E. "Common Musical Idioms in Selected Contemporary Wind Band Music." Ph.D. diss., Florida State University, 1969.

National Band Association Selective Music List for Bands

Rehrig, William H. *The Heritage Encyclopedia of Band Music.* Westerville, OH: Integrity Press, 1991.

Westrup, J. A. and F. Ll. Harrison. *The New College Encyclopedia of Music.* Revised by Conrad Wilson. New York: W. W. Norton & Company, Ltd, 1981.

Teacher Resource Guide

"Symphony No. 6 for Band, Op. 69" Vincent Persichetti

(b. 1915–d. 1987)

Unit 1: Composer

Vincent Persichitti was born in Philadelphia in 1915. He was a gifted pianist, an imaginative editor, and an informed critic. He studied composition with Roy Harris and Paul Nordoff and conducting with Fritz Reiner. In 1941, he was named head of the composition department at the Philadelphia Conservatory, and in 1947 he joined the faculty of the Julliard School of Music in New York City. He died in August 1987. Some of his other works transcribed for band include *Divertimento for Band*, *Pageant*, and *Masquerade for Band*.

Unit 2: Composition

Symphony for Band is one of many works for band composed by Persichetti. The piece was composed in the winter of 1955-56 on commission from the Washington University Chamber Band, which played the premiere performance on April 16, 1956 in St. Louis, Missouri. The piece was originally intended to be a six-minute work in the style of his *Psalm for Band*. In the course of the composition, Persichetti's six-minute work developed into a four-movement symphony. The piece has is a Grade 5 difficulty and lasts about seventeen minutes.

Unit 3: Historical Perspective

Persichetti did not consider that his interest in writing music for concerted numbers of wind and percussion instruments was anything unusual for mid-20th-century composer. He wrote 14 works for winds and percussion in a prolific catalog of over 160 opus numbers including nine symphonies, four string quartets, and twelve piano sonatas, as well as concertos, song cycles, and a variety of miscellaneous pieces. Persichetti's contributions to band literature, teachings, and

20th-century harmonic practices have—and will continue to have—a profound influence on the music world.

Unit 4: Technical Considerations

The piece has no key signatures, so accidentals abound. There are a few basic meter changes, and the tempos remain consistent within the movements; however, there is quite a bit of shifting of the metrical "feel". There are both staccato and legato articulations, so contrast is important. All instruments have several exposed sections and several solos as does the percussion section. Ranges and scalar passages are not difficult.

Unit 5: Stylistic Considerations

Articulations should be crisp, uniform and march-like. All markings in the score support this. Each movement has its own style (fast, slow, meditative, etc). The intensity and movement of the music should be equal to the phrasing, articulation, rhythms and principles of the line. This is a 20th-century work with 20th-century sounds; it should be approached with a 20th-century interpretation.

Unit 6: Musical Elements

The four movements are a reflection of 18th-century technique, including the order and style of each movement. The first movement is in sonata allegro form; the opening *Adagio* contains essential motivic material used throughout the movement. A hymn taken from Persichetti's *Hymns and Responses for the Church Year*, "Round Me Falls the Night", is the basis for the second movement. The third movement assumes the role of the dance movement and is in ABC form. The finale is a breathtaking free rondo and draws thematic material from the previous movements.

Unit 7: Form and Structure

MVMT I	No key signatures, based on opening motive
Adagio	Mm. 1 to 20 Introduction
Allegro	
Theme 1 & 2	Mm. 21 to 60 woodwinds & upper brass
il ritmo sempre...	Mm. 61 to 109
	Mm. 110 to 139 chordal long notes between woodwinds & brass
	Mm. 140 to 199 short accented notes; woodwinds
transition	Mm. 200 to 207 upper woodwinds & brass
Theme 2	Mm. 208 to 236
	Mm. 237 to 267 very rhythmic first in brass, then tutti
Coda	Mm. 268 to end

MVMT II	No key signatures, shifting tonalities
Verse I	Mm. 1-14 "Round me falls the night..."
Verse II	Mm. 14-41 "Earthly work is done..."
Verse III	Mm. 42-57 "Darkened now each ray..."
MVMT III	No key signatures, shifting tonalities, ends on C Major
A	Mm. 1-26 stated in clarinets
B	Mm. 27-61
A	Mm. 62 to 71 stated in oboe solo & upperwoodwinds
B (+A)	Mm. 72 to 89 brass, then tutti; very rhythmical and martial
A	Mm. 90 to end alto sax solo; coda
MVMT IV	No key signatures, shifting tonalities, last chord with all notes
A	Mm. 1 to 16
B	Mm. 17 to 38
A	Mm. 39 to 56
C	Mm. 57 to 72 long chords and fast crescendos
A	Mm. 73 to 104
D	Mm. 105 to 131
E	Mm. 132 to 152
(A)	Mm. 153 to 209 features clarinets & percussion; transition
(C)	Mm. 210 to 273
Coda	Mm. 274 to end

Unit 8: Suggested Listening

Vittorio Giannini, *Symphony No. 3*
Morton Gould, *West Point Symphony*
Martin Mailman, *For precious friends hid in death's dateless night*, Op. 80
Vincent Persichetti, *Divertimento for Band*
Vincent Persichetti, *Masquerade for Band*

Unit 9: Additional References and Resources

Baker, Theodore. "Persichetti, Vincent," *Baker's Biographical Dictionary of Musicians.* 6th ed., revised by Nicolas Slonimsky. New York: Schirmer Books, 1984.

Bruning, Earl Henry Jr. "A Survey and Handbook of Analysis for the Conducting and Interpretation of Seven Selected Works in the Standard Repertoire for Wind Band." Diss., Ball State University, 1980.

Fennell, Frederick. "Vincent Persichetti: Symphony for Band." *BD Guide*, September/October 1987, 5.

Hilfiger, John Jay. "A Comparison of Some Aspects of Style in the Band and Orchestra Music of Vincent Persichetti." Ph.D. diss., The University of Iowa, 1985.

Morris, Donald Alan. "The Life of Vincent Persichetti, with Emphasis on his Works for Band." Ph.D. diss., The Florida State University, 1991.

Morris, Donald and Jean Oelrich. "Vincent Persichetti Remembered: Music from Gracious to Gritty." *The Instrumentalist*, XLVII/4 November 1992, 30-38.

Morris, Donald. "Persichetti Rediscovered: The Manuscripts of Vincent Persichetti's Band-Works - Part One: Pageant and the Symphony for Band (Symphony No. 6)." *Journal of Band Research* XXVIII/1 (Fall 92): 1-20.

Mullins, Joe Barry. "Three Symphonies for Band by American Composers." Diss., University of Illinois, 1967.

National Band Association Selective Music List for Bands

Paré, Craig. "An Examination of Innovative Percussion Writing in the Band Music of Four Composers: Vincent Persichetti - Symphony for Band; Karel Husa - Music for Prague 1968; Joseph Schwantner - and the mountains rising nowhere; Michael Colgrass - Winds of Nagual." Diss., University of Cincinnati, 1993.

Rehrig, William H. *The Heritage Encyclopedia of Band Music.* Westerville, OH: Integrity Press, 1991.

Tarwater, William Harmon. "Analyses of Seven Major Band Compositions of the Twentieth Century." Diss., George Peadody College for Teachers, 1958.

Westrup, J. A. and F. Ll. Harrison. *The New College Encyclopedia of Music.* Revised by Conrad Wilson. New York: W. W. Norton & Company, Ltd, 1981.

Workinger, William Colvin. "Some Aspects of Scoring in the Band Works of Vincent Persichetti." Diss., New York University, 1970.

Teacher Resource Guide

"Symphony No. 3 for Band"
Vittorio Giannini

(b. 1903–d. 1966)

Unit 1: Composer

Vittorio Giannini was born in 1903. He studied in Milan and New York. His compositions include concertos for piano and organ, a symphony *In Memoriam Theodore Roosevelt*, *Requiem*, *Stabat Mater*, sundry chamber music, and the operas *Lucedia*, *The Scarlet Letter*, and *The Taming of the Shrew*. He taught at Julliard and became the Head of the North Carolina School of the Arts. His other works for band include *Preludium and Allegro*, *Dedication Overture*, *Fantasia for Band*, and *Variations and Fugue*.

Unit 2: Composition

Symphony No. 3 was composed on a commission (through the Mary Duke Biddle Foundation) by the Duke University Band and its conductor, Paul Bryan, during the summer of 1958 in Rome, Italy, where Giannini was spending his vacation. It was premiered the following year. Giannini said, "I can give no other reason for choosing to write a Symphony to fulfill this commission than that I 'felt like it', and the thought of doing it interested me a great deal." The piece has four movements, is a Grade 5 difficulty (NBA lists it as a Grade 6) and lasts about twenty-three minutes.

Unit 3: Historical Perspective

Symphony No. 3 was Giannini's second work for band. His father, Ferruccio A. Giannini, organized the Royal Marine Band in the early part of this century, so Giannini was exposed to band music regularly from a young age. The work was composed within an eight-year period that saw the creations of such famous symphonies for band including Hindemith's *Symphony in B-flat* (1951), Gould's

Symphony for Band (1952), and Persichetti's *Symphony No. 6* (1956).

Unit 4: Technical Considerations

The piece has no key signatures, so accidentals abound (particularly sharps). The first movement has no meter changes: the other three movements do have some basic meter changes. There are several tempo changes indicated. All instruments have several exposed sections and several solos. The first trumpet has to play up to a high D. Accuracy of articulations and sustaining of lines is quite challenging and requires mature players.

Unit 5: Stylistic Considerations

Each movement of the symphony has its own styles within. The intensity and movement of the music should be equal to the phrasing, articulation, rhythms and principles of the line. This is a 20th-century work written in a very Romantic style. The tempo changes are written for the sake of "push and pull" or Romantic expressiveness.

Unit 6: Musical Elements

In *Symphony No. 3*, Giannini uses the symphonic band medium for his classically-structured work. Each of the four movements follows the formal structure of a traditional symphony. While it is a non-referential composition without a program, it is rich in melody, texture, rhythm, color, and beauty displaying the technical and musical capabilities of the symphonic band.

Unit 7: Form and Structure

MVMT I *Allegro energico*   (sonata allegro form) Bb Major, C Major, other keys

Exposition (Theme 1)	Mm. 1 to 43
transition	Mm. 44 to 51
theme variation	Mm. 52 to 75
transition	Mm. 76 to 85
Development	Mm. 86 to 123 sax soli with low brass
Theme 1 augmented	Mm. 124 to 135
Tempo I: Theme 1	Mm. 136 to 193 in clarinets & upper woodwinds
Recapitulation (Theme 1)	Mm. 193 to 249
Tranquillo	Mm. 249 to 302
Coda	Mm. 302 to end

MVMT II *Adagio*   (A B A) B-flat minor, other related keys

Intro	Mm. 1 to 13 stated in oboe with low brass
Theme 1 (twice)	Mm. 14 to 33 stated in flutes & clarinets
Theme 2	Mm. 34 to 51 with trumpet I & clarinet solos
Theme 2 "chorale"	Mm. 52 to 66

Intro (condensed)	Mm. 67 to 72 stated in oboe with brass & saxes
Theme 1	Mm. 73 to 86
Coda	Mm. 87 to end

MVMT III *Allegretto*	(A B A B) B-flat minor, other related keys
A: Theme 1	Mm. 1 to 40 bsns & alto sax vs. flutes & clarinets
B: Theme 2	Mm. 41 to 82
A: Theme 1	Mm. 83 to 130 bsns & alto sax vs. flutes & clarinets
B: Theme 1 & 2	Mm. 131 to 170
Coda (Theme 1)	Mm. 171 to end bsns & alto sax vs. flutes & clarinets

MVMT IV *Allegro con brio*	(sonata allegro) B-flat Major, other related keys
A	Mm. 1 to 33
B	Mm. 34 to 75
false A	Mm. 76 to 116
A1	Mm. 117 to 170
Coda	Mm. 170 to end

Unit 8: Suggested Listening
Vittorio Giannini, *Preludium and Allegro*
Morton Gould, *Symphony for Band*
Paul Hindemith, *Symphony in B-flat for Band*
Martin Mailman, *For precious friends bid in death's dateless night*, Op. 80
Vincent Persichetti, *Symphony No. 6 for Band*

Unit 9: Additional References and Resources

Baker, Theodore. "Giannini, Vittorio," Baker's Biographical *Dictionary of Musicians*. 6th ed., revised by Nicolas Slonimsky. New York: Schirmer Books, 1984.

Bruning, Earl Henry Jr. "A Survey and Handbook of Analysis for the Conducting and Interpretation of Seven Selected Works in the Standard Repertoire for Wind Band." Diss., Ball State University, 1980.

Johnson, Charles E. "Common Musical Idioms in Selected Contemporary Wind Band Music." Ph.D. diss., Florida State University, 1969.

Mark, Michael L. "The Life and Works of Vittorio Giannini (1903-1966)." Diss., The Catholic University of America, 1970.

Mullins, Joe Barry. "Three Symphonies for Band by American Composers." Diss., University of Illinois, 1967.

National Band Association Selective Music List for Bands

Rehrig, William H. *The Heritage Encyclopedia of Band Music.* Westerville, OH: Integrity Press, 1991.

Westrup, J. A. and F. Ll. Harrison. *The New College Encyclopedia of Music.* Revised by Conrad Wilson. New York: W. W. Norton & Company, Ltd, 1981.

Wynn, James. "An Analysis of the First Movement of Symphony No. 3 of Giannini." *Journal of Band Research,* I/2 (Spring 1965): 19-26.

Teacher Resource Guide

"Toccata and Fugue in D minor, BMV565" Johann Sebastian Bach

(b. 1685–d. 1750)

transcribed by Erik Leidzen
(b. 1894–d. 1962)

Unit 1: Composer
Johann Sebastian Bach was born in Eisenach, Germany on March 21, 1685. He was a renowned organist, composer and violinist in Germany during his lifetime. He held positions in Weimar as court organist and Concert Master under Duke Wilhelm Ernst (1708-1717), in Cöthen as *Kapellmeister* to Prince Leopold (1717-1723), and in Leipzig as director of music in the churches of St. Thomas and St. Nicholas and cantor of the Thomasschule (1723-1750). He wrote extensive works for keyboard, including works for harpsichord, clavichord, and organ.

Unit 2: Composition
Bach considered the organ a great vehicle for creative art. Some of his grandest conceptions are to be found in his organ works, and the Preludes and Fugues include many of his greatest works for the instrument. The *Toccata and Fugue in D minor, BMV565* is classed among these. It has been speculated that this piece was originally written as a piece to test the intonation of the organ, and not as a performance work! The one-movement piece is a Grade 5 difficulty and lasts about nine minutes.

Unit 3: Historical Perspective

Bach composed *Toccata and Fugue in D minor* in 1709 when he was living in Weimar. The first edition of the transcription was published in 1942. One of the characteristic large musical structures of the late Baroque was the combination of a prelude (or toccata, fantasia) with a fugue. Most of Bach's important compositions in this form date from the Weimar period, though a few were written in Cöthen and Leipzig. Bach's preludes and fugues sum up all of the striving of the Baroque toward pure, balanced tonal architecture on a monumental scale. The piece is an example of the form established by Buxtehude in which the fugue is interspersed with sections of free fantasia.

Unit 4: Technical Considerations

The scales of D minor and its related keys are required for the entire ensemble. The rhythmic demands are very basic with the use of quarter, eighth, and sixteenth notes. Some ornaments (such as mordents) are written out in 64th notes. Accuracy in ensemble to achieve organ style is essential. In the "Toccata", the woodwinds are used for the moving lines, and the brass is used chordally to emphasize cadences.

Unit 5: Stylistic Considerations

The piece contains frequent starts and stops due to the fantasia nature of the prelude. While a certain freedom in the "Toccata" should be taken for the fantasia style, equal care must also be taken to avoid an over-Romanticized interpretation. Dynamics encompass a wide variety with several crescendos and diminuendos. Rich and full tone quality is required as well as ensemble blend to achieve the organ style. The tempo should be flexible in the "Toccata" and steady in the "Fugue."

Unit 6: Musical Elements

The piece, in the concert key of D minor and several related keys, consists of a brilliant introduction, alternating slow and fast, followed by the fugue, the subject of which is a short figure in sixteenth notes. The harmony is typical of late Baroque music, Bach in particular. The main unifying motive of the "Toccata" is the opening mordent (A-G-A). The breadth and magnificence of this music makes it ideal for transcription as a band number.

Unit 7: Form and Structure

Toccata	D minor & other related keys
Introduction	Beginning to 10; features fantasia style gestures
Section 1	Beginning to 2; establishes mordent as unifying figure
Section 2	2-4 triplets in woodwinds & cadence on D minor
Section 3	5-8 more motion and steady tempo

Section 4	8-9 return of triplets in woodwinds
Section 5	9-10 cadence on D minor to close Toccata

Fugue	D minor & other related keys
1st fugue	10-17 Fugue featuring subject based on opening mordent
Episode	17-20, running sixteenth notes between instrument groups
1st fugue 2nd x	20-23, return of 1st fugue
Closing	23-27 closing cadence on D minor

Unit 8: Suggested Listening

Johann Sebastian Bach, *Toccata and Fugue in D minor, BWV565*

Johann Sebastian Bach/arr. Stokowski, *Toccata and Fugue in D minor, BWV565*

Johann Sebastian Bach/arr. Hindsley, *Toccata and Fugue in D minor, BWV565*

Johann Sebastian Bach/arr. Hunsberger, *Toccata and Fugue in D minor, BWV565*

Johann Sebastian Bach/arr. Hunsberger, *Passacaglia and Fugue in C minor, BWV582*

Unit 9: Additional References and Resources

Baker, Theodore. "Bach, Johann Sebastian," *Baker's Biographical Dictionary of Musicians.* 6th ed., revised by Nicolas Slonimsky. New York: Schirmer Books, 1984.

Grout, Donald. *A History of Western Music,* 3rd edition. New York: W. W. Norton & Company, Ltd, 1980.

National Band Association Selective Music List for Bands

Rehrig, William H. *The Heritage Encyclopedia of Band Music.* Westerville, OH: Integrity Press, 1991.

Westrup, J. A. and F. Ll. Harrison. *The New College Encyclopedia of Music.* Revised by Conrad Wilson. New York: W. W. Norton & Company, Ltd, 1981.

Whitwell, David. "Bach—Wind Music." *The Instrumentalist,* XXI November 1966, 39.

Teacher Resource Guide

"Trauermusik"
Richard Wagner

(b. 1813–d. 1883)

Performance edition by Michael Votta (b. 1957)

Contemporary Edition by John Boyd (b. 1944)

Unit 1: Composer

Richard Wagner (1813-1883) is perhaps the most documented and discussed composer in the history of Western music. Countless recordings, biographies, analytical writings, and an autobiography have firmly established Wagner as one of the most fascinating masters of the musical arts.

Wagner was reared in a theatrical family and was exposed to the great works of the theater at an early age. He actually played minor roles in dramas and operas. Wagner decided to study music during his childhood after hearing the symphonies of Beethoven. While he sought out training in harmony and counterpoint from unknown teachers early in his life, he was primarily self-taught. This continued until he entered Leipzig University for a short, unsuccessful period. He left the University in favor of private study with Thomaskirche Kantor. This brief collaboration resulted in a few lesser known compositions including two piano sonatas and what is thought to be his only symphony.

Due to his upbringing, Wagner's true love was music of the theater. This naturally led to his composition of opera. Wagner held positions as Artistic Director of opera houses throughout Europe. Evidently he was not a very good businessman, as most of his early ventures were financial disasters. Wagner spent considerable time avoiding creditors and had to be financially rescued on several occasions. One of his rescuers was virtuoso pianist and composer Franz Liszt. Liszt admired Wagner's music and Wagner, in turn, was greatly influenced by Liszt's progressive compositional techniques. The connection between Liszt and Wagner intensified when Wagner married Liszt's daughter, Cosima. Unfortunately, this union did not meet with Liszt's approval—Cosima apparently was already married to Hans von Bulow, a noted conductor of Wagner's music.

In addition to being a composer and theatrical director, Wagner wrote numerous articles and books about opera, theater, and politics. Many of these found their way into the popular journals of the time including *Neue Zeitschrift für Musik* founded by Robert Schumann. Among his most famous writings are *Die Kunst und die Revolution*(Art and Revolution, 1849), *Das Kunstwerk der Zukunft* (The Artwork of the Future, 1849), and *Oper und Drama* (Opera and Drama, 1851). Politics and philosophy were topics of great interest to Wagner. Many of his ideas were quite radical for the time and resulted in a short exile to Switzerland in 1848. While there, he wrote *Tristan und Isolde*, one of his most famous operas.

By the time of *Tristan und Isolde*, Wagner was reshaping German opera. For many years, the well-established operatic traditions of the Italians and French dominated the musical scene. Germany's musical tradition was that of symphonists, not opera composers. Wagner incorporated and extended the advanced harmonic vocabulary and orchestrational inventiveness of composers like Franz Liszt and Hector Berlioz into epic operatic masterpieces based on stories from German folklore. Typically, German myths are full of magic and mysticism. This Wagner exploited by using a remembrance motive or *Leitmotif*. This term, originally used to describe Wagner's music, is used universally to stand for a musical passage that represents a character, idea, or event in the plot.

Wagner's most famous work, *Der Ring des Nibelungen*, is a massive tetralogy that requires approximately sixteen hours to perform and embodies all of Wagner's mature compositional techniques. Wagner called these works "music dramas" as they did not conform to the traditional form of *recitative* followed by *aria* normally found in the operas of other countries. Wagner composed the music, wrote the *libretto*, designed the sets and lighting, trained the musicians, and conducted the first performances. Furthermore, financed by the eccentric King Ludwig, he built his own theater at Bayreuth; designing it specifically for the performance of his operas. Because of his complete involvement in all aspects of production, Wagner termed his craft *Gesamtkunstwerk*, or universal art work.

Wagner's use of orchestral wind color is one of the features that sets him apart from his contemporaries. His full use of winds, to the point of inventing instruments like the "Wagner Tuba," gives his music the distinct quality we hear as "Wagnerian" in proportion. This legacy is still evolving today as composers continue to find a full and rich timbral palate when writing for winds.

Unit 2: Composition

The source material for *Trauermusik* is Carl Maria von Weber's (1786-1826) opera *Euryanthe*. It was erroneously thought that Wagner borrowed themes from *Euryanthe*. In reality, Wagner literally transcribed Weber's music, adjusting it in a

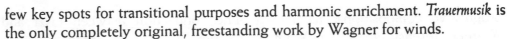

few key spots for transitional purposes and harmonic enrichment. *Trauermusik* is the only completely original, freestanding work by Wagner for winds.

Carl Maria von Weber's profound influence on Wagner should not be overlooked. Wagner took musical innovations begun by Weber and developed them extensively. Weber is considered the first important composer to write "German Opera." He is called "The Father of German Opera" due to works like *Der Freichutz*, a story from German folklore that included popular elements of magic and mysticism. The famous "Wolf's Glen" scene contains numerous avante garde compositional and symbolic techniques including dramatic chromaticism and the *Leitmotif*.

Trauermusik was composed in 1844 to accompany the burial procession of Carl Maria von Weber. Weber died in London in 1826. Twelve years later, his remains were returned to German soil for burial. An impressive torchlight procession carried Weber's body from the train station to its final resting place in Friedrichstadt. Wagner carefully selected each musical passage to pay Weber homage. Symbolism played a major role in this selection. Some clues into Wagner's thought process can be found in the actual plot of the opera itself.

Briefly, *Euryanthe* is the story of Count Adolar and his lover, Euryanthe. Adolar's sister, Emma, tragically commits suicide, which traps her spirit in a ring. A tear of innocent love touching the ring is the only way for her soul to be released to heaven. When Euryanthe is informed of the suicide, the conversation is overheard and the word gets out, casting shame on Adolar's family. He assumes that Euryanthe has betrayed him and banishes her to die in the wilderness. After much suffering, Euryanthe is rescued by hunters and vindicated. When her innocence is discovered, she sheds a tear that falls upon the ring, and Emma's spirit is allowed to ascend to heaven.

The first section of *Trauermusik* is from *Euryanthe's* overture. This music is filled with tension and melancholy. It represents the trapped spirit of Emma without hope of release. This, perhaps, represents Wagner's sadness over the loss of his friend.

The middle section is the gorgeous *cavatina* Euryanthe sings while abandoned in the wilderness. The text is primarily of a sorrowful nature tempered with a message of hope for redemption. It is not difficult to understand why Wagner chose this section. He was greatly saddened by the loss of his friend and was wishing him well in the afterlife.

Wagner's selection of music for the *coda* is also full of symbolic meaning. The music he chose can be found at the end of Act II. This is the reunion and vindication scene. Possibly, the final trumpet call of *Trauermusik* symbolizes Weber's soul ascending to heaven just as it symbolizes the release of Emma's spirit in the opera.

Trauermusik is a highly emotional work. Wagner's careful selection of each musical passage from his beloved friend's opera is a clear indication that great care and understanding should be used when preparing this work for performance.

Unit 3: Historical Perspective

Trauermusik is the original title of this work. In 1860 C.F. Meser published a piano arrangement and gave it the title *Trauersinfonie*. This publication was done without Wagner's permission. In 1926, Breitkopf and Härtle published a full score edited by Balling as part of Wagner's collected works. This edition retained the modified *Trauersinfonie* title. The most performed edition was prepared by Eric Leidzen in 1948 for Edwin Franko Goldman. Leidzen made some significant adjustments to the score to adapt it to the instrumentation of the Goldman Band. In 1992 Michael Votta prepared a performance edition that restores the integrity of Wagner's original manuscript. In this edition, Votta suggests a specific instrumentation that is true to the proportions of the original.

Fortunately, there is a great deal known about *Trauermusik*. This is due in no small part to the fine scholarship of Michael Votta and Keating Johnson.

Unit 4: Technical Considerations

There are no difficult rhythmic passages, the key signature is a minor concern, and the ranges are not extreme in *Trauermusik*. However, this should not fool the conductor into thinking that this work is easy to perform. On the contrary, slow tempos and long phrases make a musical performance exceedingly challenging. Particular attention should be paid to the shape and ending of each phrase. Intonation should be a constant concern, as most of the sonorities are open and exposed.

The conductor needs to make a decision regarding the muted drum part. It is thought that Wagner intended the sound to be very distant, deep, and hollow. Simply turning off the snares of a standard drum will not achieve this effect.

Unit 5: Stylistic Considerations

The sustained nature of this work requires careful consideration on the part of the conductor. If a phrase remains dynamically static, the listener will quickly lose interest. It is essential that the conductor look at each phrase and make decisions on direction and arrival points. Wagner provides numerous crescendo and decrescendo markings to help these decisions. One common feature is that many points of tension occur on beat four resolving on beat one of the following measure. Many examples of this can be found between mm 51 and the coda. These arrivals should be emphasized to heighten their dramatic impact.

Another issue is Wagner's articulation markings. Many examples of staccato markings underneath slurs and various accents can be observed. It would not be appropriate to perform any of these passages very short or with a pointed attack. These are indications of varying degrees of weight. Interpret them as though they are orchestral bowings.

Unit 6: Musical Elements

The harmonic structure of *Trauermusik* is fairly straight forward. The introduction is in B-flat minor and the rest of the piece, beginning at the *cavatina*, is essentially in B-flat Major. Since the music was originally written at the beginning of the Romantic era, the ensemble will encounter mostly standard tertian harmony with several upper structure harmonies added. These consist primarily of seventh and ninth chords and function as the aforementioned points of stress.

The phrasal structure is quite apparent. The introduction functions as a sixteen-measure continuous unit that can be divided into smaller components of five measures each. The extra measure can be accounted for in mm 11 with the sustained chord linking mm 10 to mm 12. Once in the *cavatina*, the phrases divide regularly every four measures with a few extensions when approaching the *coda*. The *coda* is much like the beginning. It is sixteen measures in length and can be divided down further. Like the beginning, the *coda* needs to be flowing and continuous. Finality is given to the piece by the trumpet call in mm 82. This should sound almost as if it were offstage. Be careful not to allow the player to separate the *staccato* marked quarter notes in mm 83 too much, as this would break up the line's ascension. It is appropriate to bring out the half notes in the second to last measure slightly and have the ensemble breathe before the final chord.

Unit 7: Form and Structure

As eluded to previously, *Trauermusik* has three essential parts making it ternary in form.

Introduction:	mm 1-16	(Emma's spirit)
Main Body:	mm 17-71	(cavatina)
Coda:	mm 72-end	(redemption, closely related to the intro)

Unit 8: Suggested Listening

Carl Maria von Weber, *Euryanthe*
Carl Maria von Weber, *Der Freichutz*
Richard Wagner, *Der Ring des Nibelungen*
Richard Wagner, *Tristan und Isolde*

Unit 9: Bibliography

Brusniak, Friedhelm. "Richard Wagner as Reflected Through His Music for Winds." *Journal of Band Research* XIX/2 (Spring 1984): 61-63.

Garofalo, Robert J. "Richard Wagner: Trauersinfonie." *BD Guide*, September/October, 30.

Grout, Donald Jay. Ed. Claud V. Palisca. *A History of Western Music.* 3rd ed. NY: W. W. Norton & Co., 1980.

Johnson, L. Keating. "Richard Wagner's Trauersinfonie." *Journal of Band Research* XVI/2 (Spring 1981): 38-42.

Johnson, L. Keating. "The Wind Band Compositions of Richard Wagner (1813-1883)." *Journal of Band Research* XV/2 (Spring 1980): 10-15.

Smith, Norman and Albert Stoutamire. *Band Music Notes*. Rev. ed. San Diego, CA: Kjos., 1979.

Votta, Michael. "Nineteenth-Century Transcriptions and Editions: Wagner Revisited." *Journal of Band Research* XXVIII/1 (Fall 1992): 31-56.

Votta, Michael ed., Fran J. Cipolla and Donald Hunsberger. *The Wind Ensemble and its Repertoire*. Rochester, NY: University of Rochester Press, 1994.

Wagner, Richard. Ed. Erik Leidzen. *Trauersinfonie: Funeral Music on Themes from "Euryanthe" by C.M. Von Weber*. NY: Associated, 1949.

Wagner, Richard. Ed. Michael Votta. *Trauermusik (WWV73): Trauersinfonie for Wind Orchestra*. Cleveland, OH: Ludwig, 1994.

Whitwell, David. "Wagner—His Music for Winds." *The Instrumentalist*, XX December 1965, 41-42.

Teacher Resource Guide

"Variants on a Medieval Tune"
Norman Dello Joio

(b. 1913)

Unit 1: Composer

Norman Dello Joio was born in New York City on January 24, 1913. He quickly showed remarkable aptitude and facility for playing the organ. At 14, he already was organist and choir director of the Star of the Sea Church in City Island. He attended Julliard and studied at Yale University with Paul Hindemith. He won a number of awards for composition in the United States and has written for virtually every medium including operas, incidental music, ballets, chamber music, and choral music. Dello Joio served on the faculties of Sarah Lawrence College and the Mannes College of Music. Notable works by Dello Joio include *Fantasies on a Theme by Haydn, From Every Horizon*, and *Scenes from "The Louvre"*.

Unit 2: Composition

Variants on a Medieval Tune was commissioned by the Mary Duke Biddle Foundation for the Duke University Band, Paul Bryan, conductor. It was first performed on April 10, 1963, and was first published in 1968 by Edward B. Marks Music Corp. Dello Joio was inspired by "In dulci jubilo" to compose a set of variations. They consist of a brief introduction, the theme, and five "variants" which send the medieval melody through five true metamorphoses, strongly contrasting in tempo and character, and utilizing the possibilities of the band to the highest degree. The piece is in one movement, is a Grade 5 difficulty and lasts about twelve minutes.

Unit 3: Historical Perspective

Variants on a Medieval Tune was Dello Joio's first original work for the wind medium. "In dulci jubilo" is a melody which has been used by many composers, among them Johann Sebastian Bach, as the subject for a variety of musical works. The tune was a most appropriate musical idea around which to fashion his piece. Variation in character and pace allowed him to explore what to him at the time was an untried musical medium. This piece began a period in 1963 of active band composition by Dello Joio.

Unit 4: Technical Considerations
The piece requires the keys of C Major and some related keys for the full ensemble. The meters are straightforward, and the few meter changes that do occur happen only on the quarter-note level. There are no tempo changes except between sections. The rhythmic demands are very basic with the use of quarter, eighth, and sixteenth notes. Scalar passages and ranges are not difficult; the highest trumpet note is a B-flat concert. There are no key signatures but several accidentals.

Unit 5: Stylistic Considerations
Each large section has its own style. The intensity and movement of the music should be equal to the phrasing, articulation, rhythms and principles of the line. This is a piece inspired by a melody from the Baroque period scored for modern wind band. There are some solos, and, at times, the lines are exposed. All melodies should be played in singing style. Balances are important between melody and accompaniment. A blend of sound is essential. Rhythm and style must have contrast between sections.

Unit 6: Musical Elements
The main theme is stated in C following an introduction that is something of a homage to the opening of Bach's *Toccata and Fugue in D minor*. Compositional devices used include call-and-answer ostinatos, the use of countermelodic material, and rapid pitch repetitions. It is a decidedly tonal piece using harmonies which demonstrate not only the clarity and pureness of Bach's 17th-century style but also Dello Joio's imaginative creativity in this setting. The traditional British Brass Band sonority is embellished and enhanced with the use of woodwinds and percussion.

Unit 7: Form and Structure
INTRODUCTION	C Major
	Mm. 1-12
Tema "In dulci jubilo"	C Major
Semplice	Mm. 13-34, solo flute, bassoon, clarinet I & oboe
VARIATION I	E-flat Major
Opening	Mm. 35-41

2nd phrase	Mm. 42-56, brass punctuations, tutti soft staccato
Climax	Mm. 57-62
Closing	Mm. 63-67

VARIATION II	E-flat Major, G minor, other related keys, ends on C Major
Lento, pesante	Mm. 68-84, contrasts in dynamics and articulations
Più movendo	Mm. 85-92, tutti with several mordent figures
Closing	Mm. 93-100, tutti diminuendo and rallantando

VARIATION III	
Allegro spumante	Mm. 101-108, soft staccato sixteenth-notes
	Mm. 109-120, tutti fast & rhythmical
Closing	Mm. 121-139, alternating woodwind and brass groups

VARIATION IV	
Andante	Mm. 140-159
	Mm. 160-171, climax and denouement
Closing	Mm. 172-180, trumpet I solo, chordal tutti

VARIATION V	
Allegro gioioso	Mm. 181-222
	Mm. 221-292
Closing	Mm. 293-317, tutti

Unit 8: Suggested Listening

Norman Dello Joio, *Scenes from "The Louvre"*
Norman Dello Joio, *Fantasies on a Theme by Haydn*
Norman Dello Joio, *From Every Horizon*
Gordon Jacob, *William Byrd Suite*
Martin Mailman, *Concerto for Wind Orchestra (Variations)*, Op. 89
Martin Mailman, *Liturgical Music for Band*, Op. 33
Jan Pieterszoon Sweelinck/arr. Walters, *Ballo del granduca*

Unit 9: Additional References and Resources

Baker, Theodore. "Dello Joio, Norman," *Baker's Biographical Dictionary of Musicians*. 6th ed., revised by Nicolas Slonimsky. New York: Schirmer Books, 1984.

Johnson, Charles E. "Common Musical Idioms in Selected Contemporary Wind Band Music." Diss., Florida State University, 1969.

Kopetz, Barry E. 'Dello Joio's Variants on A Medieval Tune." *The Instrumentalist*, XLIV November 1989, 21-28, 88.

National Band Association Selective Music List for Bands

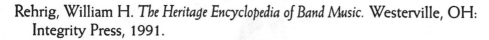

Rehrig, William H. *The Heritage Encyclopedia of Band Music.* Westerville, OH: Integrity Press, 1991.

Westrup, J. A. and F. Ll. Harrison. "Dello Joio, Norman," *The New College Encyclopedia of Music.* Revised by Conrad Wilson. New York: W. W. Norton & Company, Ltd, 1981.

Teacher Resource Guide

Variations on "America" for Band
Charles Ives

(b. 1874–d. 1954)

transcribed by William E. Rhoads (b. 1918)

based on the Orchestra Version by

William Schuman (b. 1910–d. 1992)

Unit 1: Composer

Charles Ives was born in Danbury, Connecticut in 1874. He received his basic musical training from his father, who taught him the value of "manly" classical composers like Handel, Beethoven, and Brahms. He studied composition with Horatio Parker at Yale, then opened a successful insurance business in New York City and continued to compose for all mediums. His other works for band include *The Alcotts*, *"Country Band" March*, *March: Omega Lambda Chi*, and *Overture and March: "1776"*.

Unit 2: Composition

Variations on America was composed for organ in 1891, the piece was possibly based on D. W. Reeves's *Yankee Doodle Fantasy Humoresque*. It was first published in 1949 by Mercury Music Corp. It was transcribed by William E. Rhoads in 1967 and first performed by the University of New Mexico Wind Ensemble conducted by Rhoads. The band version source was an orchestral transcription by William Schuman from Ives's original organ work. The piece is in one movement, is a Grade 5 difficulty and lasts about seven minutes.

Unit 3: Historical Perspective

George Edward Ives was a band director in Danbury, so his son Charles grew up within the New England band tradition of the late 19th century. George encouraged Charles to "stretch his ears" by exposing him to polytonal performances of

"Swanee River" and to contraptions that played quarter-tones. George would also have Charles sing a tune in one key and accompany himself on the piano in another key. Charles was inspired by such ideas as the sounds of the camp meeting choirs whose members' excitement would sometimes wreak havoc with the rhythm and sometimes even move the pitch straight up the chromatic scale.

Unit 4: Technical Considerations

The piece is centered in the key of F, but also goes into D-flat and F minor; even so, accidentals abound to create tone-clusters and bi tonalities. There are only two meter changes between large sections. There are different tempo changes for the large sections. The rhythmic demands are very basic with the use of quarter, eighth, and sixteenth notes. All instruments have several exposed sections and several solos. Scalar passages and ranges are not difficult.

Unit 5: Stylistic Considerations

Each variation has its own style. The intensity and movement of the music should be equal to the phrasing, articulation, rhythms and principles of the line. This is a 20th-century work written with contrasts between Romantic and 20th-century styles and sounds. Contrasts are important between the variations in dynamics, texture, articulation, and tone. The piece has built-in bridges between variations, which is when people would have applauded during concerts in Ives' day.

Unit 6: Musical Elements

In *Variations on "America,"* Ives uses the symphonic band medium for his classically-structured work. The piece follows the formal structure of a traditional theme and variations with two added interludes. While it is a non-referential composition without a program, it is rich in melody, texture, rhythm, tension, color, and beauty. It is a decidedly tonal piece, but with tone-clusters and bi-tonalities.

Unit 7: Form and Structure

THEME	F Major (with many accidentals)
Introduction	Beginning to C
"America"	C to D, very rhythmical
Intro 2nd x	D to F, smooth
"America"	F to G, very rhythmical
VARIATION I	F Major (with many accidentals)
	G to H, sixteenth notes in woodwinds
VARIATION II	F Major with many accidentals
	H to I, eighth notes throughout, FH I and Oboe I soli, bsn solo

INTERLUDE	F Major (with many accidentals) I to J, chorale-like

VARIATION III
  "America" 1st x
  "America" 2nd x
	D-flat Major (with many accidentals)
	J to K, Gigue-like in 6/8
	K to L, Gigue-like in 6/8

VARIATION IV	F minor (with many accidentals) L to N, very rhythmical
INTERLUDE	F Major (with many accidentals) N to O, *espr. legato*
VARIATION V	F Major (with many accidentals) O to R, fast, quasi-waltz
CODA	R to end

Unit 8: Suggested Listening
Charles Ives, *"Country Band" March*
Charles Ives, *The Alcotts*
Charles Ives, *March Intercollegiate*
Charles Ives, *Overture and March: "1776"*

Unit 9: Additional References and Resource

Baker, Theodore. "Ives, Charles," *Baker's Biographical Dictionary of Musicians*. 6th ed., revised by Nicolas Slonimsky. New York: Schirmer Books, 1984.

Burk, James. "The Wind Music of Charles Ives." *The Instrumentalist*, XXIV October 1969, 36-40.

Kopetz, Barry E. "Charles Ives' Variations on America." *The Instrumentalist*, XLV April 1991, 20-28, 75-79.

Milligan, Terry G. "Charles Ives: Musical Activity at Poverty Flat (1898-1908)." *Journal of Band Research* XX/1 (Fall 1984): 30-36.

Milligan, Terry G. "Charles Ives: Musical Activity at Yale (1894-98)." *Journal of Band Research* XIX/1 (Spring 1984): 39-50.

National Band Association Selective Music List for Bands

Rehrig, William H. *The Heritage Encyclopedia of Band Music*. Westerville, OH: Integrity Press, 1991.

Westrup, J. A. and F. Ll. Harrison. *The New College Encyclopedia of Music*. Revised by Conrad Wilson. New York: W. W. Norton & Company, Ltd, 1981.

Teacher Resource Guide

"William Byrd Suite"

Selected from the Fitzwilliam Virginal Book

by William Byrd (b. 1543–d. 1623)

Freely transcribed by

Gordon Jacob (b. 1895–d. 1984)

Unit 1: Composer

Gordon Percival Jacob was born in London in 1895. Jacob studied music at the Royal College of Music, and in 1926, became a member of the music faculty, a position which he held for forty years. A teacher, conductor, orchestrater, composer, and author, Jacob contributed several important compositions to the wind band repertoire at a time when bands had limited original literature. Notable works by Jacob include *An Original Suite*, *The Battell*, *Fantasia on an English Folk Song*, *Tribute to Canterbury*, and *Music for a Festival*.

Unit 2: Composition

Jacob set the six pieces from the Fitzwilliam Virginal Book in 1923 in honor of the tercentenary of Byrd's death. He selected appropriate music that would lie with ease within the tonal framework of the sonorous British military band. The suite was published by Boosey and Hawkes in 1924. At this time, a rare period of excellence in composition and publication of band music, Ralph Vaughan Williams also wrote his *English Folk Song Suite* and *Toccata Marziale*. The suite has six movements, is a Grade 5 difficulty (NBA lists it as a Grade 4) and lasts about eighteen minutes.

Unit 3: Historical Perspective

The pieces were originally written for the virginal, a small and simple instrument belonging to the harpsichord family. Its proportionately "small" tone and "limited" expressiveness were not restrictions to Byrd's creative imagination or his use of the available wind band forces. Jacob's sensitivity to this has resulted in these pieces being admirably suited to an "expressive medium," however distant from the original.

Unit 4: Technical Considerations

The suite requires the keys of F Major, G minor and B-flat Major for the full ensemble. The meters are straightforward. The only meter changes occur in the 6th movement between 3/4 and 9/8, quarter note equal to dotted quarter note. There are no tempo changes except between movements. The rhythmic demands are very basic, with the use of quarter, eighth, and sixteenth notes. Scalar passages and ranges are not difficult; the highest trumpet note is a written high C on the last note of the piece. Flutes, E-flat clarinet and solo B-flat clarinet must pay a C concert scale in 32nd notes at quarter note equal to 80.

Unit 5: Stylistic Considerations

Each movement has its own style. The intensity and movement of the music should be equal to the phrasing, articulation, rhythms and principles of the line. This is a Renaissance-style piece scored for wind band. There are no solos, and the lines are not very exposed. All melodies should be played in singing style. Balances are important between melody and accompaniment. A blend of sound is essential. Rhythm and dance style must have contrast between movements. Tempos should match the dance styles and the articulation.

Unit 6: Musical Elements

Jacob adds the element of instrumental texture to show Byrd's implied dynamic contrasts. Jacob only set approximately half of each original song since the songs were always extensively developed and extremely florid in figuration. It is a decidedly tonal piece, using Renaissance harmonies which demonstrate the clarity and pureness of Byrd's 17th-century style. The traditional British Brass Band sonority is embellished and enhanced with the use of woodwinds and percussion.

Unit 7: Form and Structure

MVMT 1 - "THE EARLE OF OXFORD'S MARCHE" F MAJOR

Theme		Beginning to 1 stated by clarinets
Theme	(varied)	1 to 6 tutti
Theme	(varied)	6 to 12 tutti
Coda	12 to end	

MVMT II - "PAVANA"   G minor

Theme		Beginning to 1 stated by flutes & clarinets
Variation		1 to 2 stated by brass
Theme	2 to end tutti	

MVMT III - "Jhon come kisse me now" F Major

Theme	Beginning to 1 stated by Eb & Bb clarinets & alto saxes
Variation I	1 to 2 stated by cornet
Variation II	2 to 3 stated by clarinets
Variation III	3 to 4 stated by horns, trombone 1 & low reeds
Variation IV	4 to 5
Variation V	5 to 6 stated by brass
Variation VI	6 to end stated lightly and ending softly

MVMT IV - "The Mayden's Song" F Major

Theme	Beginning to 3
Variation	3 to 4 stated by clarinets & cornet solo
Theme	4 to 5 tutti
Variation	5 to 6 tutti
Theme & closing	6 to end tutti

MVMT V - "Wolsey's Wilde" B-flat Major

A		Beginning to 1 stated in flutes
B		1 to first repeat tutti
A	(varied)	After first repeat to 2 woodwinds
B	(varied)	2 to end tutti

MVMT VI - "The Bells" B-flat Major

Theme	Beginning to 3
Variation	3 to 5 tutti rise and fall
Variation II	5 to 8 9/8 building
Bells	8 to end climax and ending

Unit 8: Suggested Listening
Gustav Holst, *First Suite in E-flat for Military Band, Op. 28a*
Gustav Holst, *Second Suite in F for Military Band, Op. 28b*
Gordon Jacob, *An Original Suite*
Gordon Jacob, *Tribute to Canterbury*
Henry Purcell/Gordon, *Air and March*
Ralph Vaughan Williams, *English Folk Song Suite*

Unit 9: Additional References and Resources
Baker, Theodore. "Jacob, Gordon," *Baker's Biographical Dictionary of Musicians.* 6th
    ed., revised by Nicolas Slonimsky. New York: Schirmer Books, 1984

Fennell, Frederick. "William Byrd Suite." *The Instrumentalist,* XXX
    September 1975, 35-41.

National Band Association Selective Music List for Bands

Rehrig, William H. *The Heritage Encyclopedia of Band Music.* Westerville, OH: Integrity Press, 1991.

Rogers, Michael R. "Gordon Jacob: A Biographical Sketch and Analysis of Four Selected Works for Band." Ph.D. diss., The University of Oklahoma, 1988.

Thompson, Kevin. "Gordon Jacob—'I Aim at Greater Simplicity Nowadays'." *The Instrumentalist,* XXXVIII September 1983, 38-39.

Westrup, J. A. and F. Ll. Harrison. *The New College Encyclopedia of Music.* Revised by Conrad Wilson. New York: W. W. Norton & Company, Ltd, 19

Grade 6

Teacher Resource Guide

"Armenian Dances, Part I"
Alfred Reed

(b. 1921)

Unit 1: Composer

Alfred Reed was born in New York City on January 25, 1921. He studied music at Baylor University and with Vittorio Giannini at the Julliard School of Music. The International Conservatory of Music in Lima, Peru honored him with a doctorate of music in 1968. He served as Professor of Music at the School of Music at the University of Miami at Coral Gables, Florida. He was conductor of the All-American Youth Honor Band on its South American tour in 1967 and its Mexican tour in 1969 as well as the Music for Peace International Concert Band on a tour of England in 1971. He is a noted composer, conductor and clinician throughout the United States, Canada, South America, Europe and Japan. He has written over 250 published works for band, wind ensemble, chorus, orchestra, and various solo and ensemble pieces. Some of his other works for band include *The Hounds of Spring*, *Armenian Dances, Part II*, *Russian Christmas Music*, and *Symphony No. 3*.

Unit 2: Composition

Armenian Dances, Part I is one of many works for band composed by Alfred Reed. The piece was completed in the summer of 1972, having been suggested to the composer by Dr. Harry Begian as early as 1963. It was first performed by Dr. Begian (to whom the work is dedicated) and the University of Illinois Symphonic Band on January 10, 1973 at the CBDNA convention in Urbana, Illinois. The *Armenian Dances*, Parts I and II, constitute a four-movement suite for concert band or wind ensemble based on authentic Armenian folk songs from the collected works of Gomidas Vartabed (1869-1935), the founder of Armenian classical music. Part II was completed in 1975, and the two parts were performed as a whole in 1976. The piece has one movement, is a Grade 5 difficulty and lasts about eleven minutes.

Unit 3: Historical Perspective
Gomidas Vartabed (1869-1935) is credited with collecting over 4000 Armenian folk songs. His legacy to the Armenian people, and to the world's appreciation of ethnic music, is invaluable, and his major contribution lies in preserving many centuries-old melodies from obscurity. As founding member of the International Music Society, Gomidas read and wrote many important papers on Armenian neumatic notation, the structure of Armenian sacred melodies and folk melodies. Four of the five songs in *Armenian Dances, Part I* are Armenian, augmented by *Gavaki Yerk*, an original song by Vartabed.

Unit 4: Technical Considerations
There are several meter changes, and the tempos remain consistent within the sections. Choosing exact tempi should be based on the size of the ensemble. The eighth note's value in the third section in 5/8 must remain absolutely constant throughout; the accents of the measures shift in irregularly recurring patterns (2+3, 3+2, etc.). There are both staccato and legato articulations, so contrast is important. There is a lengthy alto saxophone solo. Ranges and scalar passages are not difficult.

Unit 5: Stylistic Considerations
Careful attention to dynamics, clarity of attack and phrasing, based on proper tempi, is required. All markings in the score support this. Each section has its own style (fast, slow, meditative, etc.). The intensity and movement of the music should be equal to the phrasing, articulation, rhythms and principles of the line. This is a 20th-century work with 20th-century sounds; it should be approached with a 20th-century interpretation.

Unit 6: Musical Elements
Armenian Dances, Part I is an extended symphonic rhapsody built upon five different songs, freely treated and developed in terms of the modern, integrated concert band or wind ensemble. While the composer has kept his treatment of the melodies within the general limits imposed on the music by its very nature, he has expanded the melodic, harmonic, and rhythmic possibilities in keeping with the demands of a symphonic-instrumental ensemble.

Unit 7: Form and Structure
TZIRANI TZAR (THE APRICOT TREE)	F Major
Opening	Introduction & fanfare (4 measures)
Theme	M. 5 to 14 stated in upper brass & woodwinds

| | 14 to 19 stated in alto sax solo |
| Restatement of Opening | 19 to 30 fanfare & transition |

GAVAKI YERK (PARTRIDGE'S SONG)   B-flat Major, G Major
Introduction   Mm. 30 to 31
Theme   Mm. 32 to 40 stated in woodwinds
Slight thematic variations   Mm. 41 to 59
Modulated theme with closing   59 to 69

HOY, NAZAN EEM (HOY, MY NAZAN)   A minor
Introduction   69 to m. 72
Theme I   M. 73 to 87 alto sax & oboe solos
Theme I (2nd x)   87 to 101 stated in clarinets
Theme I (2nd part)   101 to m. 108
transition   M. 109 to 117
Theme II   117 to 137 alto sax & oboe solos
Theme II (2nd x)   137 to 157 stated in trumpets & trombones
transition   157 to 165
Closing   165 to 186

ALAGYAZ (AN ARMENIAN MOUNTAIN)   B-flat Major
Theme   186 to 194 tutti chorale
Theme (2nd x)   194 to 210
Theme varied   210 to m. 220
Closing   M. 221 to 224 clarinets & low brass

GNA, GNA (GO, GO)   G Major
Introduction   224 to 234 fast percussion & tutti ostinato
Theme   234 to 251 stated in oboes & alto saxes
Theme continued   251 to 268 stated in clarinets
transition   268 to 304
Theme varied   304 to 347 stated in clarinet I
Fanfare & accel   347 to 357
Furioso   357 to 402
Coda   402 to end

Unit 8: Suggested Listening

Alan Hovhaness, *Symphony No. 4, Op. 165*
Martin Mailman, *Liturgical Music for Band, Op. 33*
Alfred Reed, *Armenian Dances, Part II*
Alfred Reed, *The Hounds of Spring*
Alfred Reed, *Symphony No. 3*

Unit 9: Additional References and Resources

Begian, Harry. "Alfred Reed's Armenian Dances, (Part I)—A Rehearsal Analysis." *The Instrumentalist*, XL October 1985, 27-34.

DeCarbo, Nicholas. "Alfred Reed—Composer of Our Time." *The Instrumentalist*, XL October 1985, 20-24.

National Band Association Selective Music List for Bands

Rehrig, William H. *The Heritage Encyclopedia of Band Music*. Westerville, OH: Integrity Press, 1991.

Westrup, J. A. and F. Ll. Harrison. *The New College Encyclopedia of Music*. Revised by Conrad Wilson. New York: W. W. Norton & Company, Ltd, 1981.

Teacher Resource Guide

Selections from "Carmina Burana"
Carl Orff
(b. 1895–d. 1982)

transcribed by John Krance
(b. 1935)

Unit 1: Composer

Carl Orff's primary compositional interest was in creating a theater that combined all aspects of words, music, and movement. He also had a lifelong interest in music education, which resulted in two influential publications, *Orff-Schulwerk*, and *Musik für Kinder*. In order to develop and apply his educational theories, he and Dorothy Günther founded the *Günterschule* in 1929, creating a curriculum where music, dance, and gymnastics were highly coordinated.

Unit 2: Composition

Carmina Burana was originally a work for large orchestra, chorus, boys choir, and vocal soloists, and is subtitled "Profane songs for singers and vocal chorus with instruments and magical pictures." It is in eight large sections, with twenty-five separate movements, incorporating texts in Latin and German. The texts are secular poems of the middle ages from a manuscript found in the *Benediktbueren* Monastery in Bavaria. The songs range from simple adorations of nature to lusty and satirical drinking songs. This transcription for symphonic band by John Krance, published in 1967, consists of thirteen selected movements.

Unit 3: Historical Perspective

Orff's *Carmina Burana* reflects two important 19th-century trends, interest in historical music and the development of a "total" theater. The use of ancient texts and simple materials is a reflection of the first trend. The bringing together of large forces and the length and programmatic design of the parts are related to the second. This composition has become extremely popular with orchestral audiences and is by far Orff's most performed work. A debt to Stravinsky's *Les Noces* is obvious in the piano and percussion writing.

Unit 4: Technical Considerations
The transcription of *Carmina Burana* is generally reasonable in its technical demands. However, several movements require extreme ranges or endurance. Soloists, especially oboe, trumpet, and euphonium, are prominently featured. The percussion section is treated as an equal partner with the winds, and is skillfully incorporated into the ensemble. Some asymmetric meter is used, but it is not complex or difficult. The brass have important and exposed multiple tonguing sections.

Unit 5: Stylistic Considerations
A wide range of styles are presented in the transcription. Vocal lines are all adapted to wind instruments and require broad lyrical treatment. The insistent dance rhythms and declamatory punctuations are exuberant and vibrant. Often the ensemble is called upon to provide sensitive accompaniment for a soloist.

Unit 6: Musical Elements
The most frequently presented musical device in *Carmina Burana* is ostinato. Almost every movement of the transcription uses ostinato or a related repetitive idea. Satirical settings of text, most notably *Ego sum abbas* and *In taberna*, are faithfully captured in the transcription. The harmony is generally simple, diatonic or modal. The transcribed vocal parts are often modal, imitating elements of plainchant.

Unit 7: Form and Structure
All movements follow the form of the poetry. They are generally in repeated periods, and frequently whole movements are repeated. Some repeats are written out, and some are indicated. The analysis will treat these repeats equally, except to indicate when a whole movement is to be repeated.

I. O FORTUNA, VELUT LUNA
One four-measure phrase in D minor that ends on a half cadence and serves as an introduction.

II. FORTUNA PLANGO VULNERA
A, mm. 1-8 D minor
 One four-measure phrase repeated
B, mm. 9-24
  1, mm. 9-16, eight-measure phrase
  2, mm. 17-24, phrase repeated with added trumpets

C. mm, 25-40, 2/2, eight-measure phrase, repeated, piu mosso

III. ECCE GRATUM
A, m. 1, Introduction, F Major
B, mm. 2-9, repeated four-measure phrase, based on Introduction
C, mm. 10-13, four-measure phrase, contrasting
D, mm. 14-32
    1, mm. 14-25, repeated six-measure phrase
    2, mm. 26-32, four measure phrase
E, mm. 33-46 Coda, repeated four-measure phrase, with one-measure cadential extension

Entire movement is repeated three times with gradually increasing tempo

IV. TANZ - UF DEM ANGER
Introduction, mm. 1-4, C Major
A, mm. 5-34
    a, mm. 5-14, repeated four-measure phrase
    b, mm. 15-24, contrasting ten-measure phrase
    a, mm. 25-34, repeated four-measure phrase
B. mm. 35-54, flute and timpani duet, repeated ten-measure phrase
A. mm. 55-89
    a, mm. 55-64, repeated four-measure phrase
    b, mm. 65-74, contrasting ten-measure phrase
    a, mm. 75-89,
        1, mm. 75-78, four-measure phrase
        2, mm. 79-89, four-measure phrase with six-measure cadential extension

V. FLORET SILVA
A, mm. 1-9, Introduction, G Major
B, mm. 10-15, three repetitions of two-measure
C, mm. 16-27, 12-measure phrase
D, mm. 28-47, three-measure antecedent and four-measure consequent phrase, repeated once, with four-measure cadential extension
E, mm 48-84, 18-measure phrase, repeated once, with seven-measure cadential extension

VI. WERE DIU WERLT ALLE MIN
A, mm. 1-4, Fanfare, C Major
B, mm. 6-8, introduction
C, mm. 9-12, four-measure phrase
D, mm. 13-16, four-measure contrasting phrase
E, mm, 17-22, six-measure phrase
A, mm. 24-27, Fanfare, with one-measure cadential extension

VII. Amor volat undique
Introduction, mm. 1-4, D Major (with modal inflections)
A, mm. 5-28
    a, four-measure phrase
    a, four-measure phrase
    b, one-measure cadenza
    a, four-measure phrase
    b, one-measure cadenza
    a, four-measure phrase
    b, one-measure cadenza
    a, four-measure phrase
B., mm. 29-50
    1, mm. 29-44, five-measure phrase, repeated three times, with a one-measure introduction
    2, mm. 44-50, five-measure phrase with one-measure extension
A, mm. 51-63
    a, four-measure phrase
    a, four-measure phrase
    b, one-measure cadenza
    a, four-measure phrase

VIII. Ego sum abbas
Quasi plainchant, euphonium solo, imitating a drunken Abbot. Six solos, with band interjections and cadence. Modal

IX. In taberna quando sumus
A, mm. 1-52, E minor
    1, mm. 1-12
        Introduction, two measures
        a, two repeated four-measure phrases and a two-measure interjection
        a, two repeated four-measure phrases and a two-measure interjection
    1, mm. 13-24, repeat of preceding
    2, mm. 25-28, repeated two-measure phrase
    3, mm. 29-34
        b, repeated eight-measure phrase
        c, four-measure phrase
        b, repeated eight-measure phrase
    4, mm 49-52, Codetta
B, mm. 53-86
    1, four-measure phrase, repeated four times with different orchestration
    2, four-measure phrase

3, eight-measure antecedent, four-measure consequent phrase
Coda, mm. 87-95

X. IN TRUTINA
A nine measure phrase, repeated once, first with oboe solo, then with trumpet solo, D Major

XI. DULCISSIME
A four-measure cadenza for oboe, in D Major, that ends on a half-cadence and serves as an introduction to the next movement.

XII. AVE FORMOSISSIMA
A. mm. 1-8, four-measure antecedent and four-measure consequent phrase, D Mixolydian mode
B. mm 8-15, three-measure antecedent and two three-measure consequent phrases
C. mm. 16-19 Coda, ends on half-cadence

XIII. FORTUNA INPERATRIX MUNDI
Introduction, mm. 1-4, Literal repeat of Movement I
A, mm. 5-36
    a, four-measure phrase
    a, four-measure phrase
    b, four-measure phrase
    a, four-measure phrase
    a, four-measure phrase
    b, four-measure phrase
    Codetta, eight-measure phrase
B, mm. 37-68
    c, eight-measure phrase
    c, eight-measure phrase
    c, eight-measure phrase
    d, eight-measure phrase
C, mm. 69-77, Coda

Unit 8: Suggested Listening
Carl Orff, *Catuli carmina*
Carl Orff, *Carmina Burana* (Orchestral)
Igor Stravinsky, *Les Noces*

Unit 9: Additional References and Resources
Grout, Donald J. and Claude V. Palisca. *A History of Western Music*, 4th ed. New York: W. W. Norton & Company, 1988.

Sadie, Stanley, ed. *The New Grove Dictionary of Music and Musicians.* 20 Vols. London: Macmillan, 1980. S.v. "Carl Orff," by John Horton.

Smith, Norman and Albert Stoutamire. *Band Music Notes.* Lake Charles, LA: Program Note Press, 1989.

Stolba, K Marie. *The Development of Western Music.* Dubuque, IA: William C. Brown Publishers, 1990.

Teacher Resource Guide

"Emblems"
Aaron Copland
(b. 1900–d. 1990)

Unit 1: Composer
Aaron Copland is among the most respected composers of this century. His use of American folk idioms and open harmony created a prototypical American sound. Copland's work divides into three general periods. His early works were viewed as modernist and often featured jazz-derived material. In his middle period, where he wrote his best-known works, he made a conscious effort to simplify and make his music more accessible. *Appalachian Spring, El Salon Mexico,* and *Fanfare for the Common Man* all date from this period. Like Stravinsky, Copland began to experiment with serial technique in his last period. Copland served as a mentor to an entire generation of American composers.

Unit 2: Composition
Emblems was written in 1964 in fulfillment of a commission from the College Band Directors National Association. It was premiered at their convention on December 18, 1964 by the University of Southern California Band. The premier was not well received by people unfamiliar with Copland's late style, but *Emblems* has subsequently been recognized a 20th-century masterwork.

Unit 3: Historical Perspective
Emblems was Copland's last work for large ensemble. It is a mature work that shows elements of all of Copland's style periods. Jazz-like rhythms are incorporated, reminiscent of his early works. The well-known American hymn "Amazing Grace" is quoted, evoking his middle-period style. Polychords and harmonies reflecting his late style are featured prominently.

Unit 4: Technical Considerations

Copland fully exploits the capability of the wind instruments, creating a technically demanding work. Wide ranges, difficult intervals, fast technical passages, and dynamic extremes are expected of the performers. There are both lyrical and technical solos for the winds. In the central section of the work, performers must play very technical parts with confidence and independence. This is complicated by complex hemiola throughout this part of the work.

Unit 5: Stylistic Considerations

Emblems is written with a broad range of stylistic demands. The work opens and closes with long legato passages that range in expression from majestic and intensely lyrical to simple and serene. These are often punctuated with dramatic outbursts in marcato style. Silence is an important musical element throughout the work. The central section of the piece requires a dance-like marcato. Again, a wide range of articulations and dynamics are stipulated.

Unit 6: Musical Elements

Much of *Emblems* harmonic structure is bitonal. Like much of Copland's music, fifths play an important harmonic and coloristic part. Melodically, the work is attractive in typical Coplanesque style, including the use of an American hymn, "Amazing Grace." Motivically, the work is tightly constructed. The motive in the central section, first introduced in the percussion, is varied and developed from a single germinal rhythm.

Unit 7: Form and Structure

THREE-PART FORM, ABA, PRINCIPALLY IN C

A Section, mm. 1-107

Introduction, a and b material, mm. 1-17, F
Interlude, mm. 18-27, Bb
a and b material, mm. 28-48
c material, mm. 49-84
"Amazing Grace," mm. 85-100, A
Codetta, mm. 101-107, C

B Section, mm. 108-279, G, Variations on a rhythmic motive

Introduction, Percussion, mm. 108-120
Variation I, Piano, mm. 121-129
Variation II, Clarinets, mm. 130-136
Variation III, Soloists, mm. 137-165
Variation IV, Hemiola, 166-174
Interlude, mm. 175-187
Variation V, Hocket, mm. 188-193

Variation VI, Trumpets, mm. 194-201
Interlude, mm. 202-217
Variation VII, Sequence, mm. 218-233
Interlude, mm. 234-243
Variation VIII, Brass, mm. 244-252
Variation IX, Augmentation, mm. 253-267
Variation X, Tutti, mm. 268-279

A Section (Varied), mm. 280-366, Bb

a material, mm. 280-297
b material, mm. 298-317
"Amazing Grace," mm. 318-329, A
a material, mm. 330-335

Coda, mm. 336-356, C

Unit 8: Suggested Listening

Aaron Copland, *Inscape*
Ingolf Dahl, *Sinfonietta*
William Schuman, *George Washington Bridge*

Unit 9: Additional References and Resources

Copland, Aaron. "Aaron Copland on Aaron Copland." *The Instrumentalist*, XL November 1985, 66-69.

Copland, Aaron and Vivian Perlis. Copland, 2 Vols. New York: St. Martin's/Marek, 1984.

Cromonic, Richard. "Aaron Copland: The Vigorous Old Man of American Music." *The Instrumentalist*, XXXVIII November 1983, 24-25.

Grout, Donald J. and Claude V. Palisca. *A History of Western Music*, 4th ed. New York: W. W. Norton & Company, 1988.

Sadie, Stanley, ed. *The New Grove Dictionary of Music and Musicians*. 20 Vols. London: Macmillan, 1980. S.v. "Aaron Copland," by William W. Austin.

Smith, Norman and Albert Stoutamire. *Band Music Notes*. Lake Charles, LA: Program Note Press, 1989.

Stolba, K Marie. *The Development of Western Music*. Dubuque, IA: William C. Brown Publishers, 1990.

Whitwell, David. "The Enigma of Copland's Emblems." *Journal of Band Research* VII/2 (Spring 1971): 5-9.

Teacher Resource Guide

"Hammersmith"

Prelude and Scherzo

Gustav Holst

(b. 1874–d. 1934)

Unit 1: Composer

Gustav Holst is one of the most distinguished British composers of the early 20th century. He worked in every major genre and contributed important works that have stayed in the repertoire. He was also a professional trombonist and a teacher of composition. He was a bandmaster during the first World War, and had previously demonstrated an interest in music for the band by writing his *First Suite for Military Band in Eb* in 1909.

Unit 2: Composition

Hammersmith, subtitled *Prelude and Scherzo*, is a late work of Holst. Imogene Holst, Gustav's daughter who became a respected musician and student of her father's work, deemed it one of Holst's five best works in any genre. The work was written on commission from the BBC in 1930, but did not receive the expected premiere. It was finally premiered in 1932 by the U. S. Marine Band, conducted by Captain Taylor Branson, at the American Bandmasters Association convention. It is a monumental work for wind band and a recognized 20th-century masterpiece.

Unit 3: Historical Perspective

The title derives from Hammersmith, a western borough of London, where Holst lived and worked for thirty years. It depicts the sharply contrasting elements of life, from the peaceful Thames river to the crowded market place. It is a mature work, displaying contrapuntal virtuosity and brilliant tonal manipulation.

Unit 4: Technical Considerations

The opening Prelude demands long lyrical phrases and impeccable legato. Intonation is an extraordinarily demanding problem. The Scherzo employs wide ranges, large interval skips, and physically demanding brass parts. Controlling the distinction between duple and triple subdivision of the beat is essential. Soloists, especially woodwinds, are needed for expressive and subtle writing at the return.

Unit 5: Stylistic Considerations

The contrast between lyrical and marcato is a consideration throughout the work. The scherzo alternates between duple and triple subdivision of the beat, a stylistic change that must be performed with clarity and rhythmic precision. This problem is compounded when the contrasting meters are superimposed upon each other, which happens frequently in the Scherzo.

Unit 6: Musical Elements

The opening Prelude is a masterful example of bitonality. The opening bass line, an ostinato that is presented fifteen times, is in the key of F minor. The melody that first appears in the horns is in E Major. This striking counterpoint is handled effortlessly, using only one enharmonic common tone, Db and C#. The Scherzo begins with a fugue, which presents both the 2/4 and 6/8 material. The material is developed motivically from the harmonic scheme of the Prelude, beginning with motives on F and E.

Unit 7: Form and Structure

ARCH FORM, ABCBA

A, PRELUDE, MM. 1-61, BITONAL, F MINOR AND E MAJOR

> Ground Bass, mm. 1-45, fifteen statements of three-measure ostinato, in F minor
> Melody, mm. 1-45, in E Major
> Fanfare motive, m. 43 in piccolo, and m. 47 in trumpet
> Codetta, m. 48-61

B, SCHERZO, MM. 62-227

> Fugal Exposition, mm. 62-113
> > Subject in 2/4
> > Countersubject in 3/4
> Stretto, mm. 114-132

Subject and its Inversion
Episode I, mm. 133-145
  Subject
Episode II, mm. 146-159
  Countersubject
Episode III, mm. 160-200
  Subject in augmentation and Fanfare motive
Codetta, mm. 201-227

C, FUGHETTO, MM. 228-283

Transition from Scherzo, mm. 228-248
  Meno mosso, mm. 228-241, saxophone solo from Fugue
  Countersubject, in 3/4
  Tempo I, mm. 242-248, tuba and euphonium solos from Fugue
  Subject, in 2/4
Lento, mm. 249-283, Fughetto on subject derived from the Codetta of the
Prelude and Countersubject derived from the Fanfare motive

B, SCHERZO, MM. 284-396

Subject and Fanfare motive, mm. 284-303
Countersubject, mm. 304-310
Subject and Fanfare motive, mm. 311-334
Allargando, Subject in augmentation, mm. 335-329
Subject in stretto, mm. 330-342
Fanfare motive, mm. 343-346
Stretto, mm. 347-366
Countersubject in augmentation, mm. 367-383, 3/4
Fanfare motive, 384-396, 6/8

A, PRELUDE, MM. 397-436

Ground Bass, mm. 397-408, four statements of three-measure ostinato, in
F minor, in counterpoint with material from Fugue subject, Fanfare
motive, and Prelude Melody
Coda, mm. 409-436

Unit 8: Suggested Listening
Gustav Holst, *First Suite in Eb for Military Band*
Gustav Holst, *Second Suite in F for Military Band*
Ralph Vaughan Williams, *English Folksong Suite*

Unit 9: Additional References and Resources

Cantrick, Robert. "'Hammersmith'" and the Two Worlds of Gustav Holst." *Journal of Band Research* XII/2 (Spring 1976): 3-11.

Fennell, Frederick. "Gustav Holst's Hammersmith." *The Instrumentalist,* XXX May 1977, 52-59.

Grout, Donald J. and Claude V. Palisca. *A History of Western Music,* 4th ed. New York: W. W. Norton & Company, 1988.

Mitchell, Jon Cleander. "Gustav Holst: The Works for Military Band." Diss., University of Illinois, 1980.

Sadie, Stanley, ed. *The New Grove Dictionary of Music and Musicians.* 20 Vols. London: Macmillan, 1980. S.v. "Gustav Holst," by Hugh Ottaway.

Smith, Norman and Albert Stoutamire. *Band Music Notes.* Lake Charles, LA: Program Note Press, 1989.

Stolba, K Marie. *The Development of Western Music.* Dubuque, IA: William C. Brown Publishers, 1990.

Teacher Resource Guide

"Heroes Lost and Fallen"

(A Vietnam Memorial)
David Gillingham
(b. 1947)

Unit 1: Composer

David Gillingham, a native of Waukesha, Wisconsin, is currently Professor of Music at Central Michigan University. He studied composition with Roger Dennis, Jere Hutcheson, James Niblock and H. Owen Reed. Gillingham's work has received much attention in recent years. He is particularly praised for his evocative scoring for winds and percussion. Several of his works for percussion ensemble, including *Stained Glass*, have become staples of the repertoire. Gillingham served in the military during the Vietnam War.

Unit 2: Composition

Heroes, Lost and Fallen is written for Symphonic Band, including piano and extensive percussion. It was commissioned by, and dedicated to, Victor Bordo and the Ann Arbor Symphony Band in 1989. In 1990, it won the prestigious International Barlow Competition. The work is based on a poem, written by the composer, which is cited in the score.

Unit 3: Historical Perspective

Heroes, Lost and Fallen is a memorial commemorating those who lost their life in the Vietnam War. It is also a reflection, looking back on the events and their aftermath, and a plea for peace and unity. Gillingham writes, *"Heroes, Lost and Fallen* is about healing and hope for the world. Regardless of how people feel about this conflict—whether America was right or wrong—the music conveys that this terrible tragedy has happened and the hope that it will never happen again."

Unit 4: Technical Considerations
The work is technically demanding, but not excessively so. It exploits instrumental registers and timbres effectively. The percussion ensemble is a full partner with the winds. The piano part is essential and requires fluent technique. Although not required for all parts, principal parts often exploit wide ranges.

Unit 5: Stylistic Considerations
Both lyrical and marcato styles are consistently contrasted throughout *Heroes, Lost and Fallen*. Sudden dynamic changes and subtle timbral effects require mature performers. The work unfolds dramatically, making tempo and pacing an important element in reproducing the composer's intent.

Unit 6: Musical Elements
The harmonic structure is tonal, concluding in C Major, but often employs polychordal constructions. Musical elements are often associated with poetic images, such as martial trumpet calls and warlike drums. Both "The Star Spangled Banner" and the Vietnamese National Anthem are quoted.

Unit 7: Form and Structure
Heroes, Lost and Fallen is a tone poem in six major sections. Each section is related to programmatic aspects of the work.

I. INTRODUCTION, MM. 1—15, INSTABILITY REFLECTS THE COMING STRIFE OF WAR
   Polychordal harmony, Db/Eb
   Figures suggesting trumpet calls, m. 6
   Fragments of "The Star Spangled Banner" and the Vietnamese National Anthem

II. CHORALE, MM. 16—30, SERENE CHORALE SUGGESTS PEACE
   Diatonic harmony, Db
   Percussion ostinato

III. MARCH TO WAR, MM. 31—63
   Increasingly chromatic harmony, various keys
   Trumpet call motives, ending with a muted allusion to "Taps"

IV. WAR, MM. 64—226
   Polychordal harmony, various keys
   Trumpet call motive developed, disjunct and dissonant accompaniments

V. CHORALE RETURN AND WAR, MM. 227—273, SUGGESTS GOOD WILL ARISE FROM STRIFE
   Diatonic harmony of Chorale, Db, contrasted with polychordal

implication of "War" motive

VI. CONCLUSION, MM. 274—302, PEACEFUL CONCLUSION SUGGESTS THE TRIUMPH OF GOOD OVER EVIL, BUT QUESTIONING PERCUSSION AND TRUMPET CALL MOTIVE CAUTION THAT PEACE IS FRAGILE
Diatonic harmony concluding in C Major
Lyrical lines derived from "Peace" chorale, lingering motives from "War"

Unit 8: Suggested Listening

Warren Benson, *The Passing Bell*
David Gillingham, *Serenade, "Songs of the Night"*
Morton Gould, *Symphony for Band, "West Point"*

Unit 9: Additional References and Resources

Gillingham, David. *Heroes, Lost and Fallen.* Eugene Corporon and the University of Cincinnati College—Conservatory of Music Wind Symphony.
Compact Disc KCD—11042, 1992.

Teacher Resource Guide

"Lincolnshire Posy"
Percy Grainger
(b. 1882–d. 1961)

Unit 1: Composer
A native of Australia, Percy Aldridge Grainger began an important career as a concert pianist in 1900. During World War I, he served as a United States Army Bandsman, and became an American citizen in 1919. He became internationally known as a pianist and a noted interpreter of Grieg, whose *Concerto for Piano* he premiered in 1907. He had an enduring interest in folk music, which he transcribed and recorded with early phonographic equipment. He loved the wind band and made many significant contributions to the repertoire, including *Irish Tune from County Derry* and *Colonial Song*.

Unit 2: Composition
Lincolnshire Posy was commissioned by the American Bandmasters Association and premiered at their convention with the composer conducting. It is in six movements, all based on folk songs from Lincolnshire, England. Grainger's settings are not only true to the verse structure of the folk songs, but attempt to depict the singers from whom Grainger collected the songs. Since its premiere, it has been recognized as a cornerstone of the wind band repertoire.

Unit 3: Historical Perspective
Grainger's active life as a composer spanned a period of interest in folksong. From the nationalistic schools of the Romantics, to the works of Bartok and Kodaly, the collection of folk material became more scientific. The invention of the phonograph allowed researchers to record folk singers and transcribe their material more accurately. Grainger was one of the pioneers of this technique, making significant contributions in English and Scandinavian folksong collections.

Lincolnshire Posy is an artistic result of Grainger's interest and researches in folk-songs and the art of folk singing. Grainger dedicated it to "... the folksingers who sang so sweetly to me."

Unit 4: Technical Considerations

Grainger was a masterful orchestrator for winds as well as an early proponent of the percussion choir. Excellent and idiomatic solos are written for all instruments. The fourth movement requires some fast technical playing from the flutes and clarinets, but in general, the technical demands are more in terms of range than tempo. The third movement has some sophisticated asymmetric rhythms. All sections are required to sensitively accompany soloists throughout the work.

Unit 5: Stylistic Considerations

The predominant style of *Lincolnshire Posy* is a singing legato, as would be expected from a setting of songs. This is consistently contrasted with lilting dance movements and accompaniments. Forceful brass fanfares and punctuations occur in every movement. Indications in the score convey many stylistic indications in Grainger's own unique vocabulary.

Unit 6: Musical Elements

The simplicity of the verse structure belies the sophistication of the settings. A careful study of the text will reveal a subtle tone painting. Carefully crafted canons, such as those in movements three and four, are virtuostically handled. The freetime sections in movement five not only depict the "war song," but also the "gleeful inebriation" of the folk singer from whom Grainger transcribed the song. The harmony is tonal, with modal and chromatic alterations. In typical Grainger fashion, cadences are often elided, extended, or cleverly avoided.

Unit 7: Form and Structure

I. Lisbon (Sailor's Song)

Lisbon is the four verses of the folk song varied at each verse. The key is Ab Mixolydian.

Verse 1, mm. 1-17, muted trumpets and horns and bassoons in thirds
Verse 2, mm. 18-33, woodwinds, string bass, euphonium and timpani
Verse 3, mm. 34-49, Counterpoint, "Marlborough Fanfare"
Verse 4, mm. 60-72, includes an eight measure cadential extension

II. Horkstow Grange (The Miser and his Man: A local Tragedy)

Horkstow Grange, the folk song, has three verses and a recurring refrain that is sung to the same tune. Grainger elects to set all three verses but the refrain only once The key is Db Major, but the harmony gets quite chromatic during the last phrase.

Verse 1, mm. 1—9, simple chorale setting, Db
Verse 2, mm. 19—18, chorale setting with counterpoint, Db
Verse 3, mm. 19—28, trumpet solo, Ab
Verse 4, mm. 29—37, *Tutti*, Db, with chromatic alterations

III. RUFFORD PARK POACHERS (POACHING SONG)

Rufford Park Poachers is the five verses of the folk song in elaborately varied setting. The first two verses are set in two versions, designated A and B by Grainger. In version A, the four soloists in verse 1 are piccolo, Eb clarinet, 1st clarinet, and bass clarinet. In Version B they are piccolo, oboe, alto clarinet, and bassoon. In the second verse, the folksong is in solo trumpet in Version A and soprano saxophone Version B. In addition, Version B is a fourth lower than Version A. Grainger expressed a preference for Version B.

Verse 1, mm. 1—17, is a canon at the unison, one measure apart. It is
      virtuostic writing through complex asymmetric meters.
Verse 2, mm 18—45, trumpet or soprano saxophone solo
Transition, mm. 46—50

Versions A and B come together beginning m. 51
Verse 3, mm. 51—63, *Tutti*, loud
Transition, mm. 64—67
Verse 4, mm. 68—84, *Tutti*, soft
Verse 5, mm. 85—103, reprise of Verse 1 canon, with different orchestration

IV. THE BRISK YOUNG SAILOR (WHO RETURNED TO WED HIS TRUE LOVE)

The folksong Brisk Young Sailor has seven verses. Grainger sets only five in *Lincolnshire Posy*. It is in the key of Bb.
Verse 1, mm. 1—9, Bb, clarinet choir
Verse 2, mm. 9—17, flute, oboe and English horn
Verse 3, mm. 17—25, baritone solo
Verse 4, mm. 25—34, oboe and soprano saxophone solos in canon
Verse 5, mm. 34—43, *Tutti*, extended
Coda, mm. 43—48

V. LORD MELBOURNE (WAR SONG)

Grainger's setting of this folk song includes Free Time measures and unusual time signatures. This reflects the "gleeful inebriation" of the folksinger Grainger recorded. It is in the key of D minor

Verse 1, mm. 1—13, Free time

Verse 2 mm. 14—34, baritone solo
Verse 3, mm. 36—48, piccolo and oboe duet
Verse 4, mm. 49—59, Free time, *Tutti*

VI. THE LOST LADY FOUND (DANCE SONG)

Grainger sets all nine verses of "The Lost Lady Found". It is in the Dorian mode on D.

Verse 1, mm. 1—17, woodwinds in unison
Verse 2, mm. 18—33, brass accompaniment
Verse 3, mm. 34—48, horn with dance rhythm
Verse 4, mm. 49—65, piccolo and alto clarinet duet
Verse 5, mm. 66—81, canonic accompaniment
Verse 6, mm. 82—97, with countermelody
Verse 7, mm. 98—113, saxophones
Verse 8, mm. 114—129, *Tutti*
Verse 9, mm. 130—146, *Tutti,* with bell chords

Unit 8: Suggested Listening
Percy Grainger, *Irish Tune from County Derry*
Gustav Holst, *Second Suite in F for Military Band*
Ralph Vaughan Williams, *English Folksong Suite*

Unit 9: Additional References and Resources
Begian, Harry. "Remembering How Grainger Conducted Lincolnshire Posy." *The Instrumentalist,* XLVII August 1992, 17—20.

Bruning, Earl Henry Jr. "A Survey and Handbook of Analysis for the Conducting and Interpretation of Seven Selected Works in the Standard Repertoire for Wind Band." Diss., Ball State University, 1980.

Fennell, Frederick. "Basic Band Library: Lincolnshire Posy, Part I." *The Instrumentalist,* XXXIV May 1980, 42.

Fennell, Frederick. "Basic Band Library: Lincolnshire Posy, Part II." *The Instrumentalist,* XXXV September 1980, 15—20.

Grauer, Mark. "Grainger's Lost Letters on Lincolnshire Posy." *The Instrumentalist,* XLVII August 1992, 12—17.

Grout, Donald J. and Claude V. Palisca. *A History of Western Music,* 4th ed. New York: W. W. Norton & Company, 1988.

Knight, John Wesley. "Graphic Analyses of the Conducting Techniques for Irregular Meters and Nonmetrical Organizations Found in Selected Twentieth—Century Band Literature." Diss., The Louisiana State University, 1979.

Pittman, Daniel Sayle, Jr. "Percy Grainger, Gustav Holst, and Ralph Vaughan Williams: A Comparative Analysis of Selected Wind Compositions." Diss., Memphis State University, 1979.

Sadie, Stanley, ed. *The New Grove Dictionary of Music and Musicians*. 20 Vols. London: Macmillan, 1980. S.v. "Percy Grainger," by David Josephson.

Slattery, Thomas Carl. "The Wind Music of Percy Aldridge Grainger." Diss., The University of Iowa, 1967.

Smith, Norman and Albert Stoutamire. *Band Music Notes*. Lake Charles, LA: Program Note Press, 1989.

Stolba, K Marie. *The Development of Western Music*. Dubuque, IA: William C. Brown Publishers, 1990.

Uggen, Stuart. "Percy Grainger in Perspective." *The Instrumentalist*, XXIV June 1970, 38—41.

Wilson, Brian Scott. "Orchestrational Archetypes in Percy Grainger's Wind Band Music." Diss., The University of Arizona, 1992.

Winkle, William Allan. "Grainger's Lincolnshire Posy: An Early Masterpiece for Wind Band." Diss., University of Northern Colorado, 1976.

Teacher Resource Guide

"Masquerade"
Vincent Persichetti

(b. 1915–d. 1987)

Unit 1: Composer

Vincent Persichetti (1915—1987) studied composition with Paul Nurdoff and Roy Harris and was a conducting student of Fritz Reiner. He earned his bachelor of music degree at Combs College, and later studied at the Philadelphia Conservatory and the Curtis Institute. Persichetti headed the composition department at the Philadelphia Conservatory from 1941 to 1947, at which time he joined the faculty of the Juilliard School of Music in New York. For many years he served as Director of Publications at Elkan—Vogel Music, yet another role that allowed him to influence the course of American music. He was among the first of America's venerated composers to write serious art music for the concert band, doing so during an era when the symphony orchestra dominated the music scene. Additional works for band include *Divertimento, Psalm, Pageant, Symphony No. 6, Bagatelles, Chorale Prelude: So Pure the Star, Chorale Prelude: Turn Not Thy Face, O Cool is the Valley, Parable IX*, and *Chorale Prelude: O God Unseen*.

Unit 2: Composition

Masquerade (12:00), composed in 1965, is a realization of a set of exercises presented in Persichetti's textbook *Twentieth—Century Harmony* (1961). The composer called the work "a masquerade of the harmony book," hence the title. It was written for and premiered by the Baldwin—Wallace Conservatory in Berea, Ohio. The formal structure is that of a theme and variations, but not in the usual sense. Most variations can be traced to materials found in the textbook, although there is still organic unity rooted in the theme. Other materials are what Persichetti terms "variations upon variations." The composition became an immediate success and today remains an established staple of the band repertoire.

Unit 3: Historical Perspective

The cover note to Persichetti's *Twentieth—Century Harmony* refers to the book as "an orderly presentation of the harmonic procedures to be found in the music of the first half of the twentieth century." Offering a cohesive view of recent history can be troublesome. Time is needed to place events in the proper perspective to prioritize what is important and to excise what is not. Persichetti's 1961 book chronicles and codifies the variegated harmonic language of our time, leaning toward tonal and modal systems. Atonality and dodecaphony are afforded relatively little attention. *Masquerade* could have been a dry exercise in 20th century composition; a mechanical pastiche of compositional techniques. But the music is organicized by Persichetti's musical language, transcending whatever technique is employed.

Unit 4: Technical Considerations

Several characteristics of Persichetti's orchestrational procedures present technical problems throughout his oeuvre as well as in the present work. There is no security in numbers; performers must play with initiative, especially on the various solo and chamber ensemble passages. Tricky entrances following extended rests require razor—sharp focus and execution to succeed. Antiphonal passages between solo voices and/or consorts demand assurance and consistency. *Masquerade* is the most complex of Persichetti's band works, especially from an harmonic standpoint. Mature ears are indispensable to seeking and maintaining the correct pitch within convoluted harmonic constructs. The melodic patterns that arise from the use of traditional scales, modes, and synthetic scales (octatonic) necessitate secure technique.

Unit 5: Stylistic Considerations

It is always interesting to witness composers interacting with performers. After repeatedly conducting their own music, composers develop an inventory of special points to emphasize within a given work. Perhaps chronic misconceptions about tempo and other style issues help the composer to know where guidance is especially needed. The composer of Masquerade has provided advice to performers and conductors in letters and in rehearsal sessions. "Find a big, loud ratchet" at M. 77. At M. 83, he urged, "Play pesante, not a full staccato." Advice to the clarinets at M. 147: "Sweep with a broom (not articulate)." "Give a clear cue to the triangle" at M. 137. At M. 189 he advises, "Move from gracious to martial." This comment is especially interesting given Persichetti's belief that his music consists of two opposing forces; "gracious and gritty." At M. 420 the entire ensemble participates in a simultaneous statement of materials from throughout the piece; a favorite Persichetti technique. The composer suggests, "Allow yourself to get dizzy—but do not fall."

One additional note; the ornamentation in the oboe part at M. 169 should be performed as a single mordent before the beat.

Unit 6: Musical Elements

Persichetti uses the theme presented by the horns in MM. 7—9 to unify this kaleidoscopic work. The motive follows a universal interval sequence derived from the overtone series. Scale degrees 5—3—6 represent the first three overtones different from the fundamental pitch in the overtone series. These notes pervade much folk music of all cultures and children's incantations, and are prominent in the pentatonic scale. By M. 46, Persichetti transforms the whole step to a half—step. The new pattern (E—G—G#) resembles a tonic pitch with both major and minor thirds. By M. 60 Persichetti displaces the G# to the low octave in the timpani. This creates a major seventh intervallic motive (G to G#) that is developed throughout the remainder of the piece (M. 97, MM 124—127 develops minor ninth, MM 133—134, M. 192 adds semitone to pentatonic language, MM 358—364). The timpani reprise the motive from M. 60 in MM 410—420. The trombones join in at MM 429—434.

Within the framework of this thematic development Persichetti plants harmony examples from his textbook. The following table documents these occurrences with measure citations:

TEXT EXAMPLE	MASQUERADE MEASURES
2-16	25-28
2-17	117-129
2-11	163-166
2-35	191
9-8	202-208
7-20	223-232
2-34	235-248
2-49	257-269
11-33	352-356
11-30	358-360

Unit 7: Form and Structure

INTRODUCTION	MM1-6	Octatonic, 12-tone aggregate(M. 4)
THEME	MM7-24	Octatonic (Synthetic Scale)
VARIATION I	MM 25-49	Polymodal (E aeolian/E phrygian)
VARIATION II	MM 50-115	"Melodic exploration of basic set."

VARIATION III	MM116-169	Polytonal and Modal, Modal (E phrygian) with chromatic alterations
VARIATION IV	MM 170-201	Pentatonic melody with "foreign" chords.
VARIATION V	MM 202-222	Parallelism, Static interchange of chords, "has folk roots."
VARIATION VI	MM 223-253	Polyharmonic, Modal pentatonic. "Aaron Copland waving over my shoulder [at M. 235]."
VARIATION VII	MM 254-316	Whole-tone, Quartal
VARIATION VIII	MM 317-352	Octatonic, Mixolydian. "Gracious development of repeated—note figure and passing tone."
VARIATION IX	MM 353-373	"double pedal—point", "unison with antiphonal."
VARIATION X	MM 374-394	Summation of materials. "Six contrapuntal parts—each summing—up earlier arrival areas."
CODA	MM 395-434	Polychords, 12-tone aggregate (M. 412)

Unit 8: Suggested Listening
Vincent Persichetti, *Bagatelles*
Vincent Persichetti, *Chorale Prelude: O God Unseen*
Vincent Persichetti, *Chorale Prelude: So Pure the Star*
Vincent Persichetti, *Chorale Prelude: Turn Not Thy Face*
Vincent Persichetti, *Divertimento*
Vincent Persichetti, *O Cool is the Valley*
Vincent Persichetti, *Pageant*
Vincent Persichetti, *Parable IX*
Vincent Persichetti, *Psalm*
Vincent Persichetti, *Symphony No. 6*

Unit 9: Bibliography
Band Music Guide. 9th ed. Northfield, Ill: The Instrumentalist Company, 1989.

Casey, Patrick F. "Vincent Persichetti: Masquerade Op. 102." *BD Guide*, X/1 September/October 1995, 2—10.

Hilfiger, John Jay. "A Comparison of Some Aspects of Style in the Band and Orchestra Music of Vincent Persichetti." Ph.D. diss., The University of Iowa, 1985.

Morris, Donald Alan. "The Life of Vincent Persichetti, with Emphasis on his Works for Band." Ph.D. diss., The Florida State University, 1991.

Persichetti, Vincent. *Twentieth Century Harmony*. New York: W. W. Norton & Company, Inc., 1961.

_____. Letter to Jack Stamp, 1983.

_____. Masquerade Videotape Rehearsal. Madison: University of Wisconsin, 1976.

Sadie, Stanley, ed. *The New Grove Dictionary of Music and Musicians*. 20 Vols. London: Macmillan, 1980.

Slonimsky, Nicholas. *Baker's Biographical Dictionary of Musicians*. 8th ed., rev. New York: Schirmer Books, 1991.

Smith, Norman, and Albert Stoutamire. *Band Music Notes*. Rev. ed. San Diego: Neil A. Kjos, Jr., Publisher, 1979.

Wallace, David, and Eugene Corporon., eds. *Wind Ensemble/Band Repertoire*. Greeley, Colo.: University of Northern Colorado School of Music, 1984.

Workinger, William Colvin. "Some Aspects of Scoring in the Band Works of Vincent Persichetti." Diss., New York University, 1970.

Teacher Resource Guide

"Music for Prague 1968"
Introduction and Fanfare, Aria, Interlude, Toccata and Chorale

Karel Husa

(b. 1921)

Unit 1: Composer

Karel Husa, Pulitzer Prize winner in music, is an internationally–known composer and conductor and the Kappa Alpha Professor at Cornell University. An American citizen since 1959, Husa was born in Prague, Czechoslovakia, on August 7, 1921. After completing studies at the Prague Conservatory and, later, the Academy of Music, he went to Paris where he received diplomas from the Paris National Conservatory and the *Ecole normale de musique*. Among his teachers were Arthur Honegger, Nadia Boulanger, Jaroslave Ridky, and conductor Andre Cluytens.

In 1954, Husa was appointed to the Cornell faculty; from 1967 to 1986, he was also Lecturer in Composition at Ithaca College. He was elected Associate Member of the Royal Belgian Academy of Arts and Sciences in 1974 and the American Academy of Arts and Letters in 1993. He has received honorary degrees of Doctor of Music from the following institutions: Coe College in 1976, the Cleveland Institute of Music in 1985, Ithaca College in 1986, and Baldwin—Wallace College in 1991. Among numerous recognitions, Husa has received the Guggenheim Fellowship, American Academy and Institutes of Arts and Letters, UNESCO, and the National Endowment for the Arts awards, a Koussevitsky Foundation commission, the Czech Academy for the Arts and Sciences Prize, the Grawemeyer Award, the Sudler International Award, and the Lili Boulanger award. He is listed in *Who's Who in the World*.

Husa's *String Quartet No. 3* received the 1969 Pulitzer Prize. *Music for Prague 1968* has become part of the modern repertory, with over 8,000 performances worldwide. Husa's unmistakable musical language is characterized by a modernistic approach to melody and harmony punctuated by arresting unisons in both rhythm and pitch. His additional works for band include *Al Fresco*, *Concerto for Alto Saxophone*, *Concerto for Wind Ensemble*, *Concerto for Trumpet*, *Concertino for Piano*, *Concerto for Percussion*, *Smetana Fanfare*, and *Apotheosis of this Earth*.

Unit 2: Composition

Music for Prague 1968 received its premiere performance in Washington on January 31, 1969. The composer writes:

> Three main ideas bind the composition together. The first and most important is an old Hussite war song from the 15th century, "Ye Warriors of God and His Law," a symbol of resistance and hope for hundreds of years, whenever fate lay heavy on the Czech nation. It has been utilized also by many Czech composers, including Smetana in *My Country*. The beginning of this religious song is announced very softly in the first movement by the timpani and concludes in a strong unison (Chorale).
>
> The second idea is the sound of bells throughout; Prague, named the "City of Hundreds of Towers," has used its magnificently sounding church bells as calls of distress as well as to signal victory.
>
> The last idea is a motif of three chords, first appearing very softly under the piccolo solo at the beginning of the piece, then in flutes, clarinets, and horns. Later it reappears at extremely strong dynamic levels— for example, in the middle of the *Aria*.
>
> Different techniques of composing as well as orchestrating have been used in *Music for Prague 1968* and some new sounds explored, such as the percussion section in the Interlude, the ending of the work, etc. Much symbolism also appears: in addition to the distress calls in the first movement (Fanfares), the unbroken hope of the Hussite song, sound of bells, or the tragedy (Aria), there is also the bird call at the beginning (piccolo solo), symbol of the liberty which the City of Prague has seen only for moments during its thousand years of existence.

The following is the Hussite theme utilized in Music for Prague:

The text is as follows:

Ye warriors of God and His Law
Pray for God's help and hope in Him
That you will have final victory with faith in Him.
this Lord commands not to be afraid of corporal destructions
commands to even give life for the love of one's neighbor.

Unit 3: Historical Perspective

In 1945, Winston Churchill proclaimed, "It would be a measureless disaster if Russian barbarism overlaid the culture and independence of Europe. The eagle should permit the small birds to sing." In 1968, Czech leader Alexander Dubcek instituted his so—called "Prague Spring" reforms which he promised would lead to "socialism with a human face." The Soviets quashed Czech reform on August 20, 1968, leading an invasion with soldiers from four East bloc nations. Thirty Czechs were killed, three hundred were injured. Dubcek was seized along with other Czech Party leaders and was summoned to Moscow for a "talking—to." By October 4, the Czech leader returned to Prague a morally broken leader. Large—scale Anti—Soviet rallies in late October led to open rioting in November. By April of 1969, Dubcek was ousted as Secretary of the Czech Communist Party in favor of Gustav Husak, and the rebellion was over.

These are the disturbing events that compelled Karel Husa to compose his powerful commemoration. The composer writes:

It was in late August, 1968, when I decided to write a composition dedicated to the city in which I was born. I have thought about writing for

Prague for some time because the longer I am far away from this city (I left Czechoslovakia in 1946) the more I remember the beauty of it. I can even say that in my idealization, I actually see Prague even more beautiful.

During those tragic and dark moments...I suddenly felt the necessity to write this piece for so long meditated...I was sure that the music I would write for Prague would be scored for the concert band, a medium which I have admired for a long time. The combination of wind and brass instruments with percussion fascinated me and the unexplored possibilities of new sounds and combinations of instruments have attracted me for some time. I am not speaking here against the orchestra for this is a medium I have written much for and in addition to being an orchestral conductor, I used to play the violin. However, so much great music has been written for orchestras and strings in the past that it is difficult to produce *new* works in which orchestral musicians would be interested...

On February 13, 1990, Husa conducted the Prague premiere of *Music for Prague 1968*. Like Karel Husa, Alexander Dubcek lived to see the fall of communism in Czechoslovakia on November 24, 1989. Barely one month later, Playwright Vaclav Havel was elected President of the Czech Parliament, and Dubcek was appointed Chairman of the Parliament. Havel stated, "I learned in prison that everything is possible, so perhaps I should not be amazed. But I am. Sometimes I ask my friends if this was all a dream, a colorful and beautiful dream from which I would awake in prison. But finally, and only very recently, I began to feel that it was not a dream, and that what has happened is real and lasting."

Much of the analysis in units 4 - 7 is drawn from Mark Scatterday's article "Karl Husa's Music for Prague 1968" published in the September/October 1993 issue of the BD Guide.

Unit 4: Technical Considerations

Music for Prague is orchestrated for concert band instrumentation, including eight trumpet parts and bass saxophone (all present in the commissioning ensemble, the Ithaca College Concert Band). Husa allows for elasticity in the composition of the ensemble, realizing the idiosyncratic nature of the original instrumentation, which also includes two piccolos, English horn, contra—bassoon, Eb contra—alto clarinet, and Bb contra—bass clarinet. Husa's handling of the percussion family was revolutionary for 1968. Five percussionists are used to play timpani, chimes, marimba, vibraphone, xylophone, cymbals, bass drum, three crotales, three triangles, three suspended cymbals, three tam—tams, three tom—toms, and three snare drums. Husa provides specifications for desired usage of sticks and mallets. Parts including piano and harp are available from Associated Music Publishers G. Schirmer. Euphonium mutes are designated for use in Mvt. IV (ad libitum). They should be used when available. Use two chime players at

V in the last movement to augment the power of the part. A minimum of fifty—five players are needed for performance.

Husa provides the following performance suggestions in his preface to the score:

> The metronome markings are approximate. The Introduction, for instance, may be conducted somewhat slower than indicated and the Fanfare a little faster_not, however, so fast as to affect the clarity and rhythmic precision of the sixteenth notes.
>
> In the Aria, the melodic line of the saxophones (reinforced by low clarinets) should be predominant in the entire movement. In the Interlude, the vibraphone, although soft, must bring out its line above all the metallophones and the snare drum.
>
> The contrabass clarinets (Eb and Bb), contrabassoon and bass saxophone should be used if at all possible despite their status as "optional" additions to the ensemble: their dark color and reinforcement of the low lines are important. Some of the highest notes may be omitted at the discretion of each player.
>
> There are two types of grace notes in the score: the usual ones (slurred to the main note) and others without slurs; in the latter, both notes should be attacked (tongued) separately. In both cases, the grace note is placed before the beat.

Husa provides additional notes governing the arrangement of the percussion section:

> The technical demands in this work are such that only more advanced ensembles will be capable of mastering its intricacies. The atonal harmonic language, the rhythmic complexities, and the advanced orchestrational concepts—all will require an evolution in focused listening and precise execution on the part of the player.

Unit 5: Stylistic Considerations

Husa's orchestration often exploits unusual instrument registers. The baritone sax solo (Mvt. I — MM 30—34) begins at a dynamic of "p" on high D—a tall order for the performer. Often Husa orchestrates figures in the low registers of instruments that encounter projection problems "down low." Much of the flute writing (especially the tremolos) in the first sixteen measures of Movement I will need special care and protection to be heard. The trombone figure beginning in M. 33 of Movement IV is placed in a register made more difficult by the straight mute. The performer must compensate for the side effects of these orchestrational demands. In this way the composer challenges the performer to adapt, overcome obstacles, and grow.

There are many performance indications in Husa's scores. The performers must be held accountable for all inflections in phrasing, articulation, and dynamic shading. The composer prefers Movement II to move along and not become bogged down by its own weight. Movement IV he likes at metronome marking 126 (over the 120 also suggested). The acceleration to 132 beats per minute prior to letter O must be calibrated precisely. The tempo resolution to 44 beats per minute at letter S must bear a proportional relation of 3:1.

Unit 6: Musical Elements

Husa uses the following twelve—tone row in Movement I:

The row is announced in the solo piccolo and accompanying parts below in the second measure. The pitches C#—D#—F, found in the middle of the row are related to the Hussite theme. The twelve—tone system is loosely employed in Movement I but is more strictly adhered to in Movement II. Note the baritone saxophone solo in MM 30—34! Quartertones are used in MM 33—34 in the alto saxophone II score. The Hussite theme appears in many incarnations throughout the movement. After it is announced in the timpani, it is developed in the trumpet fanfare at M. 35, and is stated in diminution by the trumpets at M. 74.

A different row is employed in Movement II:

Husa divulges that the pitches C—C#—D#—D—E, nested in the middle of this second tone row, are related to the Hussite theme. All forms of the row are used in Movement II; P, R, I, RI. Tempo of Movement II as printed in the score should read quarter—note equals 60—66, not the eighth—note.

Husa states of Movement II:

> The title of *Aria* might be a little surprising; it is, of course, not an "aria" in an operatic sense, the word may be a little sarcastic for that occasion: it was not a happy aria. I have given it to the saxophones purposely: they have the tremendous ability to sing, sound strong and loud, and yet expressive at all times; also by their vibrating quality, it may be close to what we call *vox humana* on the organ. And this is what this melodic line was about: to say the anguish, fear and desolation in awaiting what will come next.

Movement III is scored for percussion only. The snare drum is used to symbolize the invading Soviet forces. The keyboard percussion represent the tolling bells of Prague. The composer suggests separating the percussion instruments as widely as possible to heighten the dimension of the music. Rhythmic values, dynamic markings, and timbre are serialized. Husa has constructed a musical palindrome between rehearsal letters N and P. Letter O represents the structural midpoint of this symmetry.

Movement IV contains no serialization. Husa relates his placement of articulation markings and accents in Movement IV to Czech folk dances. The Hussite theme is stated in augmentation at M. 319. Of the ending, Husa writes:

> Although *Music for Prague 1968* is not written in any tonality, the song's use at the beginning and end of the work gives it a strong "center note," which is D, even if the last unison at the end is on E. I have mentioned in the preface a few examples of symbolism. Another can be the ending of the work on the E, which is the highest note in the chorale. This note, together with the A (two measures before V) that I put one octave higher in the trumpets although the line of the song descends, is a gesture of defiance and hope.

Another motive which brings organic unity to the entire work is a series of three chords which are introduced at M. 3—4 in the flutes, horns, and clarinets. These chords, often altered, return throughout the movements.

Rhythmic problems are derived from the intricacy of patterns within beats and measures. Multimeter passages are scarce. Sections featuring rapid articulations in woodwind as well as in brass parts pose especially difficult technical problems in Movements I and IV.

Unit 7: Form and Structure

MOVEMENT I: INTRODUCTION AND FANFARE

SECTION	MEASURES	REHEARSAL AREA
A' Introduction	m. 1-34	Beginning - C
B Fanfare	m. 35-99	C - Adagio
A'	m. 100-107	Adagio - End

MOVMENT II: ARIA

A	m. 1-33	beginning - 4 after J
B	m. 33-42	4 after J - 4 before L
B'	m. 43-51	4 before L - 6 after L
A'	m. 51-68	6 after L - End

MOVEMENT III: INTERLUDE

A	m. 1-10	N - P
A'	m. 11-20	O - End

(Palindrome of A)

MOVEMENT IV: TOCCATA & CHORALE

Fanfare	m. 1-19	Beginning - A
Theme	m. 20-36	A - B
Motive/Rhythmic Development	m. 37-114	B - F
Lyrical Version	m. 115-132	F - 5 after G
Motivic Development	m. 133-228	6 after G - O
Rhythmic/Metric Restatement of Movement I	m. 229-279	O -8 before R
Augmentation of theLyrical Theme	m. 280-306	7 before R - S
Coda (Altered versionof Movement I	m. 307-315	S - T
Hussite Chorale	m. 316-330	T - End.

For detailed analyses, see: *Karel Husa's Music for Prague 1968: An Interpretive Analysis* by Bryon Adams and *"Music for Prague 1968"* by Mark D. Scatterday.

Unit 8: Suggested Listening

Karel Husa, *Al Fresco*
Karel Husa, *Apotheosis of this Earth*
Karel Husa, *Concerto for Wind Ensemble*
Bedrich Smetana, *My Country*

Unit 9: Bibliography

Adams, Byron. "Karel Husa's Music for Prague 1968: An Interpretive Analysis" *The Instrumentalist*, XLII October 1987, 19-24.

Battisti, Frank. "Karel Husa-Keeping Ties With Tradition." *The Instrumentalist*, XLIV July 1990, 11-15, 42.

Casey, Robert Lowell. "Serial Composition in Works for the Wind Band." Ph.D. diss., Washington University, 1971.

Haithcock, Michael. "Karel Husa Talks About Composing." *The Instrumentalist*, XXXVI April 1982, 22-25.

Hegvik, Arthur. "Karel Husa Talks About His Life and Work." *The Instrumentalist*, XXIX May 1975, 31-37.

Husa, Karel. "Notes on Music for Prague 1968" Unpublished, 1971.

Husa, Karel. Music for Prague 1968. Foreword and Performance Notes. New York: Associated Music Publishers, 1969.

Nelson, Judy R. "Echoing Mankind Through Music: Karel Husa." *The Instrumentalist*, October 1987.

Paré, Craig. "An Examination of Innovative Percussion Writing in the Band Music of Four Composers: Vincent Persichetti - Symphony for Band; Karel Husa - Music for Prague 1968; Joseph Schwantner - and the mountains rising nowhere; Michael Colgrass -Winds of Nagual." Diss., University of Cincinnati, 1993.

Phillips, Harvey. "Musician from Prague, An Interview With Karel Husa." *The Instrumentalist*, XLVII September 1992, 28-33.

Sadie, Stanley, ed. *The New Grove Dictionary of Music and Musicians.* 20 Vols. London: Macmillan, 1980.

Scatterday, Mark D. "Karel Husa: Music for Prague 1968." *BD Guide*, 7 September/October 1993, 32.

Slonimsky, Nicholas. *Baker's Biographical Dictionary of Musicians.* 8th ed., rev. New York: Schirmer Books, 1991.

Smith, Norman, and Albert Stoutamire. *Band Music Notes.* Rev. ed. San Diego: Neil A. Kjos, Jr., Publisher, 1979.

Sturm, George. "Music for Prague Performed in PragueAt Last." MadAminA!, 11-1 Spring 1990.

Wallace, David, and Eugene Corporon., eds. *Wind Ensemble/Band Repertoire.* Greeley, Colo.: University of Northern Colorado School of Music, 1984.

Teacher Resource Guide

"Passacaglia and Fugue in C minor"
J. S. Bach

(b. 1685–d. 1750)

arranged by Donald Hunsberger (b. 1931)

Unit 1: Composer

J. S. Bach was born to a musical family in the Thuringia region of Northern Germany. His father, a musician in the town of Eisenstadt, provided his early musical training. Left an orphan at the age of ten, Bach was adopted by his older brother Johann Christian, an organist who studied with Pachelbel. At fifteen he became a singer at St. Michael's Church, where he mastered both the violin and clavier. By age eighteen, he secured a post as town organist in Arnstadt, where he soon began to compose original works. Most of Bach's output from this period, including his tenure at the court of Duke Wilhelm Ernst of Weimar, was composed for the organ. He composed many instrumental ensemble works and clavier pieces during his time as director of chamber music at Prince Leopold's court in Anhalt—Cöthen. Bach closed his career with a 27—year stint as music director at the churches of St. Thomas and St. Nicholas in Leipzig. It was during this period that he composed many of his monumental sacred works. Although Bach was known throughout Germany as a virtuoso organist, he never achieved wide fame as a composer during his lifetime. It wasn't until Felix Mendelssohn spawned a rebirth of interest in his music nearly a century after Bach's death that his oeuvre became widely celebrated. Wagner is said to have referred to Bach's talent as "the most fantastic miracle in all music."

Unit 3: Historical Perspective

Unity was achieved in much early baroque vocal music by repeating a bassline (ground bass) while varying the melodic line on every stanza. This practice, known as strophic variation, is the basis for Monteverdi's famous aria *Possente spirito* from Act III of *Orfeo* (1607). The passacaglia is a strophic variation that arose in Spain during the late 17th Century. Although the terms "passacaglia" and "chaconne" were used interchangeably during the Baroque, a passacaglia typically denoted a work in which the bassline was left unaltered. Early passacaglia composers included Frescobaldi, Muffat, Biber, and Buxtehude. The term "fugue" denotes an imitative polyphonic work that employs a specific number of voices, usually four or five. Fugal style evolved during the final decades of the 17th and in the early 18th centuries. Early forerunners were vocal forms such as the chanson, motet, and madrigal, and instrumental forms including the canzona, fantasia, and ricercare. The fugue reached its apotheosis in the Baroque organ works of J. S. Bach. *Passacaglia and Fugue in C minor* was composed during Bach's Weimar period (ca. 1708–1717). Originally intended for the double-manual harpsichord, Bach subsequently transcribed the work for organ.

Unit 4: Technical Considerations

Organ music is truly a rich source of transcribable music for band. The band has the ability to replicate resonant sonorities commensurate with those of the pipe organ. Early organs often were equipped with stops to imitate wind instruments. Hunsberger's brilliant orchestration maximizes the organ-like character of winds en masse, yet the use of the full ensemble is saved for strategic points of emphasis. The ratio of tutti to moderate to chamber—like orchestrations is beautifully balanced. Hunsberger excludes the percussion from the instrumentation but includes a flugelhorn part. Note the subject statement in the flugelhorn in M. 40 of the *Fugue*.

The *Passacaglia* remains in C minor throughout. The *Fugue* modulates to G minor, Eb Major, Bb Major, and F minor. Rhythm patterns include multitudinous eighth and sixteenth combinations, occasional syncopations, successions of sixteenth-note triplets, and one *Passacaglia* variation featuring dotted rhythms.

Brass ranges are comfortable. Piccolo and flute parts ascend to double-high C and spend considerable time in the very high range, presumably to replicate organ registration.

Endurance will be a concern for less mature performers. The length exceeds eleven minutes (the score erroneously offers twenty minutes as the duration). Each musician must have a concept of the entire work and the energy continuum which envelopes its structure.

Many slurs of varying lengths pervade the score and are frequently coupled with additional articulation markings. Often long, sweeping sixteenth-note lines must be sustained, but all parts are reasonably idiomatic if not facile.

Unit 5: Stylistic Considerations

The obvious parallel between the present work and the "Chaconne" from Holst's *First Suite in Eb* opens the possibility for parallel instruction and comparative programming. The Baroque style features the propagation of a single rhythmic unit, in this case the eighth note which provides the underlying engine for the entire work. Although subdivisions must remain metronomic, expression can be achieved by creating lines that extend beyond the "tyranny" of the barline—even within sequential passages that invite the partitioning of phrases.

Dynamics in every section must be gauged to satisfy the dynamic contour of each movement. The fifth statement of the passacaglia theme, for example, should not overstep its relative mission within the framework of the entire piece. The passacaglia variations can be bracketed into four groups of five. Variations within each subgroup are related motivically and comprise mini-scenarios that accumulate momentum. Massive power, however, should be conserved until the appropriate moment, at which time the greatest resonance will result not from volume, but from a balanced ensemble tone, honestly projected with clean intonation.

Hunsberger makes wide use of the tenuto—when used on an arrival at the end of a phrase (M. 48), interpret the tenuto to mean full-value. When used on a repeated pitch under a slur, interpret the tenuto as a gentle re-articulation mark (M. 49). The tenuto at M. 81 should be interpreted as a soft accent, slightly separated but with length and direction.

Unit 6: Musical Elements

The fugal theme is derived from the first half of the passacaglia theme, thus bringing continuity and organic consistency to the entire composition. The current example is classified as a "double fugue", not because it contains two expositions of two distinct subjects, but because the countersubject always appears in tandem with the subject. Other theorists describe this simply as a fugue in which the countersubject appears prematurely.

The harmonic rhythm is slow generally, with quicker motion in sequential fugal episodes. The Neapolitan sixth chord in M. 117 is used idiomatically, with scale degree 4 in the bass, followed by a dominant seventh chord (in fourth inversion). The coda ends in C Major with a picardy third.

Unit 7: Form and Structure

PASSACAGLIA

Theme		MM 1-8	Theme announced in bassoon, bass clarinet, horn.
Variation	1	MM 9-16	Sequential accompaniment in ob., Eng. hn.
	2	MM 17-24	Cl., fl., continue acc. with new harmony
	3	MM 25-32	Imitation with flowing eighth pattern

4	MM 33-40	Imitation using eighths + 16ths (f dynamic)
5	MM 41-48	Addition of leaps to previous pattern, ground bass in bassoon altered to participate in imitation.
6	MM 49-56	Imitation using ascending 16ths
7	MM 57-64	Imitation using descending 16ths
8	MM 65-72	Flowing 16ths, mix of ascending + descending + contrary motion
9	MM 73-80	Imitative 16th motive leaps, ground bass in bass cl. is altered, joins in imitation
10	MM 81-88	Homophonic use of flowing 16ths, bass line is fragmented rhythmically
11	MM 89-96	Theme in tpt., fl., ob. Flowing 16th accompaniment descends to tenor/bass range.
12	MM 97-104	Theme in tpt., new bassline becomes accomp.
13	MM 105-112	Ornamented theme in Eng. hn., thin texture, no bass.
14	MM 113-120	Theme alternates between clarinet II + III, (lowest note of arpeggiations).
15	MM 121-128	Theme returns to bass, lowest notes of arpeggiation in baritone sax, bass cl., and bassoon, picc + cl. I on beat 3.
16	MM 129-136	Theme in original form, bar-long crescendos
17	MM 137-144	Triplet 16ths in accompaniment
18	MM 145-152	Theme with eighth-note pickup motive, duple 16th in accompaniment
19	MM 153-160	Four-voice imitative texture using 16ths
20	MM 161-168	Five-voice imitative texture, tutti.

FUGUE

Exposition	MM 1-23	
Subject	MM 1-5	S (subject) in E. H on C, CS (countersubject) in bssn on Eb
Answer (real)	MM 6-9	S on G, CS on Eb (real answers)
Bridge	MM 10-12	
Subject	MM 13-17	S in b.c. + t.sax on C, CS in fl. on Eb
Answer (real)	MM 18-23	S (tbn) on G, CS (low reeds) on Bb (real)
Development	MM 24-103	
Subject	MM 24-29	S (hn) on C, CS (tbn, tpt) on Eb
Answer (tonal)	MM 30-35	S (saxes) on Eb, CS (hn.) on G

Episode	MM 36-40	Sequential passage modulates to Bb
Subject	MM 40-48	S (flug.) on Bb, CS (tpt.) on D
Bridge	MM 49-52	Modulation to G minor
Answer (tonal)	MM 53-59	S (tuba+) on G, CS (tpt.+ sax) on Bb
Episode	MM 60-65	Modulates to tonic, C minor
Subject	MM 66-70	S (Tbn., bsn.) on C, CS (tuba+) on Eb
Episode	MM 71-77	Sequential passage modulates to G minor
Answer (real)	MM 78-80	S (fl+) on G, CS (tbn) on Bb
Episode	MM 81-87	Sequential passage modulates to F minor
Subject	MM 88-90	S (tuba+) on F, CS (hn.) on Ab
Episode	MM 91-103	Orchestration thins, modulation to C minor
Recapitulation	MM 104-117	
Subject	MM 104-197	S (tpt., fl., ob.) on C, CS (hn) on Eb
Episode	MM 198-117	Cadences on N6
Coda	MM 117-124	CS rhythm developed, Picardy third ending.

Unit 8: Suggested Listening

J.S. Bach, *The Art of the Fugue*
J.S. Bach, *The Well-Tempered Klavier*
Biber, *Passacaglia*
Dietrich Buxtehude, *Prelude, Fugue, and Chaconne for Organ*
Paul Hindemith, *Cardillac*
Gustav Holst, *First Suite in Eb for Military Band*
Muffat, *Passacaglia*
Claudio Monteverdi, "Possente Spirito" from *L'Orfeo*
Ron Nelson, *Passacaglia* (Homage on B-A-C-H)
Johannes Pachelbel, *Kanon in D*
Henry Purcell, "Dido's Lament" from *Dido and Aeneas*
Reger, *Introduction, Passacaglia, and Fugue*
Igor Stravinsky, *Symphony of Psalms*

Unit 9: Bibliography

Brandt, William, Arthur Corra, William Christ, Richard Delone, Allen Winold. *The Comprehensive Study of Music.* New York: Harper's College Press, 1977.

Davison, Archibald T. and Willi Apel. *Historical Anthology of Music: Baroque, Rococo and Pre-Classical Music.* 11th Printing. Cambridge: Harvard University Press, 1976.

Grout, Donald Jay. Ed. Claude V. Palisca. *A History of Western Music.* Third Ed. New York: W. W. Norton & Co., 1980.

Kohs, Ellis B. *Studies in Analysis and Synthesis*. Boston: Houghton Mifflin Company, 1976.

Parrish, Carl, ed. *A Treasury of Early Music*. New York: W.W. Norton & Co., 1958.

Sadie, Stanley, ed. *The New Grove Dictionary of Music and Musicians*. 20 Vols. London: Macmillan, 1980.

Slonimsky, Nicholas. *Baker's Biographical Dictionary of Musicians*. 8th ed., rev. New York: Schirmer Books, 1991.

Smith, Norman, and Albert Stoutamire. *Band Music Notes*. Rev. ed. San Diego: Neil A. Kjos, Jr., Publisher, 1979.

Teacher Resource Guide

"Passacaglia"
(Homage on Bach)
Ron Nelson
(b. 1929)

Unit 1: Composer

Ron Nelson (b. 1929) is a native of Joliet, Illinois. He received his Bachelor of Music degree in 1952, the Master's degree in 1953, and the Doctor of Musical Arts degree in 1956 from the Eastman School of Music. He studied in France at the *Ecole Normale de Musique* and, in 1955, at the Paris Conservatory under a Fulbright Grant. Dr. Nelson joined the Brown University faculty the following year as an Assistant Professor, attaining the rank of Associate Professor in 1960 and Full Professor in 1968. He served as Chairman of the Department of Music from 1963 to 1973, and in 1991 he was awarded the Acuff Chair of Excellence in the Creative Arts, becoming the first musician to hold the chair. He has gained wide recognition as a composer of choral, band and orchestral works. Nelson retired from Brown University in 1993 and currently resides in Arizona. His other works for band include *Rocky Point Holiday*, *Medieval Suite*, *Aspen Jubilee*, and *Sonoran Desert Holiday*.

Unit 2: Composition

Passacaglia (Homage on B-A-C-H), which lasts ten and a half minutes, was composed by Mr. Nelson in fulfillment of a commission by The United States Air Force Band, the Wind Studies Department at CCM, and the ETA OMICRON chapter of Phi Mu Alpha Sinfonia, in honor of the 125th Anniversary of the founding of the University of Cincinnati College Conservatory of Music. *Passacaglia* is conceived in a contrapuntal style reminiscent of Bach's great organ works. Mr. Nelson writes:

> *Passacaglia* (Homage on B-A-C-H) is a set of continuous variations in

moderately slow triple meter built on an eight-measure melody (basso ostinato) which is repeated, in various registers, twenty-seven times. It is a seamless series of tableaux which move from darkness to light.

Written in homage to J. S. Bach, it utilizes, as counterpart throughout, the melodic motive represented by his name in German nomenclature, i.e., B-flat, A, C, and B natural. Bach introduced this motive in his unfinished "Art of the Fugue," the textures of which are paraphrased (in an eight-tone scale) in the third, fourth, and fifth variations. The seventh variation incorporates Gustave Nottebohm's resolution (altered) of the unfinished final fugue of *The Art of Fugue*. The famous melody from Bach's "Passacaglia in C minor" appears once (also altered) in variation nineteen.

The world premiere performance of *Passacaglia* was presented by the United States Air Force Band under the direction of Col. Alan Bonner in Corbett Auditorium at the University of Cincinnati on October 3, 1992, with the composer in attendance. *Passacaglia* was awarded the 1992 NBA Award, the 1993 ABA-Ostwald Award, and the 1993 Sudler Award.

Unit 3: Historical Perspective

Unity was achieved in much early baroque vocal music by repeating a bass (ground bass) while varying the melodic line on every stanza. This practice, known as strophic variation, is the basis for Monteverdi's famous aria *Possente spirito* from Act III of *Orfeo* (1607). The passacaglia is a strophic variation that arose in Spain during the late 17th Century. Although the terms "passacaglia" and "chaconne" were used interchangeably during the Baroque, a passacaglia typically denoted a work for organ in which the bassline was left unaltered. Early organ passacaglia composers included Frescobaldi, Muffat, and Biber. Nelson's *Passacaglia* parallels J. S. Bach's monumental *Passacaglia and Fugue in C minor* of 1717. Perhaps the most famous band work employing strophic variation technique is Holst's *First Suite in Eb*, the first movement of which is entitled "Chaconne."

Unit 4: Technical Considerations

The composer suggests the following tempi:

Introduction	ca. 60-64
M 92	ca. 68-70
M 121	poco accel.
M 122	ca. 72
M 137	ca. 72
M 170	ca. 72-74 (not slower)
M 202	ca. 72, accel to ca. 74-76 by M. 208

Endurance is a material issue for the performers. The brass must have enough power left at the end to pull-off the final chord, which is intense and should sustain ideally for as long as the performers can endure. The awkward octatonic scale patterns in the woodwind parts will challenge even mature technique. Double-tonguing passages occur in the trumpets and flutes. Demanding rhythmic figures using sextuplets, septuplets, and 32nd notes abound, especially in the woodwind parts in the final third of the piece.

Unit 5: Stylistic Considerations

Nelson's orchestration is as much a musical element in *Passacaglia* as is the octatonic scale. Many details are placed within these complex textures. Ferret-out the priority lines in the musical structures and guide the performers in listening for these fine points. Nelson's orchestration is frequently organ-like in the scope and depth of sonority, recalling the original passacaglia medium. The percussion family is multitudinous and is used to add coloristic flashes as well as to create textures through ostinati. The marimba should use soft mallets at M. 17. Nelson uses the marimba to add resonance to woodwind sonorities. The composer states, "The right volume is exactly at the level where you would miss the instrument if it dropped out." The same concept is operable for the vibraphone supporting the horns at M. 97.

An important structural point begins at M. 170. The alto saxophones and percussion start the "engine" that builds inexorably to the apex. Mr. Nelson states, "All other parts should 'hunker down' in order to set up the horn statement beginning at bar 177." Be sure the planting of this seed is not overlooked; it is the beginning of the end. At the same time, the "engine" should not cover the flutes at MM. 172-177. Regarding M. 178, the composer states, "Things should be cooking just under a boil." Bring out the chimes at 202, 208, and 218. Nelson advises, "Hold nothing in reserve! It should just about demolish the set."

Strive to determine the optimal sound of each section of the piece. Certain passages should be mysterious, some beautiful, some revolting. Find the personality of each section and guage the style accordingly. For example, Nelson offers that the section at MM 162-170 should be "amorphous, almost directionless until the saxophone enters in bar 170."

Unit 6: Musical Elements

Bach's Passacaglia theme is in C minor, Nelson's ground bass is octatonic on C, as are much of the surrounding materials. The ominous bass sonority that opens the work (C-Db-Eb-E) is also octatonic.

The dark quality of the piece is defined not only by the mysterioso bassline, but by the intervallic content of the octatonic scale itself. The octatonic contains four occurrences of all interval classes, with one exception. There are eight minor thirds, double the number of any other interval. Additionally, every octatonic scale tone has a tritone counterpart. This harmonic richness actualizes the strong sense of tension and release that, in conjunction with the relentless ostinato, drives the music inexorably forward.

Messiaen identified this synthetic scale as a "mode of limited transposition." There are only three versions possible. Nelson employs the following octatonic scale:

The following seventeen chords represent all possible triads obtainable from this scale:

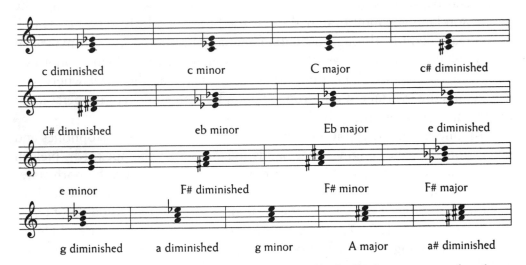

The theme appears in parallel triads at M. 186, all of which appear on the above table. Nelson harmonizes the basso ostinato with major and minor triads to add strength and weight to its statement, thereby contrasting the chattering textures above.

At M. 154 the theme is transformed into an octatonic version of Bach's C minor Passacaglia. The theme is orchestrated to simulate the "quint" stop found on the Baroque organ.

The monotonic trumpet figure in M. 4 is a Nelsonian motif that appears in similar incarnations throughout his *oeuvre*. Contrary to popular belief, this figure is not a Morse code pattern.

Nelson paraphrases portions of Bach's *Art of the Fugue* beginning in the trombone at measure 34. The trumpet I subject entrance occurs three bars later, with trumpet III and IV entrances ensuing. The second and final quotation is in four equal brass voices at MM 60-65 (the Nottebohm "solution"). Another fugue subject is referenced by piccolo and bassoon at M. 113, and in the oboe and bass clarinet at M. 118.

The B-A-C-H (Bb-A-C-B) motive was used by Bach himself in the final fugue in *Art of the Fugue*. Nelson quotes this figure, three notes of which occur in the octatonic scale pattern used as a basis for the work. It is exceptional that the non-octatonic pitch, B, is the leading tone to the tonic C. In the coda, Nelson uses this leading-tone from the Bach motive to finalize the tonality of the entire composition.

Unit 7: Form and Structure
The composer writes:

> The piece challenged my mania for trying to write "seamless" music since it closes every eight bars. I allowed a seam to show at the "Golden Section" (M. 145) where the B-A-C-H motive interrupts the ostinato and sounds on its own. Notice also, that the basso ostinato is constructed with its high point at the Golden Section. Proportions aside, my plan was to take the piece from a sort of dark embryonic contrapuntal opening through 25 variations which gradually metamorphose to a very dynamic (read that seismic) conclusion.

INTRODUCTION		1-9	B-A-C-H motive, monotonic motive
STATEMENT	1	10-17	monotonic motive
	2	18-25	Trumpets, interlocking B-A-C-H statements
	3	26-33	Inversion of above materials
	4	34-41	Art of the Fugue
	5	42-49	B-A-C-H
	6	50-57	B-A-C-H
	7	58-65	Art of the Fugue, B-A-C-H ("solution")
	8	66-73	Animando un poco, Molto legato
	9	74-81	Variation on flute motive (MM 34-36) in winds, brass
	10	82-89	Ostinato in mid-range over C pedal (tonic)
	11	90-97	Ostinato in upper range over F pedal (subdominant)
	12	98-105	Ostinato in bass
	13	106-113	Theme in horns, florid wind lines
	14	114-121	Theme in English horn, Art of the Fugue
	15	122-129	Fragmentation of theme in *durchbrochenarbeit*
	16	130-137	Fragmentation
	17	138-144	Theme in baritone sax, then horn, antiphonal
GOLDEN SECTION		145-153	B-A-C-H
STATEMENT	18	154-161	Bach's theme in "quint" voicing
	19	162-169	Monotonic motive, Theme returns to horns
	20	170-177	Fragmented theme, "machine" begins push to end

21	178-185	Theme in horn
22	186-193	Theme harmonized in low brass triads
23	194-201	Theme in tutti brass triads (including trumpets)
24	202-209	Tutti brass triads over C pedal
CODA	210-222	B-A-C-H vs. C pedals, open fifth ending

Unit 8: Suggested Listening

J.S. Bach, *Passacaglia and Fugue in C minor*
J.S. Bach, *Art of the Fugue*
J.S. Bach, *The Well-Tempered Klavier*
Biber, *Passacaglia*
Dietrich Buxtehude, *Prelude, Fugue, and Chaccone for Organ*
Paul Hindemith, *Cardillac*
Gustav Holst, *First Suite in Eb for Military Band*
Claudio Monteverdi, "Possente Spirito" from *Orfeo*
Muffat, *Passacaglia*
Johannes Pachelbel, *Kanon in D*
Henry Purcell, "Dido's Lament" from *Dido and Aeneas*
Reger, *Introduction, Passacaglia, and Fugue*

Unit 9: Bibliography

Davidson, Archibald T., and Willi Apel. *Historical Anthology of Music. Baroque, Rococo and Pre-Classical Music*. 11th Printing. Cambridge: Harvard University Press, 1976.

Grout, Donald Jay. Claude V. Palisca, ed. *A History of Western Music*. Third Ed. New York: W. W. Norton & Co., 1980.

Nelson, Ron. Letter to Eugene Corporon. 7/14/92.

Parrish, Carl, ed. *A Treasury of Early Music*. New York: W.W. Norton & Co., 1958.

Patterson, Stephen. "Profile of Composer Ron Nelson." *The Instrumentalist*, XLVIII June 1994, 49.

Sadie, Stanley, ed. *The New Grove Dictionary of Music and Musicians*. 20 Vols. London: Macmillan, 1980.

Smith, Norman, and Albert Stoutamire. *Band Music Notes*. Rev. ed. San Diego: Neil A. Kjos, Jr., Publisher, 1979.

Teacher Resource Guide

"The Passing Bell"
Warren Benson
(b. 1924)

Unit 1: Composer

Warren Benson was Professor of Composition at the Eastman School of Music from 1963 to 1993. Prior to that, he was Composer-in-Residence at Ithaca College. He has performed professionally as a timpanist with the Detroit Symphony Orchestra. He was awarded successive Fulbright Teacher Grants to Greece, where he organized the first coeducational choral group in that country. Benson's works for wind band are recognized as a significant contribution to the repertoire. His music is performed in more than forty countries.

Unit 2: Composition

The Passing Bell was commissioned by the Luther College Band in memory of a former concertmaster who died in his youth after a brief but tragic illness. It was published in 1983 by G. Schirmer Music Company. It draws freely from the Lutheran chorale prelude tradition, but is in a contemporary idiom. It is in one movement, marked quarter equals 48 to 54.

Unit 3: Historical Perspective

The Passing Bell, a highly dramatic work, uses two historic chorale tunes. The first, published in 1653, is *Jesu, Meine Zuversicht* by Praxis Pietatis Melica and is taken from the Lutheran burial service. The second, a Welsh hymn of faith, is *Merthyr Tydvil L. M. D.* by Joseph Parry and was first published in 1870. It progresses from the somber *Jesu,* in C major, to the robust hymn of faith in G minor over which elements of the former are superimposed.

Unit 4: Technical Considerations

The Passing Bell is written for large symphonic band, including five percussionists, harp (which Benson says may be played on electric piano or synthesizer) and acoustic piano. There is much *divisi* writing within parts, requiring sufficient doubling to realize the composer's intent. The slow tempo and sustained legato, coupled with wide ranges scored for all instruments, make intonation a demanding problem. Complex rhythms are also found throughout the score, including a few asymmetric meters and many compound subdivisions of the beat (e.g. five against two). Sophisticated and sensitive percussion writing is found throughout the work.

Unit 5: Stylistic Considerations

This is a work of passion, involving long phrases and very long sustained pitches, often in extreme registers. Often, melodic lines are passed hocket-like between instruments, making balance a crucial element in interpreting the score. Wide dynamic ranges are specified and particularly placed.

Unit 6: Musical Elements

The Passing Bell uses a variety of harmonic technique. Traditional tonal constructions are combined with polychords and clusters to produce dramatic harmonic effects. The tonal scheme is grounded in long pedal points that are orchestrated in a variety of textures. There is also a very effective use of unmetered events for piano, harp and percussion against the continuing meter of the winds.

Unit 7: Form and Structure

The tonal material is fluid. The conflict between C and G is never completely resolved, the final chord contains C, D, and G. The chorale tunes both have strong tonal implications, the first in C major, the second in G minor. The key indications reflect a basic harmonic movement, but should not neglect the essential tonal conflict.

A1,	mm. 1-40,	C, Serves as an Introduction
B1,	mm. 37-55	(overlaps the end of A1) C, First Chorale tune
A2,	mm. 55-59,	Serves as transition, modulating
B2,	mm. 60-74,	Second statement of First Chorale tune, modulating
C1,	mm. 75-92,	G, First statement of Second Chorale tune
C2,	mm. 76-101,	G, Second statement of Second Chorale tune
C3,	mm. 102-118,	G, Second Chorale tune in augmentation, with material from the First Chorale tune superimposed
C4,	mm. 119-125,	G, Final statement of Second Chorale tune, with material from the First Chorale tune superimposed
A3,	mm. 126-135,	G, Serves as a Coda

442

Unit 8: Suggested Listening

Warren Benson, *The Leaves are Falling*
Warren Benson, *The Solitary Dancer*
Karel Husa, *Music for Prague, 1968*
Joseph Schwantner, *and the mountains rising nowhere*

Unit 9: Additional References and Resources

Ewen, David. *A Comprehensive Biographical Dictionary of American Composers.*
    New York, G. P. Putman and Sons, 1982.

Harbison, William G. "Analysis: The Passing Bell of Warren Benson." *Journal
    of Band Research* XXI/2 (Spring 1986): 1-8.

Hunsberger, Donald. "Discussions with Warren Benson: The Leaves are
    Falling." *College Band Directors National Assocication Journal* I/1
    (Spring 1984): 7-17.

Teacher Resource Guide

"Piece of Mind"
Dana Wilson
(b. 1946)

Unit 1: Composer

Dana Wilson is a native of Lakewood, Ohio. His teachers include Samuel Adler and Hale Smith. He holds a B.A. from Bowdoin College, an M.A. from the University of Connecticut, and a Ph.D. from the Eastman School of Music. He is the recipient of many grants and commissions, and his works have been performed throughout the United States, and in Europe and Asia. He is currently a Professor of Music at Ithaca College, Ithaca, New York.

Unit 2: Composition

Piece of Mind, completed in 1987, is a musical pun on the well-known expression. It is also intended to be a musical representation of the workings of the human mind, with each movement reflecting a different aspect of the life of the mind. The work was awarded the 1987 Sudler International Wind Band Composition Prize (administered by the John Philip Sousa Foundation) and the 1988 Ostwald Prize from the American Bandmasters Association. Its subsequent publication by Ludwig Music Publishers and several recordings have led to numerous performances.

Unit 3: Historical Perspective

Wilson's music is part of a trend that Gunther Schuller has identified as "third stream," incorporating elements of jazz in traditional writing. This is an important part of 20th-century composition, the earliest proponents of which were primarily European (particularly French). *Piece of Mind* incorporates a broader palate of non-traditional technique, including minimalist-like repetitive constructions and East Indian classical music.

444

Unit 4: Technical Considerations

Piece of Mind is intricately constructed rhythmically. Complex interlocking of voices, as well as contrasting subdivisions of the beat, require clarity and precision. Syncopation and hemiola are a common element of Wilson's vocabulary. Although there are frequent changes of meter, there is no asymmetric meter or complex metric modulation. Some fluid technical playing is required. In general, the ranges are moderate. The percussion writing is idiomatic and an integral component with the winds.

Unit 5: Stylistic Considerations

Piece of Mind incorporates many different styles. "Dixieland," "Swing," and "Samba" are examples of styles requested in the score. In addition, subtle articulations, reflecting the jazz idiom, are required throughout the work.

Unit 6: Musical Elements

Piece of Mind is structured around a four-note recurring cell that is introduced at the beginning of the first movement. Each movement treats or interacts with the four-note motive in a way that relates to modes of thought. The harmonic structure of *Piece of Mind* is generally tonal, with the chromatic alterations common to the style. There are also harmonies derived from the basic four-note melodic motive, often structured as polychords. The syncopations and hemiolas also derive from the jazz idiom.

Unit 7: Form and Structure

There are four movements, each with programmatic associations related to the mind. Each uses a four note cell [0,2,3,7] which allows frequent tonal/triadic references.

MOVEMENT I, "THINKING"

Three part song form, ABA

A, mm. 1-36, Polychordal, centering on A
> 1, mm. 1-36, Repetitive patterns of different lengths, generated from the basic cell (C-A-B-E), first heard in m. 1, that are added gradually in minimalist fashion. This configuration of the basic cell suggests an A minor tonal reference, as well as a melodic turn (C-A-B), a falling fifth (B-E), and a minor sixth (C-E: inverted in movements III and IV to become the main theme, for example) which generate virtually all of the work's materials
> 2, mm. 30, saxophones introduce the intensely syncopated material that becomes important in all of the later movements. They begin with the basic cell, inverted, and transform it into a turn

B, mm. 37-79, Polychordal, centering on Eb

    a, mm. 37-55 Polychordal, centering on Eb

        1, mm 37-47, B motive (distinguished by the rhythm, still based on the basic cell) in trumpets and brass, ostinato accompaniment in percussion

        2, mm. 48-55, B motive, basic cell expanded in flutes and piano, then modified rhythmically by oboe, English horn and saxophones

    b, mm. 56-68, Polychordal, centering on E. Reintroduction of the opening tonal relationship on A over E, while piano and vibraphone continue with the B harmonic structure

        1, mm. 56-58, ostinato interrupted

        2, mm. 59-68, canonic imitation between horns, oboe, English horn and euphonium, tuba. This introduces the turn, which becomes important later, and the ascending minor sixth which introduces the opening theme of the third movement

    a, mm. 75-79, Polychordal, expansion continues

A, mm. 80-91, Polychordal, centering on A

    Repetitive patterns of beginning return

        1, B motive superimposed in trumpet, m. 82

        2, Melody derived from saxophone, m. 30

    Ends abruptly, as if interrupted

MOVEMENT II, "REMEMBERING"

This movement attempts to capture musically how we remember: from brief, vivid images to vague, floating remembrances. Here jazz styles are presented somewhat chronologically (1920's, '30's, '50's and 70's), framed by a contrasting texture [A] representing the mind itself in this process. All of the material is derived essentially from the basic cell

A 1, mm. 1-7, Eb

    static, with small motives over a sustained texture

Event I, mm. 8-11, F

    "Dixieland Style"

A 2, mm. 12-15, Polychordal, G/Ab

    more motion than A 1

Event II, mm. 16-21, F

    "Swing Style"

A 3, mm. 22-28, Polychordal, C minor/ B Major. This polychords gain significance when they are transposed in movement III to C# minor/ C Major

Event III, mm 29-35, C
> "Bright Swing"

A 4, mm. 36-49, Polychordal
> 1, mm. 36-43, Develops earlier material, allowing elements to fragment and juxtapose while staying in their respective tempi and style - the way they might in memory
> 2, mm. 44-48, 12/8, "stride piano" solo begins

Event IV, mm. 49-75, G
> 1, mm. 49-59, "Samba tempo" begins
> 2, mm. 60-61, "Stride piano tempo" returns
> 3, mm. 62-75, "Samba" continues, then fades into A 5

A 5, mm. 76-86, Polychordal, D/Db
> diminishing motion

MOVEMENT III, "FEELING"

Three part form, ABA

A, mm. 1-36, Passacaglia-like structure based on 9 statements of a four chord progression, 7 of which are the progression labeled "A," C# minor, C Major, Eb minor, D Major
> 1, A
> 2, A
> 3, A, plus bass line
> 4, A, with bass line, plus horn solo
> 5, A, with bass line and horn solo, plus alto saxophone solo
> 6, A, transposed up a major third, plus trumpet solo and woodwinds
> 7, A' [A,E,G,Gb]
> 8, A returns [C#,C,Eb,D], arpeggiated, theme in low brass
> 9, A, tutti

B, mm. 37-61, Contrasting section marked "with Anger," Polychordal, earlier chord progression now superimposed. Tempo change, rhythmic interjections from the brass, including a tense "heartbeat" in the low brass, some improvisation in the percussion

A, mm. 62-98, Tempo Primo,
> 1, mm. 62-81, Harmony is the same as A, though in different inversion
> 2, mm. 99-91, Tutti chords from Passacaglia, again creating polychords
> 3, mm. 92-98, Coda

MOVEMENT IV, "BEING"

Through Composed, in three major sections with a Coda

A, mm. 1-73, centered on G, with the D in the double bass suggesting the "second inversion" quality important throughout the work and implicit in the basic cell
1, mm. 1-5, Introduction, G/D open fifth drone
2, mm. 6-18, clarinet solo, freely based on basic cell, in the style of East Indian raga
3, mm. 18-40, oboe and flute add counterpoint to clarinet
4. mm. 41-73, 3 part counterpoint with percussion and brass ostinato

B, mm. 74-120, centered on G (with the D even stronger than before), moving to G#, via the progression from movement III
1, mm. 74-89, woodwind melody in octaves accompanied by percussion who improvise variations on a pattern
2, mm. 90-105, brass chords, derived from cell, and the same progression as Movement III Passacaglia
3, mm. 106-120, percussion ostinato, with pyramid in winds derived from basic cell, accomplishes moving the drone to G#

C, mm. 121-169, six eight-measure patterns repeated, again the harmonic progression from movement III
1, clarinet solo
2, clarinet solo with horn accompaniment
3, muted trumpet and woodwind counterpoint
4, low brass melody, woodwind counterpoint, saxophone ostinato
5, horn melody, low brass join ostinato
6, Tutti ostinato

Coda, mm. 170-177
1, mm. 170-176, trumpet chords derived from cell
2, mm. 177, motion interrupted by fermata polychord that diminuendos al niente

Unit 8: Suggested Listening
Gunther Schuller, *Divertimento, "On Winged Flight"*
Dana Wilson, *Shakata*

Unit 9: Additional References and Resources

Ferrari, Lois. "Two Symphonic Wind Ensemble Compositions of Dana Wilson: Piece of Mind and Shakata: Singing the World Into Existence." Doctoral dissertation, Eastman School of Music of the University of Rochester, 1995.

Mathes, James. "Analysis: Piece of Mind by Dana Wilson." *Journal of Band Research* XXV/2 (Spring 1990): 1-12.

Wilson, Dana. *Piece of Mind.* Eugene Corporon and the University of Cincinnati College-Conservatory of Music Wind Symphony. Compact Disc KCD-11051, 1993.

Wilson, Dana. *Piece of Mind.* Frederick Fennell and the Tokyo Kosei Wind Orchestra. Compact Disc KOCD-3569, 1994.

Wilson, Dana. *Piece of Mind.* Rodney Winther and the Ithaca College Wind Ensemble. LP MCBS-35890, 1993.

Teacher Resource Guide

"Postcard"
Frank Ticheli

(b. 1958)

Unit 1: Composer

Frank Ticheli (b. 1958) is currently Composer-in-Residence of the Pacific Symphony Orchestra and an Associate Professor of Music at the University of Southern California. His compositions for wind ensemble and concert band have received hundreds of performances throughout the US, Canada, Europe, Asia, and Australia, and have gained him several prizes, including the 1989 Walter Beeler Prize (for *Music for Winds and Percussion*) and First Prize in the eleventh annual "Symposium for New Music" (for *Concertino for Trombone and Band*).

His orchestral music has enjoyed considerable success in recent years, described as "free-wheeling, raucous, open-ended—American" (*San Antonio Express*), expressing "direct emotion, creating dramatic visceral impact" (*Orange County Register*), "lean and muscular...and above all, active, in motion" (*New York Times*). His works have received performances by the American Composers Orchestra at Carnegie Hall, the Philadelphia Orchestra, the Hong Kong Philharmonic, the Austrian Radio Orchestra, the Pacific Symphony Orchestra, Prince George's Philharmonic Orchestra, and the symphony orchestras of Louisville, Denver, Memphis, San Antonio, Austin, and others. His recent work, *Radiant Voices*, received its premiere in February 1993 by the Pacific Symphony Orchestra, and its European premiere in April of that year by the Frankfurt Opera Orchestra.

Other honors include a Charles Ives Scholarship and Goddard Lieberson Fellowship from the American Academy and Institute of Arts and Letters, the Ross Lee Finney Award, and residencies at Yaddo and the MacDowell Colony. He has received commissions and grants from the American Music Center, the Pacific Symphony, The Prince George's Philharmonic Orchestra, The Adrian

Symphony, the City of San Antonio, Stephen F. Austin State University, The University of Michigan, Trinity University, and others.

Frank Ticheli received his Doctoral and Master's degrees in composition from The University of Michigan where he studied with William Albright, George Wilson, and Pulitzer Prize winners Leslie Bassett and William Bolcom. Several of his works are published by Manhattan Beach Music, Encore Music, and PP Music Publishers, and are recorded by Koch International, Klavier, Toshiba-EMI, and Mark Records.

Additional works for band include *Music for Winds and Percussion, Cajun Folk Songs, Fortress, Gaian Visions, Pacific Fanfare, Concertino for Trombone,* and *Amazing Grace.*

Unit 2: Composition

Composed in 1991, Postcard is a brilliant, energetic work, contrapuntal in conception and written in the American vein. Ticheli exploits the tritone interval (a bisected octave) to produce a harmonic language that is both wry and mysterious, coupled with capricious rhythmic turns in mixed meter. In his preface to the score, the composer writes:

POSTCARD was commissioned by my friend, colleague, and former mentor, H. Robert Reynolds, in memory of his mother, Ethel Virginia Curry. He requested that I compose not an elegy commemorating her death, but a short energetic piece celebrating her life. In response, I have composed this brief "postcard" as a musical reflection of her character—vibrant, whimsical, succinct.

It is cast in an ABA1 form. The primary theme, first heard in the flute and clarinet and used in the outer sections, is a palindrome—that is, it sounds the same played forwards or backwards. This theme honors a long-standing tradition in the Reynolds family of giving palindromic names (such as Hannah and Anna) to their children. H. Robert Reynolds' first name is Harrah. The theme's symmetry is often broken, sometimes being elongated, other times being abruptly cut off by unexpected events.

The B section is based on a five-note series derived from the name Ethel: E (E natural) T (te in the solfeggio system, B flat) H (in the German system, B natural) E (E-flat this time) L (la in the solfeggio system, A natural). The development of this motive can be likened to a journey through a series of constantly changing landscapes.

The A1 section is articulated by the return of the main melody. This section is not identical to the A section, but is close enough in spirit to it to give the effect of a large-scale palindrome surrounding the smaller ones.

POSTCARD was completed in the summer of 1991. Its first perfor-

451

mance was on April 17, 1992 at Hill Auditorium in Ann Arbor, Michigan, by the University of Michigan Symphony Band conducted by H. Robert Reynolds.

The composer has transcribed Postcard for Orchestra, in which form it was premiered and recorded by the Pacific Symphony Orchestra.

Unit 3: Historical Perspective

Postcard shows the influence of late 20th-Century compositional trends. The frenetic rhythmic pace and iteration of a single rhythmic unit (also found in Baroque music) is reminiscent of minimalist works by composers such as Terry Riley, Steve Reich, Phillip Glass, and John Adams, although *Postcard* is not a minimalist piece. Harmonic stasis develops from prolongations of sonorities which unfold linearly, often with a quasi-hypnotic or incantation-like repetition of pitches. The idiomatic use of the tritone, especially when framed by the perfect fifth (E-A#-B in the "Ethel" theme) is quite reminiscent of Bernstein's melodic inflections. The use of palindromic melodies finds its roots in Machaut's *"Ma fin est mon commencement et mon commencement ma fin,"* in which the tenor part is the retrograde of the top voice. J. S. Bach's "Canon a 2" from *Musicalisches Opfer*, BWV 1079, is a *cancrizans*, or "crab" canon. Although the music is written monophonically on one staff (one voice reads forward from the beginning, the second reads backward from the end) the canon, though symmetrical, is not strictly palindromic. The Minuet and Trio movement from Haydn's *Piano Sonata No. 26* is comprised of perfectly constructed palindromic halves. Symmetry has been elevated to heightened prominence only in the 20th Century as composers searched for new ways to organize pitches, melodies, rhythms, and formal plans. Olivier Messaien experimented with what he termed "non-retrogradable rhythms," which are palindromic and cannot produce permutations through the retrograde operation. The following is one such example:

Ticheli uses an octatonic scale fragment that centers around the A-minor tonality in constructing his main theme. Messaien identified the octatonic scale as a "mode of limited transposition," as it has only three possible distinct forms. Stravinsky and Bartók were particularly fond of octatonic structures.

Unit 4: Technical Considerations

Postcard features irregular scale patterns and chromatic melodic fragments which pose technical challenges to the woodwinds. Brass performers must be able to perform accurately fast chromatic sequences featuring irregular intervals, and passages with fast articulations requiring double-tonguing. Rhythmic assurance on the part of all performers is a must, with a high degree of independence required; doublings are few, and absolute precision and accuracy are essential to ensure clean entrances within the context of rhythmically complex surroundings.

Unit 5: Stylistic Considerations

Performers must strive for lightness and agility in multimeter sections, always placing slurs and accents with accuracy. Be sure flutes, oboes, and clarinets, for example, bring enough attitude and energy to the style beginning at M. 66. Dynamics are used to effect changes of intensity, often resulting in rapid-fire bursts of energy. MM 98-103 contains one such passage choreographed by dynamic phasing between the trumpets, horns, and saxophones. Beginning at M. 30, the clarinets play the melody. Be sure to maximize the color possibilities in what the composer calls the "sneeze effects" in the muted trumpets (M. 32-33) and trombones (M. 34). Coach the musicians to play these parts with plenty of "snarl." Although the tempo is marked ca. 160-168, few ensembles will be able to match this clip. A slower tempo, calibrated to the ability of the group, may be more realistic. Regardless, an energetic mood should prevail.

Unit 6: Musical Elements

The dance-like personality of *Postcard* belies the composer's superb craft. One might expect dance-like music to be somewhat unsophisticated, but Ticheli's organic composition is so well-stitched that it is virtually seamless. Although this is intellectual, "planned-out" music, the listener is never diverted from the evolution of its seemingly spontaneous stream-of-consciousness.

Postcard is primarily a melodic work, dance-like in character, in which the materials are derived from several scales. The opening palindromic melody is based on a six note fragment from the octatonic scale, constructed of alternating whole- and half-steps:

The first four notes of the octatonic scale form the framework for the theme. These notes outline a symmetrical interval series (major second, minor second, major second). The palindrome features a musical representation of Reynolds' first name, Harrah. The pitches B-A-D-D-A-B, (where B = H, and D = R or "re") are placed strategically at the heart of the palindrome (the octave D to D drop is the exact midpoint). Ticheli has not treated rhythm palindromically; motivic use of rhythmic figures is maintained. The third statement (MM 21-29) presents the theme in inversion.

The central octatonic fragment is developed both horizontally and vertically throughout the piece. For example, the horn figure in MM 70-72 is derived from these four notes (transposed). The eighth-note pattern in stretto between the high woodwinds, trumpets, trombones, and euphoniums is also an incarnation of these four notes. The horn theme in MM 81-83 utilizes this melodic pattern, as do the euphonium, vibes, and trombones below. The tubas open the codetta at M. 254 with a descending pattern gleaned from this model.

The B theme, or "Ethel" motive, is also a palindromic melody (Euphonium, MM 112-116). The tritone is developed in these measures. Note the resolution of E-A# to B-D#—perfectly acceptable voice leading in the key of F# Major. The introduction of A-natural at the end of M. 113 obfuscates any tonal establishments. The tritone closes the motif, unresolved.

The prominence of the tritone is manifested also in Ticheli's use of a four-note fragment culled from the Lydian mode.

The first, fourth, and fifth degrees of this Lydian scale form the tritone/fifth pattern found in the B theme. The saxophone chord progression in MM 122-125 exploits the tritone at several levels.

These two chords, whose roots lie a tritone apart, share two pitches (Bb/A# and E) also a tritone apart. The structure of both chords is derived from the lydian (+4) scale pattern. The great extent to which the tritone pervades Ticheli's harmonic language is clear in these examples.

Measure 37 contains a descending octatonic sixteenth-note figure in the upper woodwinds comprised of a four-note symmetrical pitch sequence (Eb-E-A-Bb). This pattern recurs at M. 79-80 in the clarinets. Ticheli uses this pattern as filigree throughout the work.

Postcard is permeated with representations of these harmonic and melodic signatures. Example after example can be cited, as the composer has crystallized a highly-evolved musical language from an economy of harmonic means.

The rhythmic vernacular of *Postcard* is multifaceted. The opening theme is seemingly erratic. Multiple meters alternate, but after the theme has been stated three times, the meter stabilizes at M 30. Often Ticheli creates rhythmic ambiguity, namely through the use of hemiola. The codetta (M. 255) features one such example in the first trumpet and tuba. Both parts actualize patterns that suggest 2/4 time. The surrounding parts establish the written signature of 3/4. There are few passages in the work that project a strong, regular pulse. The often lean polyphonic texture adds to this sense, along with the multitudinous free interplay of diverse rhythmic elements.

Unit 7: Form and Structure

Form: A   (MM 1-110 [Transition 104-110])

               B   (MM 111-194)

               A1   (MM 195-265 [Codetta 255-265])

Unit 8: Suggested Listening

J.S. Bach, "Canon a 2" from *Musicalisches Opfer*, BWV 1079
Leonard Bernstein, *Mass*
Leonard Bernstein, *Symphonic Dances from "West Side Story"*
Josef Haydn, *Piano Sonata No. 26*
Machaut, *Ma fin est mon commencement et commencement mon fin*
Olivier Messaien, *Les corps glorieux:* "L'Ange aux parfums"
Olivier Messaien, *Mode de valeurs*
Igor Stravinsky, *The Firebird*
Igor Stravinsky, *The Rite of Spring*
Frank Ticheli, *Fortress*
Frank Ticheli, *Postcard* (orchestral version)

Unit 9: Bibliography

Grout, Donald Jay. ed. Claude V. Palisca. *A History of Western Music.* 3rd
    Ed. New York: W. W. Norton & Co., 1980.

Sadie, Stanley, ed. *The New Grove Dictionary of Music and Musicians.* 20
    Vols. London: Macmillan, 1980.

Ticheli, Frank. Telephone Interview with Thomas Stone. Los Angeles -
    Cincinnati. 6/12/95.

Watkins, Glenn. *Soundings.* New York: Schirmer Books, 1988.

Teacher Resource Guide

"Sinfonia No. 4"
Allegro deciso, Adagio, Vivace, Allegro molto
Walter Hartley
(b. 1927)

Unit 1: Composer

Walter Hartley is a native of Washington, D.C. He studied composition at the Eastman School of Music with Bernard Rogers and Howard Hanson. While at Eastman, Hartley earned Bachelor's, Master's, and Ph.D. degrees in music. Dr. Hartley taught piano and music theory at the National Music Camp and served as Chairman of the music department at David and Elkins College in West Virginia. He is currently Professor Emeritus at SUNY-Fredonia. Other wind compositions include *Concerto for 23 Winds*, *Symphony No. 2*, *Concertino for Tenor Saxophone*, *Bacchanalia*, *Chautauqua Overture*, *Southern Tier Suite*, and *Sinfonia No. 5*.

Unit 2: Composition

In his preface to the score, the composer has written:

> The *Sinfonia No. 4* was commissioned by the students of the Ithaca High School Concert Band as part of their unique tradition of annually commissioning new works by American composers. It was first performed under the direction of Frank Battisti at Ithaca High School's Kulp Auditorium on May 11, 1966.

> The work was composed during the spring of 1965 in London, England, where my family and I were living during a sabbatical leave from my teaching position at Elkins and Davis College. Finishing touches were applied in Belfast, Northern Ireland, and Zurich,

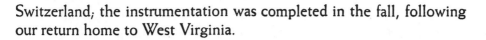

Switzerland; the instrumentation was completed in the fall, following our return home to West Virginia.

Unit 3: Historical Perspective

The 1960s witnessed an explosion in the composition of wind music in all streams. The year 1964 brought such disparate works as Chance's *Incantation and Dance*, Copland's *Emblems*, Dello Joio's *Scenes from the Louvre*, Nelhybel's *Trittico*, and Rochberg's dodecaphonic *Apocalyptica*. This snapshot demonstrates the existence by mid-decade of educational music aimed at the American high school band in co-existence with cutting-edge pieces composed without regard to level of difficulty. Hartley's *Sinfonia No. 4*, written the following year for the Ithaca High School Band and conductor Frank Battisti, although not on the compositional cutting edge in 1965, represents the work of a first-rate writer creating elevated art without adulteration. That Hartley felt comfortable doing so is a testament to the maturity of the Ithaca Band.

Unit 4: Technical Considerations

The technical complications inherent in Hartley's neo-tonal language are counterveiled to a degree by his tendency to construct melodic ideas revolving around the incantation-like repetition of a limited number of pitches. Regardless, mature technique is a must not only for clean execution, but for the processing and co-constructing of Hartley's sophisticated idiom. The orchestrations are lean; chamber music abounds throughout the four movements, and solo passages for Flute I, Oboe, Clarinets I + II + III, Alto Saxophone I, Trumpet I, and Trombone I will require the availability of at least one exceptional performer on each of these parts. The rhythmic dialect, though fresh and smart, does not pose undue obstacles. Ranges are reasonable with the exception of Trumpet I at MM. 99-102 in Mvt. III. The instrumentation excludes Oboe II and Baritone Saxophone, but calls for five trumpet parts. The percussion section, requiring four players total, is given its own soli statement at MM. 20-29 in Mvt. III.

Unit 5: Stylistic Considerations

Work to establish and sustain a definite mood in each movement. There is no filler in this concise music. Each phrase, each note has a distinct purpose in the design. Articulation markings are used sparingly, but there should be little doubt that much of the writing demands a detached style where slurs are absent.

Enlisting the ears of the ensemble is a must in performing these economical orchestrations. Guide listening toward the rhythmic activity. The greater the rhythmic interconnectedness within the ensemble the better.

Although in the score the composer provides only general tempo indications without citing metronome markings, he suggests a tempo of 46 to the dotted quarter note in Mvt. II and 76 to the dotted half in Mvt. III. Each movement, however, will work at various tempi so long as the style is maintained. With the exception of Mvt. II, the general style should be light and agile unless otherwise indicated.

Unit 6: Musical Elements

The composer discusses the materials in *Sinfonia No. 4*:

> There is much antiphonal writing between the choirs, many solo passages for a wide variety of instruments, and a general reliance on pure colors with little doubling (except for voices at the octave). The style is tonal (with free dissonance frequently producing bitonal effects) with a constant opposition of chordal and contrapuntal textures. The last two movements are lighter in mood than the first two, especially the 'finale,' which is almost but not quite a march.

Hartley's melodies frequently derive from cellular clumps of tones in close proximity. No sooner is a sequential pattern established than it is transcended by a seemingly incongruous continuation-but one that evolves in parallel logic to the composer's musical DNA. Hartley delights in the pervasive cross-relations that result. Antecedent and consequent phrases are occasionally reversed in thematic restatements (Movement I - MM 71-76).

Several figures feature accompaniment by one or more monotonic lines in rhythmic unison with the melody. The B theme of Movement I is developed in this manner at M. 26-27. The introduction to Movement IV uses a form of this pedal-point technique. An austere yet eloquent progression surrounds the pedal-point Eb in the solo trumpet at the close of Movement II. The final Eb9 sonority is both resonant and charming.

Hartley's harmonic language is characterized by complex voicings of seventh, ninth, and eleventh chords. Most often the bass movement is by thirds in avoidance of traditional movement in fourths and fifths. The latter is conserved for passages that border on satire, such as in Movement III at MM. 30-41, in which the voice movement mocks traditional "horn fifths." The opening theme in Movement IV, the most diatonic of the entire work, is accompanied by traditional bass motion.

Although generally this is juxtapositional music in which no attempt is made to meld diverse elements via slick transitions (dissimilarities are celebrated), Movement II contains a beautifully crafted elision between the second and third sections (M. 38). The reprise of the saxophone solo, foreshadowed in the previous measure, is organic and unaffected.

The rhythmic style is clever, sharp, energetic, and playful. There are few complexities, but there is hemiola at M. 97-99 in Movement III.

Unit 7: Form and Structure

In his preface to the score, Walter Hartley writes:

> The *Sinfonia*, in four movements is written in condensed classical forms of the rondo type, contrasting in tempo; each movement is designed in its own way to exploit the various facets of the modern wind-percussion ensemble in line and color.

The layout of the movements is as follows:

MVT. I (SONATA-RONDO) *ALLEGRO DECISO*

Intro	MM.	1-4
A	MM.	5-18
B	MM.	19-31
Bridge	MM.	32-34 Reprise of Introduction
C	MM.	35-43
Development	MM. 44-64 A and C themes developed over chorale	
Coda	MM. 65-76 Introduction and B theme (Consequent /Antecedent)	

MVT. II (FIRST RONDO FORM) *ADAGIO*

A	MM. 1-15	11 pitches used in opening phrase in saxophone
Transition	MM. 15-20	Foreshadows B theme with elements of A
B	MM. 20-38	Brass chorale under flute melody
A	MM. 38-46	Reprise of saxophone solo
Coda	MM. 46-55	B and A theme phrases

MVT. III (SECOND RONDO FORM) *VIVACE*

A	MM. 1-19	WW + Brass alternate antecedent and consequent
B	MM. 20-40	Percussion antecedent, brass consequent
Bridge	MM. 41-46	Chordal variant of A
A	MM. 47-70	
B	MM. 71-102	
Transition	MM. 103-105	
Coda	MM. 106-120 A theme	

MVT. IV (FIRST RONDO FORM) *ALLEGRO MOLTO*

Intro	MM. 1-6
A	MM. 7-47

a (7-20)

b (20-27)

transition on materials from introduction (28-38)

a (39-45)

transition on materials from introduction (46-48)

B   MM 49-76

Fugato, theme derived from introduction, entrances ascending in fifths. (49-69)

Transition on fugue theme (70-76)

A   MM. 77-110

a (77-93)

b (94-103)

Coda (on introductory materials) (104-110)

Unit 8: Suggested Listening

Walter Hartley, *Concerto for 23 Winds*

Walter Hartley, *Sinfonia No. 4*

Darius Milhaud, *La Creation du Monde*

Darius Milhaud, *Suite Francaise*

Poulenc, *Suite Francaise*

Vincent Persichetti, *Masquerade*

Igor Stravinsky, *Pulcinella*

Unit 9: Bibliography

Band Music Guide. 9th ed. Northfield, Ill: The Instrumentalist Company, 1989.

Hartley, Walter. *Sinfonia No. 4.* Composer's Preface to the score. Kansas City: Wingert-Jones Music, Inc., 1967.

Sadie, Stanley, ed. *The New Grove Dictionary of Music and Musicians.* 20 Vols. London: Macmillan, 1980.

Slonimsky, Nicholas. *Baker's Biographical Dictionary of Musicians.* 8th ed., rev. New York: Schirmer Books, 1991.

Smith, Norman, and Albert Stoutamire. *Band Music Notes.* Rev. ed. San Diego: Neil A. Kjos, Jr., Publisher, 1979.

Wallace, David, and Eugene Corporon., eds. *Wind Ensemble/Band Repertoire.* Greeley, Colo.: University of Northern Colorado School of Music, 1984.

Teacher Resource Guide

"Sinfonietta"
Ingolf Dahl
(b. 1912–d. 1970)

Unit 1: Composer
Although Dahl was born in Germany, his parents were Swedish. He was educated in Cologne and Zurich before immigrating to the United States in 1938; Dahl became an American citizen in 1943. He lived in Los Angeles during the war and joined the University of Southern California faculty in 1945. He was a close friend of both Stravinsky and Schoenberg.

Unit 2: Composition
The *Sinfonietta* was commissioned by the Western and Northern Divisions of the College Band Directors National Association in 1961. It was given its premiere performance by the University of Southern California Wind Orchestra conducted by William Schaeffer. Dahl described the Sinfonietta as "...the piece I had wanted to write all my life." He indicated that each movement may stand alone, identified by its individual title.

Unit 3: Historical Perspective
The *Sinfonietta* is a seminal work in the repertoire of the wind band. Although making many, very often witty, references to the traditional literature of the band, much of the work is approached from an entirely new perspective. The second movement, for instance, has no *tutti* passages for the full ensemble. The soloistic and colorful writing was a new contribution to the wind band literature that has proved to be influential. It is obvious that Dahl's technique is indebted to both Stravinsky and Schoenberg.

Unit 4: Technical Considerations

The *Sinfonietta* has demanding solos for every wind instrument in the ensemble. In addition, many lower parts have the same technical requirement as higher parts, such as the unison clarinet cadenza in the first movement. An extremely wide dynamic range, from fortissimo "bells in the air" to sounds that diminuendo to nothing. Difficult melodic intervals and wide ranges are typical of all three movements.

Unit 5: Stylistic Considerations

The predominant orientation of the *Sinfonietta* is neoclassical. Consequently, articulation and lyrical contrast are central stylistic concerns. The second movement illustrates the pattern. Broad lyrical phrases, accompanied and punctuated with dance-like staccato, is the norm. The Quasi-Gavotte, the center of the entire three movement structure, is a Stravinsky-like marcato.

Unit 6: Musical Elements

The *Sinfonietta* is constructed on a row of six pitches using serial technique. The row, Ab, Eb, C, G, D, A, was chosen to provide a wealth of triadic formations. Its inversion, at the interval of a major sixth, provides the remaining six tones of the complete chromatic scale. The second movement is almost chamber-like, having no ensemble *tutti* sections, and no dynamic mark louder than a *mezzo forte*.

Unit 7: Form and Structure

The *Sinfonietta* is constructed as an arch form spanning all three movements. Consequently, there is often more than one implication for each element of the form. The following analysis will make reference to both the form of the individual movement and the form of the entire work.

I. INTRODUCTION AND RONDO

The Introduction serves as the outside segments of the Arch Form of the work. A variation of the Introduction, in retrograde, serves as the conclusion.

The Rondo is a Rondo Form superimposed on a Sonata Form, with an extensive development and a brief recapitulation.

Introduction
      1, mm. 1-7, Lyrical introduction establishes Ab
      2, mm. 8-40, Offstage trumpet fanfare

Rondo

Exposition
      A, mm. 41-90, Ab
      B, mm. 91-142

Development

> A, mm. 143-164
> B, mm. 165-216
> *Tutti* clarinet cadenza, mm. 217-246, modulates through keys
> determined by the six note series

Recapitulation

> A, mm. 247-270
> B, mm. 271-287

Coda

> A mm. 288-301, Ab, refers to the Fanfare from the introduction and
> makes a humorous allusion to a drum "roll off" at the final cadence

II. PASTORALE NOCTURNE

The Pastorale Nocturne is an extended Three-Part Song Form, ABA. In addition, it serves as the keystone of the Arch form of the entire work. The B section, marked Quasi-Gavotte, is the center of the entire work. The return of the A section is generally a retrograde of the beginning A section.

A, mm. 1-50, Db

> introduction, mm. 1-5
> a, mm. 5-15
> b, mm. 16-46, waltz with episodes
> codetta, mm. 47-50

B, mm. 51-81, Quasi Gavotte, B minor

> c, mm. 51-69
> d, mm. 70-81

A, mm. 82-121, Db

> transition, mm. 82-92, related to codetta from first A section
> b, mm. 92-106
> a, mm. 107-112
> conclusion, mm. 113-121, related to introduction from first A section

III. DANCE VARIATIONS

The Dance Variations are a theme, based on the six-tone series, and a set of eight variations with a short recapitulation and a Coda that is derived from the retrograde of the Introduction of the first movement. This serves to conclude the Arch Form of the entire work.

Theme,	mm. 1-20, Ab
Variation, I,	mm. 22-31
Variation, II,	mm. 32-50
Variation, III,	mm. 51-65

Variation, IV,   mm. 66-75
Variation, V,   mm. 76-85
Variation, VI,   mm. 86-106
Variation, VII,   mm. 107-119
Variation, VIII,   mm. 120-155
Theme,   mm. 156-171
Variation III,   mm. 172-203
Variation, II,   mm. 204-214
Codetta,   mm. 215-239, uses material from various Variations

Conclusion,   mm 240-269, from first movement Introduction
2, mm. 240-261, Offstage trumpet fanfare, muted
1, mm. 262-269, Lyrical conclusion confirms Ab

Dahl provided an optional ending which is fast and loud. However, it is not his first choice, as it destroys the symmetry of the form.

Unit 8: Suggested Listening
Ingolf Dahl, *Concerto for Alto Saxophone*
Arnold Schoenberg, *Theme and Variations*, Op. 43a
Igor Stravinsky, *Octet for Winds*

Unit 9: Additional References and Resources
Adams, Bryon. "Ingolf Dahl's Sinfonietta for Concert Band—An Interpretive Analysis." *The Instrumentalist*, XLIII October 1988, 21-28.

Berdahl, James Nilson. "Ingolf Dahl: His Life and Works." Diss., University of Miami, 1975.

Bruning, Earl Henry Jr. "A Survey and Handbook of Analysis for the Conducting and Interpretation of Seven Selected Works in the Standard Repertoire for Wind Band." Diss., Ball State University, 1980.

Grout, Donald J. and Claude V. Palisca. *A History of Western Music*, 4th ed. New York: W. W. Norton & Company, 1988.

Kloecker, John H. "An Analysis of Ingolf Dahl's Sinfonietta for Concert Band." *Journal of Band Research* XXVIII/2 (Spring, 1993): 37-91.

Sadie, Stanley, ed. *The New Grove Dictionary of Music and Musicians*. 20 Vols. London: Macmillan, 1980. S.v. "Ingolf Dahl," by Kurt Stone.

Smith, Norman and Albert Stoutamire. *Band Music Notes*. Lake Charles, LA: Program Note Press, 1989.

Stolba, K Marie. *The Development of Western Music*. Dubuque, IA: William C. Brown Publishers, 1990.

464

Teacher Resource Guide

"Symphony in Bb"
Paul Hindemith

(b. 1895–d. 1963)

Unit 1: Composer

Paul Hindemith is one of the most important composers of the 20th century. He emigrated to the United States to avoid Nazi persecution and accepted a position on the Yale University faculty in 1940. He taught at Yale for the rest of his life. Hindemith's works have become standard repertoire in every major genre. In addition, he wrote solo sonatas for every string and wind instrument of the orchestra.

Unit 2: Composition

The *Symphony in Bb* is a landmark work for the wind band. Commissioned by the United States Army Band, it was premiered in Washington D.C. with the composer conducting. It is conceived in Hindemith's mature style and written for a professional ensemble. The work is as intellectually rigorous as it is musically attractive. Its three movements explore both the soloistic and ensemble potential of the wind band.

Unit 3: Historical Perspective

Hindemith viewed his work as an extension of the Germanic tradition. He developed a system of tonality, expounded in his famous text *The Craft of Musical Composition*, which explained his musical framework. His system, which did not recognize major or minor, asserted a hierarchical relationship of tones and an ordering of intervalic consonance and dissonance. *Ludus Tonalis,* a set of twelve fugues for piano with a prelude, postlude, and interludes, is a musical illustration of Hindemith's harmonic theory as well as his compositional technique. The

Symphony in Bb is an excellent example of Hindemith's application of his compositional theory.

Unit 4: Technical Considerations

The technical demands of the *Symphony in Bb* require a professional level of performance on all instruments except percussion. Skillful soloists are required on all wind instruments. Fast technical passages, both tongued and slurred, are required for the woodwinds, and multiple tonguing is needed in the brass. Wide ranges are used throughout the work. The orchestration, however, is masterful, exploiting the winds in a very idiomatic fashion.

Unit 5: Stylistic Considerations

Hindemith demands a wide range of styles, from intensely lyrical to heavy and martial. Very often, the technical demand of the writing intensifies the difficulty of the style. An import stylistic decision throughout the work is the treatment of hemiola. Almost all the thematic material is developed using hemiola. Balancing musical elements is also important, especially when multiple elements are presented simultaneously. This happens in all the movements.

Unit 6: Musical Elements

The *Symphony in Bb* is a textbook example of Hindemith's interest in cyclic forms. All three movements employ a simultaneous recapitulation of the previously presented material. In the second movement, the material is literally repeated with a few changes in orchestration. The third movement superimposes the expositions of a double fugue and brings back the exposition of the first movement. Hindemith also employs themes that are tightly constructed and developed motivically. As previously mentioned, hemiola is employed throughout the work.

Unit 7: Form and Structure

MOVEMENT I, SONATA FORM, BB

    Exposition, mm. 1-77

            A material, mm. 1-25, Bb

            B material, mm. 26-50, F

            Closing material, mm. 51-77

    Development, mm. 78-154

            Various keys, uses both A and B material

            Final statement uses B material and ends on 12-note chord

    Recapitulation, mm. 155-184

            A and B material simultaneously recapitulated

    Coda, mm. 185-212, Bb

            Based on Closing material from the Exposition

MOVEMENT II, SONG FORM, G
    A, mm. 1-48,
            A Theme, cornet and alto saxophone duet in Canon,
                 mm. 1-20
            Interlude, cornet and trumpet mm. 21-26
            A Theme, mm. 27-41
            Codetta, mm. 42-28
    B, mm. 49-90
            B Theme, mm. 49-72
            Interlude, flutes, mm. 73-75
            B theme, mm. 76-86
            Codetta, 87-90
    A and B Recapitulated Simultaneously, mm. 91-128
            A and B Themes, mm. 91-112
            Interrelate, flutes, cornets and trumpets, mm. 113-116
            A and B themes, mm. 117-126
            Coda, mm. 127-128

MOVEMENT III, DOUBLE FUGUE WITH CODA, Bb
    Introduction, mm. 1-9, F
    Exposition A, mm. 10-65, Bb
    Interlude, A material, mm. 66-76
    Exposition B, mm. 77-135, Bb
    Interlude, B material, mm. 136-160
    Stretto, A and B material superimposed, mm. 161-177
    Coda, A Theme from first movement superimposed on stretto,
       mm. 178-225

Unit 8: Suggested Listening
Paul Hindemith, *Konzertmusik für Blasorchester*, op. 41
Vincent Persichetti, *Symphony No. 6*

Unit 9: Additional References and Resources
Bruning, Earl Henry Jr. "A Survey and Handbook of Analysis for the Conducting and Interpretation of Seven Selected Works in the Standard Repertoire for Wind Band." Diss., Ball State University, 1980.

Ferguson, Thomas Clarence, Jr. "An Analysis of Four American Symphonies for Band." Diss., The University of Rochester, The Eastman School of Music, 1971.

Grout, Donald J. and Claude V. Palisca. *A History of Western Music*, 4th ed. New York: W. W. Norton & Company, 1988.

Hindemith, Paul. *The Craft of Musical Composition*, rev. ed. London: Schott & Company, 1945.

Knight, John Wesley. "Graphic Analyses of the Conducting Techniques for Irregular Meters and Nonmetrical Organizations Found in Selected Twentieth-Century Band Literature." Diss., The Louisiana State University, 1979.

Kopetz, Barry. "Hindemith's Symphony for Band." *The Instrumentalist,* XLIV March 1990, 24-32.

Paulding, James E. "Paul Hindemith (1895-1963): A Study of His Life and Works." Diss., The University of Iowa, 1974.

Sadie, Stanley, ed. *The New Grove Dictionary of Music and Musicians.* 20 Vols. London: Macmillan, 1980. S.v. "Paul Hindemith," by Ian Kemp.

Smith, Norman and Albert Stoutamire. *Band Music Notes.* Lake Charles, LA: Program Note Press, 1989.

Stolba, K Marie. *The Development of Western Music.* Dubuque, IA: William C. Brown Publishers, 1990.

Tarwater, William Harmon. "Analyses of Seven Major Band Compositions of the Twentieth Century." Diss., George Peadody College for Teachers, 1958.

Teacher Resource Guide

Symphony for Band "West Point"
Epitaphs
Marches
Morton Gould
(b. 1913–d. 1996)

Unit 1: Composer

Morton Gould was a native of Richmond Hill, Long Island, New York. He began to play the piano at age four and published his first original composition at six, a waltz aptly titled "Just Six." At age eight, Gould was given a scholarship to the Institute of Musical Arts, the forerunner to the Juilliard School. He later studied theory and composition with Dr. Vincent Jones, and for many years studied piano with Abby Whiteside. Gould played recitals in and around New York City, and became staff pianist at Radio City Music Hall in 1932, the year of its opening. In 1935, he began work as arranger and conductor at WOR radio and the Mutual Radio Network. He subsequently broadcast on the CBS "Schenley Cresta Blanca" program and the "Chrysler Hour." Gould's compositions were conducted by the greats of that time, including Leopold Stokowski, Fritz Reiner, Sir John Barbirolli, Arthur Rodzinski, and Arturo Toscanini. Gould guest-conducted major orchestras both here and abroad. Over the ensuing decades, Gould flourished as a composer, conductor, pianist, and recording artist. He composed music for two Broadway musicals, *Billion Dollar Baby* (1945) and *Arms and the Girl* (1950), several ballet scores, *Interplay*, *I'm Old Fashioned* (with Jerome Robbins), *Fall River Legend* (with Agnes de Mille), and *Audobon* (with George Balanchine, not produced), and a multitude of works for orchestra, band, and solo instruments. Additionally, he has written for films and television, including the CBS documentary series *World War I*, and the NBC miniseries *Holocaust*. As a conductor, Gould won numerous Grammy nominations and a Grammy Award in 1966 for

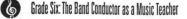

his Chicago Symphony album of music by Charles Ives. In 1986, at age 73, he added yet another dimension to his astonishingly varied career, accepting the presidency of ASCAP (American Society of Composers, Authors, and Publishers), a position he maintained until 1994. He was recognized at the prestigious Kennedy Center Honors in December, 1994, and won the Pulitzer Prize for his *Stringmusic* in 1995. Other works for band include *Ballad for Band* (1946), *Santa Fe Saga* (1955), and *Centennial Symphony* (1983).

Gould's style draws upon what the composer calls "our American vernacular", namely, folk songs, spirituals, and jazz. His oeuvre is largely tonal, with colorations of chromaticism, quartal, and quintal sonorities.

Morton Gould died on February 21, 1996 in Orlando, Florida. On the evening preceding his death, he was honored at a concert of his music performed by the United States Military Academy Band at the newly opened Disney Institute.

Unit 2: Composition

Symphony for Band "West Point" was written for the West Point Sesquicentennial celebration at the request of Capt. Francis E. Resta of the West Point Academy. The present work is the fourth symphony in Gould's entire oeuvre. It was written in January and February of 1952 and was first performed later in that year under the baton of the composer. Gould states:

> The first movement is lyrical and dramatic. The work starts with a quiet and melodic statement of the main theme and motifs that are used and expanded through the entire piece; the general character is elegiac. There is contrast between sonorous brass statements and poignant and contemplative reflections in the woodwinds. This resolves into a broad and noble exposition of one of the motifs, followed by a transition to what serves as both an extended Coda of the movement and a transformation and peroration of the preceding sections. The form here is a passacaglia based on a martial theme first stated in the tuba. On this is built a series of variations that grow in intensity. They mount to a dynamic peak, and after a final climactic variation the movement recalls the previous lyricisms, but with the passacaglia motif hovering in the background; the movement finishes quietly.
>
> The second and final movement is lusty and extroverted in character. The texture is a stylization of marching tunes that parades past in an array of embellishments and rhythmic variations. At one point there is a simulation of a Fife and Drum Corps which, incidentally, was the instrumentation of the original West Point Band. After a brief transformed restatement of the themes in the first movement, the work finishes in a virtuoso Coda of martial fanfares and flourishes.

Unit 3: Historical Perspective

Symphony for Band was conceived as part of the same West Point commissioning project that spawned Milhaud's *West Point Suite*. At the time of its composition in 1952, there were only a handful of American-written substantive band works: Bennett's *Suite of Old American Dances* (1948), Reed's *La Fiesta Mexicana* (1948), Thomson's *A Solemn Music* (1949), Persichetti's *Divertimento* (1950), Schuman's *George Washington Bridge* (1950), Mennin's *Canzona* (1951), and Piston's *Tunbridge Fair* (1951). Gould's own *Ballad for Band* (1946) was perhaps the first masterwork for band by a *bona fide*, first-rank American composer. Edwin Franko Goldman had been laboring (unsuccessfully) to persuade America's finest composers to write wind music for more than two decades. When Gould traveled to the University of Michigan to hear Revelli's band sometime around 1940, he was struck by the potential of the winds *en masse*. *Ballad* was the eventual result of this peregrination, and in the ensuing years, Gould successfully exerted his influence upon others to produce choice compositions for this burgeoning medium.

Paul Hindemith wrote his famous *Symphony in Bb* for the United States Army Band in 1951, and Reed's 1948 *La Fiesta* is regarded widely as a symphony for band. Gould's *Symphony* comes early in the development of repertoire for the band as well, and represents an exemplary work from an era when the symphony orchestra was the preeminent medium.

Unit 4: Technical Considerations

Key signatures include Eb Major, F Major, G Major, C Major, Db Major, Gb Major, and D Major. Sixteenth-note figures in brass parts of both movements may require double-tonguing, but usually on repeated pitches or triadic outlines. Rapid articulation in the clarinet parts (Movement I, MM 211-217) may be problematical. Sections pitting duple and triple meter rhythms occur in the Passacaglia of Movement I, and require rhythmic independence and maturity. Brass ranges are not unusually demanding. The score calls for marching machine, a device constructed of wooden blocks suspended by a network of cords in a wooden frame. An assembled group of people marching in time can be substituted. Listen for the many alliances between the tuba and horn sections. Gould is fond of this combination (Movement I, M. 35 and Movement II, M. 240 to name only two examples of many throughout the work).

Unit 5: Stylistic Considerations

Whereas Movement I develops two fundamental ideas, (elegiac lyricism vs. marching), Movement II is kaleidoscopic and requires facile changes of mood, energy, and intensity. The conductor must formulate a strategy for characterizing every section and each musical gesture. For example, the sequence of musical events that culminates the entire work begins at M. 415 with the percussion "roll-off." The following "fife and drum" passage is lighthearted. The ensuing section, beginning at 443, should have an allegretto quality, lighter than the previous music. The next section, M. 459, develops the opening flourish from the movement's introduction. The humoresque quality of this music should be maximized. The music at M. 475 is a bit heavier than the preceding passage and builds intensity until M. 486, where the mood turns dark and ominous, intensifying toward the coda, where an explosion of energy breaks the tension. Viewed in its entirety, Part 5 begins as a lighthearted interlude. Each new section brings a subtle exaggeration of personality. Gradual intensification heightens tension. Articulation, dynamics, and tempo decisions must be taken in light of these issues.

Unit 6: Musical Elements

It is often stated that the mark of a symphony is development. The present work certainly fills that requirement. In fact, "Epitaphs" may be viewed as one large development section from beginning to end. The opening theme of Movement I seems evolutionary, continually sampling its own "DNA" in Franckian gestures before advancing phrasally. Owing to this episodic, developmental character, it is somewhat difficult to co-construct the work in one's mind as a listener; as it evolves, it doesn't follow any prescribed formal design. The entire picture does, however, make sense in the end, and the listener is left with a great sense of satisfaction. The return of first movement materials in the second binds the work into a cyclic unit.

The Gould signature is recognizable throughout the *Symphony*. The music is filled with gestures common to Gould's *oeuvre*. There are broad, sweeping melodic lines contrasted by terse motivic interchanges. The prominence of the perfect fourth in the theme of Movement I and in the opening flourish of Movement II is a Gouldism. Seldom are sonorities purely quartal, but occasionally stacks of fourths occur within tertian structures. Melodies are triadic, but triads outlined in close proximity are frequently members of disjunct tonalities. Occasionally Gould flirts with symmetrical melodic fragments, such as in the theme of Movement I (Eb-Ab-Cb-Fb). These notes outline a symmetrical interval cycle (P4th, m3rd, P4th). In M. 72 this opening gesture appears in the trumpets. The stretto trombone statement expands both the first and last intervals into a tritone. The next statement, in the bass clarinet, transforms all the intervals to perfect fourths, maintaining symmetry. The introduction to the passacaglia announces an ostinato sixteenth-note figure that is reminiscent of similar accompanimental patterns in *Fanfare for Freedom*, *American Salute*, and *Fiesta*. A less intense example of this Gouldism occurs earlier, beginning in the clarinets at M. 50. The marching tune in the flute and piccolo at M. 187 in Movement I permits a flash of Ivesian surrealism to surface. The "drop" motive in the horns at M. 191 in Movement I is a typical Gould gesture. Similar expressions occur in *Fanfare for Freedom*, *Santa Fe Saga*, and *Ballad for Band*. Frequently Gould tampers with the direction of this motive-type, alternating between upward and downward thrusts. Listen for the "Dixie" reference at MM 125-129, and later for "The

Caissons Go Rolling Along" suggested in the trumpets at MM 186-201. The fughetta in Movement II is incredibly crafty and brims with an exuberance many composers covet but few achieve. The counterpoint is fresh and playful, and the subject entrances bring daring and imaginative modulations—yet despite their abruptness, the seamless virtue of the texture is never violated. The melodic innovation, developmental resourcefulness, conceptual scope, and compositional craft place this work in the first rank of large-scale works for band.

Unit 7: Form and Structure

MOVEMENT I

Introduction	MM. 1-34	Theme A introduced mm equal to 104, No key signature
Expansion	MM. 35-111	Thematic materials developed
Interlude	MM 112-135	B Closing theme
Transition	MM 136-146	Based on Theme A
Introduction (Pt. II)	MM 147-154	mm equal to 104
Passacaglia	MM 155-231	11 statements of ground bass, *Dies Irae* fragment at 179, G minor tonal center
Coda	MM 232-263	Passacaglia elements fragment, Theme A resumes, "Taps" motive

MVT II

PART 1

Introduction	MM 1-59	In four motivic expositions (flourishes)
Section I	MM 1-19	Eb Major key signaturemm equal to 132
Section II	MM 20-29	
Section III	MM 30-36	
Section IV	MM 37-52	
Transition	MM 53-59	

PART 2

Theme A	MM 60-76	
Interlude	MM 77-109	Antiphonal development of introductory flourishes
Theme A	MM 110-125	
Transition	MM 126-129	"Dixie" suggested at MM 125-129.
Theme B	MM 130-177	Key signature canceled
Interlude	MM 178-213	Antiphonal development of introductory flourishes. Key signature reinstated: F Major at 186. "The Caissons Go Rolling Along" at M. 186 in trumpets.
Theme C	MM 214-251	Trio-like section, G Major key signature

Interlude	MM 252-264	Extension of Theme C, F Major key signature

PART 3

Fughetta	MM 265-368	Key signatures: C, Db, Gb,D, G

PART 4

Theme D	MM 369-400	Accompanied with motive from Theme C. Key signatures of Db Major, Eb Major at 385
Transition	MM 401-418	Borrows materials from Movement I

PART 5

Introduction	MM 419-423	Percussion cadence
Theme E	MM 424-442	Fife and Drum Corps, materials related to Movement I, M. 146. ("bugle" calls accompany second statement)
Theme F	MM 442-458	Stretto, figure based on motive from M. 30
Interlude	MM 458-494	
Section I	MM 458-474	6/8 development of flourishes from Introduction mixed with inverted fragments from Movement I
Section II	MM 475-494	Transition builds to coda. Theme F accompanied by flourishes from introduction and fragments from
Movement I	(M. 191)	C Major Key signature

PART 6
Coda

Introduction	MM 495-500 Flourish motive from Introduction
Section I	MM 501-513 Theme A "Boisterous"
Section II	MM 514-539 Acceleration to end using fragments of flourishes and Theme A. Eb Major key signature.

Unit 8: Suggested Listening
Morton Gould, *American Salute*
Morton Gould, *Ballad for Band*
Morton Gould, *Fanfare for Freedom*
Morton Gould, *Santa Fe Saga*
Darius Milhaud, *West Point Suite*

Unit 9: Bibliography

"Among Famous American Composers of Instrumental Music." *The Instrumentalist*, 6 January/February 1952, 30.

Band Music Guide. 9th ed. Northfield, Ill: The Instrumentalist Company, 1989.

Evans, Lee. "Morton Gould: His Life and Music." Diss., Columbia Teachers College, 1978.

Goodman, A. Harold, ed. *Instrumental Music Guide.* Provo, Utah: Brigham Young University Press, 1977.

Gould, Morton. "The Sound of a Band." Music Educator's Journal, 48 April/May 1962, 36-47.

——————. Telephone interview with Thomas Stone, 22 November 1992, Great Neck, N.Y. - Cincinnati. Tape recording.

——————. Telephone interview with Thomas Stone, 23 June 1995, Great Neck, N.Y.- Cincinnati.

Mullins, Joe Barry. "Morton Gould: Symphony for Band, Part I." *Journal of Band Research* IV/2 (Spring 1968): 24-35.

Mullins, Joe Barry. "Morton Gould: Symphony for Band, Part II." *Journal of Band Research* V/1 (Fall 1968): 27-29.

Mullins, Joe Barry. "Three Symphonies for Band by American Composers." Diss., University of Illinois, 1967.

Phillips, Harvey. "Morton Gould: Musical Citizen." *The Instrumentalist*, XLI July 1987, 10-16.

Sadie, Stanley, ed. *The New Grove Dictionary of Music and Musicians.* 20 Vols. London: Macmillan, 1980.

Slonimsky, Nicholas. *Baker's Biographical Dictionary of Musicians.* 8th ed., rev. New York: Schirmer Books, 1991.

Smith, Norman, and Albert Stoutamire. *Band Music Notes.* Rev. ed. San Diego: Neil A. Kjos, Jr., Publisher, 1979.

Stone, Thomas. "Morton Gould-Champion of the Band." *BD Guide*, 9 January/February 1995, 2-5.

Teacher Resource Guide

"Terpsichore"
Bransle Gay–Bransel double de Poictu la Robine–Spagnoletta–Ballet des Amazones–Volte Gavotte–La Bourre–Gaillarde–Reprinses–Gaillarde–Volte

Bob Margolis

(b. 1949)

after Michael Praetorius (b. 1571–d. 1621)

Unit 1: Composer

Bob Margolis (b.1949) is a native New Yorker. He studied recorder with Bernard Krainis and pursued the study of music at Brooklyn College before transferring to the University of California at Berkeley, where he studied design. He later returned to Brooklyn College, completing his Bachelor of Arts degree in speech and television production in 1974. Margolis subsequently studied composition under William Schimmel and Robert Starer and orchestration with Arnold Rosner. He earned his Master of Arts degree from Brooklyn College in 1977. Bob Margolis began instruction on the recorder at the age of seven. His interest in this instrument has lead to the publication of several articles in *The American Recorder*, and a collaboration with Rhoda B. Weber on the teacher's manual to *The Soprano Recorder Songbook for Children*. In 1981, Mr. Margolis established Manhattan Beach Music and since has published a multitude of high quality works for band and wind ensemble, including his own *Fanfare Ode & Festival*, which has become a staple in the repertoire of the junior high school band.

Michael Praetorius (1571-1621) was a prolific and accomplished publisher, organist, theorist, and composer—a true "Renaissance man" whose writings form an important guide to the history of the music of his time. His outstanding treatise is the three-volume *Syntagma Musicum*, which deals with religious music (vol. I), musical instruments of the time (vol. II), and musical theory and notation (vol. III). Praetorius' main output was the composition of sacred music—more than one thousand compositions in all. *Terpsichore*, a collection of dances published in Germany in 1612, was Praetorius' only secular work. Terpsichore is the Greek Muse of dancing. She is one of the nine Muses, all daughters of Mnemosyne (the goddess of memory) and Zeus (the presiding Greek god). Praetorius died on his fiftieth birthday. (Adapted from notes by Bob Margolis)

Unit 3: Historical Perspective

Praetorius' *Terpsichore* has been a fertile source of performance material for latter-day composers, arrangers, and performers. The present work should be viewed as a 20th-Century composition which comments upon the past, not an arrangement of Renaissance music. Although Margolis includes the recorder in selected orchestrations, the instrumentation is decidedly 20th-Century in scope and concept despite the masterful use of consorts (even a consort of saxophones in Movement IV).

Terpsichore, composed in 1980, maintains the spirit of Renaissance orchestration within the framework of the modern symphonic band. During the 16th Century, instrumentation was left to the performers. 16th-Century descriptions of performances list an exceedingly broad range of instruments—far more (in kind if not number) than are present in the modern band. There was no international pitch standard, thus it was necessary for instrument makers to build matched sets of instruments at a particular pitch level. This grouping of a number of like instruments (for example, recorders only) is called a closed consort and is the basis of much Renaissance orchestration.

The composer has created the following consort-like instrument choirs: flute choir, double-reed choir (alone and with clarinet choir), trombone choir (alone and with percussion accompaniment), saxophone choir (with percussion), trumpet choir, wide-bore brass choir (flugelhorns/euphoniums), narrow-bore brass choir (trumpets/trombones), horn choir, and Tuba/Euphonium choir. (Quoted and adapted from notes by Bob Margolis)

Other wind works that use Renaissance materials include Ron Nelson's *Medieval Suite*, David Noon's *Sweelinck Variations*, Jan Bach's *Praetorius Suite*, Norman Dello Joio's *Variants on a Medieval Tune*, and Margolis' *Fanfare Ode & Festival* (after Gervaise).

Unit 4: Technical Considerations

The following key signatures exist in *Terpsichore*:

    1 sharp (G Major mode)
    2 sharps (D Major mode)

1 flat (F Major mode)
1 flat (D minor mode)
2 flats (G minor mode)
2 flats (Bb Major mode)
3 flats (Eb Major mode)

Terpsichore utilizes a wide variety of time signatures, after the fashion of Renaissance composers: 4/4 6/8 3/8 3/2 6/4 2/2 3/4 6/2 5/4 7/4 2/4 4/2 (in order of appearance). The greatest degree of multimeter alternation occurs at the end of the final movement. Customary practice throughout the work is to establish and sustain a meter for the duration of any given section.

Rhythmic complexities result both from original Renaissance rhythms featuring syncopations and other unexpected twists (often within the context of compound meter) as well as from Margolis' colorful latter-day gestures which permeate the score (Movement I - MM 96-99, for example). Syncopations are commonplace, as are dotted rhythms. Hemiola occurs motivically in the theme of *L'espagnollette* (Movement II - MM 44-72), which is also a wonderful example of thematic displacement between the trumpets and low brass. In his extensive preface to the score, the composer offers rhythmic simplifications that may facilitate performance for younger, less proficient ensembles. Even with simplification, this composition demands rhythmic fluency and maturity.

Brass performers must be capable of rapid articulation, usually on one continuous pitch (as in Movement I). Trumpet I ascends to high E (Movement II - M. 98), and will require a secure all-around "pro" (Movement II - 222-223). Trombone I extends to high B (Movement IV, M. 99), and the part demands technical facility in all ranges.

Endurance is a critical performance issue. Conductors may choose to program only one individual movement, or a set of two grouped movements, I and II, III and IV being the only feasible options. If Movement IV is programmed individually, the cues should be performed in MM 1-21 unless an authentic pipe organ is available.

In his preface to the score, Margolis states, "Much of the beauty of this work derives from its orchestration, and thus the first matter that must be addressed by the director is the instrumentation of his or her band."

In addition to traditional instrumentation, Margolis' orchestration features tenor recorder, contra-bassoon, Eb alto clarinet, Eb contra-alto clarinet, Bb bass clarinet, Bb contra-bass clarinet, Harp (cross-cued), and Organ (cued). A synthesizer with credible harp and organ stops can be used. The percussion score includes bongo drums, castanets, conga drum, xylophone, finger cymbals, four drums, bell tree, field drum, three suspended cymbals, dumbek, piccolo snare drum, snare drum, tubular bells, marimba, (two optional parts), small and large tam-tams, two tambourines, four triangles, whip, coconut shells (or temple blocks), claves, glockenspiel, tambourin provencal, temple blocks, large tom-

tom, bass drum, American Indian drum, frame drum, five varieties of crash cymbals, tenor drum, and vibra-slap. Margolis' impressive resourcefulness adds immeasurable scope and dimension to the entire composition.

Unit 5: Stylistic Considerations

Terpsichore, a festive holiday piece, requires high combustion throughout. The choice and sequence of dances in *Terpsichore* is the result of the predilection of the composer, not Renaissance performance practice or ceremonial usage.

Interpretation should rest upon finding the articulations that bring out the dance-like character of the melodies and provide shape to the phrases. Be careful not to let the quick passages drag, but realize that the music works at a variety of tempi. Strive not so much to find the perfect tempo, but rather to enliven the melodies. Sometimes Margolis provides accents to emphasize the linear independence of the lines, such as in the Volte at the end of Movement II. At MM 33-38 the composer has left it to the performer to decide upon articulation and placement of agogic accents.

Renaissance performance practice allows for tasteful improvisation, especially in solo instrumental parts. *Terpsichore* provides one such opportunity for license, namely in the introduction to Movement I. The recorder soloist may wish to improvise, as suggested by Margolis in the score, rendering extensions to the consequent phrase beginning at measure 6. The solo organ cadence "at pleasure" in Movement IV, M. 20 is a realization of an improvised cadence by Diego Ortiz from his "Treatise of embellishments on cadences" published in 1553.

Unit 6: Musical Elements

All Renaissance music predates the establishment of tonality, which is generally recognized to have occurred at about 1670 in the music of Archangelo Corelli. The linear dimension of Renaissance music is predominant. The bass line is beginning to function as an harmonic engine, pointing toward tonality, but the vertical dimension of Praetorius' music is still primarily modal; the inner voices maintain a contrapuntal rather than harmonic function.

Margolis' use of exacting dynamic markings, including a seventeen-fold forte, belongs to the 20th Century. Dynamics came into use in the music of Giovanni Gabrielli (Venice, ca. 1590) at the very end of the Renaissance. The use of crescendo/diminuendo markings is strictly Post-Renaissance; and Margolis employs them freely. The liberal use of articulation markings and various other latter-day inventions such as mutes also clarify that this is a 20th-Century view of antiquity.

Unit 7: Form and Structure

The following guide is included in the Composer's Preface to the score:

MOVEMENT 1

meas. 1-9	I	Bransle Gay #1, a5 ("F.C.")

This opening version of the Bransle is unusual in that the simple-triple-meter melody is forced into a double duple mold—a round peg in a square hole. Compare meas. 82-95.

meas. 10-18   Bransle Gay #1

(Note that meas. 1-9 has the tune in simple meter, and meas. 10-18 exactly the same tune in compound meter. Bransles were capable of being performed both ways.)

meas. 19-27	IX	Bransle double de Poictu, a5 ("F.C.")
meas. 27-39		Bransle Gay #1
meas. 40-51		Bransle double de Poictu
meas. 52-68		Bransle Gay #1
meas. 69-81		Bransle Gay #1, in an exact transcription of Francisque Caroubel's original five-part arrangement.

meas. 82-95   The Bransle Gay #1 again. The shift in stress from the anacrusis beginning (in the duple time version) to the downbeat beginning (in triple time version) somewhat obscures identification of the melody.

meas. 96-99   Addition.

MOVEMENT 2

meas. 1-12	XXIII	La Robine #1, a5 ("F.C.")
meas. 12-44	XXVII	Spagnoletta ("2", a4 ("M.P.C.")
meas. 44-72	XXVI	L'espagnollette, a5 ("F.C.")
meas. 73-76		Addition.
meas. 77-110	CCLXX	Ballet des Amazones, a4 ("Incerti")
meas. 111-167	CCLXVIII	Ballet, a4 ("Incerti")
meas. 168-228	CCXIV	Volte, a5 (M.P.C.")

MOVEMENT 3

meas. 1-30	I	Gavotte #6, a5 ("F.C")
meas. 31		Addition.
meas. 32-132	XXXII	La Bouree #1, #2, and #3, a4 ("M.P.C.")

MOVEMENT 4

meas. 1-21	CCXCIV	Gaillarde, a4 ("M.P.C.")
meas. 22-91	CCCIX	Reprinse #1-#17, a4 ("M.P.C.")
meas. 92-146	CCLXXXVII	Gaillarde, a5 ("F.C.")
meas. 146-147		Addition.
meas. 148-228	CCI	Volte, a5 ("M.P.C.") (The barring in the Gesamtausgabe edition is incorrect; the music actually shifts between duple and triple, as in the present band edition.)
meas. 229-230		Addition.

Unit 8: Suggested Listening
Jan Bach *Praetorius Suite*
Norman Dello Joio, *Variants on a Medieval Tune*
Bob Margolis, *Fanfare Ode & Festival* (after Gervaise)
Ron Nelson, *Medieval Suite*
David Noon, *Sweelinck Variations*
Michael Praetorius, *Terpsichore*
Susato, *Suite from "The Danserye"*

Unit 9: Bibliography

Grout, Donald Jay. Ed. Claude V. Palisca. *A History of Western Music.* Third Ed. New York: W. W. Norton & Co., 1980.

Margolis, Bob. *Terpsichore.* Composer's Preface. Brooklyn: Manhattan Beach Music, 1984.

Margolis, Bob. Telephone interview with Thomas Stone, 11 June, 1995, New York, N.Y. - Cincinnati.

Sadie, Stanley, ed. *The New Grove Dictionary of Music and Musicians.* 20 Vols. London: Macmillan, 1980.

Teacher Resource Guide

"Theme and Variations, Op. 43a" Arnold Schoenberg

(b. 1874–d. 1951)

Unit 1: Composer

Arnold Schoenberg (1874-1951) was the originator of the twelve-tone technique of composition, often referred to as "serialism." Born in Vienna, he studied with Zemlinsky before arriving in the United States in 1933. While teaching at USC and UCLA during the final period of his career, he refined the twelve-tone system, even allowing tonal elements to exist in his serial works. Schoenberg's mark on younger composers has been monumental. Webern and Berg were perhaps his most noted pupils, but his music influenced many others, including Messaien, Boulez, and Stravinsky (whose late works were conceived in the serial vein).

Unit 2: Composition

Theme and Variations, completed in 1943, was commissioned by Schoenberg's publisher, G. Schirmer. Schoenberg's mastery of motivic development is clearly in evidence throughout as virtually every note in the seven variations can be traced to the 21-bar theme. Schoenberg wrote:

> ...as far as technique is concerned it is a masterpiece; and I know it is inspired. Not only because I cannot write even ten measures without inspiration, but I really wrote the piece with great pleasure.

Unit 3: Historical Perspective

While Schoenberg intended his *Theme and Variations*, Op. 43a to be played by the average amateur band, its difficulty was such that only exceptionally advanced ensembles were able to master it. Thus he transcribed the work for orchestra as Op. 43b, and it enjoys the unusual position of being one of a handful of works that exists in the repertoire of the orchestra as transcribed band music.

It is exceptional that this composition represents a vital departure from the typical Schoenbergian language. *Theme and Variations* is late Schoenberg, written during a time when the aging master was searching for a simpler, more readily accessible musical voice. Perhaps the Neo-Romantic style is traceable to the monumental influence of Mahler, or it may be the result of the composer's reluctance to deliver a dodecaphonic work to amateur band musicians.

Unit 4: Technical Considerations

The fundamental tonality is G minor, tinged with chromatic inflections and modulations to other tonal centers. Linear passages often do not follow traditional scale patterns and will require mature technique. Brass are required to execute awkward intervallic sequences within fast and irregular rhythmic patterns. Flutter-tonguing is demanded of the flutes, horns and euphonium at measure 156. The euphonium/clarinet duet in Variation V is especially difficult.

Schoenberg continually mixes duple and triple subdivisions. These cross-rhythms, such as those found in Variation I, require devout rhythmic integrity to ensure that the duple sixteenth/eighth patterns do not lapse into quasi-triple meter.

Instrumentation includes flugelhorns, a specification endemic to the 1940's (most works written for the Goldman Band included).

Unit 5: Stylistic Considerations

Strive to heighten the Romantic aesthetic; there is great emotion in this music notwithstanding its cerebral concept and intricate compositional technique. The apex of the piece occurs at the end, and thus the Germanic/Austrian concept of building momentum to the climax should be assessed and maintained.

Schoenberg places his own interpretive markings in the score to indicate performance priorities:

1. P means principal part, the end of which has been marked with the sign .

2. S means: secondary part, the end of which has been marked with the sign.

3. ⟩ means ending of a phrase

4. ⟨ means beginning of a phrase

Seven types of articulation marks appear in *Theme and Variations*. Schoenberg's concept of articulation, envelope, and decay stem from his experience with the piano, on which articulation and decay are inextricably linked. The Romantic notion of soft, legato articulation, for Schoenberg, must cede to a new concept, relevant to the 20th Century, in which initiations are more clearly articulated and decays have a definite, prescribed shape (influence of Busoni). This explains Schoenberg's "micro-managing" or "over-notating" of articulation. Plan the seven articulations as follows:

Tenuto (–)   The softest articulation, full value.

Staccato (·)   No accent, detached, discernible decay.

Accent (>)   Accented, slightly less than full value.

Accented staccato (⋝)   Accented, detached.

Marcato (∧)   Heavy accent, long decay; slightly less than full value.

Marcato staccatissimo (⩔)   Heavy accent, very short, but longer than staccatissimo.

Staccatissimo (▾)   Abrupt accent, abrupt decay. (the shortest articulation)

Unit 6: Musical Elements

Schoenberg's theme, loosely in G minor, uses ten of the twelve chromatic tones (Db and Eb are not used). Thus the work is not constructed according to the twelve-tone system, but is freely composed. The theme consists of two main parts. Part I is comprised of antecedent and consequent phrases, ending with a brief motto which is developed throughout the piece as a separate motive.

Antecedent Phrase, Theme - Part I

Consequent Phrase, Theme - Part I

MOTTO

Antecedent Phrase, Part II - Theme

Notice that the melodic pitches in measures 10-11 form a vertically symmetrical pattern centered around A-natural. The consequent phrase to Part II is based on Part I.

The melodic movement in *Theme and Variations* is largely stepwise in all parts. The conception of the work is contrapuntal. Incidental harmonies resulting from the stacking of linear figures reflect free use of all intervallic relations, but pre-scribed vertical sonorities are tertian. Even in light of his revolutionary harmonic innovations, Schoenberg never abandoned the fundamentally Beethovenian sentence structure of his musical phrases (which appears in the present work as well).

Variation V features a canon in inversion between the clarinet and euphonium. The entrances are a tritone apart, and although there is agreement between the corresponding rhythmic values and intervals in the two parts, the direction of each interval is inverted.

The closing bars of the Finale are of special interest. It has been posited that the line in the horns, euphoniums, and tenor saxophone in MM 276-77 is a veiled tribute to Gershwin, Schoenberg's deceased neighbor, tennis cohort, and close friend. This palindromic pattern, D-E-F-Eb-D-Eb-F-E-D, bears a strong resemblance to certain of Gershwin's motives, most notably from *Rhapsody in Blue*.

Unit 7: Form and Structure

Theme	Poco Allegro	21 bars (G minor)
Variation I	(Poco Allegro)	21 bars
Variation II	Allegro Molto	42 bars
Variation III	Poco Adagio	21 bars
Variation IV	Tempo di Valzer	42 bars (Waltz - G Major)
Variation V	Molto Moderato	21 bars (Eb Major)
Variation VI	Allegro	21 bars (Fughetta)
Variation VII	Moderato	23 bars (G-Major)
Finale	Moderato	14 + 22 (Fugato) + 20 + 10 bars

Schoenberg's fascination with numerology, especially the numbers 6 and 7 (which total 13), and 23 is evident throughout his oeuvre. He chose 21 poems from Giraud's cycle of 50 to be included in his Op. 21, *Pierrot Lunaire*. The 21 movements are divided into three groups of seven. It should, therefore, come as no surprise that the *Theme and Variations* reflects numerological proportions. The 21-bar theme is followed by six variations that contain measure totals equal to multiples of seven (21, 42 [6 x 7!]). Variation VII varies from this pattern with 23 measures. Aside from its status as a prime number (a Schoenbergian enthusiasm), 23 was in itself a "hot" number for Schoenberg. It was in 1923 that he codified the 12-tone system and published the first fully serial work. His Op. 23 contains the first example of combinatoriality (in No. 3, M. 23!). The Finale, at sixty-six bars, accounts for 23% of the work (66/278)!

Unit 8: Suggested Listening
George Gershwin, *Rhapsody in Blue*
Arnold Schoenberg, *Five Pieces for Piano*, Op. 23
Arnold Schoenberg, *Pierrot Lunaire*, Op. 21

Unit 9: Bibliography
Bruning, Earl Henry Jr. "A Survey and Handbook of Analysis for the Conducting and Interpretation of Seven Selected Works in the Standard Repertoire for Wind Band." Diss., Ball State University, 1980.

Corporon, Eugene. Thematic Analysis of Schoenberg's Theme and Variations, op. 43a. Unpublished.

Nail, James Isaac. "The Concept of Developing Variations as a Means of Producing Unity and Variety in Schoenberg's Theme and Variations Op. 43a." Diss., The University of Texas at Austin, 1978.

Neff, Severine. Interview with Thomas Stone. Cincinnati, 6/7/95.

Odegard, Peter Sigurd. "The Variations Sets of Arnold Schoenberg." Diss., University of California, Berkeley, 1964.

Perlman, George. "Arnold Schoenberg." *The Instrumentalist*, XVII November 1962, 42.

Prindl, Frank Joseph. "A Study of Ten Original Compositions for Band Published in America Since 1946." Diss., The Florida State University, 1956.

Sadie, Stanley, ed. *The New Grove Dictionary of Music and Musicians.* 20 Vols. London: Macmillan, 1980.

Slonimsky, Nicholas. *Baker's Biographical Dictionary of Musicians.* 8th ed., rev. New York: Schirmer Books, 1991.

Smith, Norman, and Albert Stoutamire. *Band Music Notes.* Rev. ed. San Diego: Neil A. Kjos, Jr., Publisher, 1979.

Wallace, David, and Eugene Corporon., eds. *Wind Ensemble/Band Repertoire.* Greeley, CO: University of Northern Colorado School of Music, 1984.

Watkins, Glenn. *Soundings.* New York: Schirmer Books, 1988.

Teacher Resource Guide

"Zion"
Dan Welcher
(b. 1948)

Unit 1: Composer
Dan Welcher is gaining recognition as one of the most original and exciting contemporary American composers. He is currently on the composition faculty of the University of Texas at Austin and is an active conductor and proponent of new music. He has performed professionally as Principal Bassoon of the Louisville Orchestra, and has been Composer-in-Residence with the Honolulu Symphony Orchestra. Welcher's compositions, which span a range of genres from orchestral to chamber music, include an opera as well as music for solo piano.

Unit 2: Composition
Zion, like two of Welcher's previous works for wind ensemble, was inspired by the natural beauty of the American West. In this instance, Utah's Zion Canyon is depicted musically. The commission was from a consortium of the University of Texas at Austin, the University of Texas at Arlington, and the University of Oklahoma. It is dedicated to the memory of Aaron Copland, and uses the hymn tune *Zion's Wall*, effectively used by Copland in *Old American Songs*, Set 2, and the opera *The Tender Land*. Welcher intentionally constructed the piece to work as the final movement of a suite consisting of *Yellowstone Fires*, *Arches*, and *Zion*. The work was completed in 1994.

Unit 3: Historical Perspective
Welcher, a contemporary American composer, reflects a growing trend of using eclectic materials. His language incorporates tonal material, pre-existing melodic material, and gestural effects, as well as a wide range of 20th-century devices.

His work fits into the general trend away from strictly serial composition and has demonstrated an appeal to both the musician and the listener. *Zion* incorporates two hymn tunes, "Zion's Wall" and "Zion's Security", from an American collection of hymns, *The Sacred Harp*.

Unit 4: Technical Considerations

Zion makes use of extremely colorful orchestration that requires very wide ranges from almost all the instruments. Principal parts frequently exploit high ranges in both the woodwinds and the brass. Sustained pedal points and high tessitura make intonation a particularly important concern. The brass parts are physically demanding. The percussion writing is idiomatic and includes four mallet technique for the melodic instruments. Five percussion and timpani are required, as well as piano.

Unit 5: Stylistic Considerations

Much of *Zion* is in a lyrical legato style. Both the quoted melodies are presented in this style. Often, staccato, almost pointillistic, material is juxtaposed with the lyrical texture. Accents are incorporated for dramatic effects and are specifically marked.

Unit 6: Musical Elements

Pentatonic material, derived from the hymn tunes, provides both the melodic and harmonic content of *Zion*. The simple opening hymn tune is developed cononicaly against sustained pedal points. An unmeasured section in free time consists of structured events involving the interaction of the performers and the conductor. The overall harmonic language is consistently tonal. The effect is exuberant.

Unit 7: Form and Structure

All the material in *Zion* is derived from two hymn tunes from *The Sacred Harp*, a collection of American hymn tunes. In the following analysis they will be labeled:

A. "Zion's Security," no. 189 from The Sacred Harp
B. "Zion's Wall," no. 213 from The Sacred Harp

A1, mm. 1-30, F#, full statement of the antecedent phrase against tonic and dominant pedal points

A2, mm. 31-48, canonic statement of the consequent phrase against tonic and dominant pedal points, fragments of B material appear in accompaniment, mm. 41-48

A3, mm. 49-66, F, full statement of both phrases interspersed with material derived from B

B1, mm. 67-84, F, head motive of the consequent phrase, joined in m. 73 with the head motive of the antecedent phrase accompanied by pentatonic scales

B2, mm. 85-129, Eb, rhythmic variant of B material, faster tempo, marked "Driving"

B1, mm. 130-138, Db, material returns, still in new tempo, which is accommodated by notating B1 material in augmentation

Free Time, mm. 139-148

    m. 140, B material begins in flutes, not conducted, then is joined by solo field drum, then brass, conducted playing a full statement of A

    m. 141, B played by clarinets out of time

    m. 142-148, time begins for every one except timpani, bassoons and flutes, trumpets, trombone solo and euphonium solo play A consequent phrase.

B3, mm. 149-152, F to G, two full statements of the phrase, modulating up a step

B4, mm. 153-183, A, full statement of the phase, elements of B2 appear in m. 180

B2, mm. 184-213, material returns with fragments of A material interspersed

B5, mm. 214-231, Bb, Full statements of B over B2 material

B6, mm. 231-252, C, Full statements of B

A4, mm. 253-256, F#, last statement of A

Coda, mm. 257-287, C, begins with B2 material

Unit 8: Suggested Listening

Aaron Copland, *The Tender Land*
Joseph Schwantner, *and the mountains rising nowhere*
Dan Welcher, *Arches*
Dan Welcher, *Yellowstone Fires*

Unit 9: Additional References and Resources

Stolba, K Marie. *The Development of Western Music.* Dubuque, IA: William C. Brown Publishers, 19

Index by Title

Index by Composer, Arranger, Transcriber

About the Authors

Larry Blocher is Director of Music Education at Wichita State University in Wichita, Kansas.

Ray Cramer is Director of Bands at Indiana University in Bloomington, Indiana.

Eugene Corporon is Director of Wind Studies at the University of North Texas in Denton, Texas.

Tim Lautzenheiser is founder and president of Attitude Concepts for Today, Inc., in Bluffton, Indiana.

Edward S. Lisk is a former Director of Bands and Music Supervisor of the Oswego City School District in New York.

Richard Miles, compiler and coauthor of this book, is Director of Bands at Morehead State University in Morehead, Kentucky. He holds a Doctor of Philosophy degree from Florida State University and undergraduate and graduate degrees from Appalachian State University and the University of Illinois. Dr. Miles has 23 years of teaching experience at the university and secondary school levels, and serves nationally and internationally as a guest conductor, consultant, and clinician.